HOP

D1199091

THE PSYCHOANALYTIC
STUDY OF SOCIETY

Volume III

THE PSYCHOANALYTIC STUDY OF SOCIETY

VOLUME III

Founded as

PSYCHOANALYSIS AND THE SOCIAL SCIENCES

(Volumes I-V)

by Géza Róheim

Edited by

Warner Muensterberger, Ph.D. and Sidney Axelrad, D.S.Sc.

Editorial Board

Michael Balint, M.D., London

Viola Bernard, M.D., New York

George Devereux, Ph.D., Paris

John Dollard, Ph.D., New Haven

Erik H. Erikson, Stockbridge

Angel Garma, M.D., Buenos Aires

Martin Grotjahn, M.D., Beverly Hills

A. I. Hallowell, Ph.D., Philadelphia

Heinz Hartmann, M.D., New York

Nathan Leites, Ph.D., New York

Sandor Lorand, M.D., New York

Karl A. Menninger, M.D., Topeka

Cecily de Monchaux, Ph.D., London

R. Money-Kyrle, Ph.D., London

Herman Nunberg, M.D., New York

Paul Parin, M.D., Zürich

H.R.H. Prince Peter of Greece and
Denmark, LL.D., Ph.D., Athens

Fredrick C. Redlich, M.D., New Haven

Sidney Tarachow, M.D., New York

Robert Waelder, Ph.D., Philadelphia

George B. Wilbur, M.D., South Dennis

INTERNATIONAL UNIVERSITIES PRESS, INC.

New York   New York

Copyright 1964, by International Universities Press, Inc.

Library of Congress Catalog Card Number: 61-486

Manufactured in the United States of America

CONTENTS

MYTHOLOGY AND FOLKLORE

ANTHROPOLOGY AND SOCIOLOGY

ART

MYTHOLOGY AND FOLKLORE

MYTHOLOGY AND EGO PSYCHOLOGY

Introductory Remarks

SIDNEY TARACHOW, M.D.

The history of man's development as shown in the evolution of religion, but also particularly in the theater, shows an interesting succession of themes. Earliest was expression of conflict between the gods. This was followed by the theme of conflict between the gods and man, then the struggle between man and man. The current theme in drama is the struggle within man, his intrapsychic conflict. This stage is characterized by problems of guilt and of ego structure. I am not too certain that I would even differentiate between ego and superego. I would be content simply with an orientation based on the concepts of drive and defense.

What can be said about this progressive transition of areas of conflict? The progression can be stated in terms of attempts at solution of the ambivalence problem and the origin of the sense of guilt. Both these issues are intimately connected with problems of ego development. It is possible to state all the necessary issues regarding mythology in terms of ego vicissitudes.

The Greeks did not attempt to solve their ambivalence problem in their religious system. In terms of their religious system, they were a shame culture and not a guilt culture, i.e., their solutions were not thoroughly internalized. In the Oedipus play the hero *is* struggling with guilt and with an ambivalence conflict. Such a struggle represents an advancing stage in ego development. However, the internalization is by no means as complete as we might find in a modern neurotic. The gods and demigods are still involved as factors and actors carrying out, in an external way, some of the intrapsychic tendencies of the protagonists.

Let us return to the Greek system of gods which made very little demand on the ego organization. Every conceivable partial impulse and every conceivable part object found some *external* representation. In fact, the Greeks so relieved themselves of the burden of the ego tensions in the

---

The papers in this group were part of a Panel on Mythology and Ego Psychology presented before the Psychoanalytic Association of New York on May 21, 1962.

task of synthesis and burden of resolution of ambivalence that they had even erected an altar to "the as yet unknown or undiscovered gods." It was at this altar that St. Paul was permitted to preach in Athens. The Greeks took no chances.

What are the dangers with which the myth deals? There are external dangers and there are internal dangers. Is the myth more closely related to the social process or to the intrapsychic process? The present discussion ranging about the relationship of mythology to ego psychology is a most happy localization of discussion. I would say it is the crucial discussion. We may trace man's development from the primitive aboriginal to the modern man of science in terms of the crystallization of the ego and the secondary process.

What is the principal difficulty with reference to this ego-developmental goal? The difficulty lies in the imperfection of the result. My own private conception in approaching this issue is the conception of *the faltering ego*. Arlow (1961) made this point when he noted that the processes of identification are never completely successful. I would say that the ego is perpetually beset by the problems of the weaknesses and fluidity of its boundaries. The boundaries are laid down in two areas, one with reference to external reality and the other with reference to the unconscious. It is the eruption of the unconscious which we fear more than any external danger, even the danger of death. This leads us back to the problem of the primacy of the psychological versus the social-historical.

I regard the myth as one of a number of devices which come to the rescue of the faltering ego. Myths ease the burden of ego synthesis and/or development and facilitate a working through of disturbing problems. There is an externalizing process and an internalizing process. There is the problem of social adjustment and the problem of intrapsychic adjustment. In the sense of myths being an externalizing process, to give respite to the weary ego, they offer room for change and development, not often welcomed by the older generation. In the sense of myths being an internalizing process, they solidify character formation and stabilize relationships at a certain point. In this latter sense they contribute to ego stability, but also to a more static social process.

Some remarks could be made about the place of form, esthetic pleasure, technique, and rigidity of ritual as well as variations in detail of myths and fairy tales, or even in variations of religious belief or ritual. Form, rigidity, and technique certainly serve defensive purposes. If a joke is not told correctly it is disturbing and not pleasing. The technique of a painting serves to control the affects and anxieties and permits esthetic pleasure. Esthetic pleasure is in itself a part of the defense, the transformation of a painful affect into a pleasant one (Tarachow, 1949).

A discussion of mythology could range about the function of the constancy of myths as well as the variations of myths. Every religion has its central, fixed myth, as well as a body of related mythologies which develop, alter, or deny the central myth as time progresses. It is easier to discuss the central rigid myth than the flow of alterations and variations which confront us in the historical process. This phenomenon of change tempts us to desert the centrality of the intrapsychic process in the etiology of myths. All religions show the changes with reference to the central myth and with attempts to deal with outside, environmental factors. The medieval European Jews had collections of stories which elaborated in great detail the stories of the Old Testament (Bin-Gorion, 1914), and at the same time developed hostile New Testament Gospels (Baring-Gould, 1874), in which their antagonisms to the Christians and to Christ were developed in various fanciful ways. Myths may be adaptive or maladaptive and rebellious. "Kilroy Was Here" (Sterba, 1948) is an example of the latter.

A further aspect of importance is the matter of size, impressiveness, and the overwhelming nature of some of the stimuli to which the individual is subjected. On the Athenian stage the king wore the tallest platform shoes. Ceremonies and pageantry and ritual, as well as church spires, were immense, overwhelming. The individual is rendered insignificant and encouraged to surrender to the powers about him. The sense of separation and isolation, which is the price paid for ego formation, is readily abandoned in the face of overwhelming stimuli. Massed flags and massed bands will often make the most confirmed pacifist experience an itch to march with the soldiery. Hitler knew this very well.

The human will not readily abandon ceremony and ritual, or even the myth, which is not so formal or authoritative. They provide focal points about which the individual can organize his fantasies for identification processes and stabilize his position with reference to his family group. In that sense ritual serves a necessary defensive and ego-building purpose. A myth, even though more plastic, serves the same purpose.

BIBLIOGRAPHY

Arlow, J. (1961), Ego Psychology and the Study of Mythology. *J. Amer. Psychoanal. Assn.*, 9:371-393.

Baring-Gould, S. (1874), *The Lost and Hostile Gospels: An Essay on the Toledoth Jeschu and the Petrine and Pauline Gospels of the First Three Centuries of which Fragments Remain.* London: Williams & Norgate.

Bin-Gorion, M. J. (1914), *Die Sagen der Juden, Die Erzväter*. Frankfurt a. Main: Rütten
u. Loening.
Sterba, R. F. (1948), Kilroy Was Here. *Amer. Imago, 5*:173-181.
Tarachow, S. (1949), Remarks on the Comic Process and Beauty. *Psychoanal. Quart.,
18*:215-226.

The Madonna's Conception Through the Eyes

JACOB A. ARLOW, M.D.

It is not necessary to point out in a symposium devoted to psycho-analysis and mythology how close is the relationship between daydreams (Sachs, 1920) and myths. A considerable amount of literature has been devoted to the subject. This literature has already been reviewed by the previous speakers. The purpose of this presentation is to demonstrate how certain themes may find expression in myths which in turn serve as the central focus of religious practices and beliefs; and how these mythic themes influence character structure and neurosis in members of the re-ligion.

Especially in the context of religious teachings, myths play a very im-portant role in the education of the younger generation. Through its guiding or official mythology, a society tends to induce a climate favor-able to the realization in its members of certain desirable identifications. Such identifications with heroes or heroines of the classic or central myths point the way to the establishment of ego ideals and superego structures in consonance with the moral traditions of the society. As different societies may emphasize different ideal qualities, so one finds different types of mythology to be characteristic for different types of social organization. Róheim (1950, 1950a) discussed this problem in con-nection with varying manifestations of the oedipus complex.

The mythology which a society produces is an index to the type of unconscious conflicts common among members of that group. A recent study of the contribution which the ego makes to the structure of the myth pointed out that the central myth of a religion serves to bind the adherents to the faith by virtue of the instinctual gratification which is vicariously afforded by way of identification with the central figure of the myth (Arlow, 1961). The instinctual gratification is connected with an id impulse, with an instinctual wish of childhood, which is unconscious, which is defensively distorted by the ego, and which is integrated into the final structure of the myth in a manner which honors the superego demands. In this respect religious myth is the counterpart of tragedy.

13

Gratification of unconscious, childhood instinctual wishes is facilitated in members of the community by both the esthetic and religious sublimation on condition that the resulting conflict over the id impulse is resolved by the ego through renunciation, sublimation, and character transformation. In this manner, the members of a religious group share in common a gratifying unconscious wish together with a common conscious set of moral goals, and dedication to certain preferred character traits and ideals.

How this functions pedagogically in actual experience may be illustrated by referring to the well-known image of the Madonna. This theme, it has been demonstrated repeatedly, is connected with the fulfillment of unconscious incestuous wishes of the oedipal phase. By identifying with the Madonna, little girls achieve in fantasy the fulfillment of the incestuous wish while, at the same time, they are directed by this identification to the imitation of those ideal qualities of purity, virtue, and unselfish love which are represented by the image of the Madonna.

In the individual, the sublimations and character transformations which are achieved, in part, through the influence of religion may be undone by neurotic illness. In such instances the re-emergence of more primitive expressions of the unconscious instinctual wish leads to conflicts which serve as the basis for symptom formation. This vicissitude of the instinctual conflict furnishes us with the clinical material which gives us insight into the structure of the myth and into the role of religion in psychic economy. The clinical data for this paper are furnished by this type of situation which pertained to an identification in one of the central myths of Christianity, namely the "Annunciation to the Madonna." What was striking about this expression of incestuous impregnation was the fact that the act of conception was unconsciously fantasied as taking place by the entry of the divine light through the patient's eyes. This sublimated defensive displacement from "below to above," from the proper organ of impregnation to the eyes, interestingly enough, was also employed by medieval scholastic philosophers in their attempts to make the doctrine of immaculate conception seem plausible and acceptable. This will be discussed later in this presentation.

The classic analysis given by Jones (1914) of the medieval myth of the Madonna's conception through the ear emphasizes the original anal derivation of the fantasy. According to Jones, this myth represents an exquisite, elevated, and intensely poetic anal elaboration of an oedipal fantasy in which "we have a father incestuously impregnating his daughter (i.e., a son his mother) by expelling intestinal gas, with the help of the genital organ, into her lower alimentary orifice, one through which a child is then born. In the legend, the site of exit is completely omitted and that of ingress is denoted by the receptive organ of music, an orifice with fewer sensual implications than any other in the whole body, than the navel, the mouth, or even the eye." In the example to be cited from the analysis of a young Christian woman, an identification with the Madonna in a fantasy of impregnation through the eyes formed the basis for two hysterical conversion symptoms, headache and photophobia.

The patient was a teacher of underprivileged children in a settlement house. At the time she started treatment, she was engaged to be married to the director of the project. The imminence of her marriage and the prospect of sexual relations made her increasingly anxious, but the actual precipitation of her illness was occasioned by waiting to have blood drawn for a test. As she was thinking of the needle which was to be thrust into her arm and the blood that would flow into the tube, she was overwhelmed by panic. She had also learned that week that her sister and her supervisor were both pregnant.

Like her choice of profession, the patient's imagination and activities were dominated by rescue fantasies. This development followed upon the death of her father from a tumor when the patient was five years old. As the analysis subsequently demonstrated, she was at that time at the height of that phase of development during which the little girl usually exchanges her wish to have the father's phallus for the wish to bear his child. Unconsciously, the death of the father meant to the patient that he had gone to heaven and had thereby rendered the task of getting the phallus-child almost impossible. The hope that the father would return and fulfill this wish by impregnating her was to be seen in various fears of ghosts and intruders and in many typical rescue fantasies expressed in increasingly sublimated editions.

The editions of the rescue fantasy changed in form and content as the patient matured (cf. Arlow, 1961). As a child, she imagined saving people from shipwreck or from a pirate ship (she lived near the ocean). Later, she became a lifeguard, a Sunday school teacher and finally took up work in the slums with underprivileged children. The impending marriage to the head of her project corresponded in essence to the content of her adolescent fantasy of marrying a great leader, helping him establish a world order of justice and peace, and finally dying with him in an airplane crash while en route to perform some errand of mercy (cf. Jones, 1911).

The notion of the returning father, so close in content to the apocalyptic second coming of the Messiah, was a vivid and real concept when the patient was a child. Having been told that her father had gone away to heaven, she kept looking for him in all strangers who turned up in the vicinity of her home. She also tried to catch sight of his face by looking for it between the clouds in the skies. Anxiety-laden representations of the same wish were expressed in her fear of intruders and of ghosts as

well as in the classic nocturnal ceremonial of the "Bride of Death"
(Abraham, 1912).

Sometimes during the hypnogogic period, and occasionally as an intrusion upon her thinking during masturbation, the patient would imagine
that she saw a face, a pair of eyes, or a phallus approaching her from
above and coming toward her face, her mouth, or her vagina.

The symptoms of headache, photophobia, and fear of developing a
brain tumor were analyzed in the seventh month of the patient's analysis
in connection with the celebration of Christmas. A few weeks before
Christmas the patient and her mother had gone to visit an exhibition of
paintings which the Nazis had seized during the war and which were
now being exhibited in the United States prior to their return to their
rightful owners in Europe. One section of this exhibition had to do with
paintings of the Madonna. When the patient was in this section she kept
looking at the Christ child and especially at his penis. She was aware of
mounting anxiety to the point where she could no longer stand it, felt
very faint, and had to leave the exhibition.

On December 24, the patient observed a woman with a young child
in the analyst's office. During the session the patient expressed the thought
that the woman whom she had seen may have been the analyst's wife.
Her mind then turned to the anticipation of Christmas. She wondered
whether the analyst celebrated this holiday. She recalled listening to portions of the "Messiah" and how impressed she was by the phrase, "the
Lord with us." This led, in turn, to various recollections of Christmas
and childhood and some vague memory of her father at Christmas time.
Her next thoughts concerned an article in a newspaper about a psychiatrist whose patient had committed suicide. The details of the story led
to thoughts of possible relations between the psychiatrist and the patient.
She then thought of Fagin as he appears in Dickens' *Oliver Twist*, a vil-
lainous Jew. She also recalled occasions before her father's illness when she
feared going into a dark room. Several times her father, in order to help her
overcome the fear, would stand at the foot of the stairway while the patient
went up to her room in the dark. Throughout this, the father would keep
talking to the daughter in order to reassure her by the presence of his voice
(the sexualization of hearing had been noticed earlier in the analysis). The
next thought which occurred to the patient was a fleeting idea which she
had had when she observed the young child in the waiting room. It struck
her that in some respects this little boy resembled the analyst and she
laughed and said that she had the utterly fantastic thought that the boy
might be the illegitimate result of some sexual experience between the previous patient and the analyst. The patient then recalled that while she had
been thinking of the little boy she was aware that a headache which she
had had earlier in the day had recurred. This headache was in the middle
of her forehead, slightly above the right eye. She had noticed the headache originally when driving down for her appointment and was aware
of the fact that the pains came on when the rays of the sun shone into
her eyes.

At this point, the observation was made that on the 24th day of

December she was preoccupied with the thought of an improper relationship between the analyst and some woman and a child born out of
such a union. The patient stated that she had often felt that Jesus had
been an illegitimate child. In her early teens she wanted very much to
play the role of Mary but, much to her disappointment, was refused the
part because the teachers who cast the members of the class for the
pageant insisted that the role of Mary should be played by someone who
had dark hair. When she was about thirteen, she became furious when a
friend of hers who had blond hair was given the role although she herself had been ruled out on many occasions for this reason.

The material up to this point established that the patient was involved in a transference fantasy of bearing an illegitimate child to
the analyst and that this was a repetition of an earlier fantasy wish
in which she identified herself with the Virgin Mary in the Christmas myth. This, however, left unexplained the symptom of headache
which appeared dramatically in the midst of the patient's associations.
When this was pointed out to the patient, she recalled that the headache
felt "as a sort of tightening, expanding feeling inside as if a tumor or
something were growing." The analogy was made to a pregnancy, to
which the patient replied that on the previous Sunday, while lying in
bed late in the morning, she half opened her eyes to see the rays of the
sun streaming through the window at her. The rays were irritating and
produced unpleasant sensations in her head. Through her half-closed
eyes, the patient thought that the shaft of sunshine coming through the
curtains reminded her of a phallus directed toward her. This she associated with the hypnogogic vision of a face, a pair of eyes, and a phallus
coming toward her. When she spoke of the rays of the sun, she said, "It
seemed as if the rays of the sun entering my eyes were just like a penis
coming down towards me from above."

This material demonstrates how the professional and religious sublimations which the patient had achieved were regressively reinstinctual-
ized. They reverted to the original impulses from which they were derived. The recurrent scopophilic-incorporative wish once again became
the source of an intrapsychic conflict, thus reproducing the set of conditions which existed earlier in life and which led to the institution of the
patient's sublimations. In this instance, however, the return of the repressed id wishes resulted in symptom formation. The re-emergent wishes
found substitutive gratification in the symptoms of headache and photophobia. The fantasy upon which these symptoms were based contained a
more primitive expression of the underlying id impulse. In place of the
sublimated, divine election of the favored Madonna in the poetic setting of
the angel, the lily, and the celestial light streaming through the vaulted
windows, a disembodied phallus approaches the patient's eyes in a
shaft of light. Even in the highly stylized "superego" paintings of the medieval period (Sachs, 1920) which prescribed the fundamental features for

artistic representations of the Annunciation to the Madonna, there occurred from time to time some regressive breakthrough of the sexual significance of the symbol of the rays of light. Ordinarily, in such paintings, in the shafts of light which entered the room in which the Virgin was seated, one could see the dove, the symbol of the Holy Ghost. In some paintings, however, such as by the Master of Flemalle, the place of the dove is taken by a nude homunculus, who is pictured descending upon a shaft of light from the mouth of God bearing a cross over his shoulder.[1]

To incorporate the paternal phallus is a universal wish of children of both sexes during the oedipal phase. While incorporation by way of the mouth is the most prominent and perhaps most common expression of this impulse, any aperture or avenue of ingress to the body may be conceived as the incorporating agent, e.g., the anus, nose, ears, eyes, and even the skin (Lewin, 1930). Incorporation through the eyes has been discussed by many authors, e.g., Freud (1911), Fenichel (1937), Abraham (1927), Strachey (1930), Greenacre (1951), to mention only a few. Fantasies of incorporating the phallus visually may exist side by side with other expressions of the same wish or as variant expressions of the wish. In the Schreber case, for example, the symbolic equivalence of light and the emanation from the father's phallus is explicitly stated in connection with the delusion of being impregnated by the rays of the sun (Freud, 1911). In this instance this mode of introjection runs parallel to fantasies of anal impregnation. In the case of the prophet Ezekiel, during the process of consecration (which is the male counterpart of the Annunciation) the awesome vision of the divine phallus is followed immediately by the ingestion of the word of God in the form of a sweet-tasting scroll which is forced into the prophet's mouth. Through this act of ingestion, the prophet becomes identified with God and shares his omnipotence (Arlow, 1951a).

Hart (1949) surveyed the literature concerning the unconscious significance of the eye emphasizing how its functioning unconsciously may be conceived as active or passive, emissive or receptive, erotic and aggressive.

[1] Regressive reinstinctualization of religious sublimations, a phenomenon commonly observed in individuals during psychoanalysis, is by no means a rare occurrence in groups. The sensuality of the medieval "Black Mass" and the violent aggression of doctrinal disputes or religious wars are two examples. Another example may be cited from the ritualized rowdyism and drinking permitted groups of North African Bar Mitzvah boys (Arlow, 1951). A study of the social conditions under which large-scale regression of religious sublimations occurs would be a very important undertaking. Some aspects of what happened to religion among the Nazis in Germany bear directly on this problem (Wangh, 1962).

Fenichel (1937) compares the receptive, incorporating role of the eye with that of the mouth and states his conviction that this form of ocular activity is an important antecedent to the process of identification, a view which was re-emphasized recently by Greenacre (1958) in association with problems of sexual identity.

The childhood wish to incorporate the father's phallus is so widespread that it lends itself readily to the process of mythopoesis. Symptomatology and mythopoesis demonstrate the many fantasy expressions which this wish may take. Ocular introjection is only one form, but it is a very common form. Myths of virgins impregnated by rays of light from the sun or from fire are exceedingly numerous and have been reported from practically all areas of the world (cf. Jones, 1914). In the case of the Christian religion, this theme attains a central role in connection with the legends surrounding the miraculous birth of the Messiah.

As has already been noted, for members of a religion, the central myth plays the same role which a work of literature may serve for its readers. A community of individuals is established. They share a daydream in common. Their mutual participation in the unconscious fantasy is analogous to (unconscious) mutual exculpation (Sachs, 1920). Paintings may be regarded as graphic daydreams in common. Appealing to the visual sensibilities of the spectators, the artist may give concrete imagery to a shared fantasy, satisfying for himself and his audience voyeuristic and exhibitionistic wishes in a manner which is completely in accord with established religious teachings. The appeal to visual stimulation is obviously of primary significance in the myth of impregnation through the eyes. Such paintings would appeal not only to those individuals with sublimations of powerful scopophilic trends, but also to persons of both sexes, who in one way or another can identify themselves with the central figure on the canvas in the act of receiving the divine phallus.

Artistic representations of the Annunciation to the Madonna studied by Jones were approached from the viewpoint of his interest in the fantasy of impregnation through the ear. I would like to emphasize those elements of the fantasy which concern impregnation through the eyes. In classic paintings of the Annunciation, the rays of light usually are depicted as entering the room from Heaven or God the Father, through a window. In the midst of the rays there often appears the dove, symbol of the Holy Ghost. Reference has been made to the nude figure of a man in at least one representation of the scene. Meiss (1945), who has written an authoritative study of the symbolism of light in these paintings, states:

"The rays of the Annunciation are in essence symbols of the Holy Spirit but are usually conceived as light and in paintings of the Annunciation from the 14th century on, windows or other openings are often provided to permit the passage into the chamber of the virgin. The subtle and pervasive symbolism characteristic of the work of both these painters (Jan van Eyck and the Master of Flemalle) shows itself again in the use of precisely seven rays of these representations. In late medieval painting the number of rays in the Annunciation varies greatly from three to twelve or more; three symbolizing the trinity, are perhaps the most common, seven undoubtedly refer to the seven gifts of the Holy Ghost."

The destination of the rays of light also varies in different paintings. In some instances, the light strikes the Virgin's ear. In other cases, the rays are directed toward the eyes, forehead, and even the breast. (It will be recalled that in the case of the patient described above, the rays of light were experienced as approaching her eyes and forehead and that she suffered from photophobia and headaches, the latter associated with a fear of developing a brain tumor.)

A number of advantages accrue in psychic life from the transformation of the forbidden, aggressive, incorporative scopophilic wish to take the father's penis into the sublimated, religious myth of impregnation through the eyes. Greenacre (1947) has traced in two patients the steps which may form the path by which the aggressively voyeuristic little girl may develop into the idealized, gentle Madonna. Both these patients reported experiences of intense visual shocks connected with headache. These symptoms were derived from traumatic experiences of viewing the penis. The headaches constituted reactivations of the original trauma and mastery was attempted through "successive repetition in fantasy . . ., partial repression, or by the development of severely binding superego reaction formations of goodness which are supplemented by or converted into lofty ideals." The combination of lofty idealism and headache reminded Greenacre of the halo which appears around the head of the Madonna and other saintly figures in paintings. As in the case of the prophet, by the process of sublimation, a desexualized identification is thus attained with the (morally) aggrandized ideal image of the father, and the aggression against him is transformed into loving emulation and into doing his bidding.

In the construction of the myth of the Madonna's conception through the eyes, conflicts over the voyeuristic aggression toward the phallus and fears of retaliation from the phallus are mastered, thus freeing the individual from inhibitions or symptom formation. Strachey (1930) points out that certain reading difficulties and inhibitions are based on the unconscious connection between looking and sadistic oral incorporation of the paternal phallus. Fenichel (1937) states that the Biblical prohibition against looking at God is based on the idea that looking implies identification. If a man looks upon God face to face, something of the glory of God passes into him. It is this impious act, the likening of oneself to God, which is forbidden when man is forbidden to look at God. This prohibition finds additional expression in the injunction against the creation of any graven images. Bornstein (1930) interprets the forbidden looking at God's face as a displacement from below to above.

In the myth of the Madonna's conception through the eyes, as in the consecration of the prophet, the entire relationship is changed. Active grasping is transformed into passive receiving. An unconscious wish to steal the phallus by force is transformed into a shared fantasy of receiving a pregnancy as a gift, as an act of grace and by special selection of the divine will. The warm, gentle, life-giving rays of the sun stand in contrast to sadistic, destructive ingestion (Kris, 1939).

The imagery in which impregnation is substitutively represented by the passage of rays of light is particularly felicitous in helping overcome guilt and fear of retaliation concerning aggressive incorporative wishes directed against the penis. With the onset of her illness, the patient described above developed various inhibitions of looking as well as of learning. She felt guilty over the unconscious significance of her voyeuristic trends and of her intellectual curiosity. She punished the offending organs through the headache and the photophobia. In common with many patients who have conflicts over wishes to incorporate the phallus, she developed a fear of cancer, of a brain tumor. This was based on an unconscious fantasy that the incorporated phallus would retaliate by destroying the patient (her eyes and brain) from within. When, as in the myth, impregnation takes place through the medium of light, neither the male nor female principle, neither the active nor the passive agency is injured. Furthermore, the woman remains a virgin.

These considerations found their way into the theological disputation concerning the immaculate conception. The church authorities provided, as it were, a set of theological rationalizations which could unconsciously serve as reassurance against guilt or fear of retaliation connected with the unconscious significance of the Madonna's conception through the eyes.

Meiss (1945) writes that theologians and poets often explain the mystery of the incarnation of God by comparing the miraculous conception of Christ with the passage of sunlight through a glass window. He quotes Salzer: "Just as the brilliance of the sun fills and penetrates a glass window without damaging it and pierces its solid form with imperceptible subtleties, neither hurting it when entering nor destroying it when emerging, thus the word of God, the splendor of the Father, entered the virgin chamber and then came forth from the closed womb." He quotes Livius: "Along with these similes they spoke of Christ as a light or sometimes fire which the virgin received and bore. The virgin was regarded as a window through which the spirit of God passed to earth. From these metaphors there was developed in the 9th century or earlier the image of the sunlight in the glass. It possessed the advantage of symbolizing both stages of the miracle, the conception as well as the birth" (Meiss, 1945).

In a further quote from Salzer, one may perceive not only the reassurance against injury which is given to the receptive, incorporating or female agency, but in addition, a reassurance that the entering- penetrating symbol for the phallus is not damaged: "During the 11th and 12th centuries the simile was used by several authorities including St. Bernard. Usually it was interpreted to emphasize the virginity of Mary rather than the ghostly power of Christ. Thus St. Bridget whose vision of the nativity influenced the representation of that scene throughout Europe in the late 14th and 15th centuries is addressed by Christ in the first revelation, 'I have assumed the flesh without sin and lust, entering the womb of the virgin just as the sun passes through a precious stone. Whereas the sun penetrating a glass window does not damage it, the virginity of the virgin is not spoiled by my assumption of the human form'. . . . The theologians used to say, 'As light is colored by the radiations through stained glass, the holy spirit acquires human form by entering the sacred chamber or temple of the virgin.' St. Bernard after alluding to the ray and the unbroken window in the passage quoted above adds, '*As a pure ray enters a glass window and emerges unspoiled* but has acquired the color of the glass, the son of *God who entered the most chaste womb of the virgin emerged pure* but took on the color of the virgin, that is the nature of a man and of a comeliness of human form and he clothed himself in it' [Meiss, 1945]."

SUMMARY

1. In this analysis of the significance of the myth concerning the Madonna's conception through the eyes, an attempt has been made to emphasize the role which the central myths of a major religion may play

in shaping the education and character formation of members of the society. Through its mythology, a society tends to induce a psychological climate which favors the realization of certain desirable identifications and which fosters the institution of ego ideals and superego structures in consonance with the mores of the society. Different societies emphasize different ideal qualities and this emphasis is reflected in their mythology.

2. In their psychological function, myths may be compared to works of art. They have the following in common: they are based upon a fantasy which contains, in a disguised form, some representation of a fundamental childhood instinctual wish. Through unconscious identification with the central figure of the myth, the participant is afforded a certain degree of instinctual gratification. This is the id aspect of the myth which exerts its strong influence because of its wish-fulfilling nature. In myths which are central to religious tradition, as in great works of art, the superego elements ultimately must predominate. Central myths of a religion must demonstrate a high quality of sublimation and renunciation.

3. By sharing the myth in common the members of the religious community are bound together in their relationship of identification and mutual exculpation. This process integrates the individual into the group and gives the group a sense of direction and dedication.

4. The myth of the Madonna's conception through the eyes was examined in this light. It was interpreted as a fantasy expression of an oedipal wish to acquire the father's phallus through the process of incorporation through the eyes.

5. Regressive reinstinctualization of the sublimation of religion often lays bare the role of myth and religion in the solution of intrapsychic conflicts. Conflicts over the regressively reactivated instinctual wishes may give rise to inhibitions and symptom formation and may arouse feelings of guilt and fear of retaliation. Under special historical circumstances, changes may take place in group structure, changes which liberate the expression of unsublimated instinctualized forms of behavior. In other words, it is possible for religion to undergo regressive transformation in the mass as it does in certain individuals.

6. The role of scopophilia in religious sublimation, in religious painting, and in "saintly" character formation was discussed in connection with the fantasy of impregnation through the eyes.

7. A clinical fragment was presented in order to demonstrate the activity of the ego in integrating the id impulse with the superego demands and reality during the process of mythopoesis. In connection with

the fantasy of the Madonna's conception through the eyes, it was striking to observe how theological arguments serve as rationalizations of unconscious reassurances against guilt and fear of retaliation. The wish to steal the phallus is transformed into a fulfillment of divine purpose, and the element of injury is happily circumvented by analogy to the nondamaging passage of light through glass.

BIBLIOGRAPHY

Abraham, K. (1909), Dreams and Myths. In: *Clinical Papers and Essays on Psycho-Analysis.* New York: Basic Books, 1955, pp. 153-209.

———(1912), A Complicated Ceremonial Found in Neurotic Women. In: *Selected Papers on Psycho-Analysis.* London: Hogarth Press, 1942, pp. 157-164.

———(1927), Restrictions and Transformations of Scoptophilia. In: *Selected Papers on Psycho-Analysis.* London: Hogarth Press, pp. 168-235.

Arlow, J. (1951), A Psychoanalytic Study of a Religious Initiation Rite: Bar Mitzvah. In: *The Psychoanalytic Study of the Child,* 6:353-377, eds. R. S. Eissler et al. New York: International Universities Press, 1953.

———(1951a), The Consecration of the Prophet. *Psychoanal. Quart.,* 20:374-397.

———(1961), Ego Psychology and the Study of Mythology. *J. Amer. Psychoanal. Assn.,* 9:371-393.

Bornstein, B. (1930), Zur Psychogenese der Pseudodebilität. *Int. Ztschr. Psychoanal.,* 16: 378-399.

Fenichel, O. (1937), The Scoptophilic Instinct and Identification. *Int. J. Psychoanal.,* 18:6-34.

Freud, S. (1911), Psychoanalytic Notes on an Autobiographical Account of a Case of Paranoia. *Standard Edition,* 12:9-82. London: Hogarth Press, 1958.

Greenacre, P. (1951), Respiratory Incorporation and the Phallic Phase. In: *The Psychoanalytic Study of the Child,* 6:180-205, eds. R. S. Eissler et al. New York: International Universities Press.

———(1958), Early Physical Determinants in the Development of the Sense of Identity. *J. Amer. Psychoanal. Assn.,* 6:612-627.

Hart, H. (1949), The Eye in Symbol and Symptom. *Psychoanal. Rev.,* 36:1-21.

Jones, E. (1911), On 'Dying Together.' *Essays on Applied Psychoanalysis,* 1:9-21. New York: International Universities Press, 1964.

———(1914), The Madonna's Conception Through the Ear. *Essays on Applied Psychoanalysis,* 2:266-357. New York: International Universities Press, 1964.

Kris, E. (1939), On Inspiration. *Int. J. Psychoanal.,* 20:377-389.

Lewin, B. D. (1930), Kotschmieren, Menses und weibliches Ueber-Ich. *Int. Ztschr. Psychoanal.,* 16:43-56.

Meiss, M. (1945), Light as Form, Symbol in Some 15th Century Paintings. *Art Bulletin,* September 1945, 27(3):175-181.

Róheim, G. (1950), *Psychoanalysis and Anthropology.* New York: International Universities Press.

———(1950a), The Oedipus Complex, Magic and Culture. In: *Psychoanalysis and the Social Sciences,* 2:173-328, ed. G. Róheim. New York: International Universities Press.

Sachs, H. (1920), *The Community of Day Dreams in the Creative Unconscious.* Cambridge, Mass.: Science-Art Publishers, pp. 11-54.

————(1950), *Personal and Impersonal Art.* Cambridge, Mass.: Science-Art Publishers, pp. 55-62.

Strachey, J. (1930), Some Unconscious Factors in Reading. *Int. J. Psychoanal., 11*:322-331.

Wangh, M. (1962), *Psychoanalytic Study of Anti-Semitism.* (Dynamics of Nazi Anti-Semitism.) Paper delivered before New York Psychoanalytic Society, October 30, 1962.

On Interpreting the Oedipus Plays

MARK KANZER, M.D.

The Oedipus myth is frequently analyzed on the basis of the *Oedipus Tyrannus* of Sophocles, as though the latter represented an age-old, spontaneous and unitary fantasy of the human race, a universal dream that had been captured intact by the Greek dramatist. Similarly, the personality and even developmental stages in the life of the hero have been expounded from this same material as though it represented, in fact, the experiences of a particular individual who became somehow the allegorical representative of the male's unconscious sexual strivings everywhere and in all times. Sophocles, however, was not a dispassionate or scientific recorder of myths and, in the *Oedipus Tyrannus*, he was expressing highly personal views on political, religious, and military problems of his own time (Gassner, 1940; Gregg & Lattimore, 1959). As an ordained priest and an aristocrat, he had little taste for upstart tyrants like Oedipus who came to power because of their individual intellects and achievements, rather than a royal background and the will of the gods.

Moreover, Sophocles was submitting his play with an eye to winning the annual award of the Athenian drama critics. In this respect, it may be noted, the *Oedipus Tyrannus* was not a success. Some felt that the fault lay in a poor production, since the playwright was not able to find wealthy backers. Others were upset by sensational aspects which were regarded as an offense to good taste. For example, Sophocles employed a mask which showed blood streaming from the eyeless sockets of his hero. The Greeks, after all, may not have been closer to the unconscious than the Elizabethans, as has been suggested (Freud, 1900). The latter did not object when the eyes of Gloucester were torn from his head in full view of the audience. In any event, the Oedipus that emerges from the Sophocles classic was a dramatic hero, in many respects a contemporary sophisticated Athenian, and scarcely a universal dream that had acquired life.

There was a distinctly different version of the Oedipus myth in Homer's epics some six hundred years before Sophocles. Here there was no reference to the Sphinx; Oedipus was not blinded nor was he exiled, but lived

26

on as ruler of Thebes, afflicted by the Furies as the result of a curse by his dying mother. Ultimately, he was killed in combat and buried with honor in his own country; the version by Sophocles permits the legendary hero to die in Colonus, a suburb of Athens, where the dramatist himself had been born. Several intriguing ideas suggest themselves at this point, but we shall mention just one: the noteworthy parallel to the story of Orestes, the mother murderer, who was also afflicted by the Furies (a euphemism presumably for psychosis), and who found a haven and cure in Athens. Orestes may be regarded as representative of the negative Oedipus complex, the deeper and recessive aspect of the Oedipus myth itself. The parricidal trends appear overtly in the chronicle; the matricidal and homosexual wishes must be hidden, as through the symbolism that conceals the mother behind the figure of the Sphinx (Kanzer, 1948).

Sophocles, it appears, used as his source of information a ninth century B.C. narrative about the Kings of Thebes and the civil wars between the sons of Oedipus, which were dramatized in other plays of the Oedipus cycle (Gregg & Lattimore, 1959). In these conflicts, the greatest in Greek history before the Trojan War, Oedipus himself was assigned something of the role of an allegorical spirit, an ancestor like Adam, whose sins continued to live in and demand expiation even from his descendants. Nevertheless, it is by no means improbable, in the light of modern archeological and historical research, that a factual basis for the Theban legend exists (Reik, 1920). Velikovsky (1960), in a work which is none too convincing, suggests that Oedipus was identical with the Egyptian King Akhnaton. More substance seems to adhere to his endeavors to link the Greek and the Egyptian cities of Thebes, a matter to which we shall also give some attention.

The original chronicle of the Theban kings that Sophocles used has not been preserved. The dramatist is supposed to have adhered to it rather faithfully, though his own account about Oedipus is manifestly filled with contradictions (Gregg & Lattimore, 1959). The studies of Carl Robert (1915) suggest a derivation of the hero from a demigod, son and lover of the earth goddess Demeter. Shrines of an Oedipus cult existed in several Greek cities, the oldest probably at Eteonos, near Attica. The story of Oedipus thus becomes linked with one of the most ancient forms of worship, the spring vegetation rites which are frequently associated with matriarchal regimes and the slaying of the Winter King, real or symbolic, by the Summer King. The relationship between the kings is recognized overtly or tacitly as that between father and son.

Certain universal roots of the Oedipus legend, arising in this way, may be discovered in the play of Sophocles, which was presented in honor of the feast of Dionysos, a similar vegetation demigod and reputed in mythology to be a kinsman of Oedipus. The drama perpetuates and sublimates in art what was originally human sacrifice to procure bread and wine. It was the breakthrough of blood into the artistic mask which horrified the Greeks, not the artfully presented oedipal themes of incest and parricide, which could more readily serve for catharsis of drives that were already attenuated. The plague that the sins of Oedipus drew on Thebes were those that would be disastrous in an agricultural community; along with the inability of women to conceive or give birth, there were corresponding blights on livestock and flocks. Apollo, the god of the sun, had somehow been offended; only the advent of a fertile and blameless new king could remedy the situation. The procession of the seasons was thus linked by a nature myth with that of the human generations.

The role of Oedipus as the traditional dying god, demigod, or king, and his rebirth as the new ruler, parallel the crucifixion of Jesus and his resurrection, as aspects of a similar spring ritual. In both instances, the father is ultimately a god or king, Jehovah or Apollo, Herod or Laius, in the tradition of the family romance. The coming of the son is associated with oracular warnings to the father (renascent memories of his own infantile oedipal strivings), which lead to his efforts to dispose of the infant. The Cross derives from the sacred tree (mother) on which the old king is immolated to insure a new blossoming; the nails through the feet of Jesus correspond with those through the feet of Oedipus; the finding of the newborn child by the shepherd is a birth fantasy that belongs both to springtime and the sexual theories of children.

In the opinion of Robert (1915), this spring ritual aspect of the Oedipus legend must be separated from the narrative of the Sphinx, which seems to accrue to the myth from other sources. The slaying of a monster does belong to the spring ritual and has totemistic antecedents; he is the Winter King. The Sphinx not unnaturally presents some special riddles. It apparently originated in Egypt, where the earliest versions were masculine and without wings (Roscher, 1912). In Crete, we encounter the first female winged Sphinxes; these seem however to be secondary fusions of an imported Sphinx with local monsters, like the harpies, half human, half animal, who represented the mother goddess. The winged birdlike element in the Cretan Sphinx and the harpies bespoke, according to tradition, oracular powers and the solution as well as the propounding of riddles; the priests made prophecies by observing the flight of the birds (Robert, 1915).

The lion's body, which the Greek Sphinx shared with some of the several Egyptian varieties, invites attention to the legend of Cadmus, ancestor of Oedipus, and of his sister Europa. The Cretans, who claimed descent from Europa, and the Thebans, who claimed descent from Cadmus, both contributed to the Sphinx cult. The symbol of Cadmus was a lion; he and his sister were Phoenicians and their father Agenor was reported to have come from Egypt to the land of Canaan some five centuries before Moses traversed the same pathway (Graves, 1955). The name Cadmus itself derives from a Semitic root, *Queddem*, "the easterner." There are many curious parallels between Cadmus and Moses; both shared with Oedipus the fate of offending the gods and therefore being compelled to end their days as homeless wanderers.

Cadmus, the wandering Phoenician, is thus a legendary link between the Sphinx of Egypt and that of Greece. He is also a vehicle of familiar Semitic traditions; like Moses, he was guided by the gods to a promised land, where he proceeded to found a city for his descendants. It was the Egyptian Thebes that was the center of the Sphinx cult and its queen was the consort of the gods—a role that was often equivalent to reposing by the highway, like the Sphinx, and selecting her mate from the strangers who passed by and after a year of kingship were sacrificed to the gods. In the course of transition to patriarchy, the queens wed their own brothers —providing further material for the Oedipus myth. The Egyptian Thebes of the hundred gates was contrasted by Homer with the Greek Thebes of seven gates—in fact, the Greek name was conferred secondarily on the older Egyptian city. Quite possibly the links were furnished by migration, symbolized by Cadmus, just as legendarily Troy was linked with Rome through Aeneas.

The civic emblem of the Greek Thebes was a monster, half lion, half snake, a figure representing two familiar components of the Sphinx, (Graves, 1955). Cadmus, the lion, was reputed to have been turned into a snake in his later years as punishment for having killed a serpent sacred to the natives among whom he came to dwell and found his city. Behind this myth apparently rests a history of conflict between patriarchal Phoenicians and local snake-cult matriarchies during the second millennium before Christ. The blind Teiresias, who figures in the Oedipus legend, was originally a snake god or priest (Robert, 1915); the curse of Jocasta against Oedipus was fulfilled by the Furies, archaic winged and snaky-haired representations of the mother goddess; the fate of Oedipus was induced through the prophecies and plagues sent by Apollo, the Python god, who thus doomed the descendant of the conquering Eastern lion to be driven like his ancestor from the land belonging to the snake people. There is in this myth, with its totemistic traditions, a calendar allusion: the lion and the snake were for the Thebans the symbols of the waxing and the waning portions of the year respectively; the transformation of Cadmus from a lion to a snake would coincide with a sacrifice to denote the changing of the seasons.

The transition from lion to snake also expresses fantasies about sexual change and castration. Teiresias, who plays the part of an oracle and sage in many Greek legends and whose name ("he who delights in signs") indicates that he too was a solver of riddles, was apparently introduced into the Oedipus story only secondarily. Here he was made into an alter ego of the hero, to whom were displaced his outer blindness and his inner understanding, characteristic symbols of the internalization of character development as the oedipal phase succumbs to superego formation with the onset of the latency period. At some point in the development of the Oedipus myth, as Robert (1915) points out, the physical conquest over a monster was succeeded by a psychic victory. A symbolic parallel may be found in the traditions about Teiresias, who was reputed to have seen snakes in copulation. In a subsequent sequence of events, he was granted bisexual capacities to enjoy sex alternately as male and female. But, he offended Hera, queen of the gods, and was condemned by her to a blindness that was mitigated through his ability to foretell the future events that he would not be able to see.

It was also Hera, offended by the bisexuality of Laius, father of Oedipus, who sent the Sphinx to terrorize the people of Thebes until the monster was subdued by the intellect of the parricidal son. One may make the interpretation that homosexual dispositions of the oedipal period (rivalry with Hera), subdued by castration anxiety and superego formation, were granted a sublimated outlet during adolescent development—the subsequent regression being the point of departure for the oedipal tragedy. A cluster of myths condenses about the Tieresias-Laius theme—the rape of Ganymede by Zeus, for example, finds its parallel in the misconduct of Laius with a youth. As Reik (1920) in particular has emphasized, there is a conspicuous and unlikely duplication of events in the Oedipus narrative—two separate plagues sent down on Thebes, two different encounters of Oedipus on the road to Thebes (with Laius and with the Sphinx), and it is not improbable that (as with two dreams of the same night) there is a split which depicts first the heterosexual and then the homosexual aspect of the hero's love-making.

Our endeavor to establish the background of the Oedipus myth as distinct from the dramatized version presented by Sophocles broadens into the typical patterns which develop when a manifest content is traced through the tangles that lead to the latent content. Historical events emerge like day residues; many lands and many cultures made their contributions to the finished product for which the genius of Sophocles provided the façade of a secondary elaboration. The Oedipus myth may be viewed as a poetic chronicle of real historical value, like the Bible or the Odyssey; the experiences of individuals and of nations, the records of wars, migrations and social customs, have found their way into it. Cadmus is reputed by legend to have introduced the Semitic alphabet into Greece. A recent archeological and linguistic achievement seems to confirm this by decoding a mysterious language which suggests that the Phoenicians did in fact invade Greece and introduce their alphabet at about the time Cadmus and Europa made their appearance on the mythological scene (*New York Times*, 1961). Roscher (1912) is among the authorities with the complementary view that the Phoenicians of this period brought over the Sphinx from the Near East and ultimately from Egypt.

If myths are to be compared to the dreams of young nations (Freud, 1908), it is perhaps because dreams as well as myths deal integratively with external reality as well as with a structural hierarchy of men's wishes to which reality relates. Each dream is stimulated by immediate realistic experiences which evoke real memories of the past. It is the pattern of these memory constellations and the functions which they serve that distinguishes the dream from the myth and places both within a spectrum of problem-solving thoughts. Both the dream and the myth create symbols which expedite the transition between inner and outer reality. The dream symbol mobilizes memories which facilitate the transition to inner reality and autoplastic solutions; the myth is more of an intermediate toward outer reality and alloplastic solutions. External reality is accepted conditionally, provided there are still sufficient elements of denial admissible to safeguard the omnipotence of the ego and fulfill the wishes of the unconscious. Typical stages of myth formation indicate their early use in rituals to insure success in hunting and in planting crops. These food-procuring activities tend to become day residues for repressed impulses which threaten realistic success and must be diverted by ritual and mythmaking. Thus the myth finds its place between the oral hallucinatory satisfactions afforded by dreams and the oral mastery techniques which are part of the development of reality testing; regressively, it serves to conceal and gratify the nascent sexual drives.

The function of the myth in binding repressed instinctual impulses makes it of inherent importance in superego formation both for the needs of the individual and of the group. Where the dream represents the demands of the instincts, the myth tends to perpetuate and represent the demands of society on the mental apparatus for symbolization and acceptance. Different forms of culture evolve their own characteristic myths, and in that of Oedipus may be found deposits of the fantasies of totemistic hunting tribes, nomadic sheep tenders, agricultural matriarchies and city-founding military chiefs. The Sphinx herself is no simple nightmare figure compiled by primary process thought from infantile memories and anxieties; she is also a consciously devised emblem and ideographic description of momentous events among mature peoples.

The latent content of the Oedipus myth thus becomes truly universal. Perhaps it is possible to trace in the development of Oedipus himself that of a universal man, because the stages of individual growth find parallels among the social formations which left their fossil-like imprints among the various strata of the myth. The tribal hunt presents analogies to the oedipal stage of development and the phobias that go with it; the agricultural ritual, with seasonal death and resurrection, compares with the latency period and superego formation; the re-emergence of the sexual impulses, as these become manifest in the Oedipus drama, may be considered closer to puberty and to paranoia.[1]

In previous studies, I have discussed such individual and maturational aspects of the Oedipus legend as are recorded in the plays of Sophocles (Kanzer, 1948, 1950). His oedipal trilogy presents in essence a record of psychosocial problems from birth to death—from the actual abandonment of the newborn infant to his token sacrifice (death) and readoption (rebirth) in the circumcision rite that was symbolized by the laming of the hero. His growth is portrayed through a complex of characters who represent different dispositions and phases during his personality development—Teiresias, Theseus, Creon, even Antigone—until at Colonus his death revives ancient traditions of the slaying of the Winter King in the sacred grove of the mother goddesses.

Thus, in the Oedipus myth as depicted by Sophocles, we find that the diverse roots and fragments have been synthesized into a pattern and parable of human life generally. The very fact that so many men in so many cultures participated in the growth of the myth, each permitting it to pass through and be enriched by his own unconscious, each poet among them passing it on to other men in the idiom of his own time,

[1] "The oedipus complex too may have had stages of development and the study of prehistory may enable us to trace them out" (Freud, 1919a).

insured in the end its impersonal representation of the basic drives of mankind, illustrating paradigmatically two of Freud's observations about myths: (1) that they provide an externalization of the inner mental processes themselves and (2) that through them the individual emerges from the group (Freud, 1921). The most unique feature of the Oedipus legend and the one that distinguishes it from all others is the ability to represent in the manifest content such deeply rooted personal and social taboos as the drives toward incest and parricide. To be sure, these may emerge on condition that they are represented as a fate unwittingly undergone. The introspective insights and projective universalizations of paranoid thought would probably be contributory here—especially as the manifest content still wards off homosexual and more deeply regressive preoedipal fantasies which are permitted symbolic representation only, as in the episode of the Sphinx.

Insofar as the Oedipus of the myth is a prototype of all men, he may be said to have no special personality. He is an externalization of the intellectual processes wrestling to control the oedipal conflicts in a social setting that requires their resolution according to established form. He must serve as a scapegoat, openly presenting to the community the desires it dares not fulfill or even acknowledge consciously, and providing it with a catharsis through the suffering of the hero and the horror that the spectator may hypocritically express. The poet gives the Oedipus of an era his own special features—e.g., Shakespeare's Hamlet, the Oedipus of Voltaire, Ivan Karamazov, Don Quixote. It was the special contribution of Sophocles that he developed the Oedipus legend itself beyond its previous limits in terms of psychosocial maturation and made it a vehicle for the prevailing Greek philosophy, "know thyself!"

Where the hero had advanced with the centuries from a monster-slayer, in the externalizing tradition of a totemistic culture and the counterphobic psychotherapeutic measures that it encouraged in adolescence, and had become a more introverted and thoughtful riddle-solver, Sophocles recognized that the riddle lay not in the outer universe but within man himself. Instead of seeking to explain fate as the will of the gods (with aggression internalized through religious institutions against which the Oedipus of Voltaire rebelled), the Greek dramatist advanced toward insight into the fact that fate lies in character, in the interaction between parents and children, and in the dispositions that we now call the Oedipus complex. To that extent, he implanted his own self and that of his contemporaries on the timeless features of the hero. His very innovations in the technique of the drama, such as reducing the importance of the chorus and introducing a third actor, gave greater scope to the role of the individual man emerging from myth and ritual (Gassner, 1940). The third actor, if we may risk an interpretation, was Sophocles himself in the guise of Oedipus.

Freud (1900) pointed out that the play unfolded like an analysis, and it was actually analysis that carried the Oedipus legend to its ultimate development—not only to recognize the meaning of the riddle, but to resolve it permanently, as the catharsis provided by Sophocles could not. With analysis, the myth—with its need to invoke a denial of reality—loses its function. It is interesting to consider how, even in the earliest delineation of the Sphinx, antecedent to all subsequent elaborations and modifications, the message of self-analysis as the key to the riddles of fate and the universe is depicted. Roscher (1912) indicates that there was at first no name for the Sphinx; its origin was in preverbal visual imagery, like the dream. The earliest Sphinxes seem to have been portraits of dead kings superimposed upon the body of a lion and set before their tombs to guard their remains and treasures against intruders. In effect, King Oedipus, confronting the Sphinx, encounters his own image as a mystery to be unraveled. The situation is familiar to the analyst from mirror dreams and the phenomenon of the double, with which man seeks to preserve his identity in the face of forces like castration and death that threaten to impinge upon his ego boundaries (Freud, 1919). The sense of the uncanny, which arises under these circumstances, is the affective reaction to the encounter with the Sphinx.

The sense of the uncanny is also elicited in a characteristically oedipal phase of development by the sight of the female organ—the Medusa reaction, with the lost penis displaced upward and represented by a headless body (Freud, 1922). The Sphinx, like the Medusa, is equipped with compensatory signs of masculinity—the lion's body, the serpent tail, the wings, even the breasts (which distract attention from the lower to the upper part of the woman's body and acquire phallic significance). The Greek Sphinx, like the Medusa, is a representation of the phallic mother goddess. She now becomes the "sphincter," the vaginal strangler. We encounter the Sphinx-Medusa in the familiar blank dream with orgasm, in which the moment of visualizing or entering the female organ becomes the occasion for blacking out of the dream image and a defensive orgasm (Kanzer, 1954). The blacking out of the image, reproduced in the blindness of Oedipus and the taboo on looking required of Perseus, may be presented in attenuated form in dreams of headless persons. The oral interpretation of the blank dream phenomenon, while valid within its own context, should not distract from the inherent phallic significance of the same events.

It is the challenge of the phallic phase of development to confront the penisless body of the love object; the riddle itself is the female organ. There is an ancient tradition which suggests that the answer to the riddle is somehow contained in the name of the riddle-solver (Robert, 1915). Oedipus' "swollen foot," the sexually excited male, is the correct answer, especially as supplemented by the verbal response "Man," in reply to the phallically symbolic problem of establishing the identity of a creature with a variable number of legs. The subsequent fate of the Sphinx is confirmatory; the victorious Oedipus either stabs (deflowers) her, or she throws herself over a cliff (pregnancy—also the habitual punishment of vestal virgins who had violated their vows of chastity).

The phallic interpretation of the encounter of Oedipus with the Sphinx finds almost detailed corroboration in an ancient Egyptian myth about the sun god Ra (*Larousse*, 1959). He was a god of fertility and his image is found on the tombs of the Egyptian kings, the pharaohs, sons of the sun god, as a promise of life arising again from death. He was not all-powerful, however, for the goddess Isis sent a serpent to bite him so that he suffered cruelly until he consented to reveal to her his true name. Thereafter Isis, the Egyptian Hera, herself became the goddess of the sun and of fertility, represented with the orb of the sun and the horns of a cow on her head. Here again the name seems visibly translated into the male genitals.

However, Isis is also depicted with a cow's head set on a human body (reversing the Sphinx arrangement). The legend avers that she was decapitated by her son Horus for protecting her brother Set, who had murdered the father of Horus, Osiris. Later, he replaced his mother's head with that of a cow. Certainly Horus is the ancestor of Oedipus, of Orestes and of Hamlet; Isis is the forebear of the Sphinx. The alternating loss and possession of the penis name, the riddle of the Sphinx, is a description of sexual intercourse, mirrored again in the story of the bisexual Teiresias and in the division of the Theban calendar between the lion and the snake. Perhaps ultimately the riddle of the Sphinx, so obviously placed in the phallic phase, is to give a name to that which does not exist—the female phallus, a feat that carries animism back to its ultimate origins in the magic of thought and the use of language as a tool to replace lost objects (Freud, 1913).

Discussion and Summary

The Oedipus plays of Sophocles constitute the traditional psycho-analytic source of knowledge and theorizing about the Oedipus legend and even about myths in general. Moreover, psychoanalysis of the characters tends to treat them as real personalities whose histories and motives can be reconstructed. Nevertheless, factual research indicates that this approach, successful as it has been in producing a rich and stimulating body of literature, must proceed with caution and with a view to certain propositions which emerge from the present review:

1. The Oedipus plays themselves, and especially the personalities involved, leaned upon tradition but were creatively elaborated so as to possess dramatic appeal and contemporary significance for a particular Athenian audience. They were vehicles for the conscious views and aspirations of the dramatist himself as well as for his specific unconscious fantasies. From the analytic standpoint, the oedipal plays are to be regarded as a manifest content to be traced to its origins.

2. A sociohistoric pathway toward the latent content indicates that in the case of the Oedipus legend, as in most others, cores of historic truth may be disentangled. These spread out in a time and space continuum that apparently contains residues of different social organizations and psychologies—totemistic, agricultural, nomadic, city-founding—together with their associated customs and traditions. Here a universal origin of the Oedipus myth may be discerned.

3. The Sphinx has often been compared to a nightmare figure, a product of condensation and a recurrence of infantile fears. Analogies in the sphere of social evolution and with respect to myths as the dreams of young nations have been made. Dreams and myths have related but different functions. The dream seeks to dissipate the external reality, the myth to make it more palatable. The Sphinx of the Oedipus legend has certain roots in the nightmare—we cite especially the blank dream with orgasm and the uncanny reaction to the realities that suddenly confront us like dreams which have invaded our waking lives. As prototype, the reaction to the sight of the female genital during the phallic phase may be invoked in connection with Oedipus and the triumphs that destroyed him. The Sphinx can also be traced realistically as an emblem that leads to unknown periods of human civilization—but not necessarily to more infantile psychology than that of contemporary man. The Oedipus legend is a psychosocial record, not merely a psychological progression.

4. The mind of the storyteller is compelled to unify the data that the myth makes available to him, a work of secondary elaboration. He usually

has different versions of a myth from which to select; it is ritual that tends to establish standardized and invariable accounts because certain more authentic variants are unacceptable. The myth, or myth group, thus provides scope for a variety of psychosocial experiences and outlooks; moreover, it tends to achieve a secondary autonomy that acquires characteristic developmental patterns of its own (cf. Freud, 1913).

The universality of the myth's roots and the social stages through which it evolves ultimately eradicate the individual detail and preserve the typical, so that the psychic functions themselves come to be externalized in the characters and action. It is this very universality that makes it possible to "analyze" Oedipus as though he were a real person; moreover the submergence of the individual in the general constitutes the very condition which Freud (1908) postulated for the "mysterious transformation" from personal fantasy to the work of art. Myths, as experience has shown, constitute natural source material for dreams and for the artist, wherein preliminary working through provides an economy of creative activities.

The living progression of the Oedipus myth can be followed from prehistoric times to the epic form with which it was endowed by Homer and the sophisticated dramatization that it received at the hands of Sophocles —each of these poets finding in the legend a mirror for his own personality and era. The psychoanalyst must be aware of similar dispositions within himself, i.e., the countertransference tendency in the interpretation which actually makes each article on Oedipus a reflection not only of the analyst's own personality, but also of the contemporary theories that prevail in metapsychology (oedipal, preoedipal, identity testing, etc.). Analysis ultimately curbs the mythmaking tendency itself; but after all, it is the latter that results in the Oedipus tragedy.

BIBLIOGRAPHY

Freud, S. (1900), The Interpretation of Dreams. *Standard Edition*, 4-5:1-621, 687-751. London: Hogarth Press, 1953.
———(1908), Creative Writers and Daydreaming. *Standard Edition*, 9:141. London: Hogarth Press, 1959.
———(1913), Totem and Taboo. *Standard Edition*, 13:1-161. London: Hogarth Press, 1955.
———(1919), The "Uncanny." *Standard Edition*, 17:219-256. London: Hogarth Press, 1955.
———(1919a), Preface to Reik's *Ritual: Psycho-Analytic Studies. Standard Edition*, 17:259-263. London: Hogarth Press, 1955.
———(1921), Group Psychology and the Analysis of the Ego. *Standard Edition*, 18:69-143. London: Hogarth Press, 1955.

————(1922), Medusa's Head. *Standard Edition*, *18*:273-274. London: Hogarth Press, 1955.

————(1954), *The Origins of Psychoanalysis*. New York: Basic Books.

Gassner, J. (1940), *Masters of the Drama*. New York: Random House.

Graves, R. (1955), *The Greek Myths*. Baltimore: Penguin.

Gregg, D. & Lattimore, R. (1959), *The Complete Greek Tragedies*. Chicago: University of Chicago Press.

Homer, *The Iliad*, Book 23:366. New York: Black, 1942.

————*The Odyssey*, Book 11:159. New York: Oxford University Press, 1932.

Kanzer, M. (1948), The Passing of the Oedipus Complex in Greek Drama. *Int. J. Psychoanal.*, *29*:131.

————(1950), The Oedipus Trilogy. *Psychoanal. Quart.*, *19*:561.

————(1954), Observations on Blank Dreams with Orgasms. *Psychoanal. Quart.*, *23*:511.

Larousse Encyclopedia of Mythology (1959), Egyptian Mythology. New York: Prometheus Press, p. 19.

New York Times (1961), News Item. April 4, p. 45.

Reik, T. (1920), Oedipus und die Sphinx. *Imago*, *6*:95.

Robert, C. (1915), *Oedipus*. Berlin: Weidemann Presse.

Róheim, G. (1946), Teiresias and other Seers. *Psychoanal. Rev.*, *23*:314.

Roscher, W. (1912), Sphinx. In: *Ausfuehrliches Lexikon der griechischen und roemischen Mythologie*. Leipzig: Peubner.

Tatlock, J. (1917), *Greek and Roman Mythology*. New York: Century.

Velikovsky, E. (1960), *Oedipus and Akhnaton*. New York: Doubleday.

Ego-Psychological Implications of a
Religious Symbol:
A Cultural and Experimental Study

RENATO J. ALMANSI, M.D.

The myth, as Arlow (1961) has said, "can be studied from the point of view of its function in psychic integration—how it plays a role in warding off feelings of guilt and anxiety, how it constitutes a form of adaptation to reality and to the group in which the individual lives, and how it influences the crystallization of the individual identity and the formation of the superego." It is the purpose of this paper to present a study of a collective symbol—actually of a series of equivalent collective symbols—which are deeply steeped in religious lore and which lend themselves particularly well to illustrating these very points. Indeed, their structure and multiplicity of meaning are witness to their migration from the most elementary to the highest levels of psychic integration, from the id to the ego and superego, from primary to secondary process, from instinctual expression to defense and adaptation to reality and to the group. It will also enable us to show to what extent the use of ego-psychological concepts may deepen the psychoanalytic understanding of religious and cultural phenomena and even lead the way to unsuspected discoveries in the field of history.

One of the symbols—actually the first to come under our consideration—is that of the Hebrew Tables of the Law, whose symbolic significance had been completely obscured by the importance of the Ten Commandments inscribed on them. Indeed, only Theodor Reik (1919) had suspected that the Tablets of the Law might have a meaning of their own, and saw in them a symbolization of the stone idols of the primitive Semitic religion. Although certainly correct on one level, this view does not satisfactorily account for some of the most important characteristics of this symbol. However, if we consider that they are two in number, that each contains five commandments, if we visualize their general outline, their flat surface and rounded top margins, and think of their admonitory and threatening contents, we are easily led to the realization that they

39

do, in fact, embody another symbolic meaning—that of a pair of hands, the hands of the punitive Father-God. Some confirmatory data on this point are offered:

1. The importance of the hand in primitive magic and religious beliefs is well known; stenciled hands and occasionally feet, dating back to paleolithic times, which certainly had a magical meaning, have been found in caves in France, Spain, America and Australia (Obermaier, 1924). Hand amulets were used for millennia in Egypt (Blanchard, 1909), among the Jews, in Persia, North Africa and the Near East, and are still commonly used there today. The hand often appears as the symbol of a deity, as in the case of the god Nebo whose ideogram was a hand; the goddess Gula, "The Hand of Heaven"; the Punish mother-goddess Tanit; the goddess Ashtar; the Boetian goddess Thisbe, a "hand-goddess" who was identified as the mother of the Greek Δάκτυλοι, the finger gods. One of the ancient Sumerian signs for "lord" (bêlu) clearly portrays a hand (Fig. 1). Around the time of Moses, Aton, the supreme deity of the

FIGURE 1. Ancient Sumerian sign for "lord" (bêlu). From Langdon (1911).

religion instituted in Egypt by Amenophis IV, was represented as a solar disk with rays ending in hands. The phallic, licentious Egyptian god Bes was at times represented with a tiny body attached to a huge hand, or the hand replaced the body entirely. Some of these hands had fewer, others more, than five fingers. At times the thumb was exaggeratedly large; at other times it was missing (Grenfell, 1902). Hands or hand-shaped objects representing a deity are found in Egyptian votive tablets of the greatest antiquity. Similar representations have also been found in numerous votive steles in Phoenicia. That the hand was an object of worship in Babylonia is attested to by a Babylonian cylinder seal showing a gigantic hand upon a socle surrounded by worshippers (Fig. 2). In later times, the hand and the finger of God had a prominent place in Hebrew and early Christian religious lore and iconography, the deity often being represented as a hand coming out of a cloud.

2. A brief mention must also be made here of the problem of the decalogic arrangement of the Commandments. There are two well-known

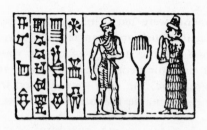

FIGURE 2. Two Babylonian cylinder seals.

definite Decalogues in the Bible—one in Ex. 20, which is known as the Ethical or Prophetic Decalogue, and that in Ex. 34, known as the Ritual Decalogue. According to biblical authorities, what we now have of the Ten Commandments in the Bible is the result of several changes, amplifications and revisions which have occurred over many centuries; the original Ten Commandments were probably one-line prohibitions which were gradually elaborated and amplified. Biblical authorities agree that, at some time in antiquity, a substitution of the ethical for the ritual prescriptions occurred, thus asserting spiritual values over religious forms and customs, but the decalogic form was not altered. This will not come as a surprise if we consider that, according to the studies of many biblical authorities, particularly Berthau, Ewald, Tillman, Briggs and Patton, the decalogic form is the general form of the early Hebrew law and traces of such an arrangement have been found throughout the Five Books of Moses; each decalogue is divided into two pentads, each pentad being devoted to a particular prescription of the law. In reconstructing the laws decalogically, they have found that this form can be more clearly evidenced in the Bible in relation to those laws which are presumably more ancient, whereas in later days the decalogic form is less evident (Kent, 1926).

All these data show the extraordinary importance of the tradition that the Commandments were ten. Bible students themselves have advanced the hypothesis that such an arrangement was related to the number of the fingers, and the ingenious explanation was given that, inasmuch as a primitive nomadic people had no way of recording the laws other than by memorization, the laws were divided into groups of ten as a mnemonic device to enable the believer to have the laws "at his finger tips."

3. The significance of the numbers 5 and 10 in ancient lore may be noted briefly. Numbers were used in ancient times to identify deities. The Sumerians represented the names of their gods by signs which became the oldest numerals. According to Newberry (1934) we have "lucky" numbers today because these numbers were once the gods of luck. For the Sumerians, there was no distinction between units and tens; 5 or 50 were the fingers of the hand and the 5 elements, and became the number of Bel, the god who shaped the universe. The numbers 1 or 10 were applied to the goddess Ishtar, deity of the earth and ocean.

Thus the earliest numbers came to represent natural forces which had been deified. Similarly, the Hebrews developed a whole mystical numerological system, the Cabala, based on the principle of the Godlike nature and power of the numbers, the first ten of which, the ten *Sefirot*, represented the potencies or agencies by means of which God manifested his existence in the creation of the Universe. *Sefirot* is the plural of the noun *Sefirah*, which originally meant *number*. According to the *Sefer Yetzirah*, 10 are the essential forms of all that is and the basis of the world plan.

4. Now we shall turn our attention to the shape of the Tables of the Law. In spite of considerable controversy among scholars as to whether the Tables of the Law might not have been fashioned and placed in the Ark of the Covenant long after the time of Moses—or even whether they ever actually existed—the preponderant opinion accepts the biblical version of Ex. 40^{20} and Deut. 10^5 and tends to believe that two such Tablets were placed by Moses in the Ark. In view of the Bible's explicit statement as to the presence of the Tablets in the Ark, it would be difficult to conceive how they could have been nonexistent, at least at the time when the narratives that form the Bible first originated.

The question of whether it can be reasonably presumed that such Tablets actually did possess the round-topped shape with which we are familiar from the representations of our day is not, strictly speaking, essentially important to our thesis; even so, it deserves particular attention because of the connection of this shape with other plastic representations of antiquity which will be discussed below. No representations of the Tables of the Law are to be found in early Hebrew iconography and no detail in this respect is contained in the Bible or early Hebrew scripts. The earliest representations known are from Christian iconography, and in them the top margin always appears as square-shaped (Good-enough, 1962). The earliest representations from Hebrew sources that we have been able to find date back only to medieval times; they are invariably round-topped and have consistently remained so up to the present day. This consistency led this author to question whether this detail does not find its roots in a very old tradition, and to undertake a very extensive study of ancient iconography of the general area in which we are interested, particularly that of the first and second millennia B.C. As a result of this study, it can be unequivocally stated that in this period practically all the tables of law and government of the East and the steles containing messages of importance featured a round-topped margin.[1]

Even more important is the fact that the Egyptian hieroglyph for tablet contains the picture of a typical round-topped tablet (Fig. 3). The vertical rectangular shape topped by a round margin is also characteristic of many tombstones in Jewish cemeteries. Interestingly enough, because of their shape, such tombstones are called *yod*, "the hand" (Róheim, 1930). The double round-topped rectangular upright shape characteristic of the Tables of the Law is also characteristic of an object of the greatest worship—the Sun Pillars, double steles the shape of which is closely reminiscent of the Mazzebots which were well known throughout the Near East and among the Hebrews (Fig. 4). Along the same lines, we may note that in India and in China the tables of religious laws are foot-shaped, i.e., the Buddhapada, or footprints of Buddha over which the laws of the Buddhist religion are inscribed (Fig. 5). It is also consistent that throughout the world the architecture of places of worship is so often based on the curved line as in roofs, domes, doors and windows, whereas the straight line is much less often employed. This also applies to government buildings, particularly those which house the administration of justice. It is a common sight in courts to see that the wall behind the judge is

[1] A few examples are: the stele of Sanherib (ca. 700 B.C.); the pillar code of Hammurabi (2100 B.C.); the plate with the victorious hymn of Merneptah (1223 B.C.); the stele of Hammurabi (ca. 1290 B.C.); the Naukratis stele (3rd dynasty); the great boundary stele of Amarna; the Serapeum stele of Psametic I; the stele of Esarkaddon; the Senjirli stele of Esarkaddon (Museum of Berlin); the Moabite Stone; the stele of Marathus in Phoenicia (6th-5th century B.C.); the stele of agreement of King Marduchi-Dinachi (1220 B.C.); the gravestone of the king "Serpent" (1st dynasty, 3000 B.C.).

panelled with round-topped niches the tallest of which is usually in the center behind the judge's seat, framing his person.

FIGURE 3.   Egyptian hieroglyph for tablet, stele (Budge, 1923).

FIGURE 4.   The Sun Pillars.

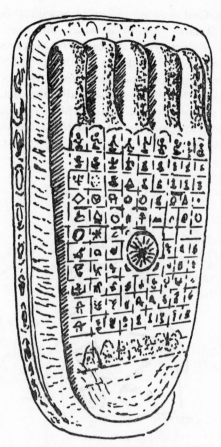

FIGURE 5. The Buddhapada.

Considering the above historical data, there appears to be sufficient evidence derived from history to support our hypothesis that the Tables of the Law do symbolize a pair of hands. At this level we may easily discern that this symbol is the outgrowth of a powerful reaction formation; it represents an expression of ego and superego control over the libidinal and aggressive drives and is a derivative of the oedipal conflicts so prominent in father religions. The hand was a common symbol of godlike power in ancient religions even before the Hebrews. To quote just a few examples: The Egyptian hieroglyph for hand is a hand attached to an arm and also has the meaning of power; in Babylon, as we have seen, the hand of God was an object of worship. In Egypt we have representations of Astarte (Fig. 6) in which the head of the asp in the uraeus, the symbol of sovereignty, is substituted by a hand. The Sumerian pictogram for king (Fig. 7) consists of the pictogram for man surmounted by the pictogram for hand—five strokes, the bottom one of which is usually longer than the others. Phonetically, the pictogram for king is rendered as *lugal,* composed of *lu* (man) which corresponds to the crude picture of the man, and *gal* (great) which corresponds to that of the hand (Mason, 1920; Langdon, 1911). When the primitive Sumerian pic-

FIGURE 6. Astarte.

FIGURE 7. Sumerian pictograms for "man," "king," and "hand" (schematic).

tographic writing evolved into the Assyrian cuneiform the same general scheme persisted; i.e., the group of cuneiform signs for king was composed of the group indicating man and the group indicating hand (Fig. 8). Similarly, the Egyptian hieroglyphic sign for prince or king is the same as for man, except that a scepter and an ankh are placed in the hands and two rounded plumes are set on the head. Thus there is no doubt that the sign of the hand above the head was an indication of royalty and power.

In Egypt, where the Jews had been so long in captivity, many male gods were represented with headdresses composed of two schematized ostrich feathers, the plumes of Amen, signifying truth, law and power (Fig. 9), the outline of which closely followed that of the Tablets of the Law, to signify their authority. The close relationship of these head-dresses to the picture of the hand surmounting the king's head in the Sumerian script had been noted by Ball (1913) who mentions that this pictogram "resembles the Egyptian sw-ti, a feather crown."

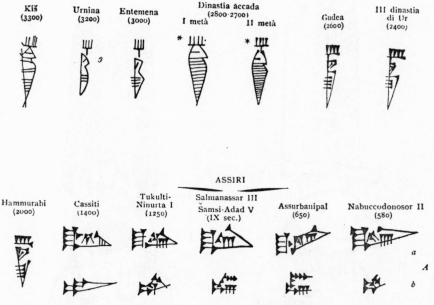

FIGURE 8. Evolution of the sign "king" (lugal). From Diringer (1937).

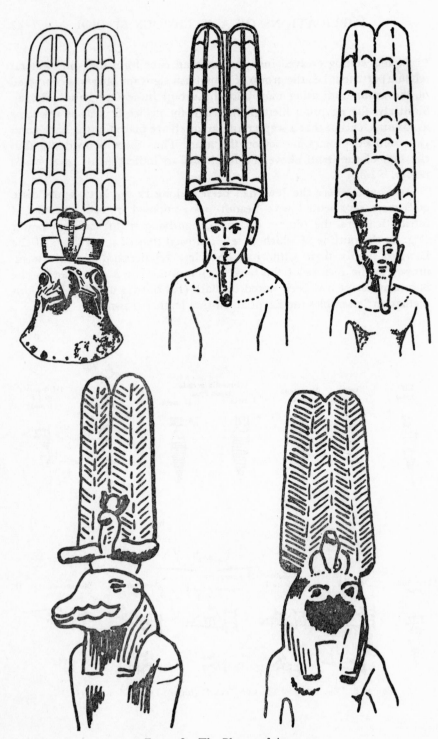

FIGURE 9.   The Plumes of Amen.

It would be impossible to go into a detailed discussion here of the fascinating subject of the headdresses of the Egyptian gods; we must limit ourselves to note that, besides the type of headdress just mentioned, we can find many other types which are highly reminiscent of the motifs discussed above: the Atef crown composed of a varying number of complex, styled, vertical finger- and handlike structures, usually five in number (Fig. 10); feather tiaras usually composed of five feathers; tablets which at times can be identified with certainty as writing tablets by the presence of a stylus (Fig. 11); as well as snakes or phalluslike protuber-

FIGURE 10. The Atef Crown and its modifications.

FIGURE 11. Bes.

ances. The observer receives the very definite impression of being confronted with a series of equivalent symbols which carry basically the same
phallic significance.

The symbol of the hand thus had a definite phallic meaning parallel
to the phallic connotation of the fingers. On the other hand, if we examine the Ka of the Egyptians, other meanings become apparent. Plasti-
cally, the Ka was represented as a pair of arms placed over the person's
head with the arms disposed horizontally from shoulder to elbow, the
forearms and hands placed vertically at right angles to the arms, the
palms facing forward (Fig. 12). The Ka stood for the fusion of the individual's very substance, his imperishable name and his totem (Nash, 1918)
and represented his "double," "genius," natural disposition, abstract personality, character, mind. While on one level it certainly also carried the
significance of dignity, virility and power, it basically represented the

FIGURE 12. The Ka.

immortal spiritual self as contrasted to the transient and corporeal.

In certain instances the hand assumed a tender and protective significance and had a life-giving and life-protecting connotation similar to that of a blessing. Even this does not exhaust the meaning of this symbol. In fact, a study of the headdresses of the gods and goddesses of Egypt shows that the rounded feathers or corresponding rounded symbolic formations were mostly a prerogative of the male gods, whereas the goddesses usually wore headdresses that were much more distinctively phallic in character (phalluslike protuberances, snakes, horns, scorpions). It is not difficult to surmise that the headdress was an element designed to complete an androgynous figure and that the feathers or their equivalents also represent a female symbol and, more specifically, a symbol of the breasts, thus paralleling the oral meaning of the fingers. This is confirmed by the fact that the common Egyptian amulet of the two fingers, in a stylized form, resembles the Tables of the Law very closely.

The study of the Tables of the Law developed, in a way which could not possibly be detailed here, into the study of what proved to be a related—actually identical—symbol: the Tetragrammaton, the ancient, highly tabooed, mysterious name of the God of the Hebrews. Its accepted spelling is יהוה. The origin and significance of the mystical Name has been one of the most puzzling and debated elements in Hebrew religion; even its exact pronunciation was a dark secret known only to the High Priests and was eventually lost forever. Out of the large number of traditions relating to the Tetragrammaton, three appear to be dominant: the unfathomed traditions of its mystery, its magical power, and its connection with the Blessing of the Kohenites. Certain details of the ritual surrounding the Kohenite Blessing are of particular interest to us. It could be administered only by people who had never killed a human being, among other moral qualifications; it could not be administered by anyone with a defect of the hands, nor before ablution of the hands. Moreover, the congregation was not permitted to look at the priest while he administered the Blessing. The connection between the Tables of the Law and the Kohenite Blessing has been studied from a psycho-analytic standpoint by Sandor Feldman (1941) [2] who saw in the position of the fingers the spelling of the word Shadai, the Almighty, and in the priestly Blessing a laying of the ineffable Name on the people who thus became identified with God. This hypothesis is based on the shape of the letters of the word as written in the square Hebrew alphabet, the Hebrew alphabet known to us today. Although quite ingenious, this explanation has a fundamental historical inconsistency because the square alphabet has been used by the Hebrews only since about the time of Christ, whereas, according to the Bible, the Blessing of the Kohenites goes back to the time of the Exodus—a lapse of about a millennium and a half. However, we are in the position of clarifying the connection between the Blessing of the Kohenites and the Tetragrammaton and of confirming the age-old tradition that the position of the fingers during the Blessing actually does spell the name of God.

In the second century A.D., Aquila, a Greek who became an extremely pious convert to Judaism, translated the Bible from Hebrew into Greek under the direction of two learned rabbis. In this translation the Name was not translated into Greek letters but was inserted into the text in the ancient characters of the North Semitic alphabet that had been used by the Hebrews before the adoption of the square alphabet. The earliest examples of the use of this alphabet go back to the sixteenth or seventeenth century B.C., and therefore well antedate the Exodus. The Name of God as Aquila wrote it (as incontestably shown in six original leaves of his translation still extant today) is spelled: ⅂ ⅂ ⅂ ⅂, that is, יהוה (י=⅂, ה=⅂). What is of utmost importance is the fact that instead of being spelled

---

[2] In this paper, the reader will find a great deal of very interesting information on the religious lore surrounding the priestly blessing.

Yod Hay Vov Hay, the name is spelled *Yod Hay Yod Hay.*[3] As there can be no question whatsoever as to Aquila's piety, his legendary literalness, his respect for the Name which he knew to be the most important word in the Bible and his intention not to defile it, one is inevitably led to the conclusion that he used as a text for his translation some ancient authoritative Hebrew manuscript in which the Name was so spelled. If we examine this spelling it is immediately obvious that we have before us two sets of five prongs equal to the fingers, and that the division of the prongs in each of the two sets corresponds exactly to the division of the fingers as used in the Kohenite Blessing (Fig. 13). Thus we have an-

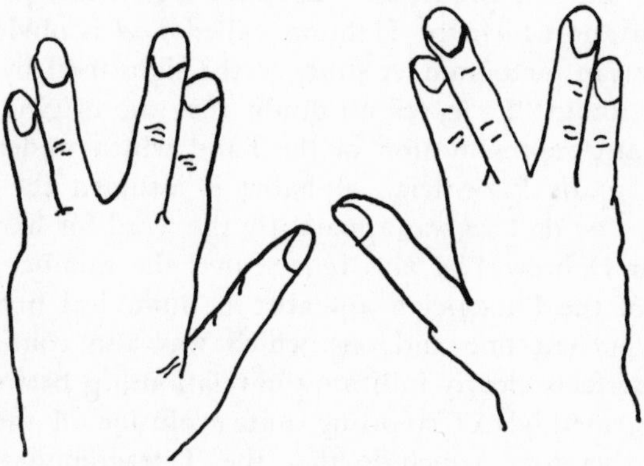

FIGURE 13. The Kohenite Blessing.

other symbol of hands exactly analogous to the Tables of the Law. This cleverly camouflaged spelling of the Name is further confirmed by Aaron's Blessing in which the act of blessing is expressed in terms of putting God's Name upon the people. To quote directly (Numbers 6:22 to 27), "And then God spoke unto Moses, saying, 'Speak unto Aaron and unto his sons, saying: In this wise ye shall bless the children of Israel; ye shall say unto them:

[3] In the Hexaplar manuscript of the Septuagint the Tetragrammaton is rendered with the letters II I II I, which was a notation introduced by Origen or Eusebius to substitute for יהוה. In Greek circles these letters were supposed to be Greek and to read πιπι. It is to be noted that the numerical value of ι was 10 and that of π was 5, exactly corresponding to those of the Hebrew letters *Yod* and *Hay*.

The Lord bless thee and keep thee;
The Lord make His face to shine upon thee
    and be gracious unto thee;
The Lord lift up His countenance upon thee
    and give thee peace.

So shall they put my name upon the children of Israel and I will
bless them.' "

A few philological remarks about the letter *Yod* will not be out of
place here. *Yod* in Hebrew means hand, a meaning which derived from
the fact that it actually evolved from a schematic representation of a
hand (other letters too have derived from the representation of other
familiar objects). The Sumerian pictogram for *Yod* represented the right
hand and arm, and the predynastic Egyptian sign which corresponds to
the Phoenician one which the Hebrews called *Yod* is obviously derived
from the Sumerian pictogram. A study of the signs used by the ancients
to express the sound "I" leaves no doubt that the original sign constituted a schematic representation of the hand which underwent several
changes until in the Phoenician alphabet it assumed the form ᄀ. Also,
in Phoenician, *Yod* or *Yud* was apparently the word for hand. It is noteworthy that in Hebrew *Yod* also represented the number 10. The use
of the letters of the Phoenician alphabet as numerical notations is certainly a very ancient one and one which was also continued by the
Hebrews. These facts clearly indicate the relationship between primitive
sign languages, methods of counting, and evolution of the alphabet.

We must, therefore, conclude that the Tetragrammaton as it has
come down to us merely represents a "security" name analogous to the
security names of many other gods of antiquity, designed to avoid the
usurpation of power attached to the knowledge of the real name of
God. ᄏ ᄏ ᄏ ᄏ was thus the real name of the new god with whom
Moses made a covenant on Mount Sinai and who became the national
and only god of the Israelites. In fact, most scholars are of the opinion
that upon the acceptance of Yahwe as the national god of Israel at Mount
Sinai, a new name of God was introduced by Moses. This view is fully
consistent with some of the views that have been expressed before.

The above interpretation does not in any way contradict that of
Abraham who saw in the position of the hands during the priestly
blessing a symbolic representation of the cloven hoof of the totem animal,
or that of Feldman who interpreted it as a condensation of the name of
God and of the paternal phallus, the blessing thus signifying a covenant
with God in which the congregation accepts castration and renounces

hostility toward the father. It merely adds a new dimension. Beyond the oral, phallic and oedipal connotations, another new and wondrous element appears—the secret of the first alphabetical notations and of the still young and mysterious art of writing. We can thus better understand the position of the initiate toward the illiterate masses. The priest was not only the representative of God and the repository of spiritual superiority, but also the wise man who possessed an arcane and infinitely valuable human knowledge which was the prerogative of the select few, the highest expression of human intelligence and achievement. Indeed, the awesome respect of the illiterate toward the learned is often emphasized even in today's literature.

The symbol of the hand, therefore, also stands for a highly specialized and adaptive human function, one which is most intimately connected with learning, communication, secondary process functioning and activity of the ego. Its religious use indicates a defense against libidinal and aggressive impulses which are repressed and sublimated, the energy thus freed becoming available to the ego for its purposes. In this way the symbol passes from id to ego interests and, paralleling normal development, from magic and omnipotence to rationality and manipulative control. Such developments imply the full emergence of the ego's defensive operations. But in the Kohenite Blessing, this transition does not yet appear to be fully completed, as shown by the large admixture of magical features which underlie it, whereas in the Tables of the Law and in the Ten Commandments we can clearly discern the almost completed results of this evolution. The God whose finger wrote the Ten Commandments on the tablets of stone is He who will protect the faithful against the urgency of the instincts and in return will offer the joys of purity and wisdom. In the adoption of this common symbol the members of the community identified with their leader and, amongst themselves, signified their bond to one another and set down the rules upon which their life together would be based.

At this point we may reasonably question why this symbolization which is so obvious and so amply confirmed by our historical study had never been clinically detected. Indeed, neither in this author's experience nor in a careful search of the literature was it possible to find any case in which the Tables of the Law were symbolically equated to hands. This lack of substantiation does not necessarily invalidate our conclusions because a particularly high degree of repression might be operative and/or because of the especially primitive character of the symbol involved. In this regard we may hypothesize that this symbolization may be based upon memory traces laid down very early in infancy, and that this symbol may therefore represent a very primitive Gestalt of an archaic object (the infant's own hands, the mother's hands).

One method which appeared propitious for the experimental investigation of this symbol was the tachistoscopic one, in view of Fisher's findings that subliminally perceived stimuli may activate unconscious processes and reappear transformed in symbolically related forms in dreams and other productions. Of particular interest in the present connection is one of his experiments in which the subliminal perception of a symbolically meaningful object (snake) brought out dreams from which the phallic meaning of the percept could be clearly evinced (Fisher, 1960). Also, in another of his experiments, parts of a tachistoscopically exposed Star of David were symbolically transformed into the urinating phallus (Fisher, 1957). It did not seem, therefore, unreasonable to expect that if the Tables of the Law were presented tachistoscopically the percept might stimulate the production of significant dreams and other material which might clarify its unconscious origins and ramifications.

TACHISTOSCOPIC EXPERIMENTS

Ten patients of Hillside Hospital (6 male, 4 female) were exposed for 1/200 of a second to a stimulus consisting of the outline of the Tables of the Law. At this speed and under the particular conditions of the illumination of the room, only a flash of light could actually be perceived consciously. Before the exposure each patient was given a brief explanation that a test of perception was being performed and that this type of study had been done elsewhere, thus giving indirect assurance. After exposure, the patients were asked what they had seen and to draw it. They were then invited to relax, to mention any images that came to mind and to elaborate upon them. If this embodied visual material, a drawing was requested. Before being dismissed, they were told that the author would see them again on the following day in order to hear about any dreams they might have had. Twenty-four hours later they were seen again and asked if they had had any dreams the night before, following the exposure. If so, they were asked to repeat the dreams, to offer whatever associations they could, and to draw the visual content of the dreams. It was not possible to interview two of the patients twenty-four hours after exposure, but they were seen forty-eight hours later.

The patients involved in this experiment were between the ages of 16 and 63. Out of the ten patients tested, four gave positive results which will be described in detail below. The other six patients were negative in all respects; they saw nothing, there was no spontaneous imagery and there were no dreams. The positive results were all found in younger patients. Also, the author had the definite impression that those patients in whom positive results were achieved were considerably less anxious and less ill than those who gave negative results.

Case 1. M. E., male, age 16. Hospital diagnosis: Chronic schizophrenia, undifferentiated. The patient was slated for discharge within a few days. He was quite cooperative although somewhat superior and supercilious in his attitude.

After exposure he said that he had seen "nothing material, nothing like an object, like the hand, face or body; nothing of that sort." There was no spontaneous imagery after the exposure. That night he had a very short dream which he could not remember. However, the next night he had the following dream: He was in a place in Queens Boulevard, and he was elongated, thin and stiff as a board. A number of people poured out of a subway station and draped themselves around him and "sort of melted into a solid whitish ball, like a stick." When asked to elaborate further, he said that it was as if "sixty people were wrapped around" him. He repeated that "they seemed to melt into one white mass; you could not see me because they were covering most of me; you could see the hands, shoulders and feet." The patient had no associations to the dream. He made two drawings of it; in the first (Fig. 14) the transversal

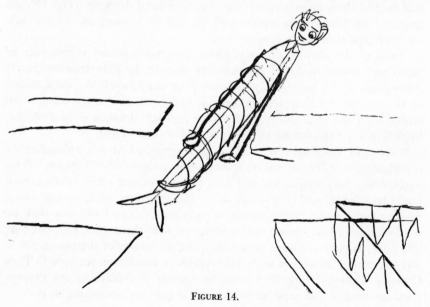

FIGURE 14.

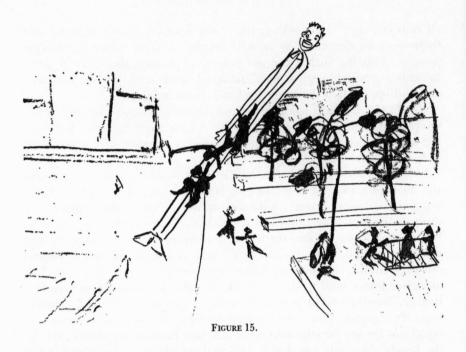

FIGURE 15.

arched lines crossing the body were explained by him to be the people who had draped themselves around him. In the second drawing (Fig. 15) the confused darkish masses represented the people coming out of the subway to drape themselves around him.

Even in the absence of associations, the masturbatory significance of the dream is unmistakable. The arched lines in the first drawing clearly correspond to the outline of a masturbating hand, while the dark masses in the second drawing are certainly a portrayal of the ejaculate. This tallies with the expression of the face in each drawing—cheerful and impish in the first, drawn and disgruntled in the second.

Case 2. M. B., male, age 25. Hospital diagnosis: Chronic schizophrenia, undifferentiated. There was no spontaneous imagery after exposure. This patient was very suspicious and had to be prodded often. Twenty-four hours later he related that shortly after the exposure, while taking a nap, he had had dreams "all jumbled up; perhaps things I did not look up to. I may have had some kind of image of something that happened on this floor, might have been some other patient or one of the personnel. It was something connected with the hospital in some way, perhaps O.T. or Creative Therapy. I think I rebelled against remembering my dreams. I volunteered in this experiment because it gave me something to do."

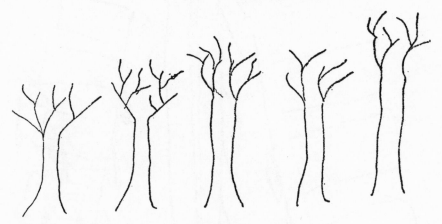

FIGURE 16.

In relation to O.T. he mentioned a painting on which he was engaged, representing a sunset in the country (Fig. 16). Associating to this sketch, he said it made him think of an apple orchard in which he, some cousins and other boys had an apple fight at the time when he lived with an aunt because his mother was sick. He had felt very bad about this and at times had fantasies that his aunt was actually his mother.

The night after the exposure he dreamed he was a policeman on duty in the city, doing what he could to curb juvenile delinquency. In this dream he saw "the law being broken by young people who were trying to find a place for themselves" and his job was to "keep the breaking of the law from getting out of hand" (he repeated this). He thought this dream took place in his old neighborhood. The buildings were familiar to him. In this area there was juvenile delinquency, as in the dream. "Mischief" was being committed in this dream; "they were not playing ball or going to school; they were not occupied in something you would see as a normal function." Associating to the dream, he said that at present he shares his room with a policeman and that there is another patient at the hospital whom he suspects of having had a run-in with the law.

The patient then made two drawings of his dream, actually of his old neighborhood. In the first drawing, (Fig. 17) he drew two rows of houses, the elevated subway tracks, and the cars parked in the street. In the second (Fig. 18) he drew the house in which he had first lived with his foster parents. It was the first family with whom he remembers living after his mother's death. He had sustained injuries in the dirt field while playing ball. Before handing me the drawing, he checked to make sure

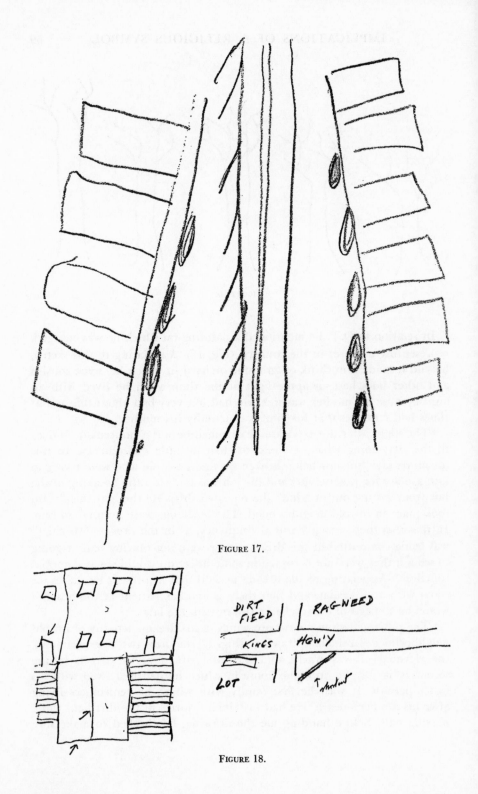

FIGURE 17.

DIRT FIELD | RAGWEED
KINGS | HGW'Y
LOT | ↑ student

FIGURE 18.

there were two doors, then concluded that it was correct. While discussing
the drawings, the patient repeatedly raised both hands to the same level,
palms forward, sustaining this position for a short period each time.

Noteworthy in this case are the handlike appearance of the trees in
the first drawing, the two rows of houses in the second (composed of 4
and 6 rectangles respectively) and the double-panelled door in the third.
The dream obviously relates to the preconscious percept of the Tables of
the Law (references to the 'breaking of the law getting out of hand') and
to "improper" sexual activities of childhood—masturbation clearly being
one of them. The connection between the subliminal percept and hands
is further emphasized by the position of his hands during the interview,
as described above.

Case 3. L. F., male, age 23. Hospital diagnosis: acute schizophrenic
attack. This patient was cooperative, interested and free from anxiety. He
was obviously convalescent.

After exposure to the stimulus, the patient said he had seen just a
flash of light which he compared to a similar experience he occasionally
had had while watching television, and once while sitting in the hospital
cafeteria. He had ascribed it to shock therapy and told his doctor about
it, but he really did not know.

In the period of spontaneous imagery following exposure, he said,
"I see a finger, sort of. It is like a thumb, really, and seems to be bending
down towards the ground. The way I distinguish it as a thumb is because

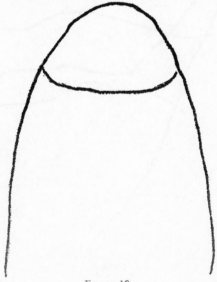

FIGURE 19.

it has a nail on it, a fingernail. There is a little bit of orange surrounding the image of the finger" (Fig. 19). Subsequently, the patient said, "I do not see anything else. There is a lot of darkness and a little bit of blue. Now I see a sort of blue ball of light and it has a sort of halo around it. There seems to be a peg passing through the center of the globe, now almost like a line running diagonally from the upper right-hand side to the lower side."

The night after exposure, the patient dreamed that he saw himself at a wedding, walking down the aisle of a synagogue or church, carrying a ring on a pillow. He offered the ring to the rabbi and, in doing so, his arms shook violently. Maybe it was a priest.

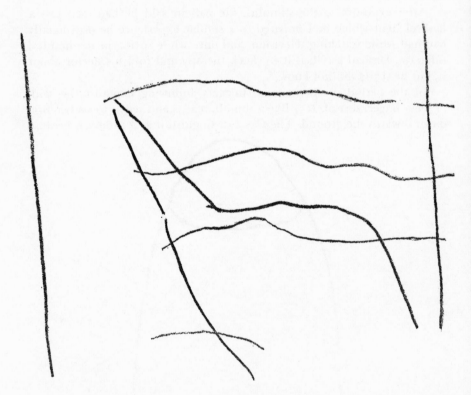

FIGURE 20.

FIGURE 21.

The patient was invited to close his eyes and to report any images in connection with the dream. He said he saw a woman writing, "like a hand writing on a sheet of paper" (Fig. 20). He then spoke of seeing a man blowing a horn or a trumpet (Fig. 21). Associating to the dream, he said that his brother was to be married soon. He would also like to get married but has difficulties about girls. His shaking in the dream was caused by fear. He had been his best friend's best man; he had roomed with this boy at school and they had been very friendly. This friend had married a "slut" but the patient liked her and did not want to believe bad things about her. He expects to be his brother's best man, too.

FIGURE 22.

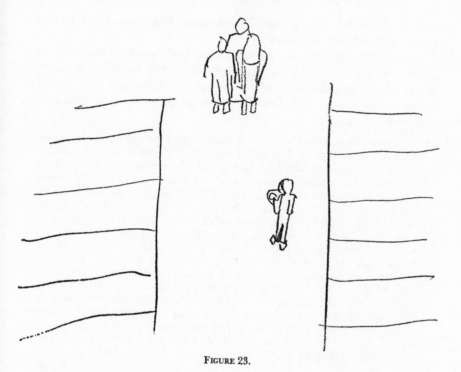

FIGURE 23.

When asked to draw the dream he first made one drawing (Fig. 22), said it was not complete, and drew another (Fig. 23). In making the first drawing (Fig. 22) he first drew the couple and added the rabbi at the very end.

At the end of the experiment, the patient was shown the stimulus picture. He saw a connection with the drawing of the finger, the wedding and the synagogue, but none with the drawing which shows a hand writing.

As in the preceding case, there is ample evidence that the patient's productions and dream were the results of the exposure to the subliminal stimulus. Of particular interest are the visualization of the finger, the hand writing and the reference in the dream to the ring and to the trembling of the arms. The emphasis on hands is confirmed by Fig. 23 which shows five rows on either side of a center aisle, reminiscent of two hands and of the two Tables with five lines inscribed on each. As in the preceding cases, masturbatory factors were also activated by the exposure to the stimulus.

Case 4. M. W., female, age 33. Hospital diagnosis: Psychoneurosis, mixed (obsessive and depressed).

Right after exposure, the patient raised both hands to the same level, palms forward, and said, "I expected something brighter, flashier. It looked like orange and blue, like a sunburst, like the sun, but instead of setting it was rising" (Fig. 24). Twenty-four hours later she related the following dream:

> I went to a friend's house. I hadn't seen her in years. She was friendly, even though I thought she wouldn't be. I started talking about her car. First she said it was old, then new, and she parked it around the corner. I never saw her child and I didn't know whether she would let me see her. Then I went to another friend but before I got there I went shopping for potatoes and cabbage. I was living in my old neighborhood. I was a little annoyed because I had a smaller cabbage left in the house. My son was playing outside. I was also annoyed because I didn't have the patience to make coleslaw. I went to another friend's house. She and her mother came down to greet me in the clothes they were going to wear to her sister's wedding. We went upstairs and there was some upset about not getting the right color for her sister's gown. I think my husband called then and it took him a long time to get there. They wanted me to sleep over and baby-sit and her husband would drive me home around 5 A.M. I think I got home and was upset about going to work.

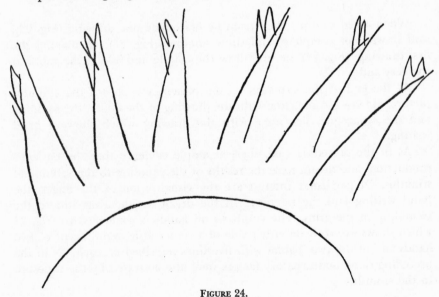

FIGURE 24.

In connection with this dream, the patient made two drawings (Figs. 25 & 26). The first drawing portrayed her old neighborhood, showing both her house and that of the first friend. In connection with the second drawing, she explained that the woman seated on the right was her friend: "This is supposed to be her shoulder—as if she were thinking—her hand is up to her chin." Her associations to this dream revolved about her feeling of worthlessness and inferiority, fear of Negroes and particularly the possibility that they might rape her, and fear of rats. All her recollections centered around her "old neighborhood." "I guess I was more hurt in the old neighborhood than anywhere else. I was very nervous in Junior High School. I used to pull on my fingers, I was so nervous." She held up both hands and pressed on the little finger, to demonstrate. "There was a pain: I can't describe it, like it was numb and I had to press it to get the numbness out. To this day I have some of it, but I don't do it as much." Her further associations related to her liking for a Catholic young man, a friendship which her mother discouraged, and her subsequent feeling of being shunned by him.

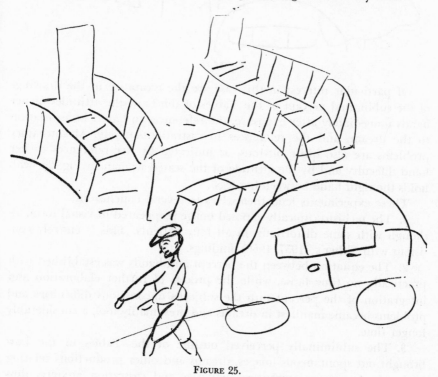

FIGURE 25.

FIGURE 26.

Of particular interest in this case are the recapture in the drawings of the subliminal percept of the Tables of the Law, the attitudes of her hands immediately after exposure, the references to hands in association to the dream, and the references to castration anxiety. Masturbatory problems are also quite obvious, as indicated by her references to her hand difficulty and by the attitude of the seated woman in Fig. 26, who holds the right hand between her legs.

These experiments lend themselves to several conclusions:

1. The tachistoscopically exposed image reappeared in visual form, although with some distortions, in all four patients. This is entirely consistent with Fisher's (1957, 1960) findings.

2. The equation between the percept and hands was established with practically no time lapse, while the process of further elaboration and integration of the percept into the subject's unconscious difficulties and problems became manifest in dreams and presumably took a considerably longer time.

3. The subliminally perceived outline of the Tables of the Law brought out spontaneous images, dreams and other productions relating to hands, fingers, masturbatory activities and castration anxiety, thus

confirming the original hypothesis which had been based on a nonclinical study. Therefore, it appears that this method, which permits a partial removal of the repression, is suitable for the activation of unconscious complexes connected to symbol formation, for the exploration of the manifold ramifications, connections, and derivatives of symbols as well as for the study of the transition of symbols into one another.

As demonstrated by the experimental and cultural data presented above, the study of the hand symbol has revealed a high degree of condensation of psychic motivations. This comes as no surprise considering the way in which the hand participates in the life and growth of the individual, the number of autonomous and drive-originated factors which participate in its operation and the increasingly complex array of functions which it assumes in the course of development. The multiplicity of meanings found in this symbol closely parallels the integration of the manifold functions of this organ. The high narcissistic and libidinal value of the hand, its fundamental role in the process of formation of the body image, in thumb-sucking, masturbation, and as an executant organ of the ego in communication and learning, all conspire to give to it a particularly complex representation in the psychic apparatus, the most complex, perhaps, of all psychic representations of bodily parts. Particularly prominent are the ego and superego derivatives, such as ego interests, recognition of reality factors, adaptation to the environment, sublimation of instinctual drives, submission to social and ethical demands, and development of social and rational attitudes.

Indeed, the hand is admirably suited to represent this aspect of the psyche as one of the chief elements of distinction between man and pre-hominidae, and the primary tool for those unique human activities that have raised our species above the others in the animal kingdom. In this respect it is not without reason that "scientists generally agree on the technical definition of man as one who made tools in a regular set pattern, as distinct from the haphazard use of sharp sticks, stones or random implements."[4] The transition of the hand from id to ego interests clearly corresponds to a change in instinctual aims and to a neutralization of libidinal and aggressive energy which leads from the pleasure to the reality ego, and from primary narcissism to object relations. In fact, in its ultimate expression, the symbol of the hand came to signify a trend away from narcissistic gratification and toward re-establishment of a mature reunion with the parental figures.

[4] L. S. B. Leakey's (1961) article in which this interesting piece of information is to be found was very kindly called to my attention by Dr. Theodore Lipin.

BIBLIOGRAPHY

Arlow, J. A. (1961), Ego Psychology and the Study of Mythology. *J. Amer. Psychoanal. Assn.*, 9:371-393.

Ball, C. J. (1913), *Chinese and Sumerian*. London: Oxford University Press.

Blanchard, R. H. (1909), *A Handbook of Egyptian Gods and Mummy Amulets*. Cairo.

Budge, E. (1923), *First Steps in Egyptian*. London: K. Paul, Trench, Trubner & Co., p. 62.

Diringer, D. (1937), *L'alfabeto nella storia della civiltà*. Florence: Barbera.

Feldman, S. (1941), The Blessing of the Kohenites. *Amer. Imago*, 2:296-322.

Fisher, C. (1957), A Study of the Preliminary Stages of the Construction of Dreams and Images. *J. Amer. Psychoanal. Assn.*, 5:5-60.

———(1960), Subliminal and Supraliminal Influences on Dreams. *Amer. J. Psychiat.*, 116:1009-1017.

Goodenough, E. R. (1962), Personal communication.

Grenfell, A. (1902), The Iconography of Bes and of Phoenician Bes-Hand Scarabs. *Proc. Soc. Biblical Archaeol.*, Vol. 4 (London).

Kent, C. F. (1926), *The Growth and Contents of the Old Testament*. New York: Charles Scribner's Sons.

Langdon, S. (1911), *A Sumerian Grammar and Chrestomathy*. Paris: Guthner.

Leakey, L. S. B. (1961), Exploring 1,750,000 Years into Man's Past. *Natl. Geogr.*, 120:564-589.

Mason, A. W. (1920), *A History of the Art of Writing*. New York: Macmillan.

Nash, W. (1918), The Totemic Origin of the Egyptian Gods. *The "Scarab Club" Papers, III*. London: Privately printed.

Newberry, J. S. (1934), *The Rainbow Bridge*. New York and Boston: Houghton Mifflin.

Obermaier, H. (1924), *Fossil Man in Spain*. New Haven: Yale University Press.

Reik, T. (1919), *Probleme der Religionspsychologie: 1. Das Ritual*. Vienna-Leipzig: Internationaler psychoanalytischer Verlag.

Róheim, G. (1930), *Animism, Magic and the Divine King*. New York: Knopf.

Ego Psychology, Myth and Rite:

Remarks about the Relationship of the Individual and the Group

MAX M. STERN, M.D.

Recent investigation of ego and group identity (Erikson, 1959) has renewed interest in manifestations of interaction between individual and group, such as myths and rites. While their function as vehicle for collective discharge of instinctual drives (Freud, 1913; Rank, 1912) refers to the id aspect, the role the ego plays in the genesis of myth and rite, and, conversely, the impact of both on the development of the ego's ability to master reality and to establish its own identity, can be regarded as the ego aspect of myth and rite.

Early, long before the inception of ego psychology, Freud recognized the relevance of findings in the individual for group psychology. His work and that of his co-workers at that period, such as Abraham, Reik, Rank, Róheim, Sachs, Jones—to name a few—revolutionized the science of man. Freud's (1913) "Totem and Taboo" belongs to the classics of anthropology. These investigations showed, as Freud expressed it, what psychoanalysis, with the means at its disposal, could accomplish toward the explanation of difficult group phenomena, by "considering details that previously had not been understood, by keeping steadily in view the relationship between prehistoric man and primitive man of today, as well as the connection between the products of civilization and the substitute structure of neurotics" (Reik, 1946). Myth and rite were explained, parallel to the dynamics of neurotic symptoms, by the need for discharge of repressed instinctual drives; they were "a receptacle for the discharge of socially unusable instinctual impulses which made possible the renunciation of uncontrolled sexual narcissistic drives dominating the behavior of primitive man" (Rank, 1912). The occurrence of narcissistic omnipotence of thought and its sexualization, both in the primitive and

Clinical Associate Professor, State University of New York.

This paper is an extended version of the original Panel presentation.

in a specific phase of the child's development, led Freud to extend the validity of Haeckel's biogenetic law to mental development.

This presentation, stimulated by the Panel on Mythology and Ego Psychology (Almansi, 1964; Arlow, 1964; Kanzer, 1964) does not deal directly with its highly interesting, rich, and valuable contributions, but rather with the tacitly underlying theoretical premises referring to the concepts mentioned above. The intention is to replace the somewhat mystical extension of the biogenetic law onto mental phenomena, with a bioeconomical concept based on the requirements of the specific biologic situation of man. It complements the discharge concept by stressing the part of the myth in the ego's mastery of external and internal reality (Kanzer, 1964).

The thesis offered is that (1) narcissistic sexualized thinking underlying myth and magic rites is conditioned to a great extent by the overwhelming anxiety in prehistoric man, evolving from his poor endowment—somatic and mental. Group formation specific for man originated in the realistic need for cooperative work, reinforced by irrational regressive wishes for mother-child symbiosis, predicated upon the long-lasting dependency on the maternal group (clinging, crowding). (2) The ego aspect of rite and myth consists in the mastery of danger through the magic act. The anxiety—emanating from the irruption of repressed infantile wishes in this act—is warded off through its displacement onto a symbol, the core of the sacral, and through the imaginary re-establishment of the mother-child union with the help of ecstatic dancing, singing, etc. This liberates the ego for the realistic conquest of reality; it creates the split between profane and sacral reality, the latter containing the "primal transference" underlying religion and group formation (Stern, 1957; Stone, 1961). The myth is a verbalization of fantasies accompanying this act. Its narration in the rites is a magic realization of their content (Hooke, 1925). In the course of development, myth and rite, the carriers of symbiotic wishes, dialectically foster individuation through increase of real mastery of reality and through identification with, and reintrojection of, wishes projected into the myth.

THE PHYLOGENETIC LAW AND THE DISCHARGE CONCEPT

Kanzer (1964) equates the stages of individual growth with social formation, comparing the tribal hunt with the oedipal stage and the phobias that go with it—the agricultural ritual with the latency period and superego formation, and the re-emergence of sexual impulses in the

Oedipus drama with puberty and paranoia. According to Almansi (1964) the evolution of mythical symbols corresponds precisely to that of id, ego, and superego: ". . . all stages of libido development participate in the formation of these symbols. Their numerous meanings bear indications not only of the different stages of libidinal development, but also of the operation of the defense process, of the superego and ego, and of the progressive integration of the drives into the totality of the psychic structure."

Arlow (1961) points out that group formation occurred through the mythmaker's sharing with fellow men fantasies which expressed the specific level—preoedipal, oedipal, etc.—of his ego development. He ascribes to myths the function of abrogating the impossible burden of instinctual renunciation which communal living demands. The Prometheus myth of stealing fire thus memorializes the stage of psychic development before the renunciation of oedipal wishes and the institution of the superego, while the Mosaic myth of stealing the tables of the Law reflects the type of ego organization associated with the beginning formation of the superego.

Arlow rejects as unsound the method used by Freud and his followers to reconstruct in precise detail the putative events of a particular period in the history of a group. "Only the shadow of a real event was necessary on which to build the structure of the myth." He proposes, therefore, to validate the study of myth solely on the response of patients to mythologic material, according to the appeal it may have in relation to specific psychologic moments in the development of the individual.[1]

Myth and Reality

This brings us to the problem of the role of reality in the genesis of the myth. Freud called myths the secular dreams of young mankind. Are these secular dreams nothing but an expression of forbidden wishes and daydreams of an individual mythmaker, accepted and shared by the

[1] It seems to me that Arlow's method of validation does not sufficiently consider the multilayered structure of myths and their multiple appeal. It may call to the fore in different patients different layers of unconscious fantasy. I would like to recall Freud's discussion of the different phase specificity of the fantasy of being eaten in Little Hans and in the Wolf Man. The myth of Kronos devouring his children might elicit in the patient wishes of various phases—oral ones, passive and active, sadistic, masochistic, homosexual ones, etc. The myth of Orestes could be seen as an expression of the negative Oedipus complex (Kanzer, 1964); to archeologists it marks the transition from the matriarchal to the patriarchal hierarchy, namely, the rebellion of the son against the aggressive Great Mother wading in blood, presented in other cultures as the rebellion against Ishtar, Anat, Tiamat, Gäa, etc.

group? We know that dreams are condensations of the impact of external reality and repressed wishes of the individual. What is a myth? We mean, of course, the term myth in its original meaning and not the metaphoric one. What appear to be myths are often later poetic elaborations like those of Hesiod and Homer, the Greek tragedians Euripides and Sophocles, down to Racine and Goethe of later days. How Sophocles transformed the original myth, adapting it to the needs of his audience, is aptly described by Kanzer (1964). Even genuine myths handed down to us from the period in which they shaped the culture of the specific group are not the creation of individual poets or mythmakers; they are the result of the elaboration of many generations bearing the imprint of external and internal vicissitudes of the group. We have to differentiate between elementary myths which are ubiquitous mythical motifs as, for example, the myths of crossing water, eating forbidden fruits, of floods, creation, paradise, battles of giants, etc., and group myths into which a number of mythologic motifs are integrated. Elementary myths originate in magic rites, that is, in attempts to cope with the dangers of reality by way of magic manipulation, which accompanies the securing of food through hunting, tilling the soil, fishing, war, migration, etc. Group myths are regarded as history of the group, providing it with the identity necessary for its functioning, e.g., to fight against enemies. Group myths often have the form of family biographies centered about tribal heroes, such as Marduk, Gilgamesh, Dionysos, Prometheus, Jacob, Moses, Cain. (In the Noah genealogy, the various races of mankind are represented by his sons, Shem, Ham, and Japhet.)

The more consolidated a particular group became through the merging of smaller tribes into larger units, the more group myths became differentiated and specific, showing the imprint of historical events, such as migrations, conquests, merging with other groups, changing economic conditions (as introduction of agriculture), etc. Yet, even elementary myths have an accidental, unrepeatable, and individualistic character. Ubiquitous mythical motifs, such as the hero splitting water and walking through it without wetting his feet, change according to historical and geographic conditions of the specific groups in which they appear, as in the procession of the Israelites through the Red Sea. Egyptian myths have another color and climate than those of Mount Sinai or Kadesh. The figure of Moses does not fit into the time of the patriarchs. Myths of many people tell of favorites of the gods receiving holy writs from their hands, but in no other myth do we hear that the hero destroys this irreplaceable gift in his wrath. Only the myth of Moses contains this individual trait. It has a historic meaning. The Mount Sinai myth in which Moses goes twice onto the mountain to meet God and comes down with the tables seems reminiscent of a historic event—the rebellion in Kadesh against the Moses of the Exodus, the rejection of his monotheism (breaking the tables of Law), his being killed on the mountain, and his substitution by the Moses of the Kadesh compromise. This conjecture is supported by the mask the latter wore when dealing with the people, possibly a totem mask with horns (quarnajim), symbolizing the regression to the Kenitic cult, and the dance around the golden calf pointing to the totem ritual of the collective eating of the totem animal.

Group myths become expanded into all-embracing *religious myths* centering around cosmic gods, such as Jahve, Zeus, Osiris. This often occurs under the influence of inspired leaders, seers, prophets, founders of religion. It is relevant for our investigation that we find two archetypes of religious myths. The first is an anthropocentric one, in which man's life originates in a state of bliss and innocence without anxiety and traumatic threats, in union with nature and life (Paradise, Golden Age), "in those times men did not know of death; they understood the language of animals and were at peace with them; they did not work and found abundant noruishment at hands' reach" (Eliade, 1960). From this paradise man is thrown out, into reality, through his own guilt. He may regain the blissful state at the end of his days in this world or in the hereafter. We encounter the paradise myth all over the world in more or less complex forms. Characteristic elements are immortality, union with creation, the oral gratification manifested in the abundance of enjoyable food, eating ambrosia, drinking with the houris, devouring the gigantic leviathan in the community of the pious.

In the second form, that of the cosmogonic myth, the universe emerges from chaos and is organized by God into a well-ordered system. A variation of it is the creation of the world out of the destroyed body of the mother, alluded to in the Biblical creation myth. It should be stressed that both archetypes are manifestations of the primordial transference to the mother. They reflect the ambivalent aspect of the Great Mother in infantile fantasies—the one representing the good mother-child symbiosis lost and unconsciously longed for throughout life, the other an aggressive response to the traumatic early oral frustration projected onto the bad mother; both reflect the undoing of early traumata.[2]

[2] We may ask whether the concept of a chaotic id, out of which organization is slowly established through ego formation, is not influenced by the primordial transference (Stern, 1963).

We may define myths as reports of supernatural happenings involving gods, demons and heroes, accepted by specific groups as truly historical. Referring to the ancestors, good and bad, myths contain psychologic projections of more or less elaborated unconscious infantile fantasies. Manifesting the primordial transference, the events reported in myths are experienced outside the realistic space-time category: the acting persons representing the ancestral family are ever-existing, as super-reality. Mythical thinking, like transference, points to a split in the individual's relation to reality which separates the sacral, supernatural world from profane reality. Existing on the level of the supernatural, the sacral part—which is the projected mythical one—represents absolute reality. The sacral originates in the need to overcome the fear of death, of mortality. This explains the tenacity with which this split is maintained—the clinging to irrational religious beliefs, obsolete traditions, superstitions, etc. Through myth, rite and religion, the group gets its identity, which unconsciously means absolute reality, and immortality.

Since myths are messages of the supernatural, of ancestors, they function as group superego; they bind its members in terms of religion.[3] Through tradition, rules and laws, they shape the behavior of the group and its members (totemism is an example of this function).

The term myth proper may be assigned to the myths of the magic period in which binding occurs on the level of magic manipulation of reality, including manipulation of the ancestors. In the religious myth, the father is a representative of the ego ideal, the impersonation of truth, justice and law. Submission to him guarantees protection from trauma and death. Its prototype is the Judaic myth of Jahve and his nation, the children of Israel.

The binding function of myths was often used for political purposes. Iconographic variations thus may reflect changes in social organization through invasions, revolutions, etc. Myths became political charters, giving the right to rule certain territories, as the myth of Abraham for the possession of Canaan; or to justify prerogatives, as the myth of Jacob for Israel's status as a chosen people, the myth of the blossoming rod of the tribe Levi for its consecration as priests. "A treacherous usurper will figure in the myth as a lost heir to the throne who has killed a destructive dragon or other monster, and after marrying the king's daughter, duly succeeds him" (Graves, 1959). Graves calls myths "dramatic short-

---

[3] Muensterberger, in a personal remark, pointed to the meaning of religare—rebinding which confirms the role of primal symbiosis.

hand records of such matters as invasions, migrations, dynastic changes, admission of foreign cults, and social reforms. . . ."

An example is the reflection of the transition from hunting and food gathering to agricultural culture in the myth of the Great Mother. War-like nomads have a patriarchal organization (Weber, 1921). We may speculate that the development of bureaucratically organized, hierarchic river societies instigated the transition to the patriarchal structure, and that this is reflected in the myth by the defeat of the Big, life-giving and destructive Mother goddess by the rebellious son. This memorializes at the same time the onslaught of bellicose nomadic tribes. In the myth of Kronos, the cruel, devouring, oral-aggressive aspect of the Big Mother goddess is transferred onto the son, who becomes the father god of the patriarchal society. In the Biblical myth of paradise, the influence of the Great Mother is denied by the fact that Eve, called in the Bible, "the mother of all beings," is born from the side of Adam.

Myths, therefore, cannot be treated as phenomena isolated from the history of the group. To interpret a myth in isolation from its back-ground would be comparable to interpreting a symptom or dream without considering the patient's personality, history, and the day residues con-veyed by free association. In the study of myth, the material provided by patients in free association must be replaced by detailed knowledge of the group, of its social, economic and historic background. This necessi-tates painstaking investigations of the origin of the myth, of its distortions —which often necessitate linguistic explorations of different variations— and of contemporary or later comments in the literature.

As an example of the interplay of infantile wishes, historic reality, and use of myth for political purposes, one may point to the Cain myth in the Bible. Cain is the tribal son-god of the Kenites, who united with the Hebrew tribe coming from Egypt at Kadesh. The Jahvistic Cain myth is the transformation of a Kenitic mother-son-god myth, in which the Great Mother is replaced by Jahve, the executor of law and justice. The myth points to the compromise between the Ichnathon concept of monotheism, grafted upon the monotheistic cult of the Hebrew half-nomads, and the Kenitic mother-son cult of Kadesh (the so-called Kadesh compromise). In the underlying Kenitic myth, Cain, the tribal father, kills his son, Abel (in Hebrew, Hawel, the "fading" one), possibly in a fertility rite "on the field." The reality aspect of the myth, its day reminis-cence, so to speak, is the struggle of the monotheistic Jahve followers, the half-nomadic cattle breeders of the south, against the sexual orgiastic fertility cult of the native Canaanitic agricultural population in the

north. Cain represents the matriarchically oriented agricultural population, and Abel, the half-nomadic cattle breeders devoted to the monotheistic Jahve cult. God's enigmatic warning in the myth, *"lapetach chatat
rowez: the sin is toward the door,"* is elucidated by the knowledge that
petach, the door, means female genital as well as furrow *(pituach).*
The meaning is that ploughing the soil equals incest. The unconscious
meaning of the myth lies in the replacement of the incestuous mother
fixation by the ambivalent homosexual submission to Jahve, specific to
the Hebrew tradition. It is assumed that the redactor of the Bible used
this myth in his political struggle in the revolt of the Jahve followers
against the king who was disloyal to Jahve. Only the investigation of the
historical background of the myth, of contemporary comments in the
Midrash, of linguistic details, enabled a full interpretation (Stern, 1943).

BIOGENETIC LAW, DRIVE CONCEPT AND MYTH

We mentioned above that Freud based his conviction of the validity
of biogenetic law on the existence of narcissistic omnipotence of thought
and its sexualization, both in the primitive and in a specific phase of the
child's ego development.

> If we may regard the existence among primitive races of the
> omnipotence of thoughts as evidence in favour of narcissism, we
> are encouraged to attempt a comparison between the phases in the
> development of men's view of the universe and the stages of an
> individual's libidinal development. The animistic phase would
> correspond to narcissism both chronologically and in its content;
> the religious phase would correspond to the stage of object-choice
> of which the characteristic is the child's attachment of his parents;
> while the scientific phase would have an exact counterpart in the
> stage at which an individual has reached maturity, has renounced
> the pleasure principle, adjusted himself to reality and turned to
> the external world for the object of his desires.... At the animis-
> tic stage men ascribe omnipotence to themselves. At the religious
> stage they transfer it to the gods but do not seriously abandon it
> themselves, for they reserve the power of influencing the gods in a
> variety of ways according to their wishes. The scientific view of the
> universe no longer affords any room for human omnipotence; men
> have acknowledged their smallness and submitted resignedly to
> death and to the other necessities of nature [Freud, 1913].

Freud (1917) expressed the belief that primal fantasies ". . . are a
phylogenetic possession. In them the individual, wherever his own experience has become insufficient, stretches out beyond it to the experience of

past ages. It seems to me quite possible that all that today is narrated in analysis in the form of fantasy ... was in prehistoric periods of the human family a reality; and that the child in its fantasy simply fills out the gaps in its true individual experiences with true prehistoric experiences."

Campbell paraphrased this concept by describing human development as an unbroken line stretching "from below the horizon of humanity, from the ritual dances among the birds, the fishes, the apes and the bees," to the paleontological level of primitive man, the hunter and early planter, to the archeological level of the beginning of high cultures of Mesopotamia, the Nile, Guatemala and Peru. He thinks that man, like other members of the animal kingdom, may possess "innate tendencies to respond compulsively in strictly patterned ways to certain signals flashed by his environment and his own kind" (Campbell, 1960). This concept is in accord with analytic concepts (Schur, 1958; Weigert, 1938; Menaker, 1942) wherein genetically fixated action patterns of lower species—i.e., inhibition of aggression in the mating of fish and birds, "the signs of humility" among wolves, the inhibition of fighting against members of the same species—are viewed as evolutionary forerunners of mental functions—i.e., superego, masochism, defenses, etc.

Of course, innate elementary responses—such as turning to or away from—operate on every organismic level. But to see in differentiated instinctual behavior patterns of lower species prototypes of human mental structure, would neglect the difference between both kinds of responses as to their structure and position in the chain of evolution. Complex, specific, instinctual behavior patterns are rather end products of an evolutionary chain and—like the antlers of deer or the shell of shellfish—possibly responsible for their arrest in evolution, which precludes their hereditary transmission to man (Stern, 1963). A member of an animal species inherits in the form of these patterns the collective experiences of the species. Yet, animals thus endowed with different instinct have been weeded out by natural selection just because of this inheritance. To see an unbroken line from the behavior of animals to that of man is to neglect the decisive turn in the process of evolution which is constituted by the substitution of instinctual behavior patterns by anticipation.

In distinction from lower species, man is born with relatively few inherited patterns of behavior. His development is based on the extensive development of the anticipatory process, specific for man, instigated by the immaturity of his brain at birth. This forces the individual into adaptation at a time when fixed pathways for action patterns are not yet developed. The quicker maturation of the brain, that is, of pathways for fixed action patterns, makes monkeys less amenable to learning than man. The compensation for man's poor bodily endowment is the possession of a large and complex brain, resulting from the replacement of fixed patterns by anticipation. As Lorenz (1957) expressed it, "in a reaction chain of an instinct, more and more instinctive links drop out and are replaced by learned behavior patterns."

Muensterberger (1955) stresses the dependence resulting from the general retardation and fetalization in man's development. In this context, I would like to concentrate especially on the decisive impact of the immaturity of the brain at birth. It is the elementary level, determined by the brain's immaturity at birth, from which ontogenesis in man starts, which accounts for his astonishing adaptive flexibility and the grandiose development of his mind.

At birth, and even soon after, the development of ganglion cells in every part of the brain is incomplete. That incompleteness of development is much more pronounced in the human infant than in any other mammalian young. The growth of the brain after birth does not consist, as does that of other tissues and organs, in the multiplication of its cells: The increase in the brain is exclusively the result of growth of fibers and arborizations which spread out from developing cells, establishing the potential for various connections. The fixed patterns of innate instinctive actions in lower species are replaced in man by the potential for innumerable responses based on the wealth of associative fibers in the brain. They are the basis for the exuberant development of the anticipatory process in man called to the fore by the necessity to meet the effects of the traumatic vulnerability of the postnatal period. This development meant crossing a definite boundary line. "Once beyond it, the course of the evolutionary process was turned into a new channel; the very method of its operation was changed. Its products became the products of a new entity, the social group; and a new heredity, the heredity of transmitted tradition, came to overshadow organic heredity. The human individual is permanently a member of a solitary social group" (Briffault, 1931).

GROUP FORMATION AND ANXIETY

Group formation originates less in the need for sharing fantasies and daydreams than from (1) the long-lasting dependency on the maternal group which grows to comprise several generations; (2) the realistic need for mutual protection due to man's poor bodily endowment in the face of overwhelming dangers of reality, such as starvation, natural catastrophies, giant animals, etc.; (3) irrational regressive wishes for the all-protective mother-child symbiosis, predicated upon the fixation to the long-lasting dependency (primordial transference). (Crowding has been described as occurring in animals in situations of stress.) The traumatic vulnerability in infancy explains the increasing permanency of the maternal group; the traumatic vulnerability of the adult requires cooperative action to succeed in coping with reality.

Group formation and the involved close proximity of its members has had manifold effects on the vicissitudes of drive gratification, which can only be alluded to in this context. The prolonged dependency, in which mastery of reality means mastery of interpersonal relations, to mother, father, siblings and group member, enforces control of libidinal, incestuous and aggressive impulses. It fosters identification and projection; it results in what we call infantile conflicts.

Dependency, be it on a mother or a group, arises from the need for protection against external anxiety; but simultaneously it fosters inner anxiety. Magic acting, which sprang from the need to protect against external threat, at the same time undoes the emerging inner anxiety.

Anxiety and Magic

Anxiety penetrates the life of primitive and of prehistoric man; it forms his habits and tradition. Gilbert Murray (1935) stressed that:

> The extraordinary security of our modern life in times of peace makes it hard for us to realize, except by a definite effort of the imagination, the constant precariousness, the frightful proximity of death, that was usual in these weak ancient communities. They were in fear of wild beasts; they were helpless against floods, helpless against pestilences. Their food depended on the crops of one tiny plot of ground. . . . It is this stage of things that explains the curious cruelty of early agricultural doings, the human sacrifices, the scapegoats, the tearing in pieces of living animals and perhaps of living men, the steeping of the fields in blood. Like most cruelty, it has its roots in terror, terror of the breach of Tabu —the Forbidden Thing. . . . The manifestation of early religion throve upon human terror; the more blind the terror, the stronger became their hold.

Anxiety explains why the primitive puts into the same category all phenomena which elicit the same emotional response. The recall of an assaulting lion, an image or a report of this, elicits in him almost the same emotional response as an actual assault. In his mind, he ascribes to all these the same power, the mana of the object.

A patient, who had an accident in which another car crashed into his, coming from the left, had in the period immediately afterwards anxiety attacks when hearing the word car; somewhat later he only felt anxiety when perceiving a car moving toward him in the street; and finally only when perceiving cars moving toward his car from a left side street. Reflex-like responses occurred before he had time to discriminate between recall and real danger.

Due to their potentiality to create a similar emotional response, the primitive ascribes to image, name, or any part of the object, such as shadow, hair, etc., the very power of the object itself. He does this not because he is unaware of the difference between them, but just because

FIGURE 1.   Engraved shaft from the Mège Shelter at Teyjat (Dordogne). According to H. Breuil. Men dancing disguised as chamois. Hunting magic (from *Larousse Encyclopedia of Mythology*, p. 2).

FIGURE 2. Engraving on limestone from La Columbière (Ain). Rhinoceros pierced with arrows. Sympathetic magic (from *Larousse Encyclopedia of Mythology*, p. 4).

of his awareness of it. To manipulate an image of the object or its name, therefore means to the primitive to master the very essence, the mana of the object. Thus, piercing the image of a bison drawn into the stone or the symbolic killing of an individual disguised as a bison, meant to kill the mana of the bison. Cave drawings of the Magdalenian period are the most early documentation of magic and mythic activities of the human mind (see Figures 1 & 2).

The same applies to the dramatic imitation of wished-for happenings. To pour water onto the earth meant getting the earth fertilized with the mana of rain. Drawing animals in caves representing the womb achieved procreation of needed animals.

Magic thinking, projecting the emotional response onto the object, paves the way for the projection of the unconscious repressed wishes of the individual. As a consequence, tilling the soil acquires the meaning of incest, killing the bison the meaning of parricide. Totemism has its origin here. Yet, irruption of traumatogenic repressed impulses was prone to interfere with the goal of magic manipulation; it threatened with punishment. Certain Indian tribes are, therefore, under the prohibition of tilling the soil; in other groups it is restricted (Frazer, 1926). In the Cain myth we have a desecration of agriculture in the rejection of Cain, the tiller of the soil.

The magic rite has a much more complex structure than abrogation of instinctual renunciation through discharge (Arlow, 1961). Apart from the attempt to master reality, it purports to counteract the threat connected with the breakthrough of the repressed, dangerous libidinal and aggressive impulses.

Another very important effect is the displacement in the mental economy of the unconscious wishes and fears from the real object, e.g., the soil, to a symbol, the fetishistic image. This liberates the real object, the soil, from the pressure of the unconscious, and the intended action, e.g., tilling the soil, from dangerous impediment. The unconscious wishes become detached from the soil and displaced onto the symbol, the magic act and myth accompanying it. The emerging anxiety is counteracted by a magic re-establishment of mother-child unity. This establishes a split between the real, the profane, and the supernatural, the sacral.

RITE AND MOTHER-CHILD SYMBIOSIS

The expected punishment for acting out the prohibited instinctual impulses is, ultimately, loss of love, or, in other words, loss of the once experienced paradise of the mother-child symbiosis, which at that phase meant death. This threat is undone through the concomitants of the magic act: endless, repetitious, monotonous dancing, for days or weeks, accompanied by exhortations and incantations mounting to a higher and higher frenzy and pitch to ecstasy, fostered by alcoholic intoxication or fasting, sexual abstinence, etc. All this produces a melting together of the participants into one ecstatic unity, achieving a magic hallucinatory re-establishment of the mother-child symbiosis.[4] (We know that monotonous repetition and fasting are, through sensory deprivation, preconditions for hallucination.) Group ecstasy achieves the undoing of the danger emanating from the symbolic acting out of repressed infantile wishes in the magic rite through establishing primal symbiosis.

The ecstatic dances of the dervishes in Cairo or Constantinople are an example of this. The dervishes sit on the floor, so close that they become one body supporting each other; one of them starts to chant; the group answers automatically, moving back and forth until their foreheads touch the earth. Their movements become quicker and quicker, wilder and wilder,

---

[4] In Elkisch's case of Stanley (Mahler & Elkisch, 1953), the child establishes symbiosis through a rite in which he, in endless monotonous repetition, puts a question to the mother, demanding again and again her immediate automatic monotonous response.

without losing their rhythmic monotony. Hours of such movement put the dervishes into a state of intoxicated daze, a frenzy which ends in exhaustion in which they feel that they enter, physically and mentally, into a union with God.

I would like to point at the mass ecstatic phenomena of many religious communities—primitive and civilized—the prophets, early Christians, the Chassidim, Negroes, etc. (I owe to Dr. Muensterberger the reference to the meaning of the Hebrew word, *chag*, holiday as dance.)

Weber (1921) stresses that in the apostolic age of Christianity, the "spirit" never took possession of the single individual but only of the assembly of the faithful. "Speaking in tongues" arose only in the midst of the congregation. It was the consequence of group togetherness. "The infinitely important significance of the congregation as a carrier of the holy spirit in early Christianity lay in the fact that it was precisely the togetherness of the brethren which created the ecstatic manifestations."

Ecstasy is being put outside of oneself, being "beside oneself." It means the ultimate bliss in feeling united with the whole cosmos. It seems to correspond to the oceanic feeling Freud has pointed at. It is defined by Plotinus as a state of exaltation of the soul, in which there is a union with the supernatural and divine. According to Eliade (1960), "during ecstasy the paradisical is recovered: through the exercise of special technique the ecstatic tries to overcome the actual conditions of human life—those affecting 'fallen man'—and to reconstitute the state of primordial man as we know it by the paradise myths. The mystic experience of primitive people is equivalent to a return to the beginning, a reversion to the mythical days of 'a lost Paradise.' "

Nietzsche, in *The Birth of Tragedy*, writes: "if one were to convert Beethoven's 'Paean to Joy' into a painting and refuse to curb the imagination when that multitude prostrates itself reverently in the dust, one might form some apprehension of Dionysiac ritual. . . . Now (that the gospel of universal harmony is sounded) each individual becomes not only reconciled to his fellow but actually at one with him. Man now expresses himself through song and dance as the member of a higher community" (Nietzsche, 1870).

Here we have to make two corrections:

1. We have defined the state of ecstasy as a regression to mother-child symbiosis. But, is it a regression to a once experienced symbiosis preceding the separation from the mother? It seems that this symbiosis was experienced only at the relief from unbearable states of frustration which ended in blissful merging with the need-satisfying object. The

fantasy or hallucination of symbiosis is a defense against the fear of loss of love, of being abandoned.

2. In the attempts in magic rites to undo the threatening loss of love by establishing symbiosis, the wishes for sexual union breaking through are acted out. In the magic rites, the presence of women is at first disturbing; they are excluded; this develops later into the sexual orgies in the rituals of the matriarchal mother-son god cult. Sexual gratification became integrated into the realm of the sacral. The façades and outside walls of Hindu temples, such as the Khajuraho of the tenth century, and Konarak of the eleventh century, are covered by life-size erotic sculptures, which are highly realistic representations of all variations of sexual intercourse, including fellatio, anal intercourse, group orgies. These were exposed to adults and children alike. In the confessions of ecstatics, the image of sexual union appears again and again, the complete frenzied and blissful merging in orgasm, with extinction of personal identity. The Upanishads state about ecstasy: "just as one who is in the embrace of his beloved wife has no consciousness of what is outside or inside, so in the experience of ecstasy there is nothing which points inside or outside. Ecstasy is entering into God, a love union with God, eating of God, breathing in of God's fire spirit. It is the unity of ego and world" (Buber, 1921). Some examples may illustrate these trends.

HUNTING RITES

The hunting rite consists mainly of dances, incantations and fasting. Catlin (Levy-Bruhl, 1923) has described the bison and the wolf dance of Indian tribes.

> Five or fifteen dancers participate in the dance; everyone has on his head the skin and the head of a bison or a mask which represents a head. He has in his hand his bow or his spear. The dance continues without interruption, sometimes two or three weeks without stopping for a single moment. It represents the hunt itself in which the bison is killed. When an Indian is exhausted, he shows it in bending over as if he would fall. But another one then aims at him with his arc and touches him with his arrow; he falls like a bison. The others draw him out of the circle by his ankles, making gestures as if to skin him. . . .
> Similar is the wolf dance of the Sioux: during this dance all voices unite in a song, addressed to the spirit of the wolves. One of the medicine men wears the skin of a whole wolf. The others wear masks of a head of a wolf. All imitate with their hands precisely all movements of that animal.

In Canada, the hunters observe fasting for eight days. They do not stop singing during the whole day. Several cut into their own bodies in different places. Before they leave for the hunt, it is necessary that some of them see wolves in their dreams. A feast is offered by the chief in which he tells stories about his hunting experiences and his dreams. In all primitive societies, the hunter must abstain from sexual relations, must observe his dreams, must clean himself, fast and paint himself in imitation of an animal (Levy-Bruhl, 1923).

FERTILITY RITES

The fertility rites among primitive people living today are probably not very different from those of antiquity. The Batschandi, for example, dig a hole in the ground, of oblong shape, and plant shrubbery around it so that it suggests the female genital. They dance around the hole with their spears held in front of them in a way suggestive of the penis in a state of erection. They dance around the hole for nights on end in ever-mounting states of ecstasy, repeating endlessly "not a hole, not a hole, but a vagina," finally thrusting their spears into the pit. During this period they observe abstinence from food and women (Preuss).

Rituals preceding tilling the soil symbolized the incestuous fertilization of the nourishing earth. Rites preceding the harvest included killing the corn spirit, i.e., a child or man, real or symbolic, meaning among other things an atonement for the incestuous action. On the partriarchal level it would correspond to killing of the first-born by Jahve. It seems to underlie the killing of Abel "in the field." Spring and fall festivals of antique Mediterranean civilization consisted of the "secret marriage" of the king, who, as the representative of the son god, had intercourse with the high priestess, the incarnation of the Great Mother, in a green hut on the roof of the temple. The ritual of the death of the son god and his resurrection three days later represented the magic repetition of the death and revival of vegetation. His resurrection, after a mourning period, was celebrated with dances, sex orgies, etc. Worship in the temple of the Great Mother included intercourse of the worshippers with the priestesses (*Quedeshot,* the sacred ones) representing the Mother, as Herodotus reported.

RITE AND MYTH

The myth emerges from the magic rite as the verbalization of unconscious fantasies breaking through in the act. The primordial vehicles for their emergence are the incantations, exhortations and magic invocations accompanying the magic act, and the dream reports used as omens for the intended action.

There are collections of these incantation texts containing the rituals for the great seasonal festivals as in the library of Assurbanipal at Nineveh. I mention the creation myth, which in the Babylonian New Year ritual had the purpose to achieve a magic resurrection of all creation. The ritual was connected with the removal of guilt and defilement of the old year and ensuring the security and prosperity of the coming year. The concept of creation at this stage was not cosmologic but ritual (Hooke, 1925). The liturgical texts for the Jewish fall holidays still reflect the Babylonian ritual to the last detail.

Recent researchers have shown that the Psalms were liturgical material, originally intended for use in the seasonal festivals and other rituals in the preprophetic stage of the Hebrew religion. They often start from imperatives and interjections, magic exhortation, directed to Jahve. The well songs (Book IV of the Bible, Chapt. 21, Verse 17) contain a magic conjuring of the well accompanying the digging.

> Rise high, oh well
> Dug by the chiefs
> Bored by the nobles of the people with their spears.

This rite is similar to the spear rite which we have already met in the fertilization as well as in the hunting rite. (According to tradition, Moses' crime at Meriba was the regression to this magic sexualized act in defiance of the command of Jahve to produce water through incantation of the name of Jahve. He was punished for this by being forbidden the entrance into the promised land, meaning, being driven away from the mother.)

DREAM, MYTH AND RITE

The content of the songs and incantations in rites was determined by dreams which had to be carefully watched and reported. As manifestations of the mana of the ancestors, they were used as sacral guideposts for the intended action. Not all dreams were equally important. "Big dreams," in distinction from the trivial ones, seem to have been nightmares with their quality of stark reality close to hallucination. It is easy to understand that the anticipation of dangerous activity, like hunting dinosaurs, which meant killing the father or mother, or the impregnation of the soil, produced anxiety dreams.

Nightmares were regarded as commands by ancestors, and required to be enacted. Levy-Bruhl and Freud (1913) gave interesting examples. We would say that they required undoing through repetition. Levy-Bruhl (1923) reports that when a man dreamed of being attacked by a person, he assembled his friends; they molded a figure of the attacker, then danced around it, destroying it by thrusting their spears at it.

This explains the nightmare character of quite a number of myths, such as that of Sodom and Gomorrah, Jahve's attack on Moses at the inn (the blood wedding), Jacob's fight with the angel, the myth of the flood in which the rising waters impersonate the all-devouring Big Mother (Tiamath, the Tehom of creation). This myth may have originated in magic rites to conjure up the inundation of the big stream fertilizing the soil. The myths of attacks at night, on Jacob, on Moses, when en route, may have originated in migration or war rites. We find the same nightmare character in Greek myths like Tantalos, Prometheus, Aktaeon, Herakles, Ikaros, Oedipus, the figure of the Sphinx, and innumerable others. Initiation rites seem to re-enact nightmares to undo the traumata of infancy (Devereux, 1951).

Through oral transmission over thousands of years, these stories, by endless repetition, became condensed and were stripped to their essentials. The typical myth appeared, but as shown before, inextricably linked with reality facts.

In the course of the development of civilization, ritual and myth become dissociated. The turning point in this development is what is called the agricultural revolution. It had far-reaching consequences. The delay between action (seeding) and visible reward, the dependence of the latter on supernatural forces, on rain, flood, or sun, fostered an exuberant growth of fantasy thinking, myths and early religious systems. The function of mass ecstasy in the rite was taken over by medicine men, seers, prophets, saints, priests—very often pathological individuals with all the positive and negative concomitants of pathology. They derived omnipotence and omniscience from their ecstatic union with God.

The split between sacral and profane becomes embodied in the separation of the temple and priesthood from the laity. The laity, assembled in the temple (the mother womb), participates in the sacral ceremony, the rituals, which magically establishes the holy union through identification with the priest, through chanting responses, etc., as in the Holy Communion of the Catholic Church, symbolizing the group's incorporation of the god.

In the ritual, the recital of the myth means magic realization of the latter, under the protective meaning of the sacral. This becomes extended from the myth itself to the holy writs. They become the magic effector of the group symbiosis, the carrier of the primal transference. The pious Jew kisses the Torah scroll and treats it like an idol; he does not uncover his head in its presence.

That myth, acting as the cement of the group, led dialectically to the individuation of its members, must be shown in a special presentation. It occurs through identification with the hero of the repressed fantasies irrupted in the myth. The myth is the bearer of the group identity, at the same time generating the identity of the ego.

We may say that the magic rite is the root out of which grows the multibranched tree of the sacral: the ritual and myth with shamans, medicine men and seers; the religion with priests, prophets and saints; and art, philosophy and science with their flag-bearers.

The split between the sacral and profane exists today as it did in the past. It goes through the mind of the individual as well as society. A scientist in his private life might be a devout Catholic. Demokritos formulated his scientific four axioms: Nothing comes about per chance but all is through reason; nothing can be created out of nothing; there is no end to the universe; in reality there is nothing but atoms and the void —not much later than Sophocles had created the Oedipus trilogy.

We therefore doubt the existence of a phylogenetic phase of magic, narcissistic mentality, as well as that of a prelogical one involving mystic participation (Levy-Bruhl, 1923). Magic narcissistic thinking existed in the so-called primitive phase—as it does in our time—side by side with sharp realistic thinking. Its extent is in any phase a function of the degree of helplessness, i.e., the lack of ability to master reality. The concept of prehistoric human beings living on a magic, pregenital or oedipal level seems to me a construct. They would never have been able to exist. Infantile phases are determined by ontogenetic conditions. It is true that there are some similarities between the behavior of primitives and children—the excessive emotionality, wishful thinking, acting out, somatic identification— but these similarities are conditioned by the prevalence of anxiety in both due to helplessness in the face of overwhelming danger.

It is still open to question whether society can exist without the function of primordial transference carried by the myth, that is, without the anxiety-relieving function emanating from the primal symbiosis. Will maturation of mankind succeed in replacing the illusion of protection, transferred to society with the help of myth, by mature love and mature reason on which the house that Freud built rests?

SUMMARY

The exceptional position of man in nature is determined by his poor body endowment and high differentiation of his brain which compensates for it. Both are the effects of man's immaturity at birth, which enforces adaptation while he is still at a primitive level of maturation. It explains prolonged dependency on the mother and family and, ultimately, group formation. Dependency—be it on a mother or a group—protects against external anxiety, but simultaneously it fosters fear of loss of the protecting object, ultimately of the mother.

Myth and rite originate in group attempts at magic mastery of a reality which threatens primitive man with overwhelming danger. In such a situation, reality and symbol—which evokes recall of reality—are equated with regard to their dynamic power (mana); both elicit the same fear. Handling the symbol is thus handling the reality it represents. In this way rites which precede vital group actions undo their danger. Magic thinking is not a manifestation of a phylogenetic phase ontogenetically recapitulated in the narcissistic phase of the child, but a response to a similar biological condition, namely, helplessness in a situation of danger.

Because of its wishfulfilling quality, magic thinking favors the transference of parental images onto reality, that is, its humanization, and with this the breakthrough of dangerous unconscious wishes. The fear of loss of object which emerges from their symbolic re-enactment in the rite is, in turn, undone by the re-establishment of the mother-child symbiosis through the accompanying group ecstasies.

This displacement of the danger onto a symbol creates the split between the actual, profane reality and the supernatural, the sacral reality, eternal and immortal, which is conceived of as being the core of actual reality.

Myths arise from verbalization of the unconscious fantasies in the rite through chants, narrations of dreams, etc. The unconscious fantasies transferred onto the sacral become sanctified and part of the group superego. This endows myths with the sacral meaning of the rite itself. They structure the group and maintain its cohesion through the group identity they create. Yet myths, while providing the group with its identity, dialectically foster in its members—via identification with the hero—the emergence of personal identity.

BIBLIOGRAPHY

Almansi, R. J. (1964), Ego-Psychological Implications of a Religious Symbol—A Cultural and Experimental Study. *This Volume*, pp. 39-70.

Arlow, J. A. (1961), Ego Psychology and the Study of Mythology. *J. Amer. Psychoanal. Assn.*, 9:371-393.

———(1964), The Madonna's Conception Through the Eyes. *This Volume*, pp. 13-25.

Briffault, R. (1931), Evolution of Human Species. In: *The Making of Man*, ed. V. F. Calverton. New York: Modern Library, p. 761.

Buber, M. (1921), *Ekstatische Konfessionen*. Leipzig: Insel-Verlag.

Campbell, J. (1951), Bios and Mythos: Prolegomena to a Science of Mythology. In: *Psychoanalysis and Culture*, eds. G. Wilbur and W. Muensterberger. New York: International Universities Press.

———(1960), The Historical Development of Mythology. In: *Myth and Mythmaking*, ed. H. A. Murray. New York: George Braziller.

Child, V. G. (1951), *Man Makes Himself*. New York: New American Library of World Literature.

Devereux, G. & Mars, L. (1951), Haitian Voodoo and the Ritualization of the Nightmare. *Psychoanal. Rev.*, 38:334-342.

Eliade, M. (1960), The Yearning for Paradise in the Primitive Tradition. In: *Myth and Mythmaking*, ed. H. A. Murray. New York: George Braziller.

Erikson, E. H. (1959), Ego Development and Historical Change. In: *Identity and the Life Cycle. Psychological Issues*, Monogr. 1. New York: International Universities Press, p. 18ff.

Frazer, J. G. (1926), *The Golden Bough*. New York: Macmillan.

Freud, S. (1909), Case Histories. *Standard Edition, 10*. London: Hogarth Press, 1955.

———(1913), Totem and Taboo. *Standard Edition, 13*:1-161. London: Hogarth Press, 1955.

———(1917), Introductory Lectures on Psycho-Analysis. *Collected Papers, 4*. London: Hogarth Press, 1925.

———(1921), *Group Psychology and the Analysis of the Ego*. Trans. J. Strachey. London: Hogarth Press, 1948.

———(1926), Inhibitions, Symptoms and Anxiety. *Standard Edition, 20*:87-172. London: Hogarth Press, 1959.

———(1937), *Moses and Monotheism*. New York: Knopf, 1949.

Goldfrank, E. S. (1948), The Impact of Situation and Personality on Four Hopi Emergence Myths. *Southwestern J. Anthropol.*, 4:241ff.

Graves, R. (1957), *The Greek Myths*. New York: George Braziller.

———(1959), Introduction. In: *Larousse Encyclopedia of Mythology*. London: Paul Hamlyn.

Hooke, S. H. (1925), *The Origins of Early Semitic Ritual*. London: Oxford University Press, 1938.

Huizinga, J. (1954), *Geschichte und Kultur*. Stuttgart: Alfred Kroner Verlag.

Jung, C. G. (1957), *The Undiscovered Self*. Trans. R. F. C. Hull. New York: Mentor Books, 1959.

Kanzer, M. (1964), On Interpreting the Oedipus Plays. *This Volume*, pp. 26-38.

Levy-Bruhl, L. (1923), *Primitive Mentality*. Trans. L. A. Clare. London: Allen & Unwin.

Lorenz, K. (1957), The Nature of Instincts. In: *Instinctive Behavior*, ed. C. Schiller. New York: International Universities Press.

Luquet, G. H. (1959), Prehistoric Mythology. In: *Larousse Encyclopedia of Mythology*. London: Paul Hamlyn.

Mahler, M. S. & Elkisch, P. (1953), Some Observations on Disturbances of the Ego in a Case of Infantile Psychosis. In: *The Psychoanalytic Study of the Child, 8*:252-261, eds. R. S. Eissler et al. New York: International Universities Press.

Menaker, E. (1942), The Masochistic Factor in the Psychoanalytic Situation. *Psychoanal. Quart., 11*:171-186.

Muensterberger, W. (1955), On the Biopsychological Determinants of Social Life. In: *Psychoanalysis and the Social Sciences, 4*:7-25, eds. W. Muensterberger and S. Axelrad. New York: International Universities Press.

Murray, G. (1935), *Five Stages of Greek Religion*. London: Watts.

Murray, H. A. (1960), The Possible Nature of Mythology to Come. In: *Myth and Mythmaking,* ed. H. A. Murray. New York: George Braziller.

Nietzsche, F. (1870), *The Birth of Tragedy* and (1887) *The Genealogy of Morals*. Trans. F. Goeffring. New York: Doubleday, 1956.

Preuss, K. T. (n.d.), Der Ursprung von Religion und Kunst. *Globus, 86*.

Rank, O. (1912), *Das Incest-Motiv*. Leipzig & Wien: Deuticke.

Reik, T. (1946), *The Psychological Problems of Religion-Ritual: Psychoanalytic Studies*. New York: Farrar, Strauss.

Schur, M. (1958), The Ego and the Id in Anxiety. In: *The Psychoanalytic Study of the Child, 13*:190-220, eds. R. S. Eissler et al. New York: International Universities Press.

Stern, M. M. (1943), The Cain Myth. Paper read before the Psychoanalytic Society of Palestine, Jerusalem.

———(1957), The Ego Aspect of Transference. *Int. J. Psychoanal. 38*:146-157.

———(1961), Blank Hallucinations: Remarks about Trauma and Perceptual Disturbances. *Int. J. Psychoanal., 42.*

———(1963), Precursor of Mental Structures. Paper read before the 23rd International Psycho-Analytical Congress, Stockholm.

Stone, L. (1961), *The Psychoanalytic Situation*. New York: International Universities Press.

Weber, M. (1921), *Gesammelte Aufsaetze zur Religionssoziologie, 3*. Tuebingen: Verlag J. C. B. Mohr (Paul Siebeck).

Weigert, E. V. (1938), The Cult and Mythology of the Magna Mater. *Psychiatry, 1*:347-378.

Remarks on the Function of Mythology

WARNER MUENSTERBERGER, Ph.D.

It is difficult for the modern mind to enter that realm of mythological imagination which the mind of primeval and primitive man displays for us. Their sense of reality, their experience of internal and external, their notions as to the nature of man tend to differ profoundly from ours. A field experience exemplifies this difference of perspective: among the Dayak of Borneo it is not uncommon for the dreamer to relate his dream to the other members of his clan, particularly if the dream content is unintelligible to him. Disturbed by the dream, he may awake his fellow tribesmen, relate what he dreamed, expect their comments and interpretations and thus share his experience. Under the conditions of this type of communal living, the other clan members found a ready-made dream and would tell me in the morning this man's dream as one each of them had dreamed. One must note the readiness for mutual identification, possibly motivated by a need to alleviate anxiety. One also can recognize how defenses become collectively mobilized and organized in that everyone tries to participate in the interpretation.

Mythology operates in a very similar manner. In aboriginal myths and legends, we find the entire range of human relations, murder and incest, eccentricity and compassion, fantastic vision and trickery. Opposing forces have free play and thus permit a limited dissociation from the demands of conscience and society. Instinctual freedom is a major theme of the mythology of all cultures. The ingenuity with which interpersonal and intrapsychic strains and stresses are described demonstrates to the present-day observer that the instincts, and hence conflicts, have always governed man's imaginative power: sons have always loved and hated their fathers; fathers have always loved and subdued their sons. Parricidal and infanticidal inclinations in overt form or by proxy have possessed our ancestors just as persistently as we recognize them in the unconscious life of modern man. Tyranny, brutality, love, and hope have preoccupied homo sapiens since his animal past. And yet, all these tendencies are superseded by the mystery of man's need to perpetuate himself and thus observe restraint and develop defense mechanisms.

However, in myths and in dreams, our internal nature finds a channel for self-expression. Through them psychoanalysis recognizes many clues for essentially regressive impulses. Here, Arlow's (1961) observations describe a part of mythology which had not been sufficiently utilized in previous studies. Almansi's and Kanzer's investigations give us new insight into the complexities which have survived all the vicissitudes of man's history and development.[1] We may characterize this development as a more or less steady increase of superego forces versus the collective conscience as exemplified by the observation made among the Dayak, and by Parin and Morgenthaler among the Dogon.

One can agree with Arlow (1961) that it is no longer sufficient for us to demonstrate the id wishes expressed in mythological form. Myths, legends, and folk tales always reflect certain types of object relationships as environmental features in various disguises, mirrored in the multiformity of projective compositions. External modalities have always found their expression in the ideational concepts of the people.

After Freud's, Abraham's, Rank's, Reik's, and Róheim's spadework we now can add our spiritual armor of ego psychology to a closer grasp of mythology and its function. Proceeding further in our effort, we see new dimensions and perspectives relating to numerous elements of developmental processes, adaptive achievements, sociopsychological types of reaction formations. Hence, we arrive at the conclusion that there are various ways to interpret a dream, a myth, or a symbol. Almansi's and Kanzer's explorations deal with the same basic problem, the oedipal theme. Sophocles' trilogy and the religious symbol of the tablets are elaborations of the ubiquitous intrapsychic struggle of the generations, the ambivalent strivings which are the matrix of law, order, etiquette, and religion.

The extraordinary achievement of Sophocles is inevitably linked to the spiritual climate of his environment: no Hebrew could or would have conceived the Oedipus drama as he was living in a theocratic society which sought religious grounds for civilized behavior. Greece, on the other hand, especially under the guidance of Solon, established individual responsibility and promoted reason as an instrument for instinctual renunciation. The Dionysiac cults were not related with the moral

[1] See the papers by Drs. Renato Almansi, Jacob A. Arlow and Mark Kanzer in this volume.

responsibility which Solon envisioned and city life promoted. It would be comparatively easy to demonstrate a different structure of ego and super-ego among the worshipers of Dionysos and the followers of the democratic city state. Murray (1912) expresses a similar thought when he says: "Certainly Greek monotheism, had it really carried the day, would have been a far more philosophic thing than the tribal and personal monotheism of the Hebrews." The Greeks could not have invented the tablets. No Hebrew could have written the Oedipus trilogy, and yet they both are rooted in the inherent conflict between the generations, and revolt finds an avenue in accordance with environmental conditions or, in other words, their particular reality and intracultural variables.

The Oedipus plays tell us about the pressures of the environment. The fear of the people of Thebes, their shared fantasy, turns into a fear of the superego. The internalization of guilt and punishment, then, seems to vary. This variability of the organizing power of the ego as well as the internalization of individual and collective superego forces has recently been explored by Parin and Morgenthaler (1956-1957) during several field expeditions in West Africa. They differentiate between *super-ego* and *clan conscience* and conclude that the superego of the natives, in contrast to our own milieu, is replaced by "important factors such as the belonging in the community life or the fact of being separated from the community, and, further, by the subject's dependency on a prestige figure."

In historical perspective, it seems evident that the integration of instinctual wishes increased considerably since paleolithic times, if we only judge by the tools and artifacts of that period. Going back to neolithic times and proceeding from there to the Bronze age and the Iron age, we find a steady increase in technological variegation and concomitantly a greater diversity of combinations, a greater intricacy of tools and machinery and hence a greater accession to abstraction.

In the face of this more or less steady progress of mechanical aptitude, man became more secure from many external dangers, while his struggle against inner ones was the price he had to pay for civilization (Freud, 1930). Thus we see a decrease of magic and mythical thinking. We also see the shift from threatening demons to more lenient demigods until the image of "sweet Jesus" appears—albeit Satan lures from behind. As a warning against incestuous wantonness, the Greeks learned their lesson from Oedipus. The medieval transformation of the Oedipus trilogy is the morality play. The steadily increasing internalization of aggressive impulses together with instinctual control had a profound effect on mythmaking as well as on the social and psychological function of the myth as such. We can agree with Arlow's (1961) view that "through its mythology, the society tends to induce a climate favorable to the realization of appropriate identifications." In today's life, however, this ancient device of the myth has gradually changed and put the burden on the superego rather than on the collective or clan conscience. Mythology, it seems to me, helps to ward off passive or active wishes, to permit or restrain instinctual desires, largely to take the part of the superego but equally aid the ego's organizing attempts. It exercises a stabilizing influence.

At present ego psychology has the focal attention of psychoanalysis. The contributions to this panel show us how ego psychology can cast new light on our understanding of mythology and vice versa, and how mythology can contribute to the ever-widening scope of psychoanalysis. Our task does not end here. Next to the global regularity of basic themes and symbols, we now recognize the differentiation due to environmental conditions and intracultural alternatives. Further studies will be needed to fully explore the psychosocial function of mythology.

BIBLIOGRAPHY

Arlow, J. A. (1961), Ego Psychology and the Study of Mythology. *J. Amer. Psychoanal. Assn.*, 9:371-393.

Freud, S. (1930), Civilization and Its Discontents. *Standard Edition, 21*. London: Hogarth Press, 1961.

Murray, G. (1912), *Five Stages of Greek Religion*. London: Watts, 1946.

Parin, P. & Morgenthaler, F. (1956-1957), Charakteranalytischer Deutungsversuch am Verhalten "primitiver" Afrikaner. *Psyche, 5*:311-330.

SOME ONTOGENETIC DETERMINANTS IN SYMBOL FORMATION

WILLIAM G. NIEDERLAND, M.D.

If judged by the number of papers in the analytic literature, the subject of symbolism and symbol formation does not appear to be one upon which current analytic thinking is focused. Part of this relative indifference may be due to the fact that the earlier and basic studies in this field by Freud (1900), Abraham (1909), Ferenczi (1913), and Jones (1916) constitute not only a well-established body of theoretical knowledge, but serve also as a useful frame of reference in the analyst's daily clinical work. It is perhaps not surprising, therefore, that the more recent contributions by Friedman (1952), Kubie (1953), Rubinfine (1961), Rycroft (1956), the present author (1956), and others have remained more or less isolated attempts to delineate the symbolic process from other forms of psychic functioning and to revive interest in the problems of symbolism.

A good part of this apparent neglect can be attributed further to the recognition that in the absence of a valid psychoanalytic theory concerning the thinking process per se we lack the instrumentality for tracing the nature and genesis of symbol formation in full detail and for differentiating this process accurately from mental functioning involving other indirect derivatives of unconscious representation. Though the importance of symbol formation in normal as well as pathological mental functioning is universally acknowledged, the pertinent concepts appear far from uniform, at times contradictory and confusing. Jones's frequently quoted criteria, for instance, of what he designated as "true symbolism" in the psychoanalytic sense (representation of unconscious material, constant meaning, independence of individual conditioning factors, linguistic connections, evolutionary basis, etc.) have been repeatedly challenged, most recently by Kubie (1953) and Rycroft (1956).

Without going into the detailed aspects of this controversy, I propose to examine—within the framework of current analytic conceptualizations

Presented in abbreviated form at the Annual Meeting of the American Psychoanalytic Association, Atlantic City, May, 1960.

—some of the ontogenetic determinants in individual cases and situations. I am deliberately speaking here of determinants or factors involved in the process of symbol formation, since in the examples offered a number of symbols (or their precursors) became manifest under certain conditions, emerging before the observer in *statu nascendi,* as it were, although the symbolic formations may have been present before and may have come to the fore due to the circumstances to be described. It is noteworthy, moreover, that, while the actual appearance of the symbols occurred clearly and in some of the cases observed rather strikingly, in no case did the subject become aware of the meaning or even his use of symbols. As "true symbols" they were unconscious and their emergence in thought or speech did not deprive them of their unconscious quality.

In the following I wish to present some examples with particular emphasis on the conditions under which the symbolic process emerged. Two of my examples are taken from the direct observation of young children, two from clinical studies of adult patients, and two from the analytic evaluation of material pertaining to historical-mythological sources.

OBSERVATIONS ON CHILDREN

Symbolism, of course, is not confined to dreams, and what follows occurred in a nontherapeutic setting. A young child, less than three years of age, suddenly complained that a particle of dust had blown into his eye. The irritation caused by the foreign body was obviously intense and the child turned to the accompanying adult for help, crying that the pain-producing particle be removed. While the adult was still considering how to help the crying child, the flow of tears had apparently swept the piece of dust out of the eye. The child stopped complaining and exclaimed: "It's gone. It's already in my stomach." He pointed to his eyes and then to his abdomen. Later he happily repeated: "It went down into my stomach." The symbolic equation between the eye and the mouth, i.e., the "devouring eye" which swallows and devours, is here highly suggestive and such well-known fantasies as ocular introjection, ocular destruction, perhaps also ocular impregnation become apparent. Here the possible connections are complex. In this group of phenomena belongs the act of looking away or spitting out, for example, when one sees a person for whom one wants to show disrespect. Of further interest is the global quality of making things disappear and vanish through the act of closing the eye which, in the above instance, is equated by the child with taking in through the eye, that is, devouring. Since every visual percept can be caused to cease instantaneously in this way, closing the eye under such circumstances would be an act of symbolic destruction via ocular introjection, and opening the eye (i.e., seeing) would be equivalent to symbolic restitution via projection. Interesting theoretical and practical perspectives open up here, which can be touched upon only in this context. If lid closure, equated in the unconscious with closure of the mouth and with an act of oral incorporation, leads to the destruction of the bad object as, in this case, to the "death" of the offending foreign body by ocular ingestion, such a symbolic "death" of the object may throw additional light on the mechanism of certain sleep disturbances in early childhood. If closing the eyes enables the young child to destroy and "ingest" the world, more specifically the object, at bedtime, it seems permissible to think of certain types of insomnia in early life as caused by infantile fears of retribution and similar anxieties.

At any rate, from the fact that the whole symbolic process, as shown in this example, emerges under the impact of anxiety, pain, and acute bodily distress in an affectively charged, organ-specific setting where magic propensities also are attributed to the eye and are implicit in other orifices (mouth, anus, etc.), we may perhaps deduce the role of such factors for symbol formation in *statu nascendi* where one aspect of the equation, that is, the drive (in the present case, the aggression) remains entirely unconscious. I also wish to point to the prevalence of tactile and kinesthetic sensations which, combined with visual experiences, characterized the incident.

My next example, again derived from direct child observation in a nontherapeutic setting, deals with the occurrence and ontogenesis of symbols in dreams of young children. In an earlier communication (1957) I described a number of dreams by a young child which the dreamer reported during the last fortnight of his mother's pregnancy. The young dreamer, Johnny, was then three years and two months old. What he communicated about his nocturnal experiences during that fortnight were all dreams about water, and, more precisely, about water in motion.

Here is the sequence of Johnny's dreams during that period when aggressive as well as regressive behavior on the child's part had become fully apparent. Awakening at his usual time, he reported as the first item one morning that he had had a "special kind of sleep." In this special kind of sleep it had been raining and "there was water jumping up and down, up and down." About a week later Johnny again informed his parents of a special kind of sleep in which "water was jumping up and down." Then he added that the water had been jumping up and down "in the street." While relating this with great excitement, the child started to jump up and down on the floor himself in an effort to show how the water had been moving violently in the street. He also mentioned that it had been raining hard in his sleep. Two days after this dream the child awoke suddenly during the night and wanted to go to the window to see the rain falling outside. Asked why he wanted to do that, he drowsily replied while remaining in a state of half-sleep: "It is raining hard and I want to see the rain. The water is jumping up and down in the street . . . ." Johnny insisted on going to the window and looking out of it to see the rain in the street. (No rain was falling; but a day or two after this incident, his mother entered the hospital from which she soon returned with Johnny's younger sibling.)

Without discussing further details which can be found in my previous communication, suffice it to say that there were no enuresis, no other aquatic experiences, no primal scene observations, and no rainfall in reality during all the days and nights in question. This series of water dreams, however, could be traced to the mother's holding the child closely and frequently during the days prior to her subsequent hospitalization, and to the definite likelihood of Johnny's perception of fetal movements in her body (the maternal body transmuted into the "street" in his dreams). The symbol *water* and its specific emergence in the dreams as "water jumping up and down," that is, as *water in violent motion*, could thus be understood as resulting from two sources: (a) from the child's tactile and kinesthetic sensations produced by his physical contact with the maternal abdomen in motion; (b) from the child's own libidinal and aggressive drives expressed, indirectly yet graphically by the child, through his violent jumping up and down on the floor (i.e., the mother or rather the mother's pregnant abdomen) in describing the appearance and impact of the water symbol.

Here also the second component of symbol formation, its drive aspect, is repressed, but the return of the repressed can be recognized in the actions (jumping) of the child. These theoretical deductions appear to be corroborated by a closer examination of what had occurred between mother and child prior to the latter's dream sequence about water, rainfall, street, and window. On detailed examination it transpired that the mother had not only held Johnny in her arms frequently and tightly during those weeks, but also had told him about the new baby growing in her belly as well as about her forthcoming separation from him; that she would have to go to the hospital because of it; that he would remain under the care of his grandmother, etc. To most of this the child had responded with considerable curiosity, but otherwise had remained out-wardly calm and collected. On the day immediately preceding the series of water dreams, however, the child, while sitting comfortably on his mother's lap, had responded with a sudden startle to a quick succession of intense fetal movements in her abdomen. According to the mother's description, there was a mixture of anxiety, surprise, bewilderment, and misery in Johnny's facial expression and from then on his behavior became more and more restless, anxious, and unruly. He also showed signs of marked regression. During the fortnight of his water dreams he threw himself repeatedly on the floor, crawling about like an infant, engaging in baby talk, and actually crying out aloud "I am a baby." Bed-wetting and bowel accidents, however, did not occur. It is worth noting, furthermore, that because of the child's intense anxiety reaction and changed behavior since the day mentioned above, the mother reduced her physical contacts with Johnny and especially avoided putting him on her lap.

It thus seems legitimate to describe the child's actual perception of specific vibratory and fluctuating movements in the maternal abdomen, the tactile and kinesthetic sensations produced by them, and the resulting intensification of the libidinal-aggressive impulses in the subject himself as ontogenetic determinants or at least co-determinants of the symbol formation in the case observed. It seems further permissible, leaving aside any discussion of identification aspects, to single out the kinesthetic experience as the key factor, an experience which, to be sure, occurred in a highly charged setting of conflict and anxiety in view of the mother's pregnancy and imminent delivery—acute separation anxiety, clinging to the mother's body, heightened aggressiveness and marked regressive features.

The other symbol in these dreams, the window against which the rain was beating hard at night (as the maternal abdominal wall had been beating hard against Johnny during the day), has been discussed as a pregnancy symbol *par excellence* by Freud in the "Little Hans" case as well as in his paper on Goethe's first childhood recollection (1917). Here also the heightened aggressiveness of the young Goethe who threw all the family crockery out of the window in connection with the birth of a sibling is reported. The meaning of the window as a pregnancy symbol (the opening in the maternal body through which the baby arrives) will be further elaborated below.

Goethe's life and creativity offer, like the creative productions of many other men of genius, impressive illustrations of symbolism. In previous papers (1956, 1957, 1960) I have presented striking examples of this symbolism in the lives and works of Byron, the poet C. F. Meyer, and others. The symbolic river-sister equation can also be found in Goethe's close and incestuously tinged relation to his sister Cornelia. Eissler (1963), in his thorough study on Goethe, publishes "the earliest certain document containing direct evidence of Goethe's relationship to Cornelia," a letter written by the young poet at the age of fifteen to his sister, fifteen months his junior. As Eissler demonstrated, the letter contains "almost undisguised sexual fantasies." What interests us here is that it was sent to Cornelia while the poet found himself, in his own words, "amidst the romantic pleasures of a well-attended spa," i.e., *Wiesbaden,* a renowned *water resort* near his *native* town Frankfurt. Years later, at his sister's death, Goethe wrote to a friend, Auguste von Stolberg, whom Eissler correctly recognizes as a sister substitute, as follows: "Thanks, Gustgen, . . . I sang recently when deep in a splendid moon night I ascended from the river that flows by my garden through the meadows; and this becomes true for me daily. I must acknowledge good fortune as my mistress, for still she troubles herself about me [lit.: she clips me again] as a beloved woman does. You will have heard of my sister's death. . . ."

Again, years later, when Goethe fled from another sister substitute, Charlotte von Stein, to Italy, the first pages of his "Italian Journey" are filled with references to rivers, their scenic beauty, course, flow, etc.

CLINICAL OBSERVATIONS ON ADULTS

My next examples deal with the occurrence of symbolic formations in the productions of adult patients as well as with the far-reaching emotional significance of the individual experiences represented by and expressed through the symbol.

Early in the analysis of patient A, who had come into treatment because of a severe washing compulsion, potency disturbances, and overt murderous impulses against several close family members, a more or less constant geometric pattern, something like a circle or a ringlike configuration, emerged in many dreams and fantasies. From this one source which for brevity I am inclined to call "the symbolic circle," sprang a number of other symbols and symbolic communications. On numerous occasions he saw himself threatened by vague, undefinable structures of a serpentine appearance and consistency which surrounded his body, especially in the region of the neck, chest, and waist, in a circular fashion. As the transference developed, he began to feel that I kept him trapped in an ever-tightening grip or encased "as in cement" on the couch which in turn became an encircling dangerous monster with polyplike arms and menacing fangs. The treatment room turned into a prison cell with walls closing in on him, while he was being held tied in various types of constricting circles made of ropes or chains. The patient was a middle-aged professional painter who had started his artistic career early in life, and even the most superficial perusal of his paintings, past and present, disclosed that they were replete with circle forms; practically all human figures painted by him showed circular indentations around the waist. Also the patient's castration fears bore the stamp of the circle configuration. They were particularly severe and centered around the fantasy of being "hanged by the neck in a noose until death" for the oedipal crime committed by him at the age of five. (The patient was five years old, i.e., at the height of the oedipal phase, when his father died.)

To return to the "symbolic circle" in its various forms, displacements, and meanings, analysis revealed that all were ultimately derived from the same source as the bodily *fons et origo* of the later symbolic formations: the patient's *congenital torticollis*. This deformity had later been repaired by plastic surgery in such a successful manner that not the slightest trace of it had remained noticeable when A entered analysis. The same deformity, however, had furnished the matrix for much of the symbolism employed by the patient and for his sometimes rather ominously sounding symbolic communications during the analysis.

My next example concerns patient B, a twenty-five-year-old man, who, suffering from the sequelae of a severe poliomyelitis attack, entered the polio ward of Mount Sinai Hospital[1] with an almost complete paralysis of both legs, both arms, both shoulders except for some residual function of his left wrist and left fingers. Virtually a quadriplegic, the patient was kept in an iron lung for a number of months. Because of his progressive muscular atrophy, developing decubitus, and his apparently intractable emotional state characterized by inertia, almost lifeless apathy and passivity, the prognosis was considered poor. I am concerned here mainly with the striking changes in this patient's condition and behavior which were observed in him under the following circumstances.

[1] The patient was psychiatrically studied and treated by Dr. Alfred Corvin, then the consulting psychiatrist of the poliomyelitis ward at Mount Sinai Hospital, and his co-workers. I am greatly indebted to Dr. Corvin for letting me see and evaluate the clinical material on this patient, and particularly the symbolic content of this material.

Prior to these changes the patient had repeatedly dreamed that he was lying dead in a coffin, and in one of these dreams his funeral took place while it was raining terribly outside. In accordance with Freud's interpretation of such dreams ("I wished it was only a dream"), I was inclined to understand the symbolism in these dreams, especially the one in which it was raining hard, as referring to birth—or rebirth wishes of the patient. A short time after the occurrence of these dreams, art therapy was initiated at Dr. Corvin's suggestion, that is, a pencil was pressed into his left hand (with its residual finger function) and he was encouraged by the art therapist, Mrs. Paneth, to scribble, draw, sketch whatever he could or wished to. Without discussing the rationale and dynamics of this therapeutic procedure,[2] I wish to mention briefly that after initially scribbling some weak lines and curves, B began to draw a series of water scenes, partly with boats, lighthouses, and vast expanses of water. Of particular interest, in this context, are his ninth and tenth pictures drawn a few weeks after the start of his art work. The outstanding feature of the former is a *bay window* with a view on water, and while producing this drawing the patient uttered as his single verbal contribution to his work the word "bay window"; in the latter the ocean can be seen as an immense, formless expanse of water and waves. (Colloquially, the term "bay window" is often used for an "expanded" abdomen, and in this way indicates "pregnancy.") Following this, more aquatic pictures were produced, altogether six out of approximately twenty.

Limiting myself to a brief comment on the symbolic content of B's productions, it is apparent that the dreams about lying dead in a coffin and the funeral in the rain, the later drawings of the bay window, the ocean, and of other water scenes point to the presence of massive pregnancy-womb- and birth fantasies which may have played a considerable role in the favorable outcome. As to the specific conditions under which the symbols emerged, it seems to me that here again the kinesthetic experiences in the iron lung (the "coffin," ultimately the womb), later in handling the pencil, the art work, etc., have to be considered as significant for the activation of the symbolic process. Although there are certainly more factors involved in it, kinesthetic stimuli of a certain intensity and type appear to be determinants or co-determinants of symbolic forma-

[2] I am further indebted to Dr. Corvin for the information that B, some weeks after completing the pictures, left the hospital in much improved condition to join his family and to start working again, in a wheelchair, on his former job. He has continued working for the past three years or so.

tions more frequently than has heretofore been recognized. At least, in the case material presented here, such kinesthetic stimuli and their trans-mutation into symbolic representations seem to prevail over visual stimu-lation. Since B was not an analytic patient, this has to remain an as-sumption in his case and corroboration will have to come from further studies. Some of the dream symbolism communicated in the literature, such as Lewin's (1958) report on a localized dental irritation and its transmutation into a direct symbolic representation in an organ-specific setting, his analysis of Descartes' dreams, Scherner's characteristic *Leibreiz-träume* mentioned by Freud (1900) and discussed by Lewin, lend support to our view concerning the essential role of kinesthetic factors in symbol formation. At any rate, in the material offered by these authors the close connection between bodily processes and the emergence of symbolic ele-ments in dreams appears as clearly established as in the cases cited above. Moreover, the ego state in the cases under scrutiny appeared altered, re-gressed, and characteristically close to the body ego.

ILLUSTRATIONS FROM HISTORICAL SOURCES

As already mentioned, symbolism is not confined to dreams; it is en-countered in folklore, fairy tales, myths, art, poetry, jokes, and in all languages of the human race. We may therefore expect that the body roots of the symbolic process can also be demonstrated by studying its occurrence and manifestations in such nonindividual material. For the purpose of illustrating this point I wish to present brief examples taken from two different areas of recorded symbolism.

The legendary figure of the *Dukatenscheisser* (Figure 1) of which Freud spoke still decorates one of the ancient buildings near the *Kaiser-pfaltz* of Goslar, a traditional residence and coronation place of the German emperors through centuries of medieval history. The fact that the small stone statue, though artistically of little consequence and de-stroyed in the past as often as later rebuilt, still exists up to the present time, is perhaps itself indicative of its hold on man's imaginative proces-ses down the ages. In its primitive directness and local proximity to the coronation seat, the little figure of an ugly deformed dwarf, shown in the act of defecating coins, suggests to the spectator much of what analysts have recognized as symbolic derivatives of the anal function, that is, money, cunning, defiance, power, anal aggression and exhibitionism, etc., as well as the unconscious sources from which so many legends about goblins, dwarfs, hoarded treasures, or the like originate.

FIGURE 1.

The body roots of symbolic creations become equally apparent when one explores the historical development of the pictographic system of writing employed by the Sumerians through the first three millennia B.C. The oldest cuneiform symbols in their original pictographic configurations, in use during the earliest period of recorded Sumerian history, are unmis-

WILLIAM G. NIEDERLAND

takable depictions of body parts or other concrete objects. In later periods these same signs assume conventionalized forms through the introduction of a phonetic, highly conventionalized system of writing and the use of clay tablets "turned on their back" (Kramer, 1959). Thus, the original pictographs changed their shape and appearance during successive centuries (Figure 2). Not being a sumerologist or a philologist and speaking with no authority whatever on the development of the cuneiform system,

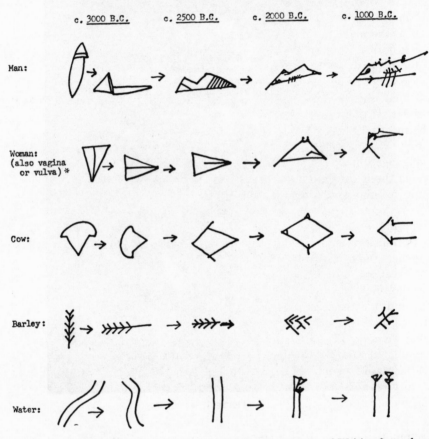

FIGURE 2. Development of the Sumerian (Cuneiform) System of Writing from about 3000 B.C. to 600 B.C.

Approximate and partial reproduction from Kramer's (1959) *History Begins at Sumer*.

* Addition by the author; characters slightly schematized.

I nevertheless deem it worthwhile to draw attention to those concrete and corporeal elements in the earliest Sumerian writings and to their gradual disappearance, to the point of near-unrecognizability of any bodily forms later on. This process of changing the character of the original symbolic signs (through the adoption of "conventionalizing" methods according to our leading sumerologists, through repression according to analytic thinking) becomes particularly manifest when one views the pictographs for a man and a woman with their gross physical resemblance to the respective genitals, during the earliest epoch of cuneiform writing (ca. 3000 to 2500 B.C.). The bodily resemblance is lost, as far as the male and female signs are concerned, in the following periods of historical development. The pictographs of some sexually indifferent objects, however, such as those for barley, cow, plant, etc., retain a measure of recognizable resemblance over the same period of time. As indicated, such a developmental course seems to be suggestive, from an analytical point of view, of the presence of unconscious repressive forces permeating here symbolic creations with no trace of individual authorship. Picture language, to be sure, is not synonymous with symbol language, though the one is presumably as ancient and primitive as the other, both corresponding to an early, archaically tinged way of expressing feelings and thoughts.

Without therefore pressing our analogies too closely (and without ignoring, in our last example, other influences responsible for the successive transformations of the cuneiform script), it may be said that from a further study of such material, taken from clinical as well as nonclinical observations, much can be gained for the understanding not only of symbolism, but also of thought development and thought processes in general. Our starting point was the search for the common matrix from which both symbols and thoughts originate, and we shall not be surprised that we may ultimately find them deriving from the same bodily sources. In this area our knowledge is as yet incomplete. No one recognized this better than Freud who, in a footnote added to the 1925 edition of *The Interpretation of Dreams,* spoke of the "to a large extent still unsolved problems attaching to the concept of a symbol."

BIBLIOGRAPHY

Abraham, K. (1909), Dreams and Myths. In: *Clinical Papers and Essays on Psychoanalysis, 2:*153-209. New York: Basic Books, 1955.

Eissler, K. R. (1963), *Goethe—A Psychoanalytic Study,* Vol. I. Detroit: Wayne State University Press.

Ferenczi, S. (1913), The Ontogenesis of Symbols. In: *Contributions to Psychoanalysis*. Boston: Badger, pp. 288-302.

Freud, S. (1900), *The Interpretation of Dreams*. New York: Macmillan, 1937.

————(1916), *A General Introduction to Psychoanalysis*. New York: Boni & Liveright, 1920.

————(1917), A Childhood Recollection from *Dichtung und Wahrheit*. *Collected Papers*, 4:357-367. London: Hogarth Press, 1925.

————(1932), *New Introductory Lectures on Psychoanalysis*. New York: Norton, 1933.

Friedman, P. (1952), The Bridge—A Study in Symbolism. *Psychoanal. Quart.*, 21:49-80.

Jones, E. (1916), The Theory of Symbolism. *Papers on Psychoanalysis*. London: Baillière, Tindall & Cox, 1948, pp. 87-144.

Kramer, S. N. (1959), *History Begins at Sumer*. Garden City: Doubleday.

Kubie, L. S. (1953), The Distortions of the Symbolic Process in Neurosis and Psychosis. *J. Amer. Psychoanal. Assn.*, 1:59-86.

Langer, S. K. (1942), *Philosophy in a New Key*. Cambridge: Harvard University Press.

Lewin, B. D. (1958), *Dreams and the Uses of Regression*. New York: International Universities Press.

Niederland, W. G. (1956), River Symbolism. *Psychoanal. Quart.*, 25:469-504.

————(1957), The Earliest Dreams of a Young Child. In: *The Psychoanalytic Study of the Child*, 12:190-208, eds. R. S. Eissler et al. New York: International Universities Press.

————(1960), The First Application of Psychoanalysis to a literary Work. *Psychoanal. Quart.*, 29:228-235.

Rubinfine, D. (1961), Perception, Reality Testing and Symbolism. In: *The Psychoanalytic Study of the Child*, 16:73-89, eds. R. S. Eissler et al. New York: International Universities Press.

Rycroft, C. (1956), The Nature of the Analyst's Communication to the Patient. *Int. J. Psychoanal.*, 37:1-4.

THE ALTERATION OF FOLK SONGS BY FREQUENT SINGING

A Contribution to the Psychology of Folk Poetry

HERMANN GOJA, M.D.

TRANSLATOR'S FOREWORD

The difficulties connected with translating this paper commenced with the title: *Das Zersingen der Volkslieder*. It was not possible to find a word or phrase which would adequately render all that "Zersingen" implies. Words beginning with "Zer" indicate a destructive process, certainly more than "Alteration" which might also be used to signify a change for the better. Not so with "Zer." Disintegration, distortion, and decomposition were considered but discarded because they suggest too much destruction. Finally, Grinstein's (1956) translation of the title, although cumbersome and not as accurate as one might wish, was accepted—in part, because it was already in print, and the use of an alternate translation would be confusing; in part, because it is hoped that the meaning Goja really intended would become clear through reading the paper.

I came across this study by Goja in the process of doing some research. Learning that I had made a rough translation for my own use, Dr. Muensterberger asked me to make it available for this publication. Both he and Géza Róheim had always considered this among the interesting and valuable papers in the early psychoanalytic literature. Dr. Muensterberger wrote: "I always' found Goja's paper of a certain historical value in the light of the development of psychoanalytic thought and insight. . . . His work, in its strange unassertive way reveals so well the spiritual

Translated and condensed by Marjorie R. Leonard from *Das Zersingen der Volkslieder. Ein Beitrag zur Psychologie der Volksdichtung. Imago,* 6:132-241, 1920.

Marjorie R. Leonard is Assistant Clinical Professor of Psychiatry (Child Therapy-Psychology) at the Albert Einstein College of Medicine.

efforts and adventures of early analysts who were like astonished discoverers. The young novice of the 1960's takes their contributions glibly for granted" (personal communication, 1961).

Despite widespread inquiries, I have not found anyone who knew Goja personally or could give me any information concerning his professional background. Obviously, he was not a member of the "inner circle" or his name would have appeared in Jones's *Biography* or in the *Minutes of the Vienna Psychoanalytic Society*. Only two other papers of his appeared in psychoanalytic literature as listed by Grinstein: "Halluzinationen eines Sterbenden" (1920) and "Nacktheit und Aberglaube" (1921).

Although apparently not known to Freudians, Goja was acquainted with and influenced by Freud's early writings. He was well aware of his own pioneering role and appears to have anticipated being subjected to the same seering criticism Freud himself had suffered. If Goja's apologetic attitude occasionally disturbs us, we should remember the courage it must have taken to introduce these concepts in an area heretofore limited to a primarily historical point of view.

Goja's theoretical explanations are frequently unclear and will often be unsatisfying to present-day readers. Nevertheless, little of the theoretical discussion has been omitted in condensing the paper since this is of particular historical interest. The careful reader will notice how gently and adroitly his thinking is guided from the viewpoint of academic psychology accepted at that time, represented by Jodl and Wundt, into the early Freudian formulations.

Goja equated song texts and fantasies, i.e., daydreams, considering their function to be wish fulfillment. Here he followed Freud's point of view (1900, p. 511): "... wish-fulfillment is a function of the system *Ucs.* (unconscious) which knows no other aim than wish-fulfillment and which has at its disposal no forces other than wish impulses." Goja postulated that alterations in the song were caused by external circumstances which altered the wish, or altered the critical attitude limiting the expression of the wish. In formulating a theoretical explanation for this, Goja's task was more difficult in 1920 than it would be today; it was not until 1924 that Freud formulated the concept of the structural parts of the psychic apparatus as the id, ego and superego in *The Ego and the Id*. Goja knew only Freud's earlier concepts apparently depending especially on Chapter 7 of *The Interpretation of Dreams*, written in 1900. Here, the psychic instances are described as the unconscious *(Ucs.)* and preconscious *(Pcs.)*. Freud considered the *Ucs.* and the *Pcs.* as systems, the second system or the preconscious being the one that "subjected the activities of the other to criticism, the result of which was exclusion from consciousness" (p. 491). Goja is referring to this when he describes the "secondary system" or "secondary thoughts," and later explains how the preconscious offers resistance to the unconscious strivings by making use of the mechanisms of condensation, displacement, omission and reversal.

The use of the term preconscious to describe both a part of the psychic "anatomy" and a critical, inhibiting function led to confusion and must have been one of the reasons for Freud's later formulation. Yet, despite the lack of tools which today we would consider indispensable, Goja was able to make very clear what he felt to be opposing forces struggling for expression through the lyrics of the song.

I have tried to reproduce as much as possible of the fascinating material Goja used for illustration. However, in instances in which I felt that Goja had proved his point, additional material was omitted to avoid redundancy. A few examples defied translation even with the able help of my husband, Alfred Leonard. Unfortunately, many of the translated lyrics have lost their charm and flavor; the dialect and old-German quaintness cannot be reproduced in English. Moreover, any resemblance to rhyme or rhythm is purely accidental; emphasis has been on the meaning and "feeling" quality of the poem.

At times it may be difficult for the reader to keep in mind that Goja is discussing song lyrics and not poetry. He rarely refers to melodies. In his capacity as musicologist, Alfred Leonard suggests an explanation for this seeming neglect on Goja's part. "Alterations" of the type investigated in Goja's study do not tend to bring about changes in the melodies of folk songs. As the "mood" of the words changes, e.g., from happy to sad, the harmonies may also change from a major to a minor key. The melody itself, however, is apt to remain unchanged. More than that, constancy would seem to be a prerequisite of the phenomenon Goja set out to investigate. If both the text and the melody were altered at the same time, we would of course no longer be discussing the same song.

INTRODUCTION

This study of the alteration of folk songs follows in the footsteps of John Meier, author of *Kunstlieder im Volksmunde* (1906b) and well known for his study of folk songs. Although Meier was aware of the need to explain the alterations many of the songs had undergone, he considered his task limited to collecting as much material as possible. At a later date someone might find the explanation. He took as a motto a saying by Goethe: "When one hazards an opinion it is like a piece pushed ahead in a game of checkers; it may be captured, but it still may well be the opening move in a game which will be won" (Meier, 1917, pp. 7-8). Meier saw himself as such a piece which must be sacrificed to gain a victory. "My opinion," says Goja, "also resembles a piece moved in a game. I will make the opening move although as yet I do not know whether it is good" (p. 132).

Most important to the study of alterations of folk songs is the collection of suitable material. John Meier encountered difficulty in identifying the original version of a song; he was unable to put the various known versions in a sequence which would show the changes from one to the next. Thus it was impossible for him to discover a rule by which to explain the development of a sequence. In contrast to this difficulty encountered in the study of the folk song, Meier (1906b) found that the alterations of the art song could be traced. In this instance the starting point of the series, i.e., the song as first conceived, is known.

Goja found that in this respect soldiers' songs are similar to art songs.[1] He made a collection of such songs and attempted to establish the manner in which variations developed within a particular regiment during the World War.[2] Besides these two sources of material, Goja suggests (but does not pursue) a third method of study not yet attempted: a comparison of two existing versions of the same song produced by the same author. If, in the life of the poet, psychological determinants of the variants could be discovered, it might be possible to find the psychological basis for the alteration and to formulate a general rule concerning the origin of new versions.

His study of soldiers' songs forms the core of this paper. Here Goja felt he had found a parallel to a phase in the development of the folk song. Accepting the impossibility of finding the first version of a folk song and tracing its development from version A to Z, he postulated: "If we have a section of the series, as for example from M to T, we might still achieve some understanding of the rule we are seeking" (Goja, p. 133). The study of soldiers' songs was undertaken with this idea in mind.

[1] Kaiserlich koeniglichen Schuetzenregiment, No. 24, vicinity of Vienna.

[2] Translator's note: All references are, of course, to World War I.

IDENTIFICATION

If at the beginning of this paper one asks why, despite much effort, one has not yet discovered the reason for the alterations, there can be only one answer: factors which are the key to the secret have been over-looked, thought of as unimportant, or irrelevant. On guard against such error, Goja commences with the investigation of one such seemingly unimportant phenomenon. The following is a verse dictated to the author by a soldier:

> And when I sold my little house,
> And then the money I got, soused,
> So, will say my Papa
> I'm a soldier
> Who's drunk it all.

This is the first verse of a well-known song popular with recruits, usually sung before induction.[3] There is nothing extraordinary about a farm boy making up a gay ditty after getting drunk on his way home from the induction station.[4] However, that someone else, a stranger, and of a different era, should sing this song years later as though he were the draftee—the "I"—this is extraordinary enough to give us reason for pause.

Goja calls this phenomenon "identification." "The singer of a song identifies with its originator; the ego of one aligns itself with the ego of the other. This of course is only possible when certain similarities exist. Exactly what these similarities are we are not yet prepared to say. Perhaps in certain instances similarities of milieu or situation suffice. We must assume that similarities in the human psyche are involved since the identification we have been able to observe is related to factors in the folk song which refer to typical human qualities" (Goja, p. 135).

Many variations appear to have developed in order to facilitate identification. For example, certain elements in old songs were changed to fit the new era and differing circumstances. In other instances, the changing mood of the soldiers brought about changes in the song. The refrain of the song *The Good Comrade* was originally:

[3] Compare Doerler (1910), Kaindl (1905), Hruschka and Toischer (1891, III, p. 297), Simrock (1851).

[4] Translator's note: The recruit received a sum of money to seal the contract before actual induction.

The little birds in the forest,
They sing so wonder-wonderfully:
In the homeland, in the homeland,
There we'll meet again [Meier, 1916, p. 57].

was changed to:

The cannons of Skoda
They shoot so wonder-wonder well:
Oh Italy, Oh Italy,
Your falsehood costs blood.

The song *Musketeers are Happy Brothers* was originally a happy hunting song:

Halli, Hallo, Hallialliallo,
Bei uns get's immer eso.
(That's how it always is with us.)

In the course of the World War it took on this plaintive tone:

Wir sterben, wir sterben,
Wir sterben als ein Held.
(We die, we die, we die as heroes.)

Here the distaste for soldiering breaks through. In a cavalry song, the words "two boots without spurs" changed later to "two boots without soles," as defeat was near and supplies were running low.[5] Another song had a phrase which spoke of strict discipline. This changed to "a bit of discipline," indicating the vanishing discipline of a defeated army.

It appears that all these variations occurred for one reason only—to facilitate identification. Some of these changes were entirely superficial, identification being achieved by bringing time, place, weapons and so forth up to date. Other changes went deeper. These were the versions which compensated for altered psychological factors, making it possible to express feelings concerning the long war with its many dead, the poor equipment, and the lack of discipline. "I believe we have found one origin of the alteration of the song, the psychological origin. . . . In any case similarity of situation is not sufficient reason for a song to be repeated. Similarity of psychological factors must exist for this to occur.

"There is one thing further we have learned to take into account: namely, that the human psyche changes just as does the milieu. Problems

[5] Translator's note: At first no spurs, later not even a horse!

alone remain constant and timeless. One such problem is the relationship of people to war. In every era, people have an opinion about war, but always a different one. For this reason in each era the songs concerning war problems are different" (Goja, p. 139).

There is a limit to the alterations a song can undergo. Alterations of a song cannot keep pace with great changes in milieu or in the psyche. When too great a change occurs, that particular song will be dropped and a new one composed more appropriate to the mood and milieu of the time. In that case there would then be two songs dealing with the same subject and the same problem. If the same subject matter is followed through various alterations, we will have some idea of its history. The transformations that might be observed in such a history are, in the last analysis, identical with the final stage of the alteration of the song.

So far, the examples quoted in connection with our theory of identification, have been songs sung in the first person singular. However, "we" songs offer the same possibility for identification since they really refer to "I" and others. Identification in the instance of a song sung in the third person is a little more difficult to demonstrate. However, for example, when a company of soldiers sings *Twenty-four Happy Brothers,* each soldier thinks of himself as one of the persons about whom he is singing: "we" could easily have been substituted for the impersonal "Twenty-four."

Nevertheless, the identification of the singer is not always so easy to see in songs sung in the third person singular, as for example, in this song from the collection by Else Priefer:

1. At the Weichsel[6] facing East
   A soldier stood his post;
   Familiar with the land
   As sentry he was assigned.

2. In the bushes suddenly he spies
   A man creeping toward him,
   Halt! Three times he called,
   And asked the secret word.

3. The password, or I must shoot,
   Your blood I must shed.
   Just as surely as I'm a Saxon,
   This bullet will shoot you dead.

[6] Translator's note: A river.

4. So now then, let's see.
   How far our bullet will go,
   Whether you must sacrifice,
   Your father on the battlefield.

5. Trembling with fear the man broke down.
   Heavens, cried he, have mercy!
   He prayed: Oh God, I must.
   And thus the deathshot was fired [Priefer, p. 212].

In this instance it cannot be taken for granted that the singer is identified with the poet or even with the hero of this song who must shoot and kill his father. The circumstances described by the song are, moreover, not in the least typical, nor would they have been likely to occur during the World War. Nevertheless, Goja's regiment sang a similar version, the chief difference being that it was sung entirely in the first person singular. This was also true of a number of other versions, evidence that identification with the hero does occur even in instances of tragedy.

However, Goja realizes that this conclusion could be questioned since these examples could be used to show that in songs sung in the third person the singer identifies with the hero; or, that the whole theory is wrong, since the example is a song sung in the first person in which the singers are not identified with the person in the song. (In the first instance, the question of how people as a group can identify with a son, a father-killing soldier, would still remain to be solved.) "I have reached a point from which there seems to be no way to proceed further. But I will say one thing more. There are many songs in the first person singular in which the identification I have been claiming does not occur. This assertion, more readily believed than my first, can easily be supported with an example" (Goja, p. 142). Referring to his earlier discussion of the recruit's song sung in the first person singular, the author points out that it is just as frequently sung by girls as by men, but the girls do not identify with the youth who has squandered all his money on drink. Moreover, many songs are sung by both sexes.

"The phenomenon of identification appears to be as complicated as that of alteration. As a result of our investigation we find a second riddle added to the one we sought to clarify. I believe, however, that this beginning had value since it showed us that an understanding of the alteration of songs must be sought in the area of psychological phenomena. For the time being, let us leave the problem of identification unanswered and attempt to search more deeply within the psyche of singers and poets" (Goja, p. 143).

Psychological Origins of Poetry

"The first chapter made us aware that the folk song stands in a much closer relationship to the state of mind of the singer than one is ordinarily inclined to believe. . . . In all probability the alteration of songs is simply a consequence of changes in our state of mind. It is now necessary to determine the relationship, or rather the nature of the relationship, between a given state of mind and its poetic expression. Once the nature of this relationship is defined, we will have the possibility to explain the song variants" (Goja, p. 143).

Goja now attempts to discover how a work of art evolves from the mind of its creator. "No one will dispute the fact that artistic creation is a human act. The basis for all acts is an effort to get rid of unpleasure (unlust) or rather to create pleasure (lust). . . . Assuming that such an awareness of unpleasure exists, there is at first an urge, a wish, to change this condition. This becomes a will toward change when a purpose, a goal, is connected with it. Purpose is here the incentive, the condition, which can bring about the disappearance or lessening of existing unpleasure, or preserve or increase existing pleasure. Reflection, supported by past experience, determines the method chosen to achieve that purpose. These reflections stimulate a variety of impulses, all but one of which is repressed. Action can then take place immediately or after a lapse of time. The carrying out of the impulse or action brings to realization the state of mind first conceived of as a purpose" (Goja, p. 144).

Thus the author describes the psychological process in altering an existing state of mind by means of an act of will. He now considers the case in which an intended purpose is blocked either because of external circumstances or because of inner resistance to carrying out the act. The process of reflection once again commences a search for new methods to achieve the goal. Repeated failures and persistent repetition of mental images bring about a condition of exhaustion. Such a condition is a prerequisite to hallucinations and fantasy. In other words, if a goal cannot be attained through action, it can be realized through hallucination or, in favorable circumstances, by a fantasy. Throughout their duration, hallucinations and fantasy have the same reality as an event achieved through appropriate action. Of course, a fantasy produced on the foregoing basis is generally more vivid than a hallucination since the physical sensations connected with the fantasy intensify the sense of reality (compare Jodl). The fantasy does not occur by chance since the stimulus for it is created consciously or unconsciously by the individual. Thus, the essence of art lies therein, that in order to satisfy an urge, a goal image is first created: the goal image is then transformed into a fantasy through the creation of external sources of stimulation. Therefore, the work of art is only the source of stimulation which, given an appropriate state of mind, makes the creation of a fantasy possible.[7]

For example, a young man is separated from his beloved, a source of an unpleasurable state of mind. The painful feelings bring about an effort toward getting rid of the source of this unpleasure. This effort first created a goal picture: being together with the beloved. The realization that this is impossible leads to exhaustion and with it to hallucinating the goal picture. In the hallucination the youth is united with his beloved and speaks with her. He speaks out loud as he would in a real union with her (the hallucination has reality for him), and this in turn creates the external source of stimulation which changes the hallucination into a fantasy. Speech in the fantasy is, however, a primal form of song; talking with the beloved is a frequent content of love songs. Thus, whatever the content might be, this act of talking becomes a means of satisfying an otherwise unrealizable striving.

"We still need to make clear the development of the idea of a goal, or purpose. Let us take as our starting point the awareness of unpleasure and follow the psychological process from this beginning to the development of the idea of a goal. This postulated awareness releases a striving which, since it is not guided by an idea of a goal, must be called a wish (Jodl, VII). The psychophysical energy released through the wish starts a chain of associations.

"The ideas that are recalled are not simply those similar to the sensations and representations contained in the prevailing state of mind; the recollections must themselves stimulate the same sensations and strivings. This would seem to be self-evident, yet consideration of this point was forgotten when associations were discovered linking together folk songs lacking overt similarity" (Goja, p. 147).[8]

[7] For purposes of exact study of the phenomenon of art creation, it is very important to distinguish three points: (1) the conscious attitude of the creative or experiencing individual, (2) the source of stimulation, i.e., the work of art, (3) the artistic fantasy.

[8] Translator's note: Since Goja believes that a clear comprehension of the process of association (at that time a relatively new concept) is absolutely necessary to the understanding of the song variants, he becomes involved in a detailed description, distinguishing between a chain of associations which appears circular, associations which appear to be a connected series, and those in which the connections are not superficially apparent. He explains that these last are linked through the underlying wishes, concluding that all associations depend on conscious or unconscious wishes or thoughts.

The train of associations stimulated by a drive does not end with the memory of a similar state of mind, but brings forth the memory of a drive-satisfying situation. The memory picture of this situation can be called the goal image, whose origin we have set out to discover.

"Herewith I have laid the groundwork upon which I wish to develop my theory of the alteration of songs. If art is nothing more than the satisfaction of an urge by means of fantasizing a goal image, the song nothing more than the basic stimulation of this fantasy, then the alteration of the folk song is nothing more than the change of the song as a result of a change in the underlying wish. We will see that this statement must be greatly supplemented before it can become a definition of the alteration of songs. It will also be found that the writing of a song is a much more complicated process than the simple fantasizing of a goal image. However, let us be satisfied for the moment to have built this foundation and let us proceed to the examination of some songs which will substantiate the wish fulfilling tendency of the poetry" (Goja, p. 147).

EXAMPLES

In order to prove this wish fulfilling tendency, songs were selected which represent a relatively clear-cut point of view on the part of both poet and singer. It would be difficult to find evidence for the proposed theory in songs which contain a complex of several wishes each of which influences the other. For this reason, we have chosen some of the oldest art songs. Even though these are not folk songs, they are still very close to them in origin. "Moreover," says Goja, "our proposed theory is equally applicable to either the art lyric or folk poetry" (p. 147).

The old minstrel songs, although written by men, frequently give the impression of having been written and sung by women. This is the result of the man's wish that the woman love him. The fantasy in the poem fulfills this wish, the woman revealing her love through the song. The following example is offered as illustration:

> Nothing seems so good and praiseworthy to me
> As the bright rose and the face of my man.
> The little birds
> Sing in the woods; this pleases some hearts.
> If my beloved doesn't come then I have no
> summer joy [Vogt, 3, 18, p. 3].

In order not to falsify the material, songs which appear to contradict the theory are also included. One of two examples of this nature mentioned by Goja is translated:

Around these parts
All the girls want
To get along without men this summer [Vogt, p. 261].

Sarcasm is expressed here; although at the moment the girls are fighting hard against loving a man, they will nevertheless soon succumb. This idea, existing only in the mind of the singer, is again a wish fulfillment.

Wedding songs also belong to the group of the oldest lyrics. However, it is not usually the bridal couple who sing during the celebration of the wedding since their desires need not seek fulfillment through poetry; they are fulfilled in reality. Those who help to celebrate the occasion do most of the singing. The meaning of these songs may be illustrated with examples:

1. Chastise the virgin bride!
   She deserves it,
   Since she had the courage
   To keep a rendezvous
   With a bachelor yesterday.

2. Chastise the virgin bride!
   Since with yearning
   She went to bed with him
   And has slept with him,
   Therefore we must punish her.

3. Chastise the virgin bride!
   And do not stop asking questions
   Until she has told
   What she was thinking
   And what she was dreaming
   [Erk and Boehme, 1892-1894, 2, p. 875b].

At a marriage feast, the group concerns itself openly with the erotic, giving the young people the opportunity to express wishes repressed at other times because of social restrictions. These songs express sexual wishes and are wish fulfillments.

Wishes are also fulfilled symbolically through the acts which are accompanied by song. The high point of the marriage festival is the ceremony of the capping of the bride. This act is a symbolic defloration. The bride is divested of her maidenly decorations, wreaths, etc., while a cap symbolizing womanhood is placed on her head. The songs which accompany such acts are either festive or delicately ironic complaints as the following:

1. Bride, where did your little wreath go?
   It was so nice and green;
   Oh, the little wreath that you liked so much,
   Alas, it's there no longer.

2. Wreaths are very becoming
   But those who always wear the wreath
   Are often made a laughing stock.
   Therefore, dear little wreath, good night!
   . . . .

5. First you do not lie alone,
   Otherwise you do not go to sleep quickly,
   Then you are quickly warmed,
   Even though it is cold in winter, etc.
   [Erk and Boehme, 1892-1894, 2, p. 873].

Another group of songs are those sung by the bride's girl friends in
taking leave of her. These are sad songs—sad because sung in a situation
of unpleasure and because the singers are denied the pleasures of love
anticipated by the bride. The songs present marriage as undesirable, full
of problems and difficulties. As opposed to this, to be single is wish
fulfilling.

Moralizing songs originated by teachers and ministers and lacking the
mark of wish fulfillment, also exist (compare Erk and Boehme, 1892-1894,
2, pp. 867, 868). However, they are not poetry, but teachings in poetic
form. If in some cases a wish fulfilling tendency exists in them, it is more
deeply hidden than in the songs of the young people.

The final type of wedding song is the bride's song of leave-taking. The
psychological process in these songs is the repression of the awareness of
unpleasure (leave-taking) by means of pleasurable (sexual) feelings. For
example:

I. Once I had to go around the mountain,
   There I saw my love standing on the path,
   First I greeted him, second he thanked me:
   "Oh, my only love, happiness is mine."

Refrain:
   I must go away. I must leave
   Dear God knows when I will come again!
   Oh, when will I come again?
   When the black raven will have white feathers.

II. I saw two roses in my father's hand:
    "Oh, dearest Father, reach me your hand!"
    I saw two roses in my mother's hand:
    "Oh, dearest mother, reach me your hand!"

Refrain:
I must go away, etc. [Erk and Boehme, 1892-
1894, 2, p. 877; compare p. 229, footnote 1].

The song commences with the fantasy of the beloved but evidence of
the process of repression follows immediately. How this is successfully
achieved the author promises to show later.

Dirges are also wish fulfillments (V. Boeckel): an attempt to satisfy
the wish that the beloved person continue to live. In this type of song
the underlying state of mind prerequisite to the development of a work
of art is especially clear: namely, exhaustion resulting from the emotional
upheaval and the restriction of mental images to one subject—ideas
related to the dead—a natural state of mind under the circumstances. In
these funeral songs, the dead are called to and spoken with, in a way one
would speak with a living person. The favorite form of address is a
question to the dead (V. Boeckel, 1906, p. 130) which develops into a
reproach for his withdrawal from life against the dictates of duty and
good sense. The dirges contain conversations of the mourners among
themselves as well as statements of the dead to the mourners. This type
of folk poetry proves that the form is just as important as the content.
Only the study of the form will bring us to an understanding of a particular type of song.

Insight into the meaning of the dirge is made difficult because of the
changes this type of song has undergone. The dirge was later no longer
sung by the family but by professional women mourners. In these instances, the wish which created the dirge does not exist. Dirges become
songs of praise for the dead, a worship of his deeds and virtues. The
dirges for Attila and Beowulf belong in this group. This is the type, possibly the only one, originally sung exclusively by women, undoubtedly because it is the women who have the closest relationship to their children
and marriage partners.

Herewith the wish-fulfilling tendency of this type of poetry has been
proven. Although hymns and sagas should be analyzed in similar manner,[9] space does not permit detailed, individual treatment, and to sum-
marize would not be convincing. It must suffice to remind the reader of
the Niebelungen Legend and of Parsifal: the first, the song of woman's
faithfulness creating the Germanic dream wife in the part of Krimhild;
the second, "the great wish poem of the middle ages" (Goja, p. 152), in
which all wishes find satisfaction. After all, the Holy Grail is that wish ob-

[9] Proof of the wish-fulfilling tendency in magical incantation is superfluous. Putting
the incantation into verse creates a method of satisfying the wish.

ject which fulfills all wishes and the end of the pilgrimage is always the realm of the dead, whether it is Klingsor's Castle, that fantasy paradise of ancient heathen legend, or Avalon, the land of ever-blooming apple trees.

Having found a tool by which the phenomenon of the alteration of folk songs can be tackled, namely, the recognition and acceptance of the psychological origin of poetry, the author has completed the introductory portion of his paper. Before continuing, however, he returns to the unsolved problem of identification, once again analyzing the song, "And when I sold my little house," seeking the underlying wish. When the song is sung by boys, it fulfills the wish to be recruited. If it is sung by a girl, the wish, basically the same, that the boy be recruited, is also fulfilled.[10] The identity necessary to the artistic creation is thus identity of the wishes, namely, the identical strivings underlying the song and the identical state of mind of the singers.[11]

CONDENSATION

It will be helpful to the discussion which follows to distinguish between the manifest content of the song, i.e., that part which can be perceived through our senses, and the latent content, the wish to which the song gives voice. The latent and manifest contents frequently differ as in the example discussed earlier, when the bride's girl friends bemoan the burdens of marriage while in reality they are wishing for its pleasures.[12]

Goja now begins the analysis of cases of alteration of songs with an example of "condensation" (Freud, 1900, p. 208). Condensation is defined as instances in which a number of songs are transformed into one new one. For an example he chooses an old Austrian army song, *Sarajevo an der Drina.*[13]

[10] The wish in both instances is thus derived from sexuality. To be recruited meant to be accepted in a socially elite group (this of course applies only to the prewar period).

[11] The question of empathy is related to these problems but to consider the problems of identification further would lead us too far afield.

[12] "The manifest content of the song is here the artistic creation; the latent content, the state of mind of the poet and the singers. I take the terminology from Freud's (1900) *The Interpretation of Dreams*, where it has been used to advantage in analyzing dreams. The manifest content of the dream (the dream picture) is comparable to the manifest content of the song, the latent dream content (the dream wish), to the latent content of the song" (Goja, p. 153).

[13] Translator's note: It is assumed that the author is speaking of a song popular during the time he himself served in the Austrian army.

I

A

1. At Sarajevo on the Drina,
   On a bright moonlit night,
   Stood a brave lad of the twenty-fourth[14]
   At his sentry post on watch.

2. A bullet flew through the air,
   A pain we all must feel,
   He lay in a foreign country
   Shot through his heart.

3. At his side I lie.
   His true Comrade.
   Yes, you were my dearest brother,
   I had a place for you in my heart.

4. Take the ring from my finger
   And all my letters in the sack,
   Give them to my parents,
   Who are in the homeland.

5. And should you be asked
   Where I rest,
   Say that I remain
   At Sarajevo on the Drin'.

6. At Sarajevo on the Drina
   On a bright moonlit night
   Stood a brave lad of the twenty-fourth,
   At his sentry post on watch.

7. Sun, moon and stars
   They shine bright and well
   They light the way for the soldier
   To his cool grave [Goja].

In examining this first version Goja does not expect the reader to find anything especially noteworthy except that it is a version resulting from considerable alteration. This becomes apparent after reading his meticulous notes on variants of different lines as well as whole verses which this version omits. In this condensation of his paper, it should suffice to point out some of the most striking omissions or condensations. Line 5, for example, is identical with a line in the old song of Uhland, *Der gute Kamerad (The Good Comrade)*, and line 9 is similar to another line of the same song.

---

[14] Translator's note: The reference is to the 24th regiment.

The song gains interest when we realize that it appears to have been constructed by putting together parts of two songs (II and III).

II

1. Near Metz on a hill
   In silent moonlight
   Stood a Bavarian guardsman
   So lonely and alone.

2. He peered with keen glances
   Into the dark night
   And kept brave watch
   Faithfully at his post.

3. He looked up to the stars
   To the silver-white moon:
   "Oh carry my heart's desire
   There where my beloved dwells."

4. A figure on the horizon—
   Then around him the sound of shots
   Quickly aiming his rifle
   The brave fighter returned the fire.

5. "To your posts Comrades!
   To arms, take aim!"
   There, as though by magic
   Stood his whole battalion.

6. The French soldiers fell,
   And cried Merciful God!
   "Where a German fighter aims
   There is only death and blood."

7. He never heard the order
   Our guardsman—oh what pain!
   He lay in enemy country
   Shot through his heart.

8. He held a little letter
   Tight in his cold hand.
   Upon it was written:
   Greetings! wife and fatherland.
   [Hartmann, 1913, No. 298]

This song probably originated after the battle of Metz during the Franco-Prussian wars and was revised following the battle of Sarajevo, becoming the basis for song I. A guardsman stands sentry and, while he peers out into the night, his thoughts turn to his beloved. This introduction is valuable to the understanding of the psychology of art as a whole. It shows clearly how an individual's attention can be divided: consciously he is standing watch, peering into the night and listening, his mind alert to danger; at the same time, unconsciously, he is dreaming, seeing himself at home with his beloved. The lines "Oh carry my heart's desire / There where my beloved dwells," simply represent the fantasy images in an associative process.

The next part of the song is presented as reality and we can accept it at first glance as an actual occurrence: a battle scene. The sentry, frightened out of his reverie by the attack, gives the alarm, opens fire, and with the help of his comrades, defeats the enemy. At the end of the battle he is slain, having saved his troops through his watchfulness and sacrifice.

If we now assume that this scene did not really occur but is an artistic fantasy as was so often the case among the song writers of the World War we must ask: what latent thoughts and wishes does it represent? The poet has made the answer easy. We need only take note of the introductory verses describing the guardsman standing sentry and dreaming of his beloved. The series of images produced by the associations to these lines are in themselves wish fulfilling; not only to the sentry who in hallucination sees himself with his loved one, but above all, also for the poet and the singer of the song. The singer's thoughts are distracted, just as are the sentry's. Thus, it is clear that the wish underlying this part of the song is to be at home, with the beloved, away from battle.

This wish arises from the awareness of unpleasure at having to be a soldier, a fact made evident in the entire spirit of the song: in its sentimentality, in particular the sentimental concept of a soldier's death, and further in the fact that the song did not become popular until the spring of 1916. By that time the early enthusiasm about the war had been replaced by war fatigue. Thus, the psychological process occurring in this portion of the song can be described as repression of an awareness of unpleasure (soldiering) by means of a pleasurable concept (reunion with the beloved).

In order to simplify our work, let us now assume that the idea complex of soldiering and the idea complex of sexual satisfaction represent two opposing forces. This being the case, the battle scene represents a moment when the complex of unpleasurable ideas has the upper hand over the pleasurable complex. However, this is only momentary since the mind immediately releases memories by means of which the painful battle scene becomes a source of pleasure. One notices that as the battle progresses these feelings of pleasure gain strength to the point at which feelings of unpleasure are completely dispelled. Goja calls our attention to verse 5 as an illustration, remarking that it sounds really enthusiastic and that it contains relatively little sentimentality. It represents an improved state of mind, even though the continuation of the sentimental melody detracts from this mood.

Seeking the psychological source for such a transformation of mood, we must discover under what circumstances the idea of soldiering might have been a source of pleasure. We are reminded, of course, of our youth when our ideal was to be a soldier, and war and battle were wish fulfillments, a means of proving our manhood and bravery. Such ideals are closely related to infantile sexuality. The painful idea of really being a soldier was repressed by the pleasurable, infantile ideal picture as seen through the transformation in the feeling tone of the song.[15]

Childhood memories are awakened through associations based on similarity since both the complex of ideas concerning the beloved and those concerning boyhood have a sexual basis. This train of thought was released through the drive to remove from consciousness the unpleasure-toned ideas about soldiering. Through this act of regression the battle scene also becomes a wish fulfillment. However, Goja considers the youth-complex of ideas secondary in contrast to the primary complex, the complex concerning the beloved.

Thus, in lines 17-24, the pleasurable ideas suppressed those evoking unpleasure. However, the latter break through successfully once more in lines 25-28—the soldiering complex describing a soldier's death. Nevertheless, the unpleasurable thoughts are once more overcome by the pleasurable representation in lines 29-32 in which a note to the beloved and the fatherland is found in the hand of the dead. Herewith ends the manifest but not the latent content of the song, the associations which it stimulates. These continue: the letter is found, brought to the maiden, who is overcome and breaks down with grief. The end of the song is the hallucination about the beloved which can unfold without restraint since the opposing train of thoughts concerning the young man's death has been completed. Thus, the unpleasurable images contained in the beginning of this song have been removed, replaced by pleasurable fantasies.

The psychological process active in this song can be summarized as the repression of an unpleasurable complex of ideas by a pleasurable complex. The manifest action of the song represents the movement of both of these complexes and is determined by them; the feelings accompanying

[15] Concerning the assumption of childhood as a source of pleasure, compare poems concerning robbers, soldiers and heroes which are also based on childhood.

the action are also mixed and, in like manner, the images of the song fantasy represent a compromise between the ideas of both complexes. The song is wish fulfilling.

Let us now suppose that the revulsion against military life has become even greater, an assumption in accord with the facts. What will be the result of such a changed state of mind? First, the elimination of unessential detail, since the pleasurable childhood memories can no longer repress the overwhelmingly numerous, painful experiences; second, the elaboration of the greeting motives (song II, lines 29-32) in order to repress the intensified opposing wish series.

We can verify these conclusions in song I: we find here the introduction so severely reduced (compare song II lines 1-12 reduced to lines 1-4 in song I) that even the pleasant associations in the introduction are repressed (they are obviously too weak to be effectual at the beginning of the song). Of the battle scene only three lines remain and are linked to the first four lines of the introduction (song I) through the insertion of a line (song I, line 5) from Uhland's song, *The Good Comrade*. The greeting motive on the other hand is threefold enlarged. Thus, song I only made use of lines 1-4 and 6-8 from song II, but incorporated also lines 9-21 of yet a third song:

III (lines 9-21)

3. He bows his head in dying
   And says "My comrade!"
   I would like to tell you something,
   That weighs on my mind.
4. Take the ring from my finger,
   When I am dead,
   And all my letters,
   That are in my knapsack!
5. And should your footsteps bring you
   By chance once more to our homeland,
   Carry with you to my beloved
   These warm greetings! [Hartmann, 1913, No. 293, 1848].

The question arises why just these particular songs were combined. It is the result of the identity of the basic wish underlying both songs—the union with the beloved.[16]

The chief advantage of combining songs is the following: with the

[16] Translator's note: At this point the author gives similar details using examples from other songs which have not been included here in this translation. They merely provide further support for his point that sections of a song are omitted because of their painful nature, or because they picture situations which no longer existed during the World War.

singing of the first lines of song I the whole song II is called to mind through a chain of associations bringing about wish fulfillment. As the song now moves into the lines from song III, a second train of thought is stimulated, leading, via the same theme (that of greeting), to the same wish fulfillment. The singer is probably acquainted also with still a fourth song (not translated) so that by means of maintaining in song I the introduction of song II the singer is able to recall three songs which lead to the same wish fulfillment.

Continuing in this manner to analyze the components of song I, Goja shows how the introduction of the two lines from Uhland's song forms an associative bridge to songs II and III, as well as to portions of two further songs which he quotes but are not translated. He traces, in all, six trains of thought stimulated through the singing of this one song, each leading toward wish fulfillment. He concludes:

> In the incorporation of parts of other songs, no matter how small these parts are, only those songs are linked together which belong together. Such coupling occurs only when the individual song is too weak to combat the complex of painful ideas . . .
> I have shown that there is meaning in the alteration of songs; it serves the purpose of wish fulfillment. Of course the associative links which I have documented did not necessarily all exist during the World War. The number of associations linked with a song depends on the number known to the singer. This number in our day was certainly very limited, but consider what a wealth of associations must have been released in the heyday of the folk song if so many were still possible in our time [Goja, pp. 165-166].

Summarizing what we have thus far learned from the Sarajevo song group: the purpose of the individual song was to repress from consciousness a source of unpleasure (being a soldier), displacing it by means of a source of pleasure (sexuality). The condensation of songs II and III into song I, with the inclusion of the song *The Good Comrade,* served to increase pleasure. If we now consider that during the World War millions of singers became aware of the unpleasure created by soldiering, and that sexuality as a source of pleasure is a common human trait, it should be possible, provided this analysis is correct, to find many songs having the same latent content as the Sarajevo Song.

That this is indeed true is documented by songs from John Meier's (1916) book, *The German Soldier's Songs from the Battlefield.*[17, 18] How-

[17] Translator's note: Several examples are cited by Goja but not translated.

[18] Buecher (1909) in his paper on *Work and Rhythm* showed that the psychological function of the work song was the repression of unpleasure (work) through the introduction of pleasure (rhythm).

ever, it would be ridiculous to assert that the process of repression is the underlying basis of all songs which combine soldiering and sexuality. In certain instances the psychic process leading to condensation is the intensification of pleasure through the introduction into consciousness of a new and pleasurable complex of ideas.

As an example of this process, Goja cites the condensation of two songs both of which are commonly learned by German school children: *Wer will unter die Soldaten? (Who wants to be a soldier?)* and *Lorelei*. Three sources of pleasure unite in bringing about the combination of these songs: pleasure in being a soldier in the first song, sexuality in the Lorelei song, and childhood memories in both.

To further illustrate this mechanism of heightening pleasure through condensation, the following collection of songs is introduced:

I

1. Upon the mountain high
   A tall house stands,
   Entered every morn
   By pretty misses three.

2. The first of these is my sis,
   The other is my friend,
   The third one has no name,
   My girl friend she must be [Uhland, 1844, No. 21B].

II

Windmill

High upon that mountain
There a windmill turns,
Grinding nothing but love
Throughout night and into day:
The mill is broken
Our love is at an end,
God bless you then, dear love!
In grief I now depart [Uhland, 1844, No. 33].

V

1. Upon that high mountain there is standing a tall house,
   And early every morning three pretty maidens look without.

2. Of one her name is Suzanna, the other one Annamarie,
   The third I dare not name, she should belong to me.

3. There down in the valley, the water drives a wheel,
   The wheel grinds nought but love from evening into day.

4. The millwheel is shattered, love has alas an end
   And when two lovers part, they reach each other a hand.

5. Oh parting, bitter parting, who would have thought of parting thus?
   All joy has left my heart, so young to grieving I am forced.

6. The garden of my grandfather, therein stand two little trees,
   On one there are some nutmegs, the other one bears cloves.

7. The nutmeg and the clove, so sweetly do they smell
   These will I send my loved one, so think she on me well
   [Bruinier, p. 34].

The first of these songs is a wish fulfillment. Because of its simple
form, it is reminiscent of songs during the early period of the German
lyric. In fact, the latent content is as simple as that of the manifest: the
singer sees his beloved in a fantasy. Only the first two lines are conspicuous
in that the picture they paint of a tall house on a mountain seems
puzzling and mysterious.

The second song is also in the old style. It is interesting that the mill
is placed on top of a mountain, while other songs place it correctly
(compare Uhland, 1844, No. 32A). Since we only possess fragments of
these songs, nothing more can be said about their original relationship
to each other or about the first two lines. In any case, the poems are
linked associatively through the similarity of the first two lines in each,
the groundwork thus established for the process of condensation which
unites both songs to form a new one (song V). We need to seek the reason
for this union. The latent content of the first song is the possession of
the maiden. What is the latent content of the second? The manifest
content is the following: a mill stands upon the mountain, grinding nothing but love all night long. The mill is a favorite image in love songs.
Sexuality lends it its pleasurable coloration. To illustrate, Goja brings
three examples of songs about mills, one of which translates:

. . . the mill lies in a voluptuous, beautiful valley,
The path leading to it is somewhat narrow,
It [the mill] is neither large nor small
Two hills enclose it gently
A dense forest shades it
And water is never lacking . . .[19] [Futilitates, IV, p. 81; compare
   also p. 140].

[19] Translator's note: The other examples are even more pointedly obscene but defy
translation.

It is clear that "grinding" (song II, line 3) can have only one meaning: coitus. From this, the reason for the union of the two songs is also understandable. In version V, the portion taken from song I expresses a wish; the portion from song II fulfills it.

As a result of the interweaving of the two songs, song II was somewhat changed. The mill was relocated once more and placed in the valley where it undoubtedly belonged. Moreover, in the process of changing song II into song V a new bond was created relating the songs more closely to each other. The first line of the new song reads: "There on top of that mountain . . ." The fifth line: "There down in the valley, there the water rushes . . ." The image of "mountain and valley," however, is one of the most common and most pleasure toned to be found in folk songs. Here the author quotes fragments of a number of songs as illustrations, some taken from pornographic and some from socially acceptable literature.

There is no doubt that the strong pleasure tone inherent in such folk poetry images is derived from sexuality. Consciously or unconsciously the singer is reminded of the sexual image, and in hearing it described (actually seeing it in fantasy), enjoys the same pleasure he would experience if he were seeing the objects in reality.

It has been valuable for the understanding of the process of condensation to have determined the meaning of these images. We have become aware that the type of condensation we are now analyzing is based on an accumulation of pleasure-toned sexual images. Further evidence of this tendency is seen in the complaint uttered in lines 6-8 in song II which is extended in song V through the addition of a stanza found in many songs. This stanza always appears in songs of leave-taking, especially in day songs[20] which either presuppose or manifestly describe love-making. In the singing of song V, all the day songs containing lines 9-10 of song V are recalled, thereby bringing to mind all the pleasure-toned ideas they embody. Songs of leave-taking, i.e., *Wanderlieder* (songs of the wanderer), typically include such phrases of parting. For this reason, song V is characterized also as a wanderer's song.

The last four lines of song V are taken from still a fourth song. This song, replete with images, uses that of lock and key in the first verse, the fountain of youth in the second, the clove and the nutmeg in the third. Since the many images used thus far in this condensed song are sexual symbols, we expect that the last named pair must be also. This suspicion is confirmed by the form of these spices: the clove is readily recognized

[20] Translator's note: Which apparently have the quality of daydreams.

as a male symbol, the nutmeg as female. Moreover the clove is frequently made use of in ribald literature, several examples of which are
cited by the author. The fact that the newly-created song ends with a
farewell gift of clove and nutmeg affirms the purpose of this condensation: intensification of pleasure by means of accumulated pleasure-toned
images.

Thus, it is evident that condensation has a twofold objective: (1)
the repression of unpleasurable idea complexes by means of a pleasurable
one, (2) the intensification of pleasure. We know that of the three basic
functions of a drive, the two functions, repression of unpleasure and the
creation of pleasure, have been chosen here and, therefore, we recognize the alteration of songs as a consequence of the drive.[21]

DISPLACEMENT[22]

Condensation is not the only form of alteration of songs—it is one
among several. Our attention is next called to the mechanism of displacement. For purposes of study a group of soldier's songs is again presented
in scholarly fashion, commencing with a song collected during the
World War.

The song *The Battle of Leipzig* is so distorted that it no longer makes
sense and can no longer be sung. Although it resembles the song *Sarajevo
an der Drina* in that it commences with a battle scene and ends with
thoughts of return to the homeland, it cannot satisfy the purpose of
wish fulfillment. The distaste for soldiering comes through too strongly
in the description of battle scenes; as a result, it is no longer sung, and
few remember it.

It is surprising to discover that this war-weary song originated with a
song of glory and triumph, immortalizing the Battle of Waterloo, a song
full of enthusiasm for fighting, ending with a hymn to Bleucher, the leader
of the army. In it the singer is wholeheartedly a soldier, and soldiering is
in itself a source of pleasure. Therefore, there is no need to repress the
thought of soldiering as a painful experience by the introduction of a
source of pleasure such as is inherent in the native-land complex. The
enthusiasm is so great that the pleasure derived from the idea of battle
is sufficient to repress any discomfort resulting from the thought that some
are lost in battle.

[21] Translator's note: Apparently the author assumes that the reader will recognize the
third function as the satisfaction of the drive.

[22] Bruinier (p. 36) calls this phenomenon "Alteration of the Song." Concerning the
psychological meaning of displacement, see Freud (1900, p. 227).

Between the Battle of Waterloo and the World War, the song went through a number of changes similar to those described in the discussion of *Sarajevo an der Drina:* as distaste for soldiering increased, the theme of the return to the homeland (representing sexuality) was added in an attempt to repress the source of unpleasure and replace it with a source of pleasure. Thus, the same psychological movement occurs in both songs. When we look at the latent content rather than the manifest, we may put both songs in the same class. In the one instance purpose of displacement (adding or replacing one theme with another) is the same as is the condensation in the other. During the World War, the attitude toward soldiering and the psychological evaluation of it had changed, and this change brought about the alteration of the song. This type of change we call "displacement."[23]

Despite the alterations which produced the song of the World War *(The Battle of Leipzig)*, it had become so strongly painful in its presentation of soldiering that it no longer fulfilled the purpose of increasing pleasure and repressing pain. For this reason it is disrupted through forgetting and misunderstanding of the uncomfortable part of its manifest content. This process will be discussed later in a discussion of "nonsense in the folk song."

Besides attempts to repress unpleasure or attain pleasure, efforts may also be directed toward the repression of a pleasurable idea. In turning our attention to examples of this nature, we will not only further our understanding of the alteration of the song but clarify certain aspects in the psychology of art as well. The song and its variations now referred to was collected by John Meier (1906b, p. xix ff.), written by Heinrich Wilhelm von Stamford, and called *Ein Maedchen holder Mienen.* It is reproduced here in the original version, together with those of the existing twenty-four variations needed for this analysis.

I

1. A maiden, fair of mien,
   Little Annie, sat on the green
   At the wheel, spinning happily.
   And: "I cannot say
   How quickly on some days
   The precious time flies by.

[23] Translator's note: Goja documents this in great detail bringing in five complete versions which preceded the final song of the World War, as well as indicating other minor changes.

2. "To get my day's work done
   Is easy and it's fun;
   Often the early morning sun
   Finds me gay and active,
   And when it descends in the evening,
   I am still wide awake.

3. "He who does not shun work
   And is happy to be alive
   The heavens are friendly to;
   Therefore, young maiden I,
   Sit spinning and spinning a thread,
   And with it sing a song."

4. She had hardly stopped singing,
   When into her view springing
   Appeared a knight young and handsome:
   "So diligent?" "Yes, to do my duty.
   If one wishes to earn his bread,
   One must of course be diligent."

5. "Your bread! You sweet maiden!
   With a little spinning wheel?
   And with such little red cheeks!
   Are your parents still living?" "Oh dear, no!
   I am by myself:
   Death took them early from me.

6. "Because of this I have nothing but blessings
   Wherever my path takes me;
   For I never suffer from want;
   A maiden who is willing to spin,
   Can easily earn so much,
   That she is never in need."

7. The knight: "Hear me, maiden!
   Leave this little spinning wheel,
   And give me your little heart:
   If luxuries will win you,
   I will spin your life for you,
   The life of a princess it will be!

8. "In my most beautiful castle,
   As big and even bigger,
   Than this little village,
   Encircled by a wall and moat,
   There will you alone rule,
   If you are agreeable.

9. "You will walk clothed in silk,
   You will wear jewelry
   Of pearls and gold;
   And whatever you desire,
   That will you be given:
   Maiden, just be gracious to me!"

10. "Sir Knight, no! This little wheel,"
    Responded the maiden,
    "This little wheel I will not leave:
    I prefer to keep my virtue,
    More than all the golden gifts,
    That your words can promise me.

11. "This little ribbon bejewels me
    (She pointed with her little hand
    to the little ribbon on her bosom.)
    Better than any gold and silk;
    For costly jewelry
    Does not become a spinner.

12. "But since you are so gracious
    So will I take your gifts
    For the needy poor:
    My neighbor close by
    Has children—nothing to live on!
    Oh, if you could only see them!"

The poem continues through five more stanzas, relating how, after listening to a further accounting of the need and worth of the poor neighbor, the knight takes flight. However, the poet suggests he might return since beauty and virtue form an irresistible combination!

II

1. A maiden fair of mien,
   Little Hanna, sat on the green
   At the wheel, sat spinning.
   She sang: "I can indeed say,
   How happily on some days
   The precious time flies by.

2. "To get my day's work done
   Is easy and it's fun,
   One can find me here early;
   Here sit I, poor maiden,
   And spin and spin my little wheel
   And with it sing a song."

3. Hardly had she stopped singing,
   When into view came springing,
   A knight young and handsome.
   "So diligent?" "Oh yes, to do my duty,
   To earn one's bread,
   One must of course be diligent!"

4. "Your bread! Oh dear maiden,
   With your little spinning wheel,
   With cheeks so fresh and red!
   Are your parents still living?"
   "Oh no, I have no one,
   I am all alone,
   Death took them early from me.

5. "Yet I have naught but blessings
   Wherever my path takes me,
   For I never suffer from lack.
   A maiden by spinning
   Can easily earn so much,
   That nothing ever fails her."

6. "But hear me, dear maiden
   With your little spinning wheel,
   Oh, give your heart to me!
   You will win luxuries
   And will spin yourself a life,
   The life of a princess!

7. "You will walk in silken garments
   You will wear lovely jewels
   Of pearls and gold!
   And whatever you desire,
   That will you be given!
   Maiden, just be gracious to me!

8. "Take, Oh beautiful one, my castles,
   A town that is far larger
   Than this little village!
   As far as the woods and the moat,
   There you alone will rule,
   If you will be kind to me!"

9. "Sir Knight, here is my little wheel,"
   Thus responded the maiden,
   The maiden of propriety!—
   The knight entered his carriage,
   Commanded immediate departure
   And suddenly he drove away [Meier, 1906b, p. xxi, No. 2].

III

1. There once was a poor maiden.
   Who sat at her wheel a-spinning
   Who spun the yarn so fine, tra la
   Who spun the yarn so fine.

2. There came a knight a-riding,
   And to the maiden he said:
   "Come with me to my castle, tra la,
   Come with me to my castle.

3. "Beautiful dresses will I give you
   Of velvet and also of silk,
   If you promise to be true, tra la,
   If you promise to be true."

4. "But I'd rather be a-spinning
   And thus my bread a-winning
   Than rich and bad to be, tra la,
   Than rich and bad to be" [Meier, 1906b, p. xxiv, No. 7].

IV

1. There sat a maiden
   At her spinning wheel
   And thereby sang a song, yes, yes,
   And thereby sang a song.

2. And as she finished singing,
   Who came along a-springing?
   A grenadier handsome and bold, yes, yes,
   A grenadier, so bold.

3. "Are your parents still living my maiden?"
   "No, I have no parents
   I am all alone,
   Death took them from me, yes, yes,
   Death took them from me."

4. "Do you have their blessing, my maiden?"
   "The blessing of my good parents
   Is mine wherever I go,
   Since I am good and diligent, yes, yes,
   Since I am good and diligent."

5. "Give me your hand my maiden,
   Forsake your little wheel,
   I say this with all my heart:
   From this moment you'll be mine, yes, yes,
   From this moment you'll be mine"
                    [Meier, 1906b, p. xxvii, No. 15].

A detailed analysis of the song is not necessary since the manifest and latent contents are immediately clear. The latent sexual wish is satisfied in the fantasy produced by the song. The manifest content divides itself into the introduction, the knight's attempted seduction, and the young girl's refusal. The exaggerated virtue and morality stressed in a most unbelievable fashion in the last part repels us more than the ambiguous middle portion.

This third part is just as distasteful to the masses as it is to us. For this reason changes are made which tend to dilute, or eliminate, this extremely moralistic attitude. For example, in version I the maiden is "spinning happily." In version II, no longer happy about her work, "She sits and spins." Moreover many passages in version I are omitted in version II, as for example:

> "He who does not shun work
> And is happy to be alive
> The heavens are friendly to;" [I, lines 13-15].

Goja also sees in the changes a subtle difference difficult to reflect in translation. Version I, he points out, intimates that so pretty a maiden need not work to earn a living; also he interprets the offer made by the knight as a bid to buy her love. He finds version II more romantic, more an offer of love than a business arrangement. Thus, it appears that the singer of version II finds as much displeasure in the conception of too much virtue and too much work as in the idea of selling love. The thought of sensual enjoyment is obviously pleasurable since it is not repressed.

Turning to version III we find increased resistance to sexuality. While in version II the rejection of sexuality was hidden in stanzas made incomprehensible through condensation (verse 9), in version III even the proposal has been enormously abbreviated as compared with the second part of version I. Resistance is focused solely on sensuality, since version II had already eliminated the element of illicit love. Actually it is directed toward extramarital libido satisfaction as version IV demonstrates. Here, resistance toward sexual content having further increased, the retention of the sensual proposal is only possible in the guise of a marriage proposal.

Although it would seem as though the resistance toward sexual wishes had achieved its end, the song nevertheless undergoes further changes. In a still later version the proposal becomes a mere conversation between the knight and the maiden. All sexuality has been repressed except within the framework of the conversation. However, it is certainly still strongly retained in the melody.

In two other versions even the conversation is eliminated so that only the situation of the orphan at the spinning wheel remains.[24] The final version cited by Meier (1906b, p. xxxi, No. 24) changes the knight into a philanthropist who strokes the orphan's cheek and promises to care for her.

> "You'll no longer be alone,
> You dear noble little one.
> I will your father be, yes, yes,
> I will your father be."

Summarizing, we can see that in this instance displacement has brought about the removal of the sexual ideas from the manifest content of the song despite the fact that sexuality is the source of pleasure. Since displacement is the result of an effort to remove unpleasure from consciousness and to create pleasure, we must conclude that sexuality can be a source of pleasure and displeasure at the same time. Sexuality actually does possess this duality of feeling. It is primarily pleasurable, secondarily unpleasurable in tone. The feelings of pleasure come from the unconscious; the unpleasure from the secondary thoughts. As a result of this secondarily acquired unpleasure, direct fantasizing of sexuality is impossible and can only occur by reaching a compromise through displacement. By means of displacement, a situation may be fantasied in which both the sexual wishes as well as the efforts to prevent their fulfillment are satisfied.[25]

As we observe the ever-increasing displacement of the manifest content of Stamford's song, we must conclude that the preconscious resistance against the satisfaction of sexual wishes has also been growing. However, to draw the conclusion that there is a morality in art would be wrong. The essence of art is in the satisfaction of the sexual wishes—the sexual drive—in direct contrast to ethics which strive for their idealization and

---

[24] Indirectly, sexuality is retained since "spinning," a sexual symbol in folk poetry, appears in the manifest content. Compare Fliegendes Blatt der Wiener Stadtbibliotek 39976, *Das Lied vom Spinnraedl, tran, tran.*

[25] Compare Freud (1900, p. 467ff). We have already encountered strivings of the preconscious against the wishes of the unconscious. They manifested themselves in the songs of leave-taking of the bride's playmates (see p. 123) where their complaints about prevented sexual pleasure were transformed into complaints about the bride's lot; in the day songs where, in place of fantasies about the moment of union with the beloved, they substituted fantasies about their leave-taking; and also in the creation of the sexual symbols we encountered (see p. 134).

control. This is proven by the regard in which folk songs are held by the church and those authorities concerned with the maintenance of public morality.

If we take another look at the original version of Stamford's song we can now recognize that the exaggerated morality of the third portion served the purpose of a compromise. Ordinarily the fantasy of the ambiguous situation would have suffered immediate repression: only by being presented in such an overly moralistic manner could it survive. The third part can be omitted at the moment when the frivolity of the second part (version I, verses 4-10) is decreased. This is the form seen in version II. In the same way we can understand the compromise inherent in the emphasis on the maiden's industry.

Up to this point we have determined the purpose of alteration of songs to be: (1) the repression of an unpleasurable complex of ideas through one which is pleasurable, (2) the increase of pleasure, (3) the increase of pleasure by means of a compromise. We have discovered two methods of alteration: condensation and displacement.

Before concluding this section a particular type of displacement must be mentioned, that of reversal. This is particularly worthy of our attention because it is the one type of alteration which is not seen in the manifest content of the song. It is an alteration without actually changing the song itself. Our study of the alteration of songs has been based on the assumption that the latent song wish, fulfilled through the fantasy in the song, undergoes a change which necessitates an appropriate alteration of the song. The changes of these wishes can be so extensive that the new song wish may be the exact opposite of the original wish.

For example, in the early days of the World War it was wish fulfilling to be a soldier. In the last days, not to be a soldier was wish fulfilling. The same songs, sung with wish fulfillment in the beginning of the war, were also sung at the end of the war without the words of the song being changed. The altered feelings were expressed by the way in which the song was sung. For example, the song *Twenty-four Happy Brothers,* sung ironically, acquires exactly the opposite meaning from that originally intended. The attitude with which it is sung as well as the remarks which people make about it leave no doubt that the intent is the opposite of the content.

The fact that the meaning of a song can be turned into its opposite places before the historian a very difficult problem. There is no way of knowing from the printed song whether it is to be interpreted by its logical meaning or as a reversal.

With these remarks about reversal Goja ends his chapter on displacement and turns to a new method of alteration of the song, namely, that of forgetting (Freud, 1901).

OMISSION

In a study of the alteration of songs, it would be out of place to devote a whole paper to the topic of forgetting or remembering the folk songs. Actually, the subject is covered in the discussion of condensation and displacement. In condensation, for example, one part is forgotten, and something else remembered instead. Moreover, now that we know that condensation fulfills a purpose, we must recognize that the same is true for remembering or forgetting. These acts do not occur accidentally, but intentionally, albeit from unconscious rather than conscious intent.

Even the choice of song in a particular situation is not accidental. The singer does not sing the song he wants to, but one he feels compelled to sing. It would be easy to bring examples (Meier, 1916) to prove this if the goal of this work were to establish a psychology of folk poetry. But since the goal is to explain the alteration of songs, this paper is limited to bringing proof that the forgetting of single lines, words, or phrases is determined in the same way as condensation and reversal.

The first example is a song *The 24th Regiment at the Battle of Lemberg*, sung to the well-known melody of *The Watch on the Rhine*. Presumably it was written shortly after the battle on June 22, 1915, at which time this Austrian regiment captured and liberated the city of Lemberg. Thereafter the date of this event was celebrated in honor of this regiment, the battle gaining added significance because of the effect of the repossession of Lemberg upon the morale of those behind the front. The song was written by a Corporal Lehner, but the troops ascribed it to an especially popular staff officer. It became the regiment's favorite song and all those who fought at Lemberg remember it. The original version, however, can no longer be found. The version discussed here was published by the regiment in March, 1917, nearly two years after the battle. This version had already undergone considerable alteration, best seen in the accounting of historical facts. The battles enumerated in the song are no longer in the order of their actual occurrence: the town names of the battles prior to the siege of Lemberg were forgotten and other names substituted, sometimes names of nonexistent places.

What causes such inexactness? Goja postulates that the unpleasurable elements in songs are repressed, and that for those who participated in a particular battle, the name of the place and the date are unpleasurably stressed. "Forgetting the names of places and dates was a common occurrence during the World War. Despite the fact that the men were always asking for the names of various towns in order to write home about it or to note it in their diaries, for the most part when they were questioned about a battle they were only able to name the country, or at best the most strategically important towns" (Goja, p. 201).

The introduction of invented names into the song, instead of the names of actual towns, is explained as a form of condensation. For example, one such neologism, "Robau," a substitute for the forgotten "Tomaszow," was introduced as a rhyme to Jaroslau and is obvious nonsense. "Robau" rhymes with Lobau, one of the favorite resort areas near Vienna, known to all the soldiers of the regiment and linked with the pleasure-toned homeland thought complex. Thus, the neologism, "Robau," formed a connection between the unpleasurably stressed Jaroslau and the pleasure-stressed Lobau-Vienna, and can be termed a condensation.

A similar case is the neologism "Grsow," which stands for Rzeszna. Although these names appear to be completely different, the difference results from ignorance concerning the writing of Polish words. "Grs" is the wrong way to spell "Rzesz." When spoken, both syllables would sound exactly alike. Therefore, "Grsow" should really be written "Rzeszow." However, this word also has no meaning. It only becomes meaningful when compared with the name Szelwow. It then becomes clear that "Rzeszow" is a condensation of Rzeszna and Szelwow: the first, Rzeszna, appeared in the original song, naming a successful battle; the second, the location of an anticipated battle which would hopefully have the same results as the first. The way in which this condensation occurs is easier to visualize when the words are written one below the other:

RZESZna

SzelwOW

RZESZOW

By bringing thoughts of Szelwow into this song about the battle of Lemberg, the mechanism of condensation satisfies this unconscious wish.[26]

The forces which created these neologisms are the same as those which brought about other changes in songs. The purpose is also the same, namely, the repression of an unpleasurably stressed idea by one which is pleasurable—the gaining of pleasure.

[26] I concur here with Freud who was the first to recognize the mechanism of the creation of neologisms in his *The Interpretation of Dreams* (1900).

Returning to the topic of forgetting, one of the most outstanding examples in the text of the song under discussion is the omission of the refrain. This omission suggests that at the time the song was written down the melody had been forgotten. This melody, however, as indicated by another version of the song, had been taken from *The Watch on the Rhine*. This is such a striking case of forgetting that it is particularly instructive. *The Watch on the Rhine* is a German national hymn which played up the relationship between the Germans of Austria and those of Germany. However, in the author's Austrian regiment there was strong antagonism toward the Germans. They held the Germans responsible for their bad luck and wanted nothing more to do with them. Therefore, the bond between the Austro-Germans and the Germans from Germany was destroyed; the German melody of the regiment's song was forgotten.

Goja points out, however, that it is not always possible to explain the omissions in a song. One can find both popular and individual versions of any given song, and it is only the popular versions, i.e., those created by the group, which can be explained when the common point of view, the group attitude, can be determined. The version created by an individual person can only be understood by an exact analysis of that individual's point of view.

At this point two versions of another war song are introduced as illustrations for the changes brought about by an individual. This particular song was sung in the streets by a war-blinded beggar who then sold leaflets containing the song. Since it was important to him to repeat the song frequently and thereby increase the opportunities for selling it, he had to shorten the original twenty-stanza version. The nine stanzas retained were selected with an audience of women in mind, the choice calculated to stir their emotions without either shocking them or giving them a feeling of wish fulfillment. Therefore, those stanzas were omitted which referred to hospitalization, the return home, or to hopes of peace. Thus, once again the alteration of a song could be explained, but this time on the basis of meeting the needs of a particular individual's situation.

Goja now pauses to reflect on the meaning of forgetting. He concludes "that the first half of forgetting results from strivings originating out of the secondary system just as in the case of condensation and displacement. The latent content of the repressed portion had aroused feelings of revulsion in the secondary system[27] therefore necessitating repres-

[27] Translator's note: Here, Goja is following Freud's earliest formulation. See Foreword.

sion" (p. 209). The purpose of forgetting in contrast to condensation and displacement is not the gaining of pleasure but the removal of unpleasure.

In the same way that we examined a case of displacement in which the mechanism was not apparent in the manifest content, our attention is now called to Tannhaeuser's song (Uhland, 1866a, No. 297a) as an example of forgetting which serves neither the purpose of gaining pleasure nor reducing unpleasure. In the early versions of this song, dating back some 350 years, two wishes are expressed. The first is sexual; the second, the one responsible for creating the conflict, is religious—the wish for immortality. The song expresses the conflicting wishes of a person living during the time of the Reformation. In the first part of the song, both wishes are striving to gain the upper hand. The primary wishes, represented in the seduction by Venus, appear to be in the lead until just before the end. The secondary wishes gain support from representations of eternal punishment and the Madonna. Tannhaeuser's entrance into Venusberg at the commencement of the song represents the fulfillment of primary wishes. The opposing feelings are first evidenced in Tannhaeuser's repentance. When Tannhaeuser wants to leave Venus, she reminds him of his oath to remain with her. This oath, preventing Tannhaeuser from leaving Venus, must be honored by the secondary wishes and strengthens the position of the primary wishes. Venus counters his attempts to be released by renewed seductions. The conflict reaches a crisis when Tannhaeuser cries out:

> Lady Venus, noble woman so gentle!
> You are a she-devil!

Herewith the second wish has conquered the first and the anxiety diminishes. At this point the image of the Madonna comes into view:

> Maria, virgin mother,
> Protect me now from this woman!

Clearly, the victory of the secondary wishes was only possible through a compromise in which the demands of religious belief were united with those of love. Such a union is seen in the figure of the Madonna. Thus, in the final analysis, the end of the first part of the story is also a victory for the primary wishes.

However, no song can end with the triumph of the secondary wish. The purpose of the song is the fulfillment of the primary wish. Here, this is brought about through the Pope who will not grant the

knight absolution but drives him back to Venusberg; although unwilling-
ly, Tannhaeuser returns to Venus. The needs of the second wish are now
directed toward the Pope who must suffer eternal punishment while
Tannhaeuser, at least in later versions, is pardoned. Thus, the primary
wishes are fulfilled.

During the centuries following the Reformation, this strong religious
belief disappeared and with it the strivings of the secondary wishes of the
song. As a result, the song became superfluous and died out, since a song
can only survive as long as it fulfills a wish. After 350 years, only the animosity against the power-hungry Pope remains. It was this animosity
which led to the Reformation and, in the song, made it possible to direct
the unpleasure derived from the feelings of secondary wishes, against the
sexual wishes. Although still in existence, this animosity is greatly dimin-
ished. The last version of this song, *The Balthaser Song* (Erk and Boehme,
1, 18e), omits Tannhaeuser's departure and his guilt, and also the damn-
ing and damned Pope, and recognizes only a righteous person.

Thus, in this instance, forgetting half the song resulted from the disappearance of the opposing drives against which the primary wish had
to assert itself. Forgetting served to remove the portion of the song which
was unpleasurably stressed and insensitive to inner feelings.

The Nonsensical in the Folk Song[28]

In the preceding chapter neologisms were analyzed which had first
seemed nonsensical, i.e., the words "Robau" and "Grsow." Closely connected with this is the study of minor alterations, if forgetting, interchang-
ing, and misunderstanding of single words can be so designated. Research
concerning the alteration of songs cannot be limited to changes in the
songs as a whole. One must also take into consideration the changes in the
smallest portion of a song.

Neologisms were seen to be the result of condensation. An excellent
example of condensation arising from misreading a poorly printed text was
found in the word "Puffernebel" in the song *The Ash Tree at Koerner-*

---

[28] "Although up to this point I have made use of both psychoanalytic and critical-
historical methods to further our understanding, I now find it necessary to drop the latter
method. The study of purely psychological problems, such as the alteration of the folk
song, must finally reach a point at which progress can be made only through the use of
the purely psychological (in my case psychoanalytic) point of view. *The advantage gained
through the application of psychoanalysis is a significant one.* This is demonstrated by the
fact that it has been possible to explain the alteration of the folk songs only two years
after John Meier's *Study of the Folksong* declared the problem insoluble" (Goja, p. 211).

gratz.[29] In the original text the words were "Tieffer" and "Nebel." The "T" was smudged as was also the "e" in the first syllable and also the dot over the "i." Thus, it was possible to misread this word as "Puffer" instead of "Tieffer." However, the word "Puffer" is the nickname for an engine of a train and trains are used to bring a person home from the front. Thus, the purpose of this misunderstanding is discovered: the neologism serves to guide the thoughts from an unpleasant picture ("tieffer Nebel" = thick fog) to one which stresses pleasure.

These three analyzed neologisms, "Robau," "Grsow," and "Puffer-nebel," correspond both in construction and purpose to the instances of condensation studied in the song groups. Proof of the correctness of this analysis lies in this parallel. Nevertheless, the author offers further proof referring to a story by Heine quoted by Freud (1905). In the story a poor lottery agent, Hirsch Hyacinth, boasts that the great Baron Rothschild treated him "as an equal and quite 'famillionaire.'" This last word is a condensation:[30]

$$
\begin{array}{c}
\text{famil i a r} \\
\text{millionaire} \\
\hline
\text{famillionaire}
\end{array}
$$

Not every case of nonsense in the folk song belongs in the group of neologisms. At times a text is changed in an attempt to write a clear copy from one which has become partially illegible. Words are than substituted which appear to fit the remaining lettering, but which do not necessarily fit into the content of the song.

Although it is always possible to explain some of the alterations in a song, other changes may defy explanation. No choice then remains but to label these changes as having been brought about by an individual singer. One can accept the idea that such changes exist and that they can be understood through an analysis of the point of view of the individual singer. Nevertheless, this could be considered too easy an explanation and one would be made skeptical of its validity if many alterations remain unexplained on that basis. What do we mean by an "individual change"? Are there specific causes for such changes? These questions can only be answered if one can produce such changes experimentally.

[29] Translator's note: A war song in the section on displacement which was not translated.

[30] Translator's note: Several other examples follow which are too difficult to translate.

The author attempted such an experiment. For this purpose he chose hymns, a form of song with written texts, so that if individual changes occurred they could always be verified. Moreover, the singing of hymns in chorus by a large group of people closely resembles the singing of a folk song. He made the experiment in the church of a monastery in which the congregation sang songs from announced texts. "I chose songs with which I was unfamiliar or knew only slightly. While the song was being sung in church, I wrote down the words, and then compared my notes with the written text. I was then in a position to determine whether I had made changes in the text and to what extent such changes reflected strivings originating from my state of mind. This inquiry was justified since all previously analyzed instances of song variations had proven to be the result of unconscious strivings" (Goja, p. 214).

Three experiments of this nature are analyzed in great detail using as a model Freud's analysis of parapraxes in his *Psychopathology of Everyday Life* (1901). In each instance Goja was able to show how thoughts and feelings which preoccupied him at the time of listening to a hymn caused him to misunderstand the words of the song as sung: in two instances words of a more familiar song intermingled with the new so that the resulting reproduction was a condensation of both songs. Moreover, that particular song was unconsciously chosen because it lent itself to the expression of feelings otherwise repressed.

"In summary, these three analyses[31] have shown us the dependency of the manner of alteration of the song on unconscious wishes and thoughts; a tendency toward a lessening of unpleasure by forgetting (I dare not assert the existence of an overriding tendency to gain pleasure); the unique character of the relationship between a particular reproduction of the song and its unconscious determinants which in this instance were established by superficial associations: the interrelationship of all the alterations in a song since they are derived from a common determinant; the purely personal quality of their origin since an explanation is

[31] "While on the one hand I have considered it my duty to observe a philological-critical method throughout this research, on the other I did not feel justified in neglecting research methods which might serve to supplement it. In the examples described above, I followed the psychoanalytic precept that every disturbance of the normal thought process, every act of forgetting, every slip of the tongue, and so forth, is determined by unconscious thoughts, etc., and that the source of these disturbances can be discovered by following the free associations to them. Through the application of this method of research it is possible to discover the source of disturbance for all cases of individual alterations of a song, and to explain each changed portion of a song, as I have demonstrated" (Goja, p. 219).

impossible without the aid of the individual who created them; the lack of any logical relationship between the alterations.

"Herewith, we are again at the point in our research from which we started. We must admit that we did not find the explanation for the alteration of the folk songs we set out to discover. We would have to leave it at that if song changes were only attributable to individuals. But objective changes also exist—changes produced not by an individual but by the masses. To explain such changes we must apply folk psychology rather than psychology of the individual" (Goja, p. 219).

Up to now, pleasure-stressed sexual and infantile complexes have been found to be part of the folk psyche. Moreover, it was seen that a change in mass attitude brought about the reversal of the emotional attitudes attached to being a soldier during the World War. It was possible to explain the alteration of songs during the World War as a result of this development of the folk psyche.

The author now attempts to explain some objective alterations. He quotes a phrase in Bruinier's book *The German Folksong* (p. 41): "Die Spatzen spielen aus Liebesfaedchen" (the sparrows play at the threads of love), which was derived from "Die Parzen spinnen am Lebensfaedchen" (the fates spin the threads of life). Of the original, only the last two syllables "faedchen" were correctly understood. Of the other syllables, only the consonants were correctly reproduced. This fact deserves special attention since ordinarily the consonants are more easily misheard than the vowels. Taking this into consideration, it seems likely that the change from "Lebensfaedchen" to "Liebesfaedchen" ("the threads of life" to "the threads of love") was determined by an unconscious factor. The introduction of words originating from the complex of sexuality is in accord with the law of folk psychology. The substitution of "life" by "love" is made easier through the circumstance that both words are often used in an alliterative formula.

Undoubtedly the noun "fates" (Parzen) was misunderstood because this concept does not exist among the masses. The substitution of the word "sparrow" (Spatzen for Parzen) is again derived from sexuality as the meaning of the word in folk poetry indicates:

Could I but swim like a swan,
Crow like a rooster,
Caress you like a sparrow
I would be the darling of every virgin [M. E. Marriage, p. 157].

The word "play" (spielen) that replaces "spin" (spinnen) has a pleasurable connotation arising from infancy and, moreover, an obscene secondary meaning in folk poetry. Thus, in these song variations the incomprehensible is substituted for by words which connote pleasure.

In both instances, alteration of the song occurs because unfamiliar words are not heard as words but as meaningless syllables. It is not a question of misunderstanding or of selecting one meaning instead of another where a series of words could have a double meaning. A double meaning does not exist for the masses; certain groups of sounds can have only one interpretation, which then becomes fixed through the writing of it. For example, the name Diana (pronounced Dee-ana in German) is heard as Die Anna; Ural (pronounced Oor-al) is heard as Urwald (Oorvald). In such instances it would not make sense to look for deeper unconscious meanings for the word change. Such changes can be considered objective.

In order to understand the conditions under which such self-explanatory objective changes came about, Goja undertook experiments which could be carried out without the help of psychoanalytic interpretation and which would therefore be more convincing than his earlier research. These investigations were based on the following considerations: if, as seems likely, the above described word changes were objective and determined by the point of view of the singer, the point of view must have been that of adult persons. The objective point of view on which these changes in the song are based, therefore, is that of an adult person. If one wishes now to determine whether this objective point of view is actually a factor in the word change (another factor is the unfamiliarity with the words of the song), one must change one point of view for another. If the same change in singing occurs even though the objective point of view is changed, then this cannot be a contributing factor. The method of investigation therefore consisted in changing the adult point of view for that of children.

The research plan was as follows: keeping in mind the previously determined conditions under which actual changes in the texts of the songs had occurred, texts were prepared which were beyond the comprehension of the pupils. These texts were dictated to the class without previous preparation or explanation. Those mistakes in hearing common to the majority of the children were then sought out. The teacher who dictated the text could be compared with the singer of the folk song. This was a fair comparison since, if a song were dictated, the words would be more easily understood than if they were sung.

As a result of this experiment[32] Goja concludes: "One fact is clearly derived from this experiment, that all cases of objective song changes are determined by the group attitude in the same way that instances of individual errors in singing depend on the point of view of the individual person, and that they represent disturbances of conscious thought by unconscious thought processes" (p. 223).

The establishment of this fact, however, does not exhaust the description of the nature of the nonsensical in the folk song. Limiting himself now to actual song changes, Goja considers a song by Ottas von Kraft. In this song one line out of thirty-four was changed during the course of the World War. The song *Auf zur Vergeltung, hurra hurra hurra!* (*Onward to Vengance, Hurrah, hurrah, hurrah!*) is a song of revenge against the Italians, and originated at the time Italy declared war. In the song, the Austrians claim never to have been beaten by the Italians and picture the time when they will march into Milan and Venice as victors, the Italians retreating before them. The line in question originally read:

> Until the brood,
> Which has never yet
> Beaten us anywhere

and was altered in the spring of 1917 to:

> Until the brood has
> Never and nowhere,
> Beaten us

Although the content of the song is not unpleasurable, unpleasure is nevertheless the cause of this one change, not because of the content, but because of the contrast between the meaning of the lines and reality. The singer was well aware of frequent defeats and had himself participated in a recent one. The change in the text in this instance is thus a denial of the content; denying not only the idea that they had never suffered defeat, but also the lines which followed describing the triumphant march into Italy. The singer no longer believes this to be a possibility. Fight until Venice is conquered? No, no! It is this No! which shows itself in the word change. Nonsense in the folk song, therefore, serves the purpose of denial of the original content.

---

[32] Translator's note: An account of the experiment is not brought into this translation since, as Goja himself says in a footnote, a large enough experiment to permit a detailed study was not possible.

This may seem like a rash statement, yet it is supported by the fact that nonsense serving the purpose of denial is a commonly used device in folk poetry. Uhland (1866b, p. 221) states: "The riddle presents the apparently impossible. Impossible things elaborate the negation. But there is one instance which stands halfway between."[33] Uhland then refers to the story of Macbeth and to the prophecy that no one born of woman would murder or conquer him until Burnham Wood would come to Dunsinane—simply a poetic presentation of never. That which was for Macbeth a decisive description of "never," finally became a riddle solved by fate. However, the described conditions are nonsense: every person must be born, no wood can wander. There is only a formal difference in the method of denial: denial through alteration of the song does not present any sort of imagery while nonsense as a device always makes use of visual pictures.

One can find numerous examples of the use of nonsense in folk poetry. For example: "It fell from heaven, was found by the shepherds, who cooked it without fire, ate it without a mouth... just as this could not happen, so should the illness return" (Petsch, 1917, p. 17). "Impossible things are often presented both seriously and in jokes as a hidden affirmation of 'no' and 'never' " (Uhland, 1866a, p. 218).

This type of folk poetry is a parallel to the instances of alteration of the song for the purpose of denying the content. Such change results from strivings of the preconscious and is a special case of forgetting in the service of avoidance of displeasure.

A further example of nonsense as a denial of the content occurs in a prewar song derived from the condensation of two songs, *The Song of Three Lilies* (see p. 159) and a song by Hoelty, *The Old Farmer to His Son*. During the World War the following stanza was tacked on to the last verse:

> Always be true and honest
> Until in your cool grave
> Then will you as a corporal
> Step down into your grave.

During the war, the word "corporal" was changed to "government official," and then to "ruler"; "grave" was changed to "mass grave," and "cool grave." What does this stanza, tacked on to this song, mean? It is of course unrelated and it is absurd to have added it to this song. However,

---

[33] Translator's note: Between the riddle and poetry.

this judgment is based on the manifest content of both portions. In the latent content, a relationship does exist. It appears that the men at the front thought of *The Song of Three Lilies* as nonsense and just tacked further nonsense on to it. The meaning of the stanza, the meaning of the alteration of the song, appears to have been discovered: a judgment, a denial, is concealed through this change. Art cannot afford a direct judgment: it can only stimulate a series of images with which the intended judgment is linked. It creates nonsense in order to say that something is absurd. In the latent content, the song and the stanza in question are equated. Comparing this with the alteration of the *Song of Vengeance,* the only difference is in the manner in which the nonsense in the manifest content is made clear. In the latter this is accomplished by altering a meaningful line; in *The Song of Three Lilies* in which no line is considered meaningful, nonsense is tacked on to it.

The content of the stanza must now be considered. This has in itself been altered. Originally it was the first stanza in Hoelty's song and read:

> Always be true and honest
> Until you are in your grave,
> And do not waver a finger's breadth
> From the path of God!

The last two lines are repressed and replaced by new ones. If this repression is a denial, it means: "To be true and honest is nonsense." The change is understandable if one is aware of the way the old song continues:

> Then will you, as though on the green meadow
> Go through life as a Pilgrim;
> Then can you, without fear or dread,
> Look Death in the eye

in the trenches. This is an ingenious condensation whereby the entire content of the song is compressed into the first verse and at the same time denied through the alteration of the last lines. If one is true and honest one will not walk on the green meadows but in the trenches; but if one is untrue and dishonest, one will be happy and rich. The rogue lives, the good and courageous bleed to death. Thus, the unconscious also improves on the altered stanza, changing the last line to:

> Step down into a mass grave.

But this song variant does not limit itself to a denial of the song content; it gives expression to yet a second train of thought. If the soldier does his duty to the end, what thanks does he get? None! He becomes a corporal. To express this train of thought the mechanism of reversal is used, since the last two lines are intended to be understood as irony, the opposite of their actual content. The meaning of the first line is also reversed: it is nonsense to be honest and true.

The next variant of the song reads:

> Then will you as government official
> Step into a cool grave.

Here the meaning of the stanza is once again reversed. To understand the meaning of this variant one must turn the first two lines into their opposites. They should now be read: "never be true and honest," etc. The thought of the stanza is thus further extended. The good and courageous not only do not receive thanks, but the thanks go to those who are not good. The hate of the singer is clearly no longer turned against his fate, but against the governing group who determine his fate. The singer considers himself a victim of that group, a victim of corruption. To bleed to death for this corrupt society is truly nonsense.

The World War brought forth a final variant, the most absurd of all:

> Then will you as ruler
> Step into a cool grave.

This variant expresses the most hate, and is therefore the most distorted. It has discovered the source of all the misery. The ruler refers to none other than the Regent, the Kaiser, although the word Kaiser cannot be used since the meaning would be too clear. If it has been proven true that in old Austria honesty did not pay, that only rogues became government officials, then the final song variant offers proof of this fact by equating the ruler with his criminal advisors. But to die for such a Kaiser is nonsense. Thus, this nonsensical stanza makes very good sense. To one who understands, it discloses the psychological development during the World War, showing the way to revolution.

Thus, small changes in the song are induced by unconscious thoughts and wishes, and serve to lessen unpleasure, to gain pleasure, as well as being a method of denial.[34]

---

[34] Another source of nonsense is the pleasure children have in rhythm. Children will use grown-up songs and alter them to serve this purpose. Examples would be superfluous.

Translator's note: Many nursery rhymes have acquired their present form as a result of just this inclination in children.

Symbolization[35]

Earlier in this paper, in the discussion of condensation, it became necessary to analyze certain word pictures as "the mill," "mountain and valley," and "the carnation" (clove). Explanations were attempted by selecting parts of songs in which the meaning of these words was unmistakable. All such examples were selected from obscene literature.

The question arises whether one has the right to assume that these word pictures have the same meaning wherever they occur, whether in illicit or licit literature. Although the answer to this question is not part of a study of the alteration of songs, a decision about it has become necessary since one form of song alteration uses the mechanism of symbolization of the offensive idea, i.e., a substitution of an acceptable, for an offensive image.

The question should be answered in the affirmative for the following reasons: it is a recognized fact today that there is no appreciable difference between licit and illicit folk poetry, and that any given singer might sing either type of song. There is only a difference of degree between the two song types resulting from a difference in the strength of the preconscious strivings against fantasies concerning the sexual wishes. The strength of these strivings is greater in the tame folk poetry than in the ribald, where in some instances they may be nonexistent. Thus, in the first instance the displacements would be greater than in the last.

Since a single person could be responsible for either type of song, there must also be uniformity to the meaning of the word picture. A singer who consciously uses an image as a sexual symbol would undoubtedly, at least unconsciously, remember the meaning of this image if he would find it again in another context. Also, undoubtedly it is the unconscious memory which determines his use of this image in another song. Further, only the assumption that the images in folk poetry are sexual symbols enables us to understand their typical character, since a comparison of the same subject within the same situation must make use of the same typical images. Moreover, the pleasurable sensations connected with them can be understood as a transference of pleasure from the original object to its image.

As a matter of fact Uhland had already recognized the double meaning in many images in folk poetry. He gave an example (1844, song 58):

[35] Compare Freud, 1900, p. 260.

God permitting, I would wish her
Two roses on one branch.

Uhland (1866b) had noted the "double meaning" and suggested comparing it with a line from Fischart's *Gargantua* (Hallenser Neudrucke, No.
65-71, p. 115): "... two cherries on one stem." It is of value that parallels
to this image can be found among the few erotic folk songs which have
been collected to date. Two variations of the same theme are:

The thorny branch is blooming,
It already has two buds [Bluemml, *Erotische Volkslieder,* 38].

and:

You didn't set the plant well,
Two roots are still outside [*Futilitates,* p. 396].

These excerpts are important in that they show how[36] one can actually
understand their meaning by comparing the images in our tame folk
poetry and in erotic poetry.

The only possible objection which can be raised to this type of interpretation is that the songs we have compared did not all originate in the
same epoch. This objection does not hold since these images are still
alive today in both tame and ribald songs. The images are as timeless as
they are universal.

It is particularly impressive that even when one refrains from making
use of the erotic folk poetry as a means of interpretation, one is forced to
the conception that the images in folk poetry are sexual symbols. By way
of illustration, Goja calls attention to a number of songs and poems in
which the word "England" occurs. A children's song translates:

A little white bean
Traveled to Engelland:
Engelland was locked shut
And the key was broken off.
(Pif, puf, paf, du bist af')
Pif puf paf, you're a monkey
[Simrock, 1857, No. 750; compare also No. 749].

[36] Compare the song, *Once I Had to Go Around the Mountain* (p. 123, line 9), "I saw
two roses in my father's hand," in which sexuality was shown to be the source of
pleasure in the latent content.

In this instance "England" was equated with the shrine in which the heart of the beloved has been locked.

The meaning of the word became clear in the fifth book of Simplicissimus (Hallenser Neudrucke, No. 19-25, p. 396) where he describes his wedding night and writes: "But the pipe soon fell into the muck, for although I intended to sail with the fair wind into Engelland, despite all precaution I came to Holland." The meaning of this excerpt is: Simplicissimus found that his wife was not a virgin.[37]

Examples of riddles further illustrate the use of both "England" and "Holland" with double meanings. The reason this occurs is, no doubt, the unconscious pleasure in the ambiguity of the words. In the alteration of the song, the riddle represents a new source of pleasure, an intensification of pleasure.

Goja believes that through similar investigation many images in folk poetry can be shown to have sexual meaning, but that it would not be justified to make this assumption without testing it in individual instances.

One instance of alteration of the song has been explained by considering symbolic meaning. The analysis of a second song, *The Song of Three Lilies,* unfortunately was not completely successful. Two versions of the song follow:

I

1. A hunter blew his horn all night,
   His blowing was to no avail.

2. "If all my blowing is for naught,
   I'd rather not a hunter be."

3. He threw his net over a bush,
   Out sprang a black-brown maiden fair.

4. "Oh black-brown maid, don't run from me!
   I have big dogs, they'll corner you."

5. "Oh, your big dogs will not hurt me,
   You don't know how high and wide I leap."

[37] Translator's note: "Enge" means narrow, or tight, while Holland, or "Hole land" means hollow or open. Other examples contrasting England and Holland appear to be based on the meaning "Engel," angel, contrasted with "Hoelle," or hell. Goja was particularly interested in interpreting the meaning of "England" to explain its occurrence in a song introduced earlier in the paper which was, however, not possible to translate.

6. "Your high, wide leaps will not help you.
   You know that it is today you die."

7. "Then if I die, I will be dead,
   Let me be buried, buried, 'neath the rose red.

8. Oh 'neath the rose, 'neath the clay,
   Nothing can touch me ever more."

9. Three lilies grew upon her grave,
   There came a rider to break them off.

10. "Oh rider, just let the lilies stay
    They shall be pluck'd by a hunter young"
    [Uhland, 1866a, No. 103].

II

1. Three lilies, three lilies,
   I planted on my grave,
   Walera
   There came along a proud rider
   And broke them off.

   Refrain:

   > With Juwiheirasasasasasasa
   > With Juwiheirasasasasasasa,
   > There came along a proud rider
   > And broke them off.

2. Oh rider-man, oh rider-man,
   Let the lilies remain,
   Walera
   My love should see them
   Yet once again.

   Refrain:

3. What care I for your lover
   What care I for your grave,
   Walera
   I am a proud rider
   And broke them off.

   Refrain:

4. And if I die today,
   So am I dead tomorrow
   Walera
   Then will the people bury me
   Tomorrow morn.

Refrain:

5. Tomorrow morn, tomorrow morn
   Then buried I will be.
   Walera
   So sleep my dear, my love,
   So still, so well,

Refrain: [Goja].

Although this song (version II) was a favorite in the author's regiment during the World War, no objective variations developed—proof of how well suited it was to the state of mind of the singer.

Commencing with the analysis of version I, Goja points out that the song fails to supply an explanation of why the hunter blows his horn (verse 2 has evidently already undergone change). This must be learned from other songs, for example, *The Happy Hunter* (Erk and Boehme, 1892-1894, *3*, No. 1456):

> The hunter blew into his horn,
> He blew the game right out the corn.

He blew it, therefore, to chase the game from its lair. However, this does not explain version I, line 2. The following fragment gives the clue:

> I am a hunter and I blow a horn
> All that I hunt is lost,
> . . . .
> Yet I will hunt day and night
> Until I find a steady love [Uhland, 1844, No. 102].

Thus, the "hunt" is seen to be an image: hunter and game are none other than man and maiden. This is, of course, a well-known and accepted fact and did not need such elaborate proof. The reason for the hunter's anger in verse 2 is now understandable: no matter how much he blows his horn, no animal jumps out—he blows in vain. It must then, of course, go badly for the maiden when caught as his "game." The need for the alteration is somewhat clarified: the rationalization of the image was unsuccessful.

The hunter throws his net, catches a maiden and commences to speak with her, ending with a threat of death:

> You know that it is today you die.

Herewith a point of controversy has been reached.

However, to continue: if the hunt represents love, then the image, "killing the game," can only be interpreted as "the rape of the maiden." Seduction is the only consequence one can expect if one follows the train of thought expressed in the song. This is supported by the fact that from this point on the song has been greatly altered. The fantasy of rape must release resistance on the part of the preconscious, which becomes evident in the distortion of the manifest content. There is no need to refer to a theory concerning the alteration of songs in order to verify this conclusion. Versions of this song in which the verse in question is missing, and which present on the whole a much milder version of the song, indicate the love-making which followed upon the capture of the maiden:

> He threw his net around her body
> All-the-while at night:
> Thus she became the young hunter's wife,
> All-the-while, all-the-while the hunter's wife,
> All-the-while at night [Erk and Boehme, 1892-1894, *1*, 19d].

The killing of an animal in the hunt as a representation of love-making is typical of our folk poetry. For example:

> If I were a hunter
> I'd shoot a dove
> That had red cheeks
> And coal-black eyes [M.E. Marriage, p. 139].

or:

> I'm not shooting me a buck
> I'm not shooting me a doe
> I shoot my Teresa
> And I do not hurt her [M.E. Marriage, p. 141].

The double meaning in the following is evident:

> As Hans sprang over the heather
> He shot at a dove;
> He shot the dove, a feather fell off
> And he let her fly away [M.E. Marriage, p. 139].

Marriage explains this: "It is clear from the context that Hans had seduced a maiden (shot a feather from the dove), and deserted her (let her fly away)."

Just to show that erotic folk poetry also uses such images, the following examples are included:

> I like to follow her
> Until she stands still[38]
> Then I shoot her
> When I can see the target.

> If I meet with a bitch
> And then I discover
> That she is mortally wounded
> I quickly let her run away [*Futilitates*, 1, LXIII, 4].

or

> If you do it once, so let's keep it up
> Hit it again, so the bed creaks, yes the bed creaks
> [Bluemml, xxxix, 2, verse 14].

The images in these erotic folk poems show clearly the value and purpose of the resistance originating in the preconscious. This resistance is almost entirely missing in the conscious mind of the person who permits such images to form. Those persons in whom the striving toward sexual fantasies immediately releases resistance of the preconscious do not find these images pleasurable. On the contrary, they create unpleasure. It is only possible to experience pleasure through representations resulting from a compromise of both strivings as seen in the first of these examples.

These many examples lead to the conclusion that the killing of the maiden in the song under consideration stands for rape. The meaning of burial still needs to be clarified. No interpretation has as yet been convincing although much has already been written about the three lilies in the lines

> Three lilies grew upon her grave,
> There came a rider to break them off.

It should be noted that in these two lines, two symbols have been condensed—that of three lilies and that of picking a rose. In yet another song, the breaking of a rose represents love-making. It is perhaps a breakthrough of this formula when in some versions of the song, three roses grow on the grave.

[38] Translator's note: The double meaning, "Until it wants to stand."

They planted three roses on my grave.
Then came my love and broke them off [M.E. Marriage, p. 139].

Here, again, is an alteration resulting from condensation as in the song *Upon the Mountain High* (p. 132). In seeking an explanation of the three lilies, the number three can be disregarded. It is not essential to the image since in some versions of the song there is only one lily. The number three, however, has a meaning of its own which will be discussed later. However, the lily itself does not appear in all versions, but is often displaced by the carnation.[39] For example:

A carnation grew out of my grave,
There came a proud hunter and robbed me of it,
Oh hunter, dear hunter! Let the carnation stand,
My most dearly beloved should see it once more [M.E. Marriage, p. 133].

Lily and carnation are identical. Having come to know the carnation as a sexual symbol, the lily must be the same. This assertion may seem monstrous in view of the fact that the lily is the symbol of purity. The conception of purity attached to this symbol is, however, understandable. It is a camouflage, a way of covering up, in order to disarm the resistance of the preconscious. That the lily is the symbol of the male genital in folk poetry is proven by the fact that on the one hand it changes places with other phallic symbols and on the other hand is paired with the rose, the favorite symbol of the female genital. Compare:

No rose, no carnation
Can bloom so beautifully
As two souls in love
When they stand together [M.E. Marriage, p. 106].

with:

Three lilies in the garden
Three roses in the field
I must marry now
Or I'll be too old [M.E. Marriage, p. 108].

Even more convincing is the section of the text from Erk and Boehme (1892-1894, *1*, 19b):

[39] Translator's note: The German word "Nelke" refers to both the spice "clove" and the flower "carnation." See discussion of "clove," p. 135.

12. The third was a lily white, lily white,
    He stuck into his hat with might.
13. This he did with abandon great, abandon great.
    Which rarely bode well for the farmer maid.

The verse already cited (p. 158) as having a double meaning, also belongs here:

> God permitting, I would wish her
> Two roses on one branch.

In the oldest text of the song, according to Erk and Boehme, the three lilies are omitted in the significant verse. That part of the song is as follows:

9. It was barely the third day, the third day
   When three flowers grew out of her grave.
10. The first was a little rose red, rose red,
    Grown of the dearest love, dead.
11. The other was a little clove, a little clove,[40]
    Grown from my dearest love
    [Erk and Boehme, 1892-1894, *1*, 196].

Goja sees a progression in the different versions, the clearest symbol being that of the branch and two roses. Two branches and one rose is a reversal of the original, the final version being three branches, i.e., three lilies. Even though the parallel is no longer so clear in the images themselves, it is maintained through the addition of the symbol three, for three is also a genital symbol. "Because they are accustomed while virgins to sell their lovers nulls instead of threes," writes Fischart (Hallenser Neudrucke, No. 65-71). Recognizable, once again, in the transformation of symbols, is the effect produced by the resistance of the preconscious which in the course of development gains increased strength.

It was determined above that the image of breaking off the three lilies represents a condensation; it is now clear that this is a condensation of the image of two roses on one branch, with the breaking of the rose and with the image of three. This, however, does not complete the series of the images here united. In a folk song called *Laughing and Crying*, which again represents seduction by a hunter in its manifest content, the third verse reads:

[40] Translator's note: Here the word is "Naegelein," literally "little nail," but is also used to mean the spice "clove."

They went together to the mountain top.
They sat down under a tree in the woods.
He broke off a green branch
And made the maiden to his wife.
Then the maiden laughed so much [Simrock, 1851, No. 102].

In this verse the image of the breaking off of a twig has the same meaning as the breaking off of the rose. Obviously both images were originally independent. The breaking of the twig appears elsewhere in the folk song and always with the same meaning.

From a little apple tree,
I break a twig,
Of an intrepid maiden,
I make myself a wife [Simrock, 1851, No. 114].

Thus the idea is expressed by the next to last verse of yet another song. It is not surprising to find this image also in quite frivolous songs. One singer relates how a man went to the woods and in the month of May broke off a branch. He then goes to the window of his beloved and asks to be admitted. But the maiden sees through his ruse and says:

The May branch you want to bring me,
leave outside [Simrock, 1851, No. 108].

The substitution of the lily for the branch is made possible through the similarity of the two. The lily is substituted because the maiden is pure.[41]

Summing up what has thus far been recognized as the content of the changed verses, there were two representations for rape—the killing of the victim and the breaking of the branches.

One manifest content of the song is still confusing: the rider suddenly appears in verse 9 (p. 160). If the analysis has been correct so far, then this rider is incomprehensible. The rider may not break the lily, but the hunter may; if the maiden begs her seducer for mercy, she should direct her cry toward the hunter, not the rider, much less should she cry out:

"Oh rider, just let the lilies stay
They shall be pluck'd by a hunter young."

The question is whether the hunter and the rider are not one and the same person. The expression to ride, used in erotic literature for coitus, is

[41] We see in this the effect of religious symbols.

one of the expressions that has found the most verification. A heretofore unpublished example from Goja's collection reads:

> De-ulioeh, de-ulioeh,
> Riding is my life, hi-ho!
> De-ulioeh, de-ulioeh
> Riding is my life.
> Without reins or curb
> I'll ride me a wench at home,
> De-uhlioeh, de-uhlioeh,
> Riding is my life.

At the beginning of the song *(Three Lilies)*, while the man pursues the maiden, he is appropriately designated as hunter; now at the end, and in accordance with the situation, he is characterized as a "rider-man." Thus, the words of the maiden prove the correctness of the analysis. The song is a song of seduction. The youthful eager hunter in verse 10 (p. 160) is the lover of the maiden.

Except for the image "to be buried under a rosebush," everything has been explained. Goja admits that he has not found a convincing parallel to assist the explanation, but guesses that the image of the grave and that of the rose is identical. He derived this idea from:

> And should I once be parted,
> Where will they bury me?
> In my beloved garden
> Where the red rose blooms [Simrock, 1851, No. 154].

Since the garden of the beloved is her lap, the grave of the loved one is also determined. This supposition is supported by the following song from which the significant lines are reproduced:

> 6. Good little Hans let his little horse be shoed,
>   It should carry him up the high mountain.
> 7. How high the mountain, how deep the valley!
>   It is sad that little Hans must die.
> 8. "And if I die then I am dead
>   So they will bury me under the rose red.
> 9. So they will bury me at the same spot
>   Where you my love were unfaithful to me"
>   [Uhland, 1866a, No. 150].

Here we have the image of mountain and valley preceding the grave, and fitting in with our supposition.

The analysis showed that an explanation of the many versions of a song is only possible if one accepts the images of folk poetry as symbols which are transformed as changes occur in the character of the people (Volksseele). Alterations in songs by means of the use of symbols always occur under the influence of the resistance of the preconscious and serve the gaining of pleasure in the highest degree. In this process, one can differentiate: (1) the displacement of a particular thing by its symbol, (2) the change of the symbol itself through singing.

The transformation can be seen through displacement of a hunter's song into that of a song of the rider (the soldier). For this reason the beginning of the original version has disappeared. The new song begins with the plea of the maiden, is followed then with a rough (new) answer by the rider, and ends with the surrender of the victim to the one who dishonored her. In the picture of dawn (Morgenrote = red of the morning), sexuality[42] is mingled with the image of the soldier.

"Herewith, I have reached the end of my work. There exist no other types of alteration of songs through singing than those resulting from condensation, displacement, omission, and symbolization. This paper has shown that alteration of folk songs does not occur by chance, but is determined by changes in the temperament of the people and that the alterations always serve the purpose of removing unpleasure or gaining pleasure. In this context, the paper has also shown that art has only one purpose and always fulfills it: that of making people happy" [Goja, p. 240].

[42] See Aigremont (1908, p. 111) regarding the remark concerning the color red.

BIBLIOGRAPHY

An attempt has been made to rearrange the author's list of references in accordance with the method customarily used by this publication. Also, references occurring in footnotes, although not originally included, were added to the bibliography when they were not too fragmentary. Nevertheless, compared with present-day standards, the bibliography remains incomplete: dates are frequently omitted; it is often unclear whether "herausgegeben" means "edited" or "published"; in many instances the publisher and place of publication are omitted completely.

Aigremont (1908), *Volkserotik und Pflanzenwelt.*
Das Ambraser Liederbuch (1582).
Angermann, R. (1911), *Der Typus des Leidvollen in der deutschen Volksballade.*
Bergreihen: ein Liederbuch des XVI Jahrhunderts (1891). Herausgegeben von J. Meier. Hallenser Neudrucke, No. 99-100.
Bluemml, E. K., *Erotische Volkslieder aus Deutschoesterreich.*
———*Futilitates, I-IV.*

Boeckel, O. (1885), *Volkslieder aus Oberhessen.*
——(1908), *Das deutsche Volkslied.* Handbuch etc.
Boeckel, V. (1906), *Psychologie der Volksdichtung.*
Boehme, F. M. (1895), *Volkstuemliche Lieder der Deutschen im XVIII und XIX Jahrhundert.*
Brecht, W. (1915), *Deutsche Kriegslieder sonst und jetzt.*
Bruinier, J. W., Das deutsche Volkslied. *Natur und Geisteswelt,* Band 17.
Buecher, C. (1909), *Arbeit und Rhythmus.*
Carmina Burana (1847), lateinische und deutsche Lieder aus Benediktbeuern. Herausgegeben von Schmeller.
Daur, A. (1909), *Das alte deutsche Volkslied.*
Das deutsche Volkslied. Zeitschrift herausgegeben von Pommer, 1899 und folgende.
Doerler, A. (1910), Volkslieder aus Tirol. *Zeitschrift des Vereines fuer Volkskunde, 20.*
Erk, L. & Boehme, F. M. (1892-1894), *Deutsche Liederhort, 1-3.*
Freud, S. (1900), *Die Traumdeutung.* Leipzig, Vienna: Deuticke, 1914. [The Interpretation of Dreams. The Basic Writings of Sigmund Freud. New York: Modern Library, 1938, pp. 181-549.]
——(1901), *Zur Psychopathologie des Altagslebens [The Psychopathology of Everyday Life].* Berlin: Karger, 1912.
——(1905), *Der Witz und seine Beziehungen zum Unbewussten [Wit and Its Relation to the Unconscious].* Leipzig, Vienna: Deuticke, 1912.
——(1916-1917), *Vorlesungen zur Einfuehrung in die Psychoanalyse [Introductory Lectures on Psycho-Analysis].* Leipzig, Vienna: Heller.
——(1924), *The Ego and the Id.* London: Hogarth Press, 1947.
Futilitates, I-XLV. Hallenser Neudrucke, No. 19-25.
Goja, H., *Handschriftliche Sammlung der Lieder des kaiserlich koeniglichen Schuetzenregiments, No. 24, Umgebung von Wien.*
——(1920), Halluzinationen eines Sterbenden. *Int. Z. Psychoanal.,* 6:357-359.
——(1921), Nacktheit und Aberglaube. *Int. Z. Psychoanal.,* 7:63-78.
Grinstein, A. (1956), *The Index of Psychoanalytic Writings.* New York: International Universities Press.
Hartmann, A. (1913), *Historische Volkslieder und Zeitgedichte vom XVI bis XIX Jahrhundert.*
Hoffmann von Fallersleben, A. (1900), *Unsere volkstuemlichen Lieder.* Herausgegeben von K. H. Prahl.
Hruschka, A. & Toischer, W. (1891), *Deutsche Volkslieder aus Boehmen.*
Jodl, F., *Lehrbuch der Psychologie.*
Jungbaur, G. (1908), *Volksdichtung aus dem Boehmerwald.*
Kaindl, P. (1905), Deutsche Lieder aus Rosch. *Zeitschrift des Vereines fuer Volkskunde, 15.*
Koehler, C. & Mayer, J. (1896), *Volkslieder von der Mosel und Saar.*
Marriage, E. A. (1902), *Volkslieder aus der badischen Pfalz.*
Marriage, M. E., Poetische Beziehungen des Menschen zur Pflanzen und Tierwelt im heutigen Volkslied auf hochdeutschem Boden. *Alemanina, 26.*
Meier, J. (1906a), *Kunstlied und Volkslied in Deutschland.* Hallee: M. Niemeyer.
——(1906b), *Kunstlieder im Volksmunde.* Hallee: M. Niemeyer.
——(1916), *Das deutsche Soldatenlied im Felde.*
——(1917), *Volksliedstudien.*
Muendel, C. (1884), *Elsaessische Volkslieder.*
Petsch, R. (1899), *Neue Beitraege zur Kenntnis des Volksraetsels.*
——(1917), *Das deutsche Volksraetsel.*
Priefer, E., *Zeitschrift des Vereines fuer Volkskunde, 4.*

Rebieczek, F. (1913), *Der Wiener Volks- und Baenkelgesang, 1800-1848*.

Reuschel, K. (1903), *Volkstuemliche Streifzuege*.

Rieger, F. (1908), *Des Knaben Wunderhorn und seine Quellen*.

Simrock, R. (1851), Die deutschen Volkslieder. *Die deutschen Volksbuecher, 8*.

——(1857), *Das deutsche Kinderbuch*.

Tobler, L. (1884), *Schweizerische Volkslieder*.

Tschischka, F. & Schottky, J. M. (1819), *Oesterreichische Volkslieder*.

Uhland, L. (1844), *Alte hoch- und niederdeutsche Volkslieder in fuenf Buechern*.

——(1866a), Alte hoch- und niederdeutsche Volkslieder. *Uhlands Schriften zur Geschichte der Dichtung und Sage, 3*.

——(1866b), Anmerkungen zu den Volksliedern. *Uhlands Schriften zur Geschichte der Dichtung und Sage, 4*.

Venus-Gaertlein (1890), Herausgegeben von M. F. von Waldberg. Hallenser Neudrucke, No. 86-89.

Vogt, F., *Des Minnesangs Fruehling 3*, 18.

Volks- und Gesellschaftlieder des XV und XVI Jahrhunderts. I. Die Lieder der Heidelberger. Handschrift Folio 343, herausgegeben von A. Kopp, 1905.

von Arnim, A. & Brentano, C. (1906), *Des Knaben Wunderhorn*. Herausgegeben von Grisebach.

von der Hagen & Buesching (1807), *Sammlung deutscher Volkslieder*.

von Ditfurth, F. W. (1855), *Fraenkische Volkslieder, 2*.

——(1871), *Die historischen Volkslieder des bayrischen Heeres*.

——(1871-1872), *Historische Volkslieder der Zeit von 1756 bis 1871*.

——(1874), *Die historischen Volkslieder des oesterreichischen Heeres, 1638-1849*.

——(1877), *Die historischen Volkslieder, 1648-1756*.

von Kobell, Fr. (1860), *Oberbayrische Lieder*.

von Liliencron, R. (1865), *Die historischen Volkslieder der Deutschen vom XIII bis XVI Jahrhundert*.

von Oppeln-Bronilowski, F. (1911), *Deutsche Kriegs- und Soldatenlieder 1500 bis 1900*.

von Soltau, F. L. (1836), *Ein Hundert deutsche historische Volkslieder*.

——(1856), *Deutsche historische Volkslieder*.

Wackernell, J. (1890), *Das deutsche Volkslied*.

Wegener, P. (1879), *Volkstuemliche Lieder aus Norddeutschland*.

Wolfram, E. (1894), *Nassauische Volkslieder*.

Wossidlo, R., *Mecklenburgische Volksueberlieferungen, 1*.

Wundt, W., Die Kunst. *Voelkerpsychologie, 3*.

Zeitschrift des Vereines fuer Volkskunde, 1891 und folgende.

ANTHROPOLOGY AND SOCIOLOGY

THE WESTERN TRIBES OF CENTRAL AUSTRALIA: THE ALKNARINTJA

GÉZA RÓHEIM, Ph.D.

1. IN MUNDANE LIFE

One of the most important personae of both mundane and ritual life is the *alknarintja*. None of my informants were clear as to whether the *alknarintja* was an actual woman or a mythical being. The name is used to refer to real women and to characters in the myths and rituals of the people. The *alknarintja* of the myth owned the *tjurunga* in times long past. She owned the bull-roarer as well, which, at a later time, was passed on to the men. She is described as having hair the color of smoke. Her primary characteristic was that she avoided men. She would respond, however, to the one man who performed a love incantation for her. When he wanted her, she would rush to him from a great distance in a highly excited state.

Old Yirramba told me that a real woman could also be an *alknarintja*. The word itself means "eyes-turn-away." He said that all women become *alknarintja* when they are very small, i.e., they begin with an attitude of avoiding men. Spencer (1927, pp. 471-472) refers to the *alknarintja* as a woman who will not go with a man unless he has performed love magic for her. She is said to prefer men from distant places. I do not feel that his remarks on the *alknarintja* give enough importance to the significance of the *alknarintja* concept in myth or in everyday life.

Editor's Note.—The following paper, published posthumously, edited by Warner Muensterberger, is a chapter from Géza Róheim's *Magnum Opus, The Western Tribes of Central Australia,* his as yet unpublished field report from the Aranda, Lurittya, Pitjentara, among whom the author did his most comprehensive psychoanalytic-anthropological field work.

In editing the present chapter of *The Western Tribes of Central Australia,* Dr. Muensterberger was assisted by Miss Elise Wechsler.

Copyright by the executors of the Géza Róheim Estate, Sandor Lorand, M.D. and Warner Muensterberger, Ph.D.

Before we can discuss the mythical attributes and their meanings, we must first discuss the role that the *alknarintja* plays in mundane life. I was told that in the beginning every woman is an *alknarintja*. She continues to be one until her resistance has been broken by the man who has "sung" her. The man who wishes to win an *alknarintja* must smear the small bull-roarer with blood taken from his subincision hole. The bull-roarer is swung while the man chants the proper incantation. (The incantations, the *ilpindja*, will be discussed in the next section.) When he has done this, the woman sees his *altjera* (ancestral spirit or double) penetrating into her body and calling her by name. She, who until this time had had nothing to do with men, now falls in love. She continues to resist the advances of all other men and will give herself only to the man who has "sung" her.

The Pindupi and the Yumu call an *alknarintja* an *aninpa*. She lives in the girls' camp. The men who live nearby all advise their friends to take her. The girl takes great pains to hide herself from the men. When she leaves the camp, she walks on the grass in order to leave no track. At night, she does not stay in the camp with the others, but erects a windbreak in the bush and stays there. In the morning, when she goes to gather seeds with the other women, if a man should approach her, she runs away and hides in the bush. Finally, when the man who has made her into an *alknarintja* appears, she succumbs to him, and he takes her by the arm and marries her.

From this description we can see that the *alknarintja* may be a woman who has resisted the advances of men since she was a baby, or she may be a woman who has become an *alknarintja* after having been "sung" by one man. Although, to begin with, every woman may be an *alknarintja*, it must be noted that there are no spinsters among the Central Australians, and that therefore no woman lives and dies an *alknarintja*. It should also be noted that all the men with whom I spoke had had intercourse before the age of puberty. Nonetheless, the *alknarintja* attitude of the woman is not merely a conventional façade to be cast aside as soon as the opportunity presents itself. The custom of *mbanja*, which is directly related to the *alknarintja* concept, often requires real force on the part of the man and real struggles on the part of the woman and her friends.

Strehlow (1913, Vol. I, Part 1, p. 97) has recorded the myth of the Alknarintja of Iloata (Mt. Conway) which illustrates the relation of the *alknarintja* concept to the custom of *mbanja*. A group of *alknarintja* women met a man of the Little Hawk totem and asked him if he were related to them. He replied that he was their husband. He then put his spear thrower under his arm in the typical *mbanja* attitude and tried to drag off one of the women. She bit his hand until he released her. Then she and her friends hit him with their yam sticks.

The *alknarintja* is connected in some fashion with the small bull-roarer. Motna, a southern Aranda, told me that the small bull-roarer was originally owned by an *alknarintja* called Djirindjira (Grass-woman). She later gave it to the men. He said that when a man wishes to charm an *alknarintja,* he throws the bull-roarer in her direction and then pulls it back toward himself. The woman then dreams of the man and embraces him. When a woman conceives, the same thing occurs.

Having seen the role that the *alknarintja* plays in mundane life, we can now focus our attention on the *alknarintja* of the mythical period. The collection of myths and songs which follows has to do with the *alknarintja*. They are used at various totemic rites· In those cases where I saw or obtained a description of the corresponding ritual, that information is included.

2. THE MYTHS AND SONGS OF THE *Alknarintja*

1

The following song of the Honey Ant totem was given to me by Old Yirramba. The song, and the myth which corresponds to it, are used in a totemic rite at which a ceremonial pole is erected.

The Alknarintja of Aroulbmoulbma[1]

The alknarintja woman is tired.
She refuses to move.
She sits very still.
Near her is an ants' nest and a ti tree bush with
 its branches stuck together.
All the alknarintja women are tired.
They sit down and refuse to move.
Near them are erijila flowers and a tnyelinga bush.
They are sitting near a big camp.
They sit on the flat sand.
About them grow many tnatata flowers.
The pollen of the flowers fills the air.
They bend down the branches of the mulga tree and pick
 its flowers.
They pick the tnata flowers.

[1] Free translations of the songs are presented here.

The branches of the mulga tree are laden with flowers and
    bending with the weight.
Beyond where they sit is a narrow gap in the hills.
Beyond the gap are many camps.
The ants crawl on the ground.
They look like decoration marks.
They look like decoration marks.

One of the concepts found frequently in the mythology of the
alknarintja is introduced in this song. The *alknarintja* women are
motionless. They refuse to move. Not only are the women immobile, but
the objects in their environment are also motionless, i.e., the branches
of the bush are stuck together and so the bush cannot move. The burgeon-
ing fertility of the bushes stands in sharp contrast to the rejecting attitude of the *alknarintja*. The following myth is related to this song.

Many *alknarintja* women of the Honey Ant totem lived at Aroulb-
moulbma. They collected undjiamba flowers, brought them back to their
camp and soaked them in a bark vessel. They also found red flowers and
mulga flowers. They went out looking for the flowers of the iron-wood
tree and for *tjuarka*. All the flowers were soaked in water which the women
drank. They then went to a place called Ipmana-pundja (Black-piss-ant)
where they found black piss ants. Again they soaked mulga flowers,
tjuarka, iron-wood flowers, ti tree seed, and the branches of the witchetty
bush in water. Then they returned to Apma-kapita (Snake-head), where
they gathered the flowers of the ti tree bush and took them to the ances-
trial cave. They went out again and found many different kinds of flowers.
They went back to the ancestral cave where they became *tjurunga*. They
were Pananga and Pangata women. They owned ceremonial spears and
decorated themselves all day. Their leader was Tnatjilpaka (Stand-up).
She stood up at Indotapa (Boomerang) and became tired. A gum tree
stands there now.

2

The following myth and song were related to me by Aldinga of the
Merino group. The Merinos are a group of Lurittya of the type that
would be called "half-Aranda" by the natives. The song is used at a multiplication ceremony. Only the initiated are permitted to attend. The
performers make a hard surface of the sand by permitting blood from
wounds made in their subincision holes to drip onto it. The men make
marks in the sand and then toss the sand into the air. The old men sit
motionless, holding their shields and wearing their large *tjurunga*

("body" *tjurunga*) on their heads. They eat euro meat before singing the song. The ritual ensures the reproduction of the euro.

> The two men are wandering in search of euro.
> They see a woman far off on the road.
> They cook the fat of the euro in its skin.
> They strike the erultja bush with their ceremonial spears.
> Near them is a red salt bush.
> It is bad, for salt bushes should be blue.
> They make spears from the branches of this bush.
> The spears are crooked.
> They do not want to hunt euro now.
> They want to hunt women.
> They see the nest of the arkana bird among the rocks.
> As they run along, they decorate themselves and put on their
>   arm strings.
> They dance. Their feet thud on the ground.
> Their feet thud on the rock where the bad spear bush grew.
> They think to themselves, "We will make a spear."
> "We will make a spear that the women may know we want them."
> They see the women standing in a row.
> Again they see the arkana bird.
> It reminds them of the old blind woman back at the camp.
> The bird's cave is black.
> It has been burnt black by the bird's fire.
> The men sit down in a dry bush.
> The bird flies away.
> They hear the women approaching.
> The men dance on the rock.
> Their feet thud.
> They dance on the ground.
> Their feet thud.

Before we attempt an interpretation of this song, it will be necessary to relate the myth associated with it. The myth differs from the song most strikingly in that there is no mention made of the women (presumably *alknarintja* women), whom the men see in the song.

An old woman and two men lived at Alknarintja-arakutya-indara (Alknarintja-woman's-vagina). She was their father's sister. The elder of the two men gave her kangaroo meat, but the younger did not. She would ask him, "Have you killed any euro?" and he would answer, "No." She was blind and so she could not see what the younger man was doing.

He left the camp one day and went to the southwest. There he killed two kangaroos. He brought them back and cooked them in the camp. Then he fell asleep beside the fire. The elder brother went to get some eagle down with which to decorate himself. The old woman smelled the meat. She took it out of the fire and ate it. When the elder brother returned to the camp, his body was covered with eagle down. When the younger brother saw him, he shouted, "Wah! Wah!" and danced around him.

Each of the brothers made a ceremonial spear. They placed them so that they formed a cross. There is a big stone there today to mark the spot where the two spears stood. The brothers then went to the north where they killed an euro. They found a big white rock on which there were many euros. The younger brother speared the euros and cut them up on the spot. He took only the fat back to camp to cook. The older brother went to the south where he found two euros which he brought back to the camp. Then the younger brother went back to the place where he had hidden the euro meat. He dug it up and brought it back to the camp where both men cooked their meat.

The older brother gave some of his meat to the old woman, but the younger one gave her nothing. Neither of them gave her any fat, but she smelled it cooking. "Why don't you give me any fat?" she asked. Even the elder brother had never given her any fat. Then she made many *tjurunga*. She decorated herself and put the *tjurunga* on her head. The two men went back to the cave. There they found a great deal of eagle down. They all became *tjurunga* together in the cave.

This myth is a variant of one which I attempted to interpret in a previous work. In it, a blind *tneera* (this word means "beautiful woman," but it is also another name for the *alknarintja*) of the Euro totem lived with her two nephews.

The two men were good hunters, and always had success when they went to spear the euro. The two brothers would never give their aunt any fat. One day, however, the younger one gave her some caul fat. She rubbed this on her eyes and was instantly cured of her blindness. Thereupon, she spat on the euro bones which lay about the camp. The bones were immediately transformed into live euros which sprang up and began to jump about. Previously, all the euros had been blind and therefore easy to spear, but now the euros could see. When the nephews heard the thuds of the euros' feet upon the ground, they knew what the old woman had done. They were very angry that she had spoiled their hunting and tried to kill her, but instead, she seduced them. After they had had intercourse with her, she taught them how to kill the euros with their spears and with black magic.

This myth, as well as the one previously related, is used in ceremonies which ensure the multiplication of the euro. "To gain eyesight" is a euphemism for "being born" in several Central Australian languages. A statement that the young kangaroos are jumping about and have gained their eyesight really means that they have jumped out of their mothers' wombs (or pouches) and have been born. It should also be noted that the Central Australian youth frequently refer to their mothers as *"banga"* (the blind one). Since multiplying one's own totemic species is symbolic incest, we need only rearrange the sequence of events in the myth just related for it to become perfectly comprehensible. The nephews first have intercourse with the old woman, i.e., they have incestuous coitus. She is thus made pregnant and gives birth to the young of the species. Since the Central Australians are among the few peoples of the world who regularly eat their own totemic animal, the old woman is able to teach the young men how to kill the euros. Nonetheless, there is a difference between killing the totemic animal and killing any other animal, and so, they must rely upon black magic.

The myth and the song previously related differ from this myth in several respects. In the song, the old woman (as a sexual object) has been transformed into the *alknarintja* woman, whom the men are trying to win through the use of the *ilpindja*. No mention is made of their having sexual intercourse with the *alknarintja* in the song, and in the myth there is neither the transformation of the old woman into an *alknarintja* nor mention of coitus with the aunt. All overt sexuality has been repressed. It is obvious that the *alknarintja* is a distorted form of the original incestuous love object. Lest there be a breakthrough of the repressed, mention both of coitus and of the multiplication of the species must be omitted. The *alknarintja* is the representative of the incestuous love object.

3

I learned the myth and song which follow from Mulda, Wapiti's classificatory brother. They are used in connection with a "making" ceremony. It is not quite clear as to what they are intended to "make." In my notes, I found a statement to the effect that the wombs of the women open during this ceremony, from which one can conclude that the song and myth are intended to "make" love. The meaning of this song and myth would therefore appear to be approximately the same as that of the other song and myth I learned from Mulda. However, at the same place in my notes I found another statement that the *alknarintja* menstruate a great deal, and so this ceremony may be intended to "make" menstruation.

The alknarintja are menstruating.
The blood flows out.
They tie their arm strings tightly to stop the flow.
As they walk, they pass a ti tree bush laden with flowers.
They see a tjora bush bent under the weight of its seeds.
The branches are hanging down under the burden of their seeds.
They sit down near a lupulupa bush.
They cover their vaginas with their heels.
Far off they see the track of a man.
It is a clear track and far away.
Within their bodies, they hear the growling of the bull-roarer.
The bull-roarer talks.
The bull-roarer thunders.
"I am breaking up,"[2] cries one of the women.
"My womb has opened at the sound of the bull-roarer.
It has entered into me and become a child in my womb.
I am in love."
The bull-roarer talks loud.
The man of the Iwupa Worm totem stands with his tjurunga tied
    to his back.
He is excited.
He bites his beard.
He whirls the bull-roarer.
The string breaks!
The bull-roarer whizzes through the air.
The women stand, holding their yam sticks.
The bull-roarer talks!
The bull-roarer talks!
The ground is cold.
A cool wind blows.
The man is excited.
His Adam's apple tightens.
The women rise up from the grass.
Again the bull-roarer talks.
The man's Adam's apple tingles.
He has performed an ilpindja.

It is morning again.
The heat rises.
The sun rises.
The alknarintja women walk softly.
They have decorated themselves.

[2] In most songs the term "breaking up" when it follows the words "the bull-roarer talks" refers to the bull-roarer itself. There are two possible interpretations for this use of the term. In order to make a bull-roarer, the natives must split a piece of wood. This is the first possible meaning. The words may also mean that once having been made and used, the bull-roarer splits and is broken. My informants led me to believe that in this song the term should be translated as I have done.

The pointed antara bush grows by the road.
Its flowers smell foully of urine.
The women sit quietly, playing the oracle game.
They sit still on the ground and hit the leaves.
They sit in one place and hit the leaves.
They tear up the branches of the bushes.
They make a soft ground for the camp.
They blow out the fire.
One woman puts on her headband and walks quietly into the
    scrub.
"Where are you going?"
"I have taken everything I own.
I want to go back to the men."
The other alknarintja beg her not to go.
Her eyes are blurred with tears, but the feeling in her womb draws
    her on.
The others remain, seated about the dead fire.
Their wombs itch.
Their menstrual blood has ceased to flow and their wombs itch.
They sit in a circle.
In one place, without moving, they sit together.

This song contains, as did the previous ones, a description of the immobility of the *alknarintja* and the contrast between it and the over-ripe fertility of their environment. A new element, common to many of the *alknarintja* songs, is introduced in this one. The *alknarintja* are menstruating and therefore unable to have sexual intercourse. At the same time they are extremely excited. As we continue with our presentation and interpretation of the *alknarintja* data, it will be seen that almost every statement made about them is followed almost immediately by its exact opposite. The reason for this will be explained later. The following myth is related to this song.

Two *alknarintja* women lived together at Aningittja-ampingi (Walk-walk-softly). They had a baby.[3] Every day they left the camp to look for food and witchetty grubs. When they returned they erected a big cere-monial pole and performed ceremonies. One day they went to the south-west and found many wichetty grubs in a big tree. They returned to the camp and decorated themselves for the ceremonies. Then they went to another tree and found more grubs. When they returned to the camp they worked on the ceremonial pole. Then they went to the northwest to find more witchetty. When they returned to camp they worked once more on the ceremonial pole. Then they went to hunt for opossums, and when they had found three they went back to the camp where they

---

[3] The impossibility of this statement was not perceived by the informant.

erected several very high ceremonial poles. Then they went to the east
where they found more witchetty. When they returned they made a
short ceremonial pole. Then they went north for more witchetty and
when they returned they performed an *illapangura*. They left again, this
time going south, and when they returned they erected a very high ceremonial pole.

Then they went to the northwest and there they saw men of the
Mosquito and Iwupa Worm totems. These men were in the classificatory
relations of son to their child. One of the men had killed three euros. He
gave two to the women and kept one for himself. The two women
made a camp and the man camped nearby alone. There was a pool between the two camps. The women continued to go out in search of
witchetty grubs and perform ceremonies while the man hunted for
euro. Then the women and the man felt very tired. The women went
right into the earth and a fruit tree marks the spot where they went in.
The man also went right into the earth and a ti tree marks that spot.

4

The myths and the song that follow belong to the tradition of the
Honey Ant totem. The two myths are used in conjunction with the one
song. They are included because they add significantly to our understanding of the latent meaning of the *alknarintja* concept. The song is
sung at the totemic ceremony that forms the last part of the initiation
rites. Ceremonial poles are employed at this ceremony and the men wear
bark vessels on their heads in place of the more customary *tjurunga*. In
accompaniment to the song, the old men and the youths dance, circling
around the ceremonial poles. However, the myths are also connected
with the fertility rite of one class of the totem. Instead of the shields
used in most fertility rites, bark vessels, called *tmara,* are used. This rite
is performed at Ljapa. Only the old men are allowed to witness it. They
sit on the ground and sing. They do not dance in circles around the
ceremonial poles. The song of the old men will be given later.

> Yirramba and the young men walk in a row.
> They walk in a straight line.
> They hear the alputakaputa bird, the familiar of Yirramba, talking.
> Yirramba and the young men make ant holes in the earth.
> On either side of the road they make holes.
> The alputakaputa bird talks again,
> And Yirramba and the young men make more holes.
> Like ants, they creep up to the mulga flowers.
> The leaves of the mulga are dry.
> The young men, the ants, crawl into the mulga bush.
> They have the vessel used for collecting ants.
> The alknarintja women go into the bush with them.

There they erect a ceremonial pole.
The ceremonial pole keeps the alknarintja women from running away.
Their Adam's apples tingle.
Their penises become erect.
They have kept the alknarintja from running away.
The ants scratch the sand.
They throw the sand about.
They make a big noise.
This is the home of the ants.
This is the bark-covered tree in which they live.
Again they make a big noise.
They return to the place from whence they came.
They sit down.
They look like iwupa worms with long eye lashes.
The little holes of the ants' nest are empty.
In the big hole is the tjurunga.
The young men, the ants, carry the tjurunga about with them.
They carry it in their armpits as they hunt for mulga flowers.
Ilpmana, the alknarintja, the mother of the honey ants, goes everywhere with them.
They come to a camp with a fire.
By the great light of this fire they sit down.
They sit down all together in the men's camp.
Their tjurunga are covered with the bark of the root of the mulga.
They carry their tjurunga with them as they wander.
They carry their tjurunga with them as they go right into the earth.
There they find the dry leaves of the mulga.
Ilpmana, the alknarintja, goes right into the earth with them.
The letipa bird, the father and the chief of the honey ants,
He goes to the north with his sons and the alknarintja.
They go away to the north.
They walk in a line.
They walk in a straight row.
Along the Ljapa road they make their camp.
The father and his sons are together.
The alknarintja woman camps apart from them.
They have come a long way along the road.
Now they sit down.
Along the Ljapa road, as they wandered toward Ljapa, they saw the smoke of many campfires.
There were campfires all around them, but far off.
And so they grew sad.
Their tracks in the sand have been hardened by the rain.
They make new holes in the earth.
They throw the sand all about.
They make the little holes of the ants' nest.
They make the holes in a row.

In this song, the realistic and the mythical elements are welded together. The ants are particularly suitable objects for symbolizing the life of the ancestors. The ants dig holes in the earth and live underground, and the ancestors "go right into the earth" and find their eternal resting place under the ground. All the uterine symbols—the holes in the ground, the caves in which the *tjurunga* are stored, the bark vessels in which ants are collected—are used in the song and ritual. Instead of the more customary *tjurunga* worn on the heads of the participants in the rite, bark vessels are used.

Perhaps the most noteworthy feature of the song is the fact that the *alknarintja* woman is the mother of the totem. She partially fulfills the wishes of the sons: she abstains from intercourse with the father. The following myths are related to this song.

Myth A

Yirramba was the greatest chief of a place called Kourpula (Blackhead). The young men who stayed there with him made a big mound of sand and performed totemic ceremonies on it. Then they made another mound of sand, a long one. They left the camp and a short distance away came to a big swamp called Etuna (Sand). They sat down and made a camp. There they performed ceremonies. Then they went and camped at Ipmanapuntja (Ipmana-ceremony) near a big water hole. Then they went to a place in the west called Altuna and finally to a place called Wotta (Swamp). There they decorated themselves and again performed ceremonies. They left Wotta and went to Erkirinja (Sores).

At Erkirinja, Yirramba scratched at the sand all day until he had scratched a round vessel in it. He continued to scratch at the sand as he walked to a place called Arumbia (Clay-pond). He carried the vessel of sand on his head like a *tjurunga* until he came to a second place called Arumbia. Then he and the young men went to a place called Engua (Cave). He went away again, continually scratching at the sand and fashioning it into vessels. He went to another place called Engua where there was another chief of the Honey Ant totem and his young men. The two groups united and performed ceremonies. Yirramba was very white. The other chief and his young men came to see Yirramba and the vessel of sand which he carried on his head. Then the second group went away. Yirramba kept scraping at the sand until he went halfway down into it and came to a place called Ngurra (Place). Then all the young men went into the sand. There was a big camp inside. Then Yirramba went right down into the earth and became a *tjurunga*.

Myth B

Yirramba made a big ceremony in a big camp in a place called Arumbia. The initiates ran around him in the ceremonial dance. Another group came and joined them and they all went to a second place called Arumbia. There was a big ceremony going on there in which ceremonial poles and bark vessels were used. Yirramba and his young men made a cave in which to perform their ceremony. There they stayed and did not wander away. They all became *tjurunga* in a stone and went right into the earth. They descended on their ceremonial spears. The whole group, with their pubic tassels and their bull-roarers, hung onto the ceremonial pole. Wotta was the chief of the place to which they came. He lived under the ground. The sand vessels went right into the earth and they too became *tjurunga*. They are all still there.

These myths are used at a fertility rite as well as during totemic ceremonies. In the former instance, the following song is used with them.

This is the big place where the honey ants are made.
They turn around in the sand.
It rains when the honey ants are made.
And the toadstools grow.

5

I learned the following song and myth from Wapiti. I saw him and his friends perform the ceremony associated with it. Before they began the ceremony, they wound string around a yam stick. They let blood pour from small cuts in their subincision holes onto the string and then affixed charcoal and eagle hawk down to it. They dug a small hole in the ground and let their blood pour into that. Eagle hawk down was placed in the little pool of blood and then a ceremonial pole was stuck in the hole. The pole (or spear) was decorated with the feathers of the night hawk.

Mulda and Ilntjirilka played the roles of the two *alknarintja* women. They wore head rings with *alpita* tassels hanging down about their ears. Their faces were decorated with white paint and eagle hawk feathers. On their chests were painted circles which represented the breasts of the *alknarintja* women. They circled around the ceremonial pole on their knees. They appeared almost to glide. As they crawled, they brushed away the sand with boughs held in their hands. I was told that the ritual represented the *alknarintja* women cleaning themselves after menstruating. The gliding movements were frequently interrupted as the two men got to their feet and ran around the ceremonial pole in the usual ritual manner.[4]

---

[4] This myth, with some difference in detail, was told to Strehlow, probably by the same informant. Cf. Strehlow (1913, Vol. II, p. 44).

Looking out over the vast reaches of the country,
The hawk sings.
The alknarintja women cut their breasts.
On their breasts they make scars.
They slap their thighs.
They strike the ground and the seed bush that grows there.
They walk about, stepping on the hard ground.
They blow their noses.
As they pass the seed bush, they stamp their feet on the ground.
A rat jumps up and frightens them.
They see the white leg of the kangaroo.
They see the kangaroo's leg, the white leg of the kangaroo.
They walk over many hills, past many bushes.
They carry their yam sticks.
Now they are tired.
They sit on the ground.
"My sister has a red string," says one of the women.
"My sister has a red string."
They stand on a sand bank.
The sun is very hot.
A man, sitting at the top of a big tree, watches them.
At Uralpminja they make a camp.
They are menstruating.
Their flanks are wet with blood.
They talk to each other.
They make a bull-roarer.
They split the wood to make this bull-roarer.
The bull-roarer talks.
As the bull-roarer talks, another answers it.
Alas, the bull-roarers have split!
Their sound is louder.
The bull-roarers thunder.
The bull-roarers talk.
One talks from here, the other answers from there.
Alas, they have both split!
The bull-roarer of the woman of the Pigeon totem talks incessantly.
The alknarintja women clean their camp.
They make a hard place on the sand.
They raise dust all about them.
The baby cries and cries.
He walks on all fours.
He walks holding his little stick.
The women don their arm strings.
They throw sand about them.
They sit down.
They are menstruating.
The blood is perpetually flowing.

A tall ilpila tree grows where they sat.
The red string is bad.
The strings are tied cross-wise.
At Uralpminja the alknarintja women make a camp.
There are leaves on the ground.
There are feathers on the ceremonial pole.
    Take them down.
They cut a straight bush.
    Take them down.
They go to the north.
    Take them down.

This song, like the previous ones, contains many of the typical *alknarintja* motifs. Again, there is the ambiguous statement, "The bull-roarer splits." In this song it probably is referable to castration anxiety rather than to the manufacture of the bull-roarer. From the mention of the crying baby, it would appear that the women have conceived and given birth. The sound of the bull-roarer entering into their wombs caused them to conceive. In the myth which is related to this song, the women are again the owners of the bull-roarers. A man is introduced, but the women will have nothing to do with him.

There was a big camp of *alknarintja* women at Uralpminja (Ashes). In the morning they went out of their camp to find seeds, and when they returned they whirled their bull-roarers. One day, when they had returned to the camp, they divided themselves into two groups. One group went to the west and the other went to the east. The leader of the first group was a woman called Mutta (Little-rat). While she was gathering yams, a euro saw her. The euro was frightened and ran away. Then she and her women went back to Uralpminja. From there they went to Aningi-tjampi (Short-ceremonial-spear), where they found other *alknarintja* women who whirled their bull-roarers day and night.

The group that had gone to the east went right down into the earth as they kept whirling their bull-roarers. The strings attached to the bull-roarers were broken as they did this and the bull-roarers flew into the air and landed at Ltalaltuma. The bull-roarer of a woman of the Pigeon totem flew to Aningi-tjampi. There, the women who found it made a ceremonial spear of their yam sticks and whirled the bull-roarer all day long.

A man of the Opossum totem came to their camp and tried to take one of the women, but he could not get her to go with him. He then went to Atunguma (Guts) and found several women there, whom he took to Ipmilkna. The *alknarintja* women at Aningi-tjampi and at Uralpminja became *tjurunga*.

6

The next song and myth were used at the next to the last rite of the initiation ceremony. The uncle of the initiates and all the women of the group dress themselves as *alknarintja*. They wear headbands and arm strings. While the women who have dressed as *alknarintja* act as spectators, the initiates, one by one, climb to the top of a ceremonial pole, and each takes one of the *tjurunga* which is hanging there. They then turn around and climb down very quickly. This maneuver is repeated several times. When the uncle has finished singing the *alknarintja* song, he takes the headbands and the arm strings from the women and gives them to the boys, who wear them from that time on.

> The alknarintja sit with their smoky heads turned away from the man.
> As they stand up, they hold their yam sticks to show that they will not go with him.
> As they sit, they wear their head rings.
> As they stand, they hold their yam sticks.
> They decorate themselves.
> They wear their nose bones.
> They whirl their yam sticks, their bull-roarers.
> Alas, they have split!
> The bull-roarer, the loud singer, splits.
> The yam stick, the long bull-roarer, sings.
> The bull-roarer sings.
> They stand by a tall fig tree.
> The young tree has grown.
> They say, "I won't go with you."
> "I will remain an alknarintja."
> They whirl their bull-roarers.
> They stay where they are.
> They sit very still.
> The man wants them to say, "I will go with you."
> But they remain where they are.
> They hear the bell bird, the messenger of love.
> The bell bird talks.
> The women, the fat lovely women, remain seated.
> They have gathered seeds.
> They rub them in their vaginas.
> They wear their head rings.
> The bull-roarer talks.
> The bull-roarer talks.
> But they sit still and avert their gaze.

Of all the songs that we have seen, this is probably the clearest and easiest to understand. In any myth, an *alknarintja* may be recognized by the fact that she is constantly decorating herself with red ochre, that she wears a head ring with *alpita* and arm strings, and that she is usually associated with water. The bell bird tries to take the women to the men. It appears when an *ilpindja* has been performed. The following myth is associated with this song.

Many women of the Alknarintja totem, who were themselves *alknarintja* and would have nothing to do with men, lived at Ilpila. They belonged to the Purula and Kamara classes. They collected many seeds, but since they had no water with which to prepare them, they were forced to use urine. The next day they again found many seeds and also some guanos and rats. Again they prepared the seeds by urinating on them. This went on for several days.

A man called Patu-walanpa (Hatchetman), a Purula of the Alknarintja totem, decorated himself with a nose bone, a headband, and a white pubic tassel made of the skin of an euro. He saw one of the *alknarintja*. She was a Kamara and a very pretty one, a fine fat woman. His penis immediately became erect. He caught hold of her, knocked her down, and had intercourse with her all day long. Finally, he pulled his penis out of her vagina, sat down in the shade, and went to sleep.

In the morning, the man went to hunt for euro and the women went to gather seeds. In the evening, they all came back to the camp. The man wanted the same woman and he tried to pull her along with him, but she resisted and would not go with him to his camp. The *alknarintja* women had found a soakage. They drank some water and rubbed the seeds that they had found with the water and ate them.

The next day, the *alknarintja* women found some seeds and guanos while the man killed a euro. All that day he had been watching the woman he wanted. Finally, he went over to where the women were standing, took the one whom he wanted by the arm and dragged her off. He pulled her right into her camp and cohabited with her then and there in the presence of all the others. He had intercourse with her all night long until the daylight came.

In the morning, the women went to the east for seeds while the man hunted euros. In the evening, the women returned to the camp with many seeds. Then they climbed a big rock where there were many caves. The man joined them and they all whirled their bull-roarers the whole night long. They erected a big ceremonial pole and fastened their bull-roarers to it. Then they all went into the cave and became *tjurunga*.

This myth and song are particularly significant in that they form a part of a ceremony in which the women participate and in which they are permitted to see *tjurunga*. The women, who represent *alknarintja,* are the owners of the objects which the young men are given as the symbols of their manhood. The fact that the *alknarintja* was the original owner of the bull-roarer and was considered to possess a penis is certainly the determinant here. Whether the participation of the women in the rite is to be considered a survival of an earlier form or the result of the breakthrough of the original idea cannot be ascertained.

7

Many alknarintja women walk about leaning on their yam sticks.[5]
All of them carry their tjurunga with them as they walk about
    leaning on their yam sticks.
Finally, they sit down.
They had passed around a dense scrub carrying their tjurunga on
    their heads.
The yalka grew so thick that they were like a fig tree.
Suddenly the women stand up and divide into two groups.
They shout to one another.
It is raining and very cold.
The women cry because of the cold.
The rain falls.
One old alknarintja woman begins to sink into a boggy place.
She scratches at the earth trying to get out.
She sees a duck as she struggles.
The duck has a big belly.
It sits down near the women.
The smoky-haired alknarintja dig for yalka.

In this myth as in earlier ones, we see the motif of the bushes being so thick and so pressed against each other that they cannot move separately. Again the association with water, this time rain, is present. The duck with the large belly is undoubtedly symbolic of pregnancy, but its exact meaning in this song is difficult to ascertain. In the myth associated with the song, the meaning of certain elements of the song becomes clearer.

In the Tjoritja Aranda country there was a place called Indankangua (Seed-place). Many *alknarintja* women of the Honey Ant totem were staying there. They were of the Paltara and Pananga classes and they had originated there. They gathered indanga seeds and yams which they ground up and ate as soon as they found them. There was a water hole nearby in which a kunia snake lived. In order to find water they set out many times for other places, but they could never get away because

---

[5] *Editor's Note.*—No source was given for this song.

they were surrounded by lakes and there were many swamps in which they got stuck. They would start out, be forced to return, and then start out again in search of another gully. Then there was a big rain which caused a flood. The *alknarintja* women went back to the place where they had originated and became *tjurunga* there. They were all covered by the flood.

It is apparent from the mention of the snake that the rain is symbolic of semen. This would explain the pregnant duck.

8

The following myth and song were told to me by Mulda. They, and another shorter song related to them, are used at the Mbatjiaalkatjuma ceremony. They are performed in order to arouse the participants to the extent that they will have intercourse with anyone present at the ceremony, including those forbidden to them by the kinship regulations. The men taking part in the ceremony rub little stones against a rock and "sing" them:

Lumps in the flesh of he who cohabits wrong.
He who cohabits wrong.

Porcupine grass is stuck into a rock by a man who then kneels and goes through the motions of coitus with the rock. The rock is called the Iwinjiwinji (Mosquito) rock. This rite is also performed as part of the Nankura ceremony.

The ground is cool.
The ground is cool where the alknarintja sit.
A feeling in their wombs had drawn them on toward their eternal
    camp.
Now they know that they are at the right spot.
They know because of the feeling in their wombs.
They walked all in a row and saw a "beautiful man."
The women tremble with desire for him.
The ground is cool.
A breeze blows.
But the alknarintja, the committers of incest, tremble with desire
    for the man.
They are hot with desire even while the cool wind blows over
    them.
Their wombs tremble, these committers of incest!
They cannot sleep.
They lie awake and think of the man.

O the man of the Mosquito totem!
O the man on the road!
Now the women and the man go right down into the earth.
They become tjurunga.

The "feeling in their wombs" which drew them on was caused by the *ilpindja* which the "beautiful man" had performed for them. The magic drew them to the spot where the man waited. Instead of the coitus which usually follows the performance of an *ilpindja,* the man and the women "go right down into the earth" and join the ancestors.

A man of the Mosquito totem, from a place called Pangatuma (Hit-dry-grass), went to a place called Akantjirkni (Ceremonial-pole) where he erected a ceremonial pole. Then he went to Yutarinda (Porcupine-grass-sleep). There he made a windbreak of porcupine grass and went to sleep. From this place he went to a place called Inimba (Semen). There he saw two *alknarintja* women. He was urinating as he watched them and his semen came out.

One of the women stood in the relationship of wife to him and the other in the relationship of mother-in-law. He followed the urine and their track until he returned to Pangatuma. There he found an empty camp. He picked up their track again and followed it until he came to a water hole called Tulpurta (Salty-ground). From there he tracked the two women to Ngunmurkna (Gum) and then to Indutakungura (Normal-healthy-place). There he found them.

He was a normal healthy man. He had intercourse with both of them, first with the woman who stood in the relationship of wife and then with the woman who stood in the relationship of mother-in-law. Then they all went to Aningu-tjampi (Walk-step) and from there to Itjititjita (Bush) and finally to Iwinjiwinji (Mosquito). Then they all became *tjurunga.*

9

This song and myth which follow are part of the ceremonial rites of the Allaparindja totem. They were related to me by Old Yirramba whose father's mother belonged to the Allaparindja totem. The women referred to are often called *labarindja* women. I was told by my informants that a *labarindja* is a real woman who is "wild," i.e., who refuses to have anything to do with men. They are described as having blue skins and smoky-colored hair which are the characteristic features of the *alknarintja*. However, the *labarindja* are also considered demons. Old Yirramba told me that if a man had intercourse with a *labarindja* woman he might die because the *labarindja* have evil magic in their vaginas.

The ceremony in which the song and myth are used consists of the usual dancing and singing. The old man who represents the *labarindja* in the ceremony dresses like the woman in the myth.

> The Allaparindja women sit on the gravel, on the hot ashes.
> They sit very still on the hot ashes.
> Their vaginas look black.
> Their vaginas look black.
> They wear the feathers of the black cockatoo.
> They are shy.
> They say, "We two are shy."
> They put their seeds into their vaginas.
> They put their seeds into their vaginas.
> They are fat seeds, good seeds.
> The women sit down.
> Their vaginas are pointed to the labia.[6]
> They play with two little sticks.
> They strike them together.
> "We hit them," they say.

It is obvious that the *labarindja* have most of the attributes of the *alknarintja*. My informants considered the most important characteristic of the *labarindja* the fact that after having coitus with them a man was sure to die. At the beginning of this chapter we mentioned that there is a tendency to regard every young girl as an *alknarintja*. A conclusion may be drawn that the Central Australians regard coitus as an extremely dangerous and anxiety-provoking act. In the song, the women's movements are at a minimum. In the myth, they are constantly moving.

Two *Allaparindja* women of the Kamara class originated at Ljalapuntja (Gravel-place). They both had big *tjurunga* on their heads and strings around their necks. One of them was called Allaparindja and the other was called Naierambuma (Red-tail-feather-of-the-cockatoo). From Ljalapuntja they went to Indora (Hot). There they ground seeds. Then they went to Ljipa (String). There they made string. Then they went to Kultjinanga (Arm-string). There they made arm strings. From there they went to Ipija (Rock-hole) and from there to Ndadaquarinja (Round-hill). From there they went to Ikundja Creek and then to Arata (Arata-bush). There they made a long string and then climbed a big hill at Kwalpa (Sand-wallaby). After that they went to Itarka (Itarka-bush) and then to Yuta (Porcupine-grass). There they gathered eagle hawk down and decorated themselves. They had a great deal of string with them. They

---

[6] A term of opprobrium.

had many *tjurunga*. They sat on the ground close together. Then they all went right into the earth and became *tjurunga*.

Strehlow (1913, Vol. I, pp. 28-29; Vol. III, Part I, p. 117) has recorded several *alknarintja* myths and songs which are similar to the ones related here.

3.   THE MEANING OF THE *Alknarintja* CONCEPT

It would appear that originally each totem had its own *alknarintja,* that all the women of the totem were the *alknarintja*. First, and most important, the *alknarintja* is a representative of the mother imago. The "eyes-turn-away-woman" is the mother who resists the demands of her son. She is also the person who originally owned the *tjurunga*. The *tjurunga* is a symbolic penis. The mythological *alknarintja* owned the *tjurunga* and then gave them to the men. In the initiation rites, men or women representing *alknarintja* give the symbols of manhood to the initiates.

The Central Australian women sleep on top of their small sons in a position that was described to me as being like that of a man lying on top of a woman during coitus. Anuinga told me several of her dreams. In one of them, two men sneaked up behind her. They were carrying axes. She was so frightened that she awoke. She fell asleep once more and had the same dream which again awakened her. Although she was very frightened, she did not move, but went to sleep again on top of her small son. Nyiki, her son, was one of the children who dreamed of a female demon with a penis. It is not difficult to recognize Anuinga, his mother, in his dream. The position of the woman on top of the man is greatly feared by the Central Australians. They state that the woman might break the man's penis by sitting on top of it. The old men counsel the young men to make every effort to awaken if they dream of an *alknarintja* for she might attempt to get on top of them and have intercourse. Were this to happen, either the penis would break, or they would die.

The *alknarintja* is the phallic mother, the mother with a penis. The small boys must frequently have erections when their mothers sleep on top of them. However, the penis is attributed to the mother, for has she not taken the masculine position? Not only is the *alknarintja* the phallic mother, she is also the castrator of men. She appears to be avid to regain the penis which she gave up, the *tjurunga* which she gave to the men. It is just this object which is used in wooing the *alknarintja* and all other women. The *namatuna*, the small bull-roarer, calls the women to the men. When the sound of the bull-roarer enters into the womb of a woman, she conceives, and so the *alknarintja* is also the pregnant mother. Pregnant women are the only ones who are allowed to cohabit in the inverted position.

In myths, the *alknarintja* is pictured in two diametrically opposed ways. She is either sitting absolutely still and refusing to move, or she is in rapid motion, rushing toward the man who has bewitched her. The immobile *alknarintja* is the result of two constellations of ideas. She is the mother who resists the demands of her son. But she is also the fulfillment of one of the son's wishes. She is also resisting the demands of the father by refusing to move. Perhaps the best example of this is the *alknarintja* myth of the Honey Ant totem. In this way, the *alknarintja* becomes the virgin mother. The second picture of the *alknarintja*, that of her in rapid motion, is also the result of two constellations of ideas. She is the mother as she was observed by the son during the primal scene. The rapid motion is that of coitus. This picture of the *alknarintja* also represents a fulfillment of one of the son's wishes. She is the woman rushing toward him in a highly excited state because he has won her through his magic.

The *alknarintja* is frequently represented as menstruating copiously. It would at first appear that this is another instance of the *alknarintja's* resistance to men, since a menstruating woman must refuse to have intercourse. On the other hand, she is also pictured as having a copious vaginal discharge and as urinating profusely. These last two are regarded as signs of great sexual excitement. This seeming contradiction can be resolved by the realization that the *alknarintja* as a menstruating woman is a primary love and anxiety object in Daly's sense.

The bull-roarer is the symbol of the penis which was once owned by the *alknarintja*. The swinging of the bull-roarer is like the sexual pulsation, and indeed we find the same sort of symbolism in the dreams of American and European patients. The rapid motion of the *alknarintja* toward the men also represents coitus. When the bull-roarer is swung in the performance of the *ilpindja*, it is done so in the magical belief that like will produce like. This is an instance of magic by analogy.

The natives of the Cape York peninsula have several kinds of bull-roarers. One represents a young girl just prior to the age of puberty, and the other, a fully mature young woman. The former corresponds to the *namatuna* (the small bull-roarer) and the latter corresponds to the *tjurunga mborka* (the large or "body" *tjurunga*) of the Central Australians. They are presented to the boys at different stages of the initiation rite. The mythology associated with these bull-roarers is similar to that of the Central Australians. The bull-roarers are believed to be a husband and wife and are supposed to represent the inside of the genitals (Mc-Connel, 1935). The bull-roarer was originally the property of the women because it is symbolic of the girl herself. "The bequeathing of the bull-roarer at the beginning of time for the men to swing is subtly symbolic of the yielding by the woman of herself to a man as also of man's interest in what 'belongs to her.'" "The swinging of the bull-roarer appears to symbolize the interest of the girls in a sex relationship which is as yet forbidden."

If the above is true, then we can understand why the women are not permitted to see or touch the bull-roarer. Sexual desire, the rhythmic swinging of the bull-roarer, is considered male and the women are therefore forbidden to see or touch it or the glans penis.

Among the Aranda, an old woman is called a "woman father." From the infantile point of view, there is an element of maleness in the concept of mother. Such things as the inverted Oedipus complex and castration anxiety are universal human features. The unconscious determinants of the behavior of Central Australian males and their unconscious fantasies, which we have pointed up in this chapter as being specifically Central Australian, take their origin in a particular infantile trauma—that of the male child sleeping under his mother. Such a custom must go far to strengthen the negative or inverted oedipal attitude of the adult male, and it is this custom which is specifically at the basis of the mythology of the *alknarintja*.

BIBLIOGRAPHY

McConnel, U. H. (1935), Myths of the Wilmunkan and Niknatara Tribes. *Oceania*, *6*:68, 69, 70, 72.
Spencer, B. & Gillen, F. J. (1927), *The Arunta, II*. London: Macmillan.
Strehlow, C. (1913), *Die Aranda- und Loritjastämme*. Frankfurt: Baer.

EGO AND ORALITY IN THE ANALYSIS OF WEST AFRICANS

PAUL PARIN and FRITZ MORGENTHALER

The authors studied thirteen normal adults of the Dogon people in Mali. The primary aim of the investigation was to learn about the psychodynamics and the psychic structure of these individuals, rather than to generalize about the personality of the Dogon or of West Africans. A secondary purpose of the study was to evaluate the appropriateness of the psychoanalytic technique as a tool in understanding the inner life of people living in a traditional West African society.

Our preliminary studies of the Dogon culture were based on the ethnological and sociological publications of Marcel Griaule, his collaborators and successors (Palau-Marti, 1957). The interviews were conducted in French since many Dogon of traditional manners and customs attended French primary schools (managed by African schoolmasters) which were erected in some villages thirty to fifty years ago.

Our technique was, so far as possible, the usual psychoanalytic one. The investigation was interrupted after twenty to forty sessions, at a time too short for the establishment of a firm transference-neurosis.[1] We derived our findings mainly from the resistances and from the transference reactions which were provoked by our interpretations.

This paper summarizes some results of the investigation. The case histories (expanded by the results of one hundred Rorschach tests) and the discussion of them in the frame of the anthropological background has been published recently (Parin et al., 1963). The following abstract is to be understood as a reconstruction such as occurs in an analysis intended to further psychoanalytic views about the connection between ego functions and the vicissitudes of the instinctual drives.

Presented at the twenty-third International Psychoanalytical Congress in Stockholm, July 1963.

[1] Whether psychoanalytically conducted sessions interrupted after twenty to forty sessions may be called psychoanalysis is not relevant to this paper.

Some characteristics of the "normal" ego of the Dogon would, if encountered in Europeans, be incompatible with clinical normality. The Dogon ego oscillates between one form of gratification and another. It is capable of simultaneously admitting instinctual demands which stem from different stages of the development of the instincts, with neither anxiety nor inhibitions. There are no signs of disintegration. Judging by the stage of development of the various admissible instinctual urges, we would have to speak of a tendency toward total regression. Owing to the reversibility of the process and because the total personality involved in it remains intact, it is better to say that this ego displays a high degree of flexibility. The relationship to objects is also alternating: sometimes one object is exchanged for another, at other times the relationship to one and the same person is altered. In particular, different readily distinguishable forms of identificatory relationships can replace one another, the Dogon having at their disposal a copious repertory of well-developed modal identifications.

We derive these ego characteristics from the evolution of the instinctual strivings out of the oral stage. Oral urges undergo an extraordinary differentiation and gain admittance into the ego of the adult.

We will shortly describe some facts of Dogon infancy and childhood, laying stress on these events necessary for the understanding of the inner life of all thirteen adults. These events lead to inner experiences which shape an integral part of the psychological make-up of the Dogon.

The Dogon mother, as a rule, nurses her child until around the end of its third year. During this time it enjoys an immediate gratification of all wishes which the mother can satisfy. The child never has to wait for nourishment: it is nursed the instant it expresses the slightest discomfort; at night it can suckle whenever it likes. The mother never leaves the child alone for a single moment. In the daytime she carries it naked, bound to her by a cloth, on her naked back. The child shares all the mother's movements and accompanies her to work and to dance. At night it lies in her arms. It sometimes happens that the mother hands the child over for some minutes or hours to another woman, who gives it exactly the same treatment. The child is never laid down alone; after its first attempts to walk it is picked up again every time.

The mother observes strict sexual continence until the child is weaned. She is thus all the more emotionally bound to the child. The Dogon maintain that a child would never put up with being weaned, and thus separated from the mother, and at the same time experiencing the arrival of a brother or sister.

During the nursing period there is no sort of discipline or training, no alternation between the mother's demonstrations of love and her withdrawals of interest. Her behavior is not characterized by granting and refusing, but rather by unconditioned yielding to the child's demands.

The child is not trained in cleanliness by the mother. Sphincter mastery is learned later by imitation of older playmates, with no sort of compulsion being involved.

The child is weaned abruptly. It is left alone with its group of companions, seldom taken up on the mother's back again, and eats and sleeps with a troop of playmates of the same age or older. It is in this community that it remains.

As the children grow older separate groups of boys and girls are formed. The adults of the same sex in the whole consanguinity, beginning with the elder brothers or sisters, constitute an ascending hierarchy of "parental" authorities, with the actual parents playing a leading role. The disciplinary functions of upbringing are exercised by all older persons.

It is in this context that oral strivings mature. The urge to appropriate is often mitigated by the wish to distribute. Against the cessation of a gratification there is mobilized the tendency to substitute any other gratification at hand. The mitigation and aim inhibition of the instinctual demands from the oral stage appear to be facilitated by kinesthetic and tactile experiences. Working together and participating in communal singing and dancing pacify these urges, which during the long nursing period were linked with other oral demands. Greed or envy hardly ever appear in the behavior of adults.

The primary omnipotence on the part of the child is obviously not surrendered, as among Europeans, to the mother. The child acquires the mastery of inner and outer stimuli in unison with her: it shares its omnipotence with her. Later in life self-esteem does not depend so much on the independence of the individual, or on the harmony of the ego with internalized demands in the superego. Close integration with a group, communal rhythmic movements, and communal eating and drinking reconstitute self-esteem, should it be shaken.

Imminent loss of an object leads to depressive feelings of loss and forlornness. If an object is lost it may be easily replaced by another one. It seems that separation anxiety is experienced relatively late and that experiences of primary anxiety are less traumatic than ours. Adults have no pronounced tendency toward anxiety in connection with physical threats. But they experience castration anxiety provoked by the oedipal conflict as a fear of being neglected or abandoned by the sexual partner.

It is impossible to prove the existence among these people of the experience of defiantly confronting an object, of feeling cut off from it, which we inherit from our experience of the sado-anal stage. Hostility does not separate. It does not have to be internalized in order to spare the loved object. Love and hate can be directed concurrently to the same object. This ambivalence generates but slight tension.

The Dogon appear to preserve all the possibilities of oral gratification for the phallic stage of development. What is most striking is the very slight fusion of these urges with aggressiveness. Since the anal fixations as well are lacking, aggressiveness is not internalized. Rather there is no separation from objects.

These circumstances exert a great influence on further development, having such an influence on ego formation that they not only apply to the child at the beginning of the phallic stage but, as it were, can be detected unaltered in the oral characteristics of the ego of adults. In this connection, however, the Dogon lack other features which we should otherwise rightly expect in the case of oral fixations. They do not suffer from "primary guilt feelings" and have but a slight tendency toward anxiety. To be sure, they easily project their emergent fears onto the external world, but they are capable of quickly retracting these projections, in that their ego orients differently to objects and that anxiety-laden objects are easily exchanged for reassuring ones.

To understand how the Dogon manage the oedipal conflict, which for them as for us is inevitable as soon as the phallic demands of the boy are directed toward the mother, we should recall a peculiarity which Freud (1905) ascribed to the ancient Greeks: instead of, like us, warding off the impulse, they exalted it even when it was returned toward an unworthy object.

The Dogon do not experience their incest demand as we do, with an anally-influenced desire to possess the mother and to kill the father. The conflict refers more to the incestuous object than to the instinctual demand. They demand that the mother not turn away and they wish to obtain further gratification from her. At the stage of oral regression an exchange of one gratifying object for another is possible. The way has already been prepared for the capacity to make such an exchange in the experiences of the nursing period. Among Europeans, incestuous love develops in accordance with the object-oriented type. We expect gratification from the exclusive possession of the desired object. Every other gratification of urges has been frustrated by premature weaning. The confrontation with the disciplinary mother in the anal stage has confirmed the first refusal and warding off of impulses and strengthened the fixation on the object.

Owing to the fact that among the Dogon the oedipal conflicts often coincide with the period of weaning, the shifting of castration anxiety onto the mother is facilitated. Later in life the Dogon man fears that his wife will leave him (or that he will have no children from her), if incestuous demands are mobilized. The castration anxiety then is, at least in part, lived out at the oral level.

This account neglects not only the significance of phallic-narcissistic wishes but also the role played by the father. The father is felt to be the rival for the phallic-aggressive urges. The sadistic wish to kill the father, however, does not appear as it does among Europeans. Rather there emerges the wish to incorporate the father, to devour him (or to be merged in him), to be devoured by him.

The conflict with the father is experienced in an "oral" way. Passivity and activity rapidly alternate. Devouring and being devoured are, again, less object-bound, not fixated on the nonpermissive authority figure. The outcome of this struggle is not the permanent introjection of an aggression-laden object. What emerges, rather, is a readiness to identify with partners of the same sex, a readiness which is maintained throughout life.

There is no doubt that in the oedipal conflicts lasting ego modifications are acquired. The opportunity offered to the child and the youth to integrate on a basis of identification with shifting but firmly organized social groups leads to the moulding of these ego modifications into several characteristic modes or forms of identificatory relationships. A Dogon can simply feel like a comrade of all those of his age and sex who were circumcised at the same time. Or, he can be integrated in the hierarchical line of his younger and elder brothers, extending up to the fathers and the dead ancestors of the whole people, he himself being subordinated to his elders and ranking above those younger than himself. A description of these and still other possibilities of identifying that are available to the adult Dogon would far exceed the scope of this paper.

We should like to stress what all these ego modifications have in common. Above all, they are always identificatory relationships to several (at least two) persons, and generally to an entire group. The tendency to identify is from childhood on the basis for the eminent capacity for social cohesion possessed by the Dogon people. It is probably based on the experience of the ego of entering into alternating identifications with the aggressor in the face of the oedipal threat. This becomes clear in the subordination to the elder brother and the simultaneous authority over the younger brother. Adult Dogon behave as if they had gone through the positive and the negative outcomes of the oedipus conflict concurrently, the former to be sure, without sadism, the latter without any anal or masochistic development.

For the Dogon, identification is not merely a means of social integration. It replaces or accompanies the most important possibilities open to the adult to gratify his urges. For this reason we can speak of identificatory relationships just as Freud regarded identification as a preliminary stage of object relationship on the genital level. Many of these relationships, as follows from their origin, have as their inherent character mutual incorporation, and this is much more clearly evident than it is among normal Europeans. All of them, however, lead to a state of placidity and repose only if instinctual demands were wholly neutralized.

The ego of the Dogon can come to terms with mature oral instinctual demands without experiencing guilt or anxiety. With this inherent safety factor their ego can adapt to various other instinctual demands. It remains elastic and flexible. However, it is also quite dependent on the attitude of all the partners. Without them it can orient itself only with difficulty and easily loses all hope of gratification. It functions as a group ego.

BIBLIOGRAPHY

Freud, S. (1905), *Drei Abhandlungen zur Sexualtheorie*. London: Imago, 1949 (Footnote p. 48.)
Palau-Marti, Monserrat (1957), *Les Dogon*. Paris: Presses Universitaires de France. (Contains a complete bibliography of the Dogon up to 1957.)
Parin, P., Morgenthaler, F., & Parin-Matthèy, G. (1963), *Die Weissen denken zuviel*. Zurich: Atlantis. (Psychoanalytic studies with the Dogon in West Africa.)

PSYCHOLOGICAL PROBLEMS OF A GROUP OF APACHES: ALCOHOLIC HALLUCINOSIS AND LATENT HOMOSEXUALITY AMONG TYPICAL MEN

L. BRYCE BOYER, M.D.

In this communication will be illustrated some aspects of the relationships between institutionalized trauma and personality development as observed in a transitional, reservation-bound tribe of American Indians. A summary of relevant data pertaining to aboriginal and current social structure and socialization processes will demonstrate that (1) in previous times the groups which amalgamated to form the observed tribe reared

Principal Investigator, Project for Field Research in Anthropo-Psychoanalytic Techniques, Department of Anthropology, University of New Mexico.

The research which made this communication possible was partially supported by National Institute of Mental Health Grants M-2013 and M-3088.

During the summer of 1958, Dr. David M. Schneider and I were assisted by Dr. Ruth M. Boyer (Grant M-2013). We conducted a preliminary survey to determine whether conjoint anthropological and psychoanalytic work was feasible on the Mescalero Indian Reservation. Dr. Harry W. Basehart and I were assisted in the field by Dr. Ruth M. Boyer and Dr. Bruce B. MacLachlan for fourteen months of 1959 and 1960. The purpose of our investigation was to study the interactions of social structure, socialization processes, and personality. Dr. Ruth M. Boyer and I spent two additional months in the field in 1961. Basehart and the Boyers will continue collaborative work for the next few years (Grant M-3088).

I am indebted to many individuals who have discussed various aspects of the material incorporated into this manuscript and its possible meanings. Drs. Edward C. Adams, Sidney Axelrad, and Harry W. Basehart, Dr. and Mrs. Peter Blos, Drs. David Beres, Charles B. David and Ruth M. Boyer, Mrs. Marjorie Leonard, and Drs. Anna Maenchen and Hilda S. Rollman-Branch have read various versions of the communication and offered most helpful suggestions and criticisms. I am particularly grateful to them. However, I am ultimately responsible for the presentation, hypotheses and conclusions and whatever deficiencies exist in them. I wish also to express my deep appreciation to Mrs. Rosalyn Olguín, whose patient, devoted and uncomplaining secretarial and stenographic assistance has been of great help.

their children formally and informally in such manners that specific personality problems resulted and sanctioned means were provided for the discharge of attendant anxieties, whereas (2) the present-day tribes continue to rear their children in such ways that the same problems exist but there are only very inconsistent avenues for anxiety discharge. Special attention will be focused on two manifestations of Apache personality problems, (1) the high occurrence of alcoholic hallucinosis among adults and (2) the prevalence of latent, passive homosexual yearnings among men.

Kardiner (1939, 1945) focalized the viewpoint that personality patterns were to be found among societies which could be considered typical for the group, and Gladwin and Sarason (1953) noted that the personality structure of the "typical" member of a group often coincides with patterns which have come to be known in Western psychiatric conceptualizations as diagnostic of personality disorders. Among the Apaches of the Mescalero Indian Reservation, the preponderance of individuals exhibit a constellation of characteristics matching a syndrome which would be named character disorder among members of a Western culture. Their psychopathological state corresponds to a combination of the hysterical and impulse personality disorders (L. B. Boyer, 1961, 1962; Klopfer & Boyer, 1961) and they have a proclivity to develop schizophreniform psychoses.

During their infancies, they are most inconsistently cared for by mother figures who are largely psychologically unrelated, and the differentiation of id and ego is stunted. When they are between eighteen and twenty-four months old, they are abruptly and grossly displaced by new babies and their regressive reactions to psychological abandonment are handled in such manners that primitive defensive mechanisms are supported, even institutionalized. Throughout their childhoods, they are subjected to repeated observations of overt sexual behavior of adults, actions which are associated with brutal physical expressions of hostility. They are reared in an environment in which males are nominal leaders but women are obviously dominant in family relations. At least the male children leave the oedipal situation with a negative orientation and few are able to resolve oedipal problems in such a manner that they emerge with a clear masculine identity. The present-day society does not provide unambiguous masculine roles to which the boy can aspire. The adult roles which girls are trained to fulfill are more clearly defined, and females have less difficulty in establishing a sexual identity. The Apache goes through life with an essential attitude in which the world is (at least) unconsciously perceived as a breast and the usual male has strong, latent, passive homosexual yearnings. He distorts his oral dependency into pseudogenital terms.

In this paper, case material obtained in psychoanalytically oriented investigative interviews with two typical young men who suffered from alcoholic hallucinosis will be supplemented by data obtained through standard anthropological techniques. There are two reasons for inclusion of the latter material: (1) The history of a group in which an individual is reared and his total environment provide elements which are introjected to determine his attitudes, conceptualizations and behavior, or, as Cohen (1961, pp. 11-39) and Henry (1936) have indicated, the personality of an individual cannot be understood apart from the social structure in which it has its being. (2) Because of the brevity of contact I had with the two men who provided the clinical data, it was not possible to learn from their individual case histories information which is relevant to the arguments of this essay. The supplemental data will serve the purpose of illustrating some of the phenomena which surround the socialization of typical modern Apaches.

No implication is intended that all Apache families consist of individuals designated under the rubric "typical." However, some of the elements of the changing social structure and organization have provided common heritage and environment for all of the Apaches. The socialization processes have been carefully studied and are surprisingly uniform (R. M. Boyer, 1962, pp. 199-366). Thus, in addition to their commonality of broad environmental background, most Apache babies grow up in a family situation such as will be depicted below.

SETTING

Rather more information is presented here concerning the history and aboriginal and modern social structure and socialization processes than is strictly necessary for the theses of this paper. This course has been chosen because, when shorter versions have been presented, audiences have requested such data, and they are not readily available in the anthropological literature. The relevant writings are unpublished, printed in obscure books and journals, or to be found only in large, specialized libraries.

It should be remembered that growing children are regularly deeply affected by the givens of the environment within which they are reared. Their everyday observations, perceived through all sensory channels, serve to shape their psychological development. The material which follows illustrates the main elements that combine to shape the environment of Apache children.

Perhaps ten centuries ago, groups of hunting, gathering, and raiding nomadic Indians who spoke the language stock known as Southern Athabaskan (Hoijer, 1938) migrated southward from northwestern Canada (Boas, 1911; Hall, 1944; Huscher and Huscher, 1942; Kluckhohn & Leighton, 1946, p. 3; Worcester, 1947). During the ensuing seven hundred years or so, the assemblage divided (Shepardson, 1961); one portion was influenced by the sedentary Pueblos and became the Navaho, while the other continued their earlier pattern of living and became the Apache, who have been popularized in so much fictional and objective literature (Albert, 1957; Betzinez with Nye, 1959; Burnett, 1956; Calhoun, 1849; A. Davis, 1929; Forster, 1958; Lummis, 1952; Santee, 1956; Sonnichsen, 1958), and by television programs. Of them, Cremony (1868, p. 203) wrote: "In point of intellect, in cunning and duplicity, in warlike skill and untiring energy, in tenacity of purpose and wondrous powers of endurance, [they] have no equals among the existing Indians in North America." Schwatka (1887, p. 42) and Chittenden were awed by the ability of the Apache to humiliate the governments of Mexico and the United States; the latter wrote (1902, p. 883): "In their whole career of more than two centuries, the Spanish and Republican governments . . . seem to have existed only by their sufferance."

The Apache gradually formed a number of tribes, which claimed large, overlapping areas of land for their food pursuits. The principal hub of activity of the Mescalero Apache was in recorded aboriginal times in the area of the present reservation, south central New Mexico. The Lipan, who roamed from northern New Mexico and Colorado apparently separated from the Jicarilla and Kiowa Apaches some three hundred years ago, were driven into Texas and northern Mexico, primarily by the Comanche, and, to a lesser extent, the Kickapoo. Encounters with Mexicans and the United States military and settlers completed their destruction as functioning groups. The few known living remnants of the Northern Lipan became associated with the Mescalero in 1863 and the nineteen known members of the Southern Lipan trekked to Mescalero at the turn of the century. The Chiricahua, whose activities radiated from southeastern Arizona, were taken as prisoners of war by the United States soldiery in 1886, following the capitulation of Geronimo, and removed to camps, first in Florida, then in Alabama, and finally, in 1894, in Oklahoma. In 1913, the majority of the Chiricahua were moved to the Mescalero

Indian Reservation (Basehart, 1959, 1960; R. M. Boyer, 1962; Kunstadter, 1960; M. E. Opler, 1933, 1955; Opler & Opler, 1950; Sjoberg, 1953; Thomas, 1959, 1959a, 1959b).

In the past, Apache children were systematically informed of their tribal heritages and lore. Particularly during the cold months, family units gathered around the campfire and were regaled by group elders with stories, legends, and myths. Although this practice has grossly deteriorated and many children have not been thus formally instructed, they have heard the gossip, distortions, and complaints of older generations and are aware of the fierce independence of the aboriginals and the treatment to which they were subjected by whites. Hostility toward the *indâh*, a word which means both white man and enemy, is ingrained within them. However, they know, too, of the humiliating defeat of their forebears and the dissolution of ancient tribal ways resultant from contacts with their mortal enemies. They fear, respect, and envy the prospering Caucasian, reflecting attitudes of their parents.

The reservation was established in 1873 and occupies some 461,000 acres of pine forests and grazing land ranging in altitude from 6,000 to 12,000 feet. The three groups which comprise the major stocks of the Apache Tribe of the Mescalero Indian Reservation are the Mescalero, Chiricahua and Lipan (L. B. Boyer, 1962, Appendix I). They number some 1200 individuals. Although they retain some affiliation with their original ethnic groups, all usually call themselves Mescalero and they share the obligations and privileges of a single tribal membership. All but the very old and the very young speak at least both Apache and English. Although tribal dialects vary, they are mutually comprehensible.

Much more is known concerning the aboriginal social structure and organization of the Mescalero and the Chiricahua than the Lipan. From the standpoint of the present study, however, a knowledge of the old ways of the Lipans is not necessary. They had disappeared for practical purposes by the time the Lipan joined the Mescalero and the actual number of Lipan Apaches on the reservation is very small. Basehart (1959, 1960) has collected what information is available concerning the subsistence patterns and sociopolitical organization of the aboriginal Mescalero and Chiricahua. Although differences were demonstrated by his studies, there are similarities sufficiently great so that certain blanket statements concerning both are valid. It should be remembered that the social organization of the Chiricahua was grossly disrupted by their having been systematically subjected to total, near-idle dependency upon the government of the United States; although the tribal government and

economic patterns of the Mescalero were less abruptly destroyed, their
confinement to a reservation which was very small compared to their
former living area resulted in great changes in their previous ways.

In the old days, kinship was reckoned bilaterally, and the significant
kinship unit was composed of the matrilocal extended family. The majority of marriages began with a period of initial residence with the
wife's parents. After the birth of several children, the married pair were
free to go where they chose (Basehart, 1960, p. 112). Sociopolitical organization was influenced strongly by the necessity for mobility stemming
from subsistence practices. The largest solidary group conceptualized
was the tribe. The greatest concrete political unit centered about a
particular male leader. He and his followers formed a "band." Basehart
(1960, p. 118) wrote: "A relative group of the leader formed the nucleus
of each band; in consequence, the proportion of relatives in a band was a
function of the size of the group." The distribution of resources and
variations of climate favored regular seasonal movements. To quote
Basehart further (1960, p. 10): "The subsistence pattern appears to
represent a balance between hunting and collecting. However, the most
dependable and consistent contribution was provided by the collecting
activities of the women." The men and older boys who had proved themselves sometimes left old people, women, and children in the camps
while they hunted or raided. They were occasionally gone for weeks or
months, as when they travelled to the Plains to seek bison (although, at
times, the entire band moved to the Plains for this purpose), or raided
deep into Mexico, on horseback or foot. Despite the importance of the
bands, Basehart (1960, p. 104), wrote

> . . . no Mescalero was committed to a permanent affiliation with a
> specific group; he could go where he liked, becoming a member of
> another leader's group or not, as he chose. Nor was any Mescalero
> bound to any particular territory.

The Mescalero placed a high value on movement as such. According
to Basehart (1960, p. 105):

> Gukeiya, "our country," was "our country" equally for all; in
> terms of the jural norms of the society, trespass was meaningless
> where members of the tribe were concerned. The only rules in
> this connection were rules of politeness, but if they were trans-
> gressed, the offenders were subject to no physical sanctions. Gossip
> and the weight of public opinion, however, were potent incentives
> for proper behavior.

The leaders, while respected, had no definite authority over members of a band. A follower went on a hunting party or a raid if he thought the journey wise and, once with the group which was travelling, was free to turn away if he decided to do so. Leaders exerted influence with their exhortations, but they may have been astute individuals who listened carefully to group opinions and then advised action which accorded with majority sentiment. The band, when camped together, was an important economic group. There was much emphasis on cooperation in production. For such endeavors as the bison hunt, groups from several bands would at times collaborate. Subsistence products circulated throughout the band. Various family units became linked through a network of mutual economic obligations.

Little appears to be known concerning Apache farming during pre-reservation days (Basehart, 1960, p. 58; Castetter and Opler, 1937; Kunstadter, 1960, pp. 98ff). Just before the Mescalero were conquered, there was harvesting of stick-planted corn, squash and beans in a few isolated areas. Essentially, the Apaches appear to have scorned farming as being suitable only for the sedentary Mexicans or women (Betzinez, 1959). They have remained uninterested in tilling the soil and have not responded to continuous inducements by the government to this day. A few family gardens exist, but the sole commercial crop is alfalfa, which is bought by the Cattle Growers' Association.

The principles related to herding were not understood by the roving Apache (Kunstadter, 1960, pp. 100-101, 196-205, 634-636). The government abandoned its effort to train them to become cattle herders by 1897 and then was successful in persuading some few families to raise sheep and goats. However, in the early 1930's, cattle were reintroduced. At present, the tribe claims some cattle and others are owned by individuals. Stock is raised and sold by a Cattle Growers' Association, composed of cattle owners. A hired white outsider supervises operations. Individual Apache owners have nothing to do with the actual work involved, although they may be hired. They receive checks from cattle sales.

While depicting the anomie of the Sioux, Erikson (1945; 1959, p. 21) indicated that their historical group identity as romantic bison hunters stood counterposed to the occupational and class identity of the American civil service employee. The historical group identity of the Apaches, still retained by individuals of the older two (and in some instances three) generations, is that of the hunter, warrior, and raider. A masculine model of the Apache man during late aboriginal days was that of horseman. Skilled equestrians have been admired throughout reservation times. A major social event has been the rodeo. Until recent years, two rodeos were held on the reservation each year and competition among Indian riders was keen. However, outside participants have usually won most of the awards. Apache contestants seldom participated in rodeos sponsored off the reservation. The games and fantasies of boys frequently illustrate their hope that they will become expert horsemen. The only practical application for their aspiration nowadays is to become cowboys, but this potential life goal must be thwarted. Almost the sole occupational use for the role of skilled cowboy is working for the Cattle Growers' Association, since the Mescalero thus far have been almost totally unable to adjust to life off the reservation. Because Apaches have proved to be undependable employees, the Cattle Growers' Association now hires few. More and more men are becoming employees of the Bureau of Indian Affairs and the tribal government and achieve some satisfaction in the role copied from the governmental employee. But those who do are met with mixed reactions from their peers, including ridicule.

In modern times, kinship remains reckoned bilaterally. There is a trend toward neolocality but matrilocality remains the grossly dominant pattern (R. M. Boyer, 1962, pp. 93-122, 329-369). Restriction to the reservation has removed the migratory pattern as it pertains to subsistence. The old plant foods are gathered nearby and, with the exception of piñons, are used almost exclusively for ceremonial purposes. Hunting is performed solely on the reservation and almost entirely during the seasons which are legal throughout the state. Residence studies reveal a clear remnant tendency toward roaming. It has been unusual, even since the Apaches have had tribal houses, for them to remain in a single location for periods lasting more than a few months. The residence pattern today remains almost identical with that of aboriginal periods, despite confinement to the reservation. It may be that the psychological effects of perpetuation of roaming and housing constitute one of the most important elements which permit the Apaches to continue to identify themselves as a solidary group. Apaches who leave the reservation to seek livelihood, whether spontaneously or sponsored by the government, almost always return.[1] Bands have disappeared. The tribe is governed by the Business Committee, a council of ten members who are elected to serve terms lasting two years. In recent times, some of them have been women. A short time ago, a woman served two years as president of the

[1] Dr. Edward C. Adams, in a personal communication, has suggested that the tendency to roam and then return may have meaning in terms of the young child who attempts to master being left by the mother, as Freud discussed in his *Beyond the Pleasure Principle* (1920).

Business Committee. There is a tribal court, consisting of elected tribal judges (MacLachlan, 1962). They have jurisdiction over nonfelonious crimes which are committed on the reservation. There is an appointed tribal police force. The leaders now probably have more actual power than they wielded in olden times, due to the length of their tenure and to their being supported by the local superintendent, a representative of the Bureau of Indian Affairs, who, depending on his personality, directly or indirectly guides the decisions of the Business Committee. In addition, there is no practical way for tribal members to forsake their leaders and join other groups. Nevertheless, the attitude of the followers remains much as it did earlier, in that their criticisms of the leaders are frequently unstinted and they retain a fierce independence regarding which laws they will follow and which they will transgress. There is little respect for law as such, especially since the current legal system is based upon white philosophies, some of which seem ridiculous to Apaches. The example set by members of the Business Committee does not always encourage responsible behavior on the part of reservation residents. There was a recent financial scandal involving certain members. The ostensibly most moral and responsible (and the most powerful) member and others have incurred huge debts at the tribal store and refuse to pay them. No punishment resulted from the scandal and the members are not forced to settle their accounts. Operations of the Business Committee are sometimes grossly inefficient because no member wishes to make a decision which might incur the hostility of any group. The tribe has sources of income which are used to support the tribal government, to care for needy people, and to supply scholarships for college aspirants. The largest source of tribal revenue is from exploitation of the local luxuriant pine forest.

An economic survey was done of the individual 1959 cash incomes of 1148 persons, constituting 209 households and 248 family units (R. M. Boyer, 1962, pp. 123-153). The combined individual incomes amounted to some $702,000, of which 64 per cent was earned through employment. The 36 per cent unearned income stemmed almost entirely from cattle sales payments, pensions, and relief. The earned income was derived largely from unskilled wage work, 55 per cent of which was provided by the tribe, the Bureau of Indian Affairs, and the USPHS Hospital. The husband contributed 100 per cent of the family income in 21 per cent of the cases and 51 to 99 per cent in 56 per cent. The wife contributed 100 per cent of the income in only 1 per cent of the cases and 51 to 99 per cent in 9 per cent. The average household income was $3,795. In 70 per cent of the families in which there were children, there was more than one income contributor. The male emerged as the predominant breadwinner, in contrast to prereservation days during which the woman provided over half of family subsistence with her gathering procedures. However, only 27 per cent of the men who worked held jobs for nine months or longer per year, whereas 40 per cent worked less than three months. Women contributed 31 per cent of the total income and 47 per cent of their contribution was unearned.

Despite the fact that these Indians have almost no necessary living expenses beyond food, clothing, utilities (if present) and some transportation, a great many live on the verge of abject poverty due to their impulsive expenditures. Although there are a few gross exceptions, in general there is no correlation between consistency of work and standards of living. In aboriginal times, much work performed by all physically fit adults and most teenagers was necessary for group and individual survival and prestige was to be gained from productive occupation. Although the males were held in high respect and their activities were more spectacular, many were away from their families much of the time. The authority wielded by females in family matters must have been great at all times. Perhaps that of the men was concerned more with decisions pertaining to the larger group. From the standpoint of the child, despite the fact that when father came home his word was probably powerful, the person who wielded daily authority was a female. There remains strong solidarity among female kin. The researchers found very few families in which it appeared that a male figure had an ultimately authoritative role; this was true whether or not the male was accorded the status of a powerful tribal governmental figure. There is reason to suspect that some decisions ultimately formalized by the Business Committee are made by women while they gamble or gossip and then transmitted to their husbands for action. Women, as noted above, are gradually taking over formal political roles.

Aboriginally, then, these Apaches were self-sufficient, independent, hardy people who had stable but internally flexible social structures and had clearly defined roles for men and women. Currently, dwelling on the reservation as a tribal member consists of a "protected" existence. The inconsistently administered governmental policies, although called paternalistic, have coincided in fact more with what Apaches expect from maternal figures, and supported dependency and lack of personal responsibility. Apache immaturity has been and is fostered by tribe, state and nation (R. M. Boyer, 1962; Kunstadter, 1960). The diluted and attenuated aspects of reservation life which were demonstrated by Mead (1932, pp. 64-75) hold for the Mescalero.

The growing child assumes that the attitudes and practices of his societal elders, particularly those of his own family, are appropriate and generally applicable. Among the Apaches, to be sure, formal instructions differ grossly from informal, and confusions result. The child of this group learns that true *indéh*, the people, eschew permanent location of domicile although it is customary to remain within the same restricted geographical location; tillage of the soil is to be scorned; gaining a livelihood without physical or time-taking exertion is quite acceptable; the white man's law is to be ridiculed when it differs from native concepts, although lip service is to be paid; periods of residence within the "jailhouse," although irksome, are to be expected and result in some temporary mild shaming but scant permanent reduction of esteem by societal co-members; although females are formally supposed to be dependent upon male wisdom and subsistence provision, in fact, the female position is stronger, and males are dependent upon their women in many ways.

In the past, the old-time religion of the Mescalero, Chiricahua and Lipan overtly influenced every action and thought. Today, although there has been consistent contact with Christian teachings for almost a century, their meanings have been modified, as a rule, to make them consistent with Apache ideologies. The aboriginal religion still affects the preponderance of action and thought, although such influences are frequently covert.

The basic concept of the religion of these Apaches is that of diffuse supernatural power. To quote M. E. Opler (1947, p. 1), speaking of the Chiricahua:

> This force floods the universe and renders even ostensibly inanimate objects potentially animate. However, in order to become effective, it must "work through" humankind. Its method is to utilize the animals, plants, natural forces, and inanimate objects familiar to the Chiricahua, as channels by means of which to get in contact with men. After this contact has been made, the power appears in a personified guise and offers a ceremony or supernatural aid to the person approached.

According to one version of the Mescalero myth of their origin, there was in the remote past, in the central area of their residence, a race of men. A giant and four huge flesh-eating animals devoured all of

them but one virgin girl, White Painted Lady. She was magically impregnated by He Created Us and produced Child of the Water, a son who
killed or subdued the giant and the carnivores. From him and some
unstated or unknown woman arose the Mescalero. Today, the three
principal mythical characters are alternately known as God, Virgin Mary,
and Jesus. The only formal rite remnant from the aboriginal religion
is the puberty ceremony for girls (Breuninger, 1959; Hoijer, 1938a;
Nicholas, 1939; M. E. Opler, 1941; Pellman, 1950) which in certain respects
constitutes a re-enactment of the myth of the birth of the Child of the
Water.

The practical application of the aboriginal religious beliefs was very
broad. According to M. E. Opler, who used the word shaman to include
any person among the Mescalero and Chiricahua who was considered to
possess a ceremony (1941, p. 200), the ancient Apaches were a nation of
shamans (1935, p. 70). M. K. Opler (1959), as late as the 1930's, thought
practically every adult of the Mescalero reservation to be a shaman. Our
information revealed that current informants, including the aged, dis-
agree with the Oplers' understanding of the definition and incidence
of shamans (L. B. Boyer, 1962, 1964). Nevertheless, in the old days, all
Apache behavior and whatever happened to the Apaches were considered
to be ultimately under the influence of the supernatural. The administration of powers was thought to be in the hands of the shamans, some
of whom were very important. Cochise was a great Chiricahua band
leader. After his death, his elder son Taza, who had been trained in The
Medicine and thought to have received supernatural powers, died. A second son, Naiche, had not achieved the status of shaman and the leadership was transferred to Juh. But Geronimo was a more powerful shaman
and usurped the leadership, not because of his prowess as a warrior (in
fact, modern Chiricahua who knew him claim he was lazy and a coward
and state his Indian name was "Sleepy Head"), but because of a combination of his position as a powerful shaman and his hostility toward whites,
which pleased many renegade Chiricahua (Nicholas, 1961, 1961a). This
was true despite Geronimo's apparently having been a member of a different band (Basehart, 1959, p. 62). One interesting function of shamans
was the practice of love magic. In this concept, a person could hire a
shaman to perform a ceremony which would cast a spell on any person
and make him or her irresistibly attracted to any designated person of the
opposite sex. Functionally, a sexual transgressor could be pardoned for
illicit behavior by claiming love magic had been practiced. Ceremonies
were performed in private and the involved shaman would choose to

keep his action secret, since love magic was considered to be akin to witchcraft. However, so far as we could determine, love magic was never practiced for the purposes of incest or homosexuality.

Early contacts with the Christian religion were sporadic and transient. Although some Mescalero were known to have recited Catholic prayers in 1863 (Steck, 1863), the influence of Christianity upon aboriginal patterns was minuscule in prereservation days. Due to the influence of Catholic missionaries who were backed by the Indian Service, apparently all the Mescalero and Lipans became nominally Catholics by the turn of the century. According to present-day informants, while the Chiricahua were in prison camps in the southern states, all were forced to be baptized Catholics. When they were in Oklahoma, the Dutch Reformed Church learned of their plight and provided an orphanage and substantial relief. With very few exceptions, the Chiricahua renounced Catholicism and affiliated themselves with that Protestant sect. Catholic and Dutch Reform churches were built on the reservation and, until 1950, no other Christian denominations influenced the Apaches at Mescalero. Then, missionaries from the Church of Jesus Christ of Latter Day Saints (Mormons) made their appearance and a few families of Indians were converted to their faith. Three years later, a minister of the Assembly of God came to the reservation and remained. Probably due to his personal magnetism and the Apache's attraction to faith healing (L. B. Boyer, 1964), the Assembly of God has flourished.

In 1959, R. M. Boyer (1962, pp. 154-198) obtained information concerning church membership and attendance of 519 adults. Two hundred sixty-two were formally members of the Catholic, 171 of the Dutch Reform, 75 of the Assembly of God, and 11 of the Mormon Church. Of the 519 adults, 53 per cent never, 20 per cent occasionally, and 27 per cent frequently or regularly attended church functions. There was a tendency toward males as nonattenders and females as attenders.

The precise role played by the old-time religion in shaping current Apache belief and behavior is probably not subject to rigid determination. The influence of the Christian faiths has been strong, and the effects of their philosophies have probably changed understanding of the ancient mythologies . . . and perhaps the mythologies themselves (M. E. Opler, 1941a, 1946a; L. B. Boyer, 1964a). The Mormon and especially the Assembly of God Church have been overtly hostile toward continuation of formal Apache religious ceremonies. The attitude of the Dutch Reform and particularly the Catholic Church has been more tolerant. The tenor of the preaching of the ministers of those faiths on the reservation has been that there is good to be said for Apache and Christian teachings. Apaches are bewildered concerning religious philosophies. They desperately seek supernatural guidance. They no longer find security in their old beliefs, but neither do they find adequate succor in the varying Christian ideologies. Many Apaches assume a resigned eclectic viewpoint, hoping they can receive spiritual largess by attending various churches and believing in or pretending to believe in the dogmata of different churches at different times. Some church attendance, however, appears to be motivated by the wish for largess of a more material type.

The Apache believe that when a human dies, his spirit becomes, in most cases, a malevolent ghost, called *ch?idneh,* who is either lonely for his loved ones and attempts to drive them crazy in order that they will suicide or foolishly get killed and join him in the Other World, or seeks revenge on someone who has harmed him during his lifetime (L. B. Boyer, 1962, 1964; M. E. Opler, 1945, 1946b). The word *ch?idneh* means both ghost and devil, concepts which are fused in Apache thinking.

In past days, group unity was fostered in part by war and raiding training for males (Opler and Hoijer, 1940). All non-Apaches were considered to be hostile and, accordingly, were hated. Aggressions were and are projected onto ghosts and witches. Protection against the hostilities to be expected from ghosts and witches was and is afforded by shamans who were and are endowed with supernatural powers. The powers of the shamans are individual and secret.

The Apache child, then, grows in an environment within which there is constant evidence that *indéh* remain in close contact with the supernatural, although both formal and informal teachings are contradictory and lead to insecurities. His world is peopled by ghosts, witches, and supernatural powers which can assume the form of plants, animals, and natural phenomena. Only the faith-healing shamans can mediate for him with the dangers to be expected from the actions of *ch?idneh,* *enti[n]* and *diyi[n]* or *nant?a* (L. B. Boyer, 1964). He observes that despite overt teachings which encourage faith in and obeisance to Christian doctrines, attendance in the churches is low and irregular, clear evidence his parents put limited trust in the efficacy of these white man's ways. He is taught to project his hostilities onto supernatural agents and eschew personal responsibility for his actions.

Data concerning the drinking patterns of the Apaches before contact with the whites are sparse. They made *tiswin,* a fermented beverage of low alcoholic content made from corn and wheat. The native beer was brewed for parties and celebrations and on those occasions drunk in considerable quantities by males and females alike. However, there may have been no drunkards. At present, *tiswin* is made only occasionally and drunk more or less in secret by small groups for home parties. Beer, whiskey, and especially sweet wine are much easier to procure and constitute the constant source of liquor.

Alcohol is a great problem among present-day Apaches. Kunstadter (1960, pp. 269-287) reviewed tribal court records and found the Mescalero to have a crime rate ten times greater than the national average and five times larger than the Mountain States' incidence. Tribal court records do not include data concerning felonies. Seventy-eight per cent of all cases reported in the tribal court records of 1955-1957 involved the use of liquor. Our research teams estimated the actual incidence of drunkenness to be perhaps tenfold greater than reflected in official court statistics. The occurrence of alcoholic hallucinosis is widespread, although determination of the exact incidence may be impossible. Individuals of both sexes and all ages from the middle teens onward are known to suffer from the disorder. However, few acute psychotic episodes result in the victim's being hospitalized because they are attributed to the actions of ghosts and witches and accordingly treated by shamans, if at all. The disorder is usually transitory and a victim is given one or more curing ceremonies, each of which may last four nights, and is required to abstain from alcohol intake.

When sober, the Apaches are as a rule courteous, gentle, humorous, shy, modest people. Rules for ideal behavior are well defined and generally obeyed. Remarks pertaining to sexual matters are usually omitted when the two sexes are together, and intragroup physical violence is proscribed. When intoxicated, their behavior is quite otherwise. Humor becomes boisterous, and practical jokes are cruel. Modesty disappears, speech becomes "dirty," and violence is to be expected. (During one month of the summer of 1961, I tabulated statistics pertaining to official arrests and obtained information from individuals who had been arraigned and their relatives, as well as from jailers, policemen and judges. There were 81 arrests, 65 of which were associated with drinking. Physical violence was involved in 38 instances and publically lewd behavior in 8. According to a special federal officer hired to teach the judges and the police, the incidence of violence would have been much higher except for the fact that extra policemen had been hired during this period, who were able to get drunken individuals to jail before fights began.) Suppressions seem to evaporate. Among these Indians, conscious aspects of the superego dissolve in alcohol, to paraphrase an old comment. A drunken man will shout from his porch to a woman who is walking by. He will reveal his knowledge of her escapades, brag of his sexual prowess, and invite her to share his bed, his floor, or the nearby brush. Such behavior and sexual relations will take place in the presence of onlookers of any age. A drunken woman will be dragged into the bushes and subjugated to serial intercourse by several men. Kunstadter (1960, p. 279) has stated the incidence of arrest of females to be approximately eleven per cent of total arrests for the nation as a whole and about thirty-two per cent for the Apaches of the Mescalero Reservation. In the presence of intoxication, the release of most brutal hostilities is sanctioned. For example, a woman had an automobile. Her brother, after a night of drinking, demanded in the presence of children and adults she lend him the car. He had previously wrecked another of her automobiles while drunk. She refused. He knocked her to the ground, kicked her with his pointed boots, and raked her with his spurs. No one interfered until her skull had been fractured and she was severely lacerated. When she regained consciousness some days later, she was amazed when requested to sign a complaint against her assailant. She exclaimed, "But he was drunk!" Even murder unusually results in sentence. This attitude is encouraged by federal courts. A wife cuckolded her husband with his best friend. After the husband had for months ignored the affair, of which he had full knowledge, the two men drank together. While intoxicated, the wronged husband shot his friend, probably in the presence of witnesses. He slept, rifle in hand, at the side of the corpse. Months later, he was brought before a judge to enter a plea. His lawyer said the client was a drunken Indian and, although he had confessed the murder, one cannot take the word of a drunken Indian. The case was forthwith dismissed on the basis of "insufficient evidence." No plea was entered.

Although there are a few Apaches who have been teetotallers throughout their lifetimes, the great majority of Indians have been at some period drunkards and promiscuous and violent while intoxicated. It is my impression, although I cannot substantiate my contention with statistics, that most Indians who have been drunkards have suffered acute psychotic episodes while intoxicated or during the period immediately succeeding an alcoholic bout.

The Apache, despite assertions to the contrary, generally believe that an immoderate tendency to drink is inborn, and one's urges to attain drunkenness are not truly controllable, inasmuch as they are constitutional. The notion is prevalent that a strong desire for alcohol was placed within older generations through the actions of witches, angry "powers," and the schemings of whites, who wished to destroy the Indian through causing them to become drunkards, and then visited upon their offspring through heredity. Today, Indian drunkenness is blamed also upon white vintners, distillers, and brewers. The attitude of many Apaches is that if alcoholic beverages were not made to be purchased, there would be no general drunkenness.

The Apache child, then, is reared in an environment within which drinking alcohol is common and its effects upon the behavior of individuals are starkly evident. Although he hears repetitious platitudes concerning the evils of drink, he observes drunkenness to be an ambivalently received way of life. He grows to realize that drunkenness is an acceptable means of expressing one's dependent needs and provides a state within which one can abrogate formal rules of morality, whether they pertain to sexual or aggressive behavior, without serious negative sanction. He learns that excessive drinking is thought to result from one's inherent constitution and is outside the realm of one's personal responsibility.

Although, in the past, boys received active, rigorous training in preparation for their anticipated adulthood roles of hunters and warriors, now their future is cloudy and their preparation for manhood haphazard and confusing. Girls have a somewhat easier transition into adulthood, since they are still usually expected to become homemakers only and are trained accordingly. Their coming into womanhood is publically celebrated, whereas no recognition exists for the physical maturation of a boy. Nevertheless, the integrity of the Apache girl has likewise deteriorated. Early traders and soldiers often commented that Apache women, unlike squaws of other tribes, were not easy marks for sexual games. Husbands slit the noses of adulterous women. Girls were married soon after their pubertal ceremonies. Table 1 demonstrates the current tendency toward sexual looseness. It should be remembered that the figures presented concerning incidence of premarital and particularly extramarital birth rates constitute understatements.

TABLE 1

INCIDENCE OF MOTHERS UNMARRIED, PREMARITAL BIRTH AND EXTRAMARITAL BIRTH IN 1959

Age of Mother	Per cent of Unmarried Mothers	Per cent of Mothers Who Had Children Premaritally	Per cent of Married Women Who Had Children Extramaritally
14-29	23	59	7
30-49	4	29	17
50 and over	0	15	5

There has been, in recent times, extensive intermarriage and interbreeding with outsiders (L. B. Boyer, 1962). Of the mothers (one of whom has ethnically "Mexican" parents) who are 29 years of age or younger, 100 per cent have had children premaritally. The incidence of prostitution cannot be accurately determined, but it is common among women who are 35 years of age and younger, whereas only a few older women have ever practiced it.

As will be discussed below under Typical Childhood, male Apache youths must "prove" their masculinity through promiscuity. Tacitly, men are expected to continue such actions postmaritally, and most do. Although policemen are exhorted to set moral examples, most, at least among those under 40 years of age, are said to routinely "rape" drunken women and girls whom they have arrested, and sometimes men and women alike snigger when they discuss policemen who do not have sexual relations with intoxicated female arrestees.

Our work revealed only two instances of overt male homosexuality and perhaps none among females. Nevertheless, formal psychoanalytically oriented investigative interviews with 45 individuals of both sexes, ranging in age from 5 to 65 years and involving from one to 140 hour-long *vis-à-vis* sessions per informant, have indicated the presence of much latent homosexual yearning among males. The attitude of the Apache toward homosexuality is confused. The most common defense employed is massive denial of its existence, although the two instances are publically known. Adults claim overt homosexuality to be an inborn character defect which cannot develop from or be influenced by environmental situations and at the same time aver that those Apaches who become homosexuals learn the abhorrent behavior from outsiders. M. E. Opler (1941) found that witches were considered homosexuals at times. At present, there is one woman who is uniformly accorded the status of witch. She is reputedly training another woman in witchcraft. They have been seen dancing together nude. While their behavior is considered socially deviant, some adults claim that it is not truly homosexual but merely an unusual requisite step in witchcraft education. A male shaman, who is at times accused of being and sometimes claims to be a witch, dances naked with some male clients. He is not accused of being a homosexual. We heard of no instances of aboriginal overt homosexuality. No myths, legends, or tales manifestly involving homosexuality have come to our attention.

According to modern informants, from the earliest known times incest has been defined as sexual intercourse between individuals who could trace mutual relationship to any person in the grandparental generation.

Aboriginally, incest was equated with witchcraft. In recent times, a person who is accused of sexual relations or marriage with a "close relative" is sometimes thought to be a witch (M. E. Opler, 1941, p. 250). In the past, one who broke the incest tabu could expect to be killed as a witch, cast from his band, receive supernatural punishments, or, at least, be ridiculed and beaten. At present, although the old definition holds in the stated ideal, sexual relations among relatives of the same generation seem to be common in childhood and adolescence and occasional in adulthood. Transgression is punished only by gossip and mild ostracism. Intercourse between fathers and daughters or uncles and nieces may not be rare and the only retribution is indignant gossip. At the turn of the century, a minor Mescalero leader impregnated his mother and her sister. The infants were killed at birth. Although the events were common knowledge, the only punishment afforded the man was a degree of ostracism. He retained his leadership, but no girl would marry him. Apparently the women suffered from nothing beyond gossip. There are instances of marriage between stepmother and stepson, following the death of the husband-father. Such occurrences result in nothing more than raised eyebrows. We learned of half a dozen instances of father-daughter or stepfather-stepdaughter relationships from which children resulted. Neither partner had been punished, although two of the cases occurred in the last quarter of the nineteenth century.

In-laws are not considered to be relatives. Sororal bigamy was common in the past. Today, a man who marries his deceased wife's sister is approved, as is a woman who weds her dead husband's brother. One woman lives openly with her husband and his brother. Disapproval is expressed in jokes which are tinged with envy.

Incestuous relations are not uncommon in the manifest content of Apache stories. Chiricahua and Mescalero versions of "Coyote Marries His Own Daughter" have been published (Hoijer, 1938a, pp. 25-27, 182). In the published stories, Coyote was severely punished for having tricked his wife into permitting him to marry his daughter. According to the Chiricahua variation, his wife retaliated by crushing his head with a stone; in the Mescalero, he escaped unharmed, although she attempted to kill him with an ax. In current versions of the same story, which is known also to Lipans, Coyote sometimes is able to discard his wife and retain his daughter as a sexual partner. In one story I heard, Coyote was able to keep both wife and daughter as alternate bedmates.

It would appear that the need for group defense against homosexuality is greater than that against incest.

It is difficult to learn what elements contributed to status and reputation in former times. Today, the concept of status is somewhat vague and its determinants are diffuse and individual. It is clear, however, that it does not depend upon possession of property, judicious use of income, or a sense of responsibility, and there may be no connection between status and the degree of formal education. A person may be or have been a drunkard and frequently jailed for disorderly conduct, adultery, contributing to the delinquency of a minor or failure to support dependent persons, and retain high status. Perhaps leadership qualities, generosity, and the reputation of one's forbears are the significant determinants. However, the impression is gained that the power one wields, for whatever reasons, is the most important item. Reputation seems to depend, in the case of the woman, on her being primarily oriented toward holding her family together and caring for her children. In the case of the man, criteria are less obvious. Ideally, they seem to involve morality as preached by Christian sects, but this attitude seems to be superficial. A man's reputation may be practically determined by his conforming to an indefinite picture of manhood which includes such elements as bravery, the ability to exploit outsiders, exhibition of sexual prowess, skills at hunting and riding, and the ability to withstand the demands of women. In fact, we learned of very few men who could directly and successfully contradict females.

Before we turn to a resume of these further aspects of the general environment, aspects which provide informal educative messages which are transmitted to growing children, let us turn to a brief discussion of the role played by formal education.

The early policy of the Bureau of Indian Affairs concerning education was to remove children from their parents and send them to distant boarding schools or to reservation boarding schools, where they were taught English and "civilized" trades. The aim was to accelerate de-Indianization. Parents and children responded to such attempts at education with sharp ambivalence, mostly colored by hostility (Kunstadter, 1960, pp. 74-75, 109-113). Since individuals who were married were not forced to attend school, prepubertal girls were married to grown men who simply "played with them." From the early part of the twentieth century, the Apaches have had sharply mixed feelings toward the "educated." Nowadays, Indians are encouraged by the tribe to mime whites and assume white patterns of achieving success, but when they do, they are ridiculed and may even be brutally beaten by their peers (R. M. Boyer, 1961). Formal education is officially approved, but many parents do little to help their children even to attend school. Although school authorities lean over backwards to permit Apaches to graduate from high school, Kunstadter (1960, p. 175) found 343 adults to have some grade-school and 150 to have some high-school education. A small group of tribal members stems from Mexican captives, some of whom have intermarried with Apaches. Of the few tribal members who have graduated from high school, the majority have been of "Mexican" descent. Although some twenty tribal members have received grants to attend college, the vast majority have failed during their first year, and only one was graduated during the last half-century. In recent years, some girls have continued education after graduation from high school. They have attended vocational schools (Marintsek, 1960; Zintz, 1957-1960). A few individuals of both sexes have been able to put their formal education to practical use, becoming white-collar workers.

Let us turn now to these additional elements of the environment from the viewpoint of the growing child, bearing in mind that such data provide elements which will be introjected and serve as internalized criteria for acceptable attitudes, concepts, and behavior.

The celebration of the girls' physiological sexual maturation provides a forceful bit of evidence that females are considered more valuable than males by the group, and boys are envious, although resigned. Girls have a reasonably clear example of an adult role toward which they can aspire, whereas boys are provided with no consistent picture of manhood toward which they can aim. When boys and male teenagers are asked to delineate ambitions, they are usually surprised at the questions. The few who have thought in such terms give highly unrealistic responses, as a rule. Typical of the latter group is the series of responses provided by one teenager, a slight, unathletic lad who had been held back twice in grammar school and who had failed in his second year of high school. When he was asked what he planned to do in the future, he responded that he was going to get a football scholarship at a university and become a doctor. A week later, he reported he had sent to a correspondence school for lessons which would enable him to become a hairdresser. No reservation Apache women have their hair cared for professionally; at the time of our stay, there was no barber. At a later time, he said he was going to become a truck-gardener. In fact, he remained a parasitic loafer.

The lessons to be learned from the discussion of status determinants are obscure and do not contribute positively to the child's picture of desirable adulthood. Those from the results of formal education are also confusing.

TYPICAL CHILDHOOD

During aboriginal times, when the Apaches were nomadic hunters, gatherers, and raiders, they lived in a hostile environment, beset by human and nonhuman enemies. Survival depended upon the maintenance of optimal numbers of tribal members and the development of hardy people who were accustomed to privation and cruelty, each of which was to be accepted without too great psychological disturbance of group members. Perhaps because of the difficulties entailed in keeping infants alive and the likelihood they might be lost through capture, it was necessary for parents to develop a particular kind of emotional distance, that the removal of small children might not result in hampering grief reactions. We find that the old-time Apache did not consider a newborn to be a human individual until he had reached the age of eighteen to twenty-four months. The child's innate aggressive and erotic drives had to be abetted and channeled into attitudes and practices designed to support group survival.

So far as we have been able to determine, the birth of a baby was uniformly consciously welcomed. M. E. Opler (1941, pp. 5-76) stated great love for children characterized the Chiricahua society. Tabus concerning pregnancy, childbirth, and infant care were obeyed, and numerous ceremonies were performed. Psychoanalytic insight into some of the tabus and ceremonies, however, suggests the presence of latent hostility toward the pregnancy and/or the baby. For example, a piece of turkey gobbler's neck skin, which held long, stiff, hairlike feathers, was often used to decorate the cradleboard. Its purpose was to avert the infant's being struck by lightning. There was an aboriginal custom of killing one of newborn twins. Such behavior was justified by modern informants by the difficulties of infant care while the band was on the move. Old women said: "A mother could not have enough milk for two babies." Yet infants of mothers who died were wet-nursed. One method of killing the unwanted baby was to place it on an ant hill. Some modern Apache mothers rear twins. Others, it would appear, simply let one starve. M. E. Opler (1941, p. 411) found twins to have been considered evidence of unfaithfulness.

The care afforded infants by Apache mothers nowadays is startlingly inconsistent. They are usually very tender and considerate in their physical relationships with their babies. There is much bodily contact. Nursing times are generally determined by the baby's cry, and every distress is greeted first by the nipple of a breast or a bottle. At the same time, mothers have a very limited sense of responsibility so far as child care is concerned, and the impression gained is that the mother's tenderness for her baby is based upon her bestowing upon the infant care she herself desires as an adult. A great many mothers abandon or give away children—babies they had been nursing lovingly only a week before. Apaches very accurately name this practice "throwing the baby away." Not only do they feel scant conscious guilt for this behavior, but at times they are overtly delighted to have been able to rid themselves of the burden. In some instances, mothers who have given children away, "forget" they ever had them. The usual Apache mother believes physical care is all an infant requires. She has little or no compunction about leaving her baby with just anyone at all while she impulsively leaves to gossip, shop, gamble or drink and "fool around." Ideally, the mother entrusts her baby to a sister or older female relative. In aboriginal times, such an arrangement was almost always possible. At present, even a nursling is temporarily abandoned at the whim of the mother, and the physical results of gross infant neglect are obvious (Clements & Mohr, 1961; Kunstadter, 1960, pp. 334-336). In an extreme example, a mother frequently left her infants to the care of children three to five years of age for many hours at a time. On three separate occasions, the family dwelling burned to the ground. Some of her babies have starved to death; others have been simply permitted to die when ill, although the family lives within a mile of the hospital, and one of the mother's favorite loafing-sites is within a few hundred yards of that hospital.

In aboriginal times, cradleboards were used in the care of all Apache infants (Mason, 1889). The use of the cradle is still almost universal, although generally concealed from whites (R. M. Boyer, 1962, pp. 216-223). The effects of cradle employment and swaddling on physical development have been subjects of prior investigations and speculations (Benedict, 1949; Dennis & Dennis, 1940; Erikson, 1950, p. 120; Leighton & Kluckhohn, 1948, pp. 18-26; Mead, 1954). In the old days, the cradle served a double purpose for the Apaches: (1) as protection for the infant against potential damages inherent in the rigors of travel and hardy semi-outdoor living, and (2) convenience for the mother. Currently, both reasons are applicable. Apache mothers do not prevent visiting children from handling their infants roughly. Should such a youngster shove a baby to the floor or poke it with some object, whether by chance or intent, nothing is done, since to "cause trouble" with the mother of the visiting child is strongly disapproved. Cradles also protect babies from jostling afforded by reckless driving over rough roads, etc.

However, the cradle is rarely used at night. The infant sleeps with his parents in almost all cases. The effect of the use of the cradle on the psychical development of the Apache child would be very difficult to assess. It is obvious that the infant finds much security from the warmth and physical security the cradle affords. Apache babies obviously want to be placed in the cradle after they have nursed. Apache adults rarely assume the fetal position in sleep or when they are in a drunken stupor. Instead, they commonly assume the cradle-board position, lying on their backs, with their legs together and straight.

There have been a few instances in which the occipita of neglected children have been flattened, probably from pressure caused by lying supine in the cradle too long (Clements & Mohr, 1961). Most Apache infants, however, are not cradled until a month after their births, and then are kept on the cradleboard only four to six hours per day.

Erikson (1950, pp. 219-222; 1959, pp. 55-65) has stressed that an essential component of a healthy personality is developed during the first year of life, the "sense of basic trust."[2] With the grossly inconsistent and ambivalent treatment he receives from his unrelated mother, it is difficult to conceptualize how he *could* develop a sense of basic trust.

Within the limits described above, then, the infant is king or queen until the next baby is born, an event which usually transpires within two years, if the mother is under thirty years of age. At that time, he is most commonly removed from his parents' bed at night. He is quite literally and brutally pushed aside. No longer does he receive prolonged, tender baths. At times when the crying, displaced child seeks proximity to his mother while she is caring for the new baby, she will kick him in the face. If the screaming sufferer then looks for solace from an older sibling or the father, he may or may not be petted briefly. Usually, he is ignored and finds his thumb or a crust of bread. For the next few years, he will be seen to be eating almost constantly. Throughout his life, he will seek close physical contact avidly.

The displacement of the Apache child occurs during the stage of muscular maturation in which a youngster should obtain "autonomy"

---

[2] In a personal communication, Peter Blos has written: "... 'basic trust' seems to me an idealization of Western culture childhood, or rather infancy. Generally, as general as orality which is based on the function of the maturing organism, it seems to me that the oral phase survives in its positive or adaptive and integrative aspects by evolving modalities which do not negate psychosexual progression and fit into acceptable culture avenues. This concept is much broader than basic trust. There the Apache seems to be without any selectivity or resourcefulness. This must have its basis in the early abandonment and unrelatedness of the mother."

(Erikson, 1950, pp. 222-224; 1959, pp. 65-74). During this period, a child must learn self-control; limit his emotions and overt behavior to those proper within his society. He must learn to please and influence those about him. Among the Mescalero, toilet training per se is practically non-existent. An older child may take a younger to the outhouse or he might mess anywhere at all. Feces-laden diapers remain on some walking babies for hours or even days, or they may be thrown by the most fastidious woman into a corner where they are covered with flies. No one heeds the stench. The child is not rewarded outwardly for learning bowel control. However, he quickly learns another type of control which clearly involves muscles, that of his aggressions toward younger children.

Thus, an Apache toddler cannot gain approval and support from, or control over, his mother through regulation of excretory activities. He must demonstrate maturation by learning to accept his displacement by the new arrival and to handle his rage and disappointment in sanctioned manners. He soon discovers that overt expression of hostility toward the newcomer is tabu. He may for some weeks direct anger toward the mother herself without being punished by more than mild rebuke. However, an effort to hurt the infant results promptly in physical punishment administered by the mother, who also ridicules him. She and other family members call him "crybaby," "naughty," "bad," "dirty," or "no good." As will be amplified below, a typical and extremely consistent means of disciplining the child is that of telling him $ashi^n$, meaning a ghost or other frightening being is coming to get or hurt him. It is known that this is an ancient form of discipline. All older Apaches remember having been taught, during their early childhoods, that if they cried "too much," jajadeh, the whippoorwill, would come to carry them away in a basket (L. B. Boyer, 1962). Most elderly Apaches now laugh at the memory of their childhood terror of jajadeh, but some are still consciously afraid of the little bird. The displaced child is permitted to strike and torment other children or destroy their beongings without fear of retaliation, if the actions occur in the presence of parents. However, within a few months, the older manage to discourage the younger children from direct, painful attacks on them. The toddler is permitted the most violent torture of small domestic animals. If he strikes, gouges or burns a puppy, no one will reprimand him. Such behavior toward animals, especially small ones, persists into the adulthood of many Apaches. The displaced child, then, is systematically trained to develop reaction formation as pertains to those who are younger and smaller than he, to project and displace his hostilities onto the supernatural and other objects he has been trained to fear, to express his aggression directly but with attenuated intensity to older and larger children, and to express his rages in full force in sadistic attacks on harmless or helpless animals. In addition, from the earliest times when he can comprehend language, he hears his parents speak with rancor about outsiders, whom they blame for a great many of their (largely self-imposed) troubles. No doubt, this pattern is an attenuation of the old-time need to inculcate enmity toward non-*indéh*.

By the time the toddler is three, he has learned that a tantrum is rarely rewarding, and by the time he reaches four, he looks upon such uncontrolled activity with disdain. But the disappointments still exist in early childhood, so what does the three-year-old do? If he cries, and he usually does, he tries to do so silently, for he has learned by now that a mother will tolerate a quiet child—one who does not "bother" her. Sometimes she may even show affection if he is near, and remains unobtrusive. The unhappy three-year-old may undergo certain distinctive bodily maneuvers. His torso becomes rigid and his general posture resembles that of attack. His knees bend slightly, his fists clench at his sides and his facial muscles become tense. His jaws are locked together. The muscles of his abdomen tighten and, for a brief time, he may hold his breath. In large measure his posture resembles that of a two-year-old, but then a change takes place. Instead of casting himself to the ground or floor, the three-year-old controls his muscular system. Slowly, his fists relax, his arms grow limp and he stands erect. His face becomes poised, his color pales and his eyes grow deep and disinterested. He seems to retire inside himself. In other words, he has accomplished two things in the course of a year's time: mastery of his muscles and control of his emotions. He has become passive, and he appears unconcerned. This is the first evidence we have of Apache passivity, of the stoicism displayed throughout his life. To be sure, the toddler has varying degrees of success in his attempts at mastery, but a basic pattern of reaction has been created. Later, as an adult, he will often [when sober and insecure or frustrated] assume the facial response and the bodily control which he found to be most acceptable in early childhood days. He will look as though he were uninterested. . . . In terms of muscular coordination, the Apache child's ultimate mastery of his reactions to frustrations involves "whole-body" passivity, or relaxation, following a period of extreme tension. In many ways, this sequence of controls corresponds to sphincter mastery required in the course of toilet training. . . . Although the focus of the mother's interests are different, an Apache child, just like an American, must learn *when* he can "let go," *when* and *what* he must "retain," and which muscles he must master. Both societies require a sense of timing and restraint [R. M. Boyer, 1962, pp. 238-240; 1962a].

In the above passage, the positive, adaptational aspects of the development of resignation and passivity in Apache children are stressed. However, we cannot overlook Winnicott's (1961) often supported experience that the abrogation of rebellion in the face of separation constitutes a reaction of hopelessness and often heralds subsequent severe psychiatric illness. Khan (1962), too, has contributed a relevant datum. He indicates that some mothers are relatively adequate in their handling of infants but reveal psychological weaknesses when their babies become toddlers. Khan states that the mother's inability to tolerate the child's shift from primary identity to seeking recognition of independence results in inconsistent precocious ego development in the child. The Mescalero data clearly support his stand, even though the Apache mothers seem to have been less adequate in their handling of infants before they have begun to seek recognition of independence than were the mothers of whom Khan writes.

If the Apache child has not become a thumb-sucker before a rival appears, he almost certainly will do so then. Almost all Apache children suck their thumbs and many twist their hair and pick their noses, during preschool years. In the absence of whites, their mothers pay no heed to such activities. Children who are tired, bored, or upset suck their thumbs into their early teens. Nail-biting is common in adolescence. Nocturnal enuresis occurs in all households and occasions little or no comment. Only an unusual child continues to wet the bed after he attends grammar school.

Erikson (1950, pp. 224-226; 1959, pp. 74-82) states that the next stage of psychosexual maturation is concerned with the locomotor-genital system and that it involves the development of initiative. The four- or five-year-old child has sufficient mastery of language and muscular motility to permit concentration in a new field, daydreaming. He now becomes intensely interested in comparisons of sizes and particularly in sexual differences. Erikson (1950, p. 225) calls this the stage of the castration complex and writes that "the fear of losing the (now energetically eroticized) genitals as a punishment for the fantasies attached to their excitements" now occurs with force.

Children indulge in much of their early childhood sexual explorations in the outhouse, to which they never go alone. Playroom interviews with young boys frequently revealed serious preoccupation with castration fears. Girls as young as two years overtly express penis envy. One small girl tearfully asked her mother to buy her a penis, so she could "have a gun like those boys." She wanted to enter the contest as to who could urinate the farthest over the bank of a nearby hill. Tiny boys express overt breast envy. All sexual activities, and even new underclothes, are uniformly called "dirty" by the Apache.

Each August, injections are given to children who are going to attend school for the first time. The "shots" are given into the upper arm at that time of the year. Yet, during August and September, in every Apache home in which there are small children, all dolls which are not absolutely new are found to have holes from one-eighth to one-half inch in diameter in at least one buttock. The mothers state their children love to play "hospital." The identification with aggression (A. Freud, 1936, pp. 117-131) appears, here, to be fused as well with sexual behavior in which phallic activity is fused with anal sadism.

In addition to mutual exploratory behavior of the sort usually reported in western cultures, among these Indians, sexual intercourse occurs with very small children. Men reported to me that they had been seduced before they were six years old by teen-age girls. They said they, in turn, had had intercourse with girls four and five years of age when they reached their own adolescence.

It is impossible that adults do not know of the outhouse sexual relations of children. Anyone walking near outside toilets will hear the children's giggles and pantings from time to time. Adolescent premarital sexual relations are condoned by most parents. The young lovers simply move in with the parents of one or the other participant.

The early training through ridicule continues throughout the childhood of the Apache. Adults are apprehensive particularly of the laughter of whites and convey this message very strongly to their offspring. In grammar school, the child is usually a fearful, passive observer, afraid to speak up lest he err and be ridiculed (R. M. Boyer, 1962, pp. 261-281). Apache children are not taught to compete with one another. It will be recalled that a smaller or younger child automatically wins a contest, simply because he is small or young. White grammar school teachers are frustrated when they cannot stimulate Apache children to work harder or to actively participate in classroom activities by attempting to get them to compete with one another. The teachers usually display their annoyance through ridicule.

According to present-day sources, during aboriginal times, the treatment of boys and girls was very similar until they were four or five years of age. Both were often dressed in girls' clothes. Parents were grossly indulgent toward their young children, so far as imposing tasks upon them was concerned. Their few chores, apparently done more volitionally than under duress, were similar. Both performed identical camp functions, such as collecting firewood, caring for younger children, fetching water, gathering berries, and doing simple cooking. However, it would seem that a change of parental attitude took place when the child reached about six years of age, the period which corresponds to the onset of the latency period in our culture. Then a clear differentiation of dress occurred; the boy began his elementary training in hunting techniques, and the girl was indoctrinated into collecting larger plant products, such as the mescal, and the tanning of hides.

Today, most children are dressed differently by the time they are two years of age. As before, they have no early separation of duties and tasks are usually performed voluntarily. However, there is a clear difference between current and past handling of children who have reached six years of age. Now, they continue to perform similar duties and there is no distinctive, formal training of boys. Mostly, the responsibility to discipline and duty indoctrination is turned over to the schools, and further development of distance between parent and child is fostered.

By the time the child attends grammar school, he has learned more about permissible forms of expression of anger. He has been told and has seen that expressions of hostility within the group are permissible only when a participant is intoxicated and officially irresponsible. He knows that anger toward outsiders, especially neighboring "Mexicans," is sanctioned hypocritically. He has also determined that although his parents initially seemed anxious that he attend school, in fact they are not much concerned whether he attends or not. Their primary concern is in having the child attend sufficiently often so that the parents are not hauled before the court. The mothers often contribute to the child's tendency toward truancy by failing to provide him with clean clothes. No Apache child, with his fear of being laughed at, wants to go to school in soiled or wrinkled clothes. The children also soon determine that although their parents tell them to study and learn how to succeed in the white man's way (as represented usually by the Bureau of Indian Affairs employee), neither mother nor father much cares. In addition, the school child's peers ridicule him if he does well.

The role of the father in child-rearing is remarkably similar to that of the mother. Aside from actual breast feeding, he willingly performs all of her tasks, with equal gentleness, affection, and bodily contact, when the mood strikes him. There appears to be a difference in quantity but not in quality of ministrations. Both parents, however, consider the mother to be the rightful agent of discipline for the growing child. The father either abstains or takes cues from the mother, whose discipline he supports periodically and briefly. The father is with his children much more than are whites, unless he be the unusual Apache who holds a permanent and steady job. Most fathers have been charged in court for failure to support dependent persons. Both parents are equally willing to dispose of infants and children. Despite the amount of actual time spent in the vicinity of his children by the Apache father, he is even less dependable a caretaker for them than is their mother. The principal example he sets for his children is that of a seldom-working, irresponsible individual whose life pursuits are dictated by the urge to immediately gratify his desires, but who is much of the time fearful of supernatural aspects of his environment.

It is a rare father who spends time formally instructing his children. Periodically, he may teach them the construction of simple drums and some Indian songs and dances. Otherwise, they learn from him almost exclusively through observation. Most fathers have little to do with their latency sons, aside from occasionally offering them some transient physical affection. Boys in their early teens expect money, candy, cigarettes or "things" from their fathers and uncles, and contacts are limited to requests which are almost always granted, regardless of what the boys' behavior may have been during the period which preceded the asking. Youths in their later teens drink with their fathers and uncles.

Mothers and fathers alike, when intoxicated, may brutally beat their young children, and records indicate that parents have killed infants either by rolling on them, thereby crushing or smothering them, or by striking them. Such infanticides are never punished in the courts and cause no more than transient gossip. They are frequently attributed to supernatural causes or witchcraft.

When drunken behavior results in homicide of adults, the murderer expects retaliation by the ghost of the deceased or by witchcraft bought or practiced by relatives of the dead person. The killer also fears physical retaliation from a relative. In actual practice, the murderer is sometimes temporarily ostracized by the relatives of the dead and ridiculed by gossip in the community.

Sexual activities of adults for the most part seem to occur in conjunction with drinking. Since mother-in-law avoidance practices have been abandoned almost entirely, dwellings have become crowded. During one period of our study, twenty-nine Indians of all ages slept the whole of a long winter season in a small four-room house and an adjacent tent, as they had done during other cold periods. They, especially the children, were scattered over the floors. Several shared a blanket. Most of the adults were frequently drunk. There were new births every year. One man sired children by his own and another man's wife. From direct observation, it is known to the investigators that men and women who have been drinking engage in sexual relations in public during daytime or nighttime. If they have been drinking or not, some indulge themselves sexually in private at any time, whether or not there are children about. It is unlikely that there are any children, whether their own parents do or do not imbibe, who have not observed openly conducted sexual relations, in addition to brawls.

Apache children, nevertheless, are thought to know *nothing* until they are four or five years of age. They are overtly taught to consider themselves totally ignorant and "no good" through high school. Despite the facts outlined above, adults appear to believe sincerely children are kept in complete ignorance of sexual matters until they are of grammar-school age and that they learn such "dirty things" only from other children.

Although sexual relations among children are disapproved ideally, they appear to be the rule. The research teams have little evidence of masturbation and homosexuality among children. The young seem to imitate the scenes they have witnessed and which have excited them. Analysts know from clinical work that small observers of primal scenes interpret them according to their level of maturation and take on the excitements of both partners. It is commonplace knowledge that confusion about one's sexual identification can be fostered by such experiences.

Discipline of Apache children appears to begin with the birth of the next sibling, or in cases in which there are no new births, after the child is two or more years old. It is most haphazard. Discipline is the domain of the mother figure, who regularly uses promises of rewards and threats of punishments she has no intention of fulfilling. In the past, as mentioned earlier, educative stories were related, apparently with constructive effect (L. B. Boyer, 1964a; Hoijer, 1938a; M. E. Opler, 1938a, 1940, 1941, 1942). At present, that practice has been abandoned almost entirely. The children are inconsistently taught aboriginal and Christian ideals of behavior, but they learn primarily through observation and testing. One uniform disciplinary measure is the systematic teaching of obedience through fear. Such training has a number of manifest contents. "If you cry, I'll put you in the dark closet with the mouse." "If you're not good, I'll put you outside in the dark where there are dangerous lions, bears, owls, crows, wild men, ghosts, drunks, dogs, whippoorwills, etc." Any Apache who is displeased with or who simply wants to taunt a young child will say *"ashi^n."* The implied threat of desertion is effective. The child becomes terrified and obeys for a time. In their attempts to master such fears, children of three play games alone or with others in which they say *"ashi^n"* aloud and then laugh. Very soon, however, they are frightened of the vision they have conjured. Few children denied having experienced hallucinations, and it is our impression that hallucinations are common among individuals of all ages and perhaps universal among children in their teens and younger. Phobias relating to bears, coyotes, darkness, dogs, ghosts, lions, snakes and wild men are found in almost all Apaches.

The weight of the threat of desertion may be somewhat lessened because the reasons for punishment are inconsistent; identical behavior will result in reward or discipline depending on the mood of the authority at hand. However, the threat becomes even more real to the growing child who, within his first few years, will observe the practice of "throwing children away." As noted previously, in prereservation days, when there were bands, there was group cooperation. Then, children who had no parents or whose parents were away, were automatically cared for by relatives or families with whom there were mutual cooperative agreements. Today, children whose parents have simply gone away and left them for periods varying from hours to weeks will wander about seeking shelter and food and not uncommonly be turned aside even by close relatives.

Conscious guilt does not play an important part in the behavior of most of the Indians studied. The majority fear social sanctions and consciously determine their actions and verbal revelations largely on the basis of whether they anticipate punishment. Although promiscuity is the rule, nonpsychotic subjects interviewed while sober never spoke of their own sexual relations in any but the most general of terms.

Apache adults are aware of their proud heritage and their social degradation. They are aware of being a vanishing people and are fundamentally pessimistic. They see no convincing purpose in preparing for the future with hard work and regular lives. Yet they long for their old pride and dream of ways in which their children might be brought up as individuals who were able to obtain the best from both Indian and white ways. This can be illustrated by their attitude toward me. I spent two years trying to learn the grammar and subtleties of the relevant Apache dialects, tongues so difficult to master that professional linguists were aghast when they learned I had decided to study them. Initially, many Indians were suspicious of my motives. Some men, who continued to think in terms of warring and raiding, recalled that during the second World War, Apache was one of the languages used by the United States military for secret communications. They took as implicit that we would soon be at war with the Soviets and decided I was a Russian agent, sent to learn the language in order that the meanings of confidential messages would be understood. I had been introduced to the tribal Business Committee as a psychiatrist; the Apache synonymized psychiatrist and shaman. Shamans have supernatural powers which they can use for good or evil purposes as they choose. Those who employ their powers for profane purposes are called witches. Although the practice is attentuated, Apache are still taught to view outsiders and particularly whites as enemies. Many gave me the name of *indah enti*ⁿ, white witch, and thought I was among them to discern their religio-medical secrets, in order to exploit them more easily, to their loss and my gain. Naturally, learning their secret lore would be easier if I understood their language.

The Apache language has degenerated into a mockery of its former purity, and many Indians cannot really understand each other's use of their native tongues. The elders rue the inability of young people to speak properly. After we had been among the Apaches for about a year, perfect understanding was generally ascribed to me, and it was assumed by some that I knew the pure, old-time language, not only of the Mescalero, but of the Chiricahua also. In addition, it was believed that I knew more accurately than did any but a few older Apaches the entire native mythologies and the tenets of their religious and medical practices. Although the "powers" of shamans are thought to be secret and the ceremonies which make the powers operate are individual and jealously guarded, eventually, several shamans offered to "give" me all their lore. One shaman requested that I officiate at the "coming out" of a relative in the puberty ceremony. I was later asked to become the leader of that rite and to become "chief" Apache shaman, a role which apparently would be newly made, since there is no record of its prior existence. I was to become an ideal leader who would teach future generations the old-time language and make certain they understood aboriginal tenets and mores. One old man said: "We want you to be the father of our children; that they can grow up to be real Apaches. The language is dying and the old beliefs are getting lost. We need a good man who knows everything to bring up our children to be real Apaches. Maybe you can bring back the old days." There was no shaman who was universally respected except one aged woman. It was assumed I was an important and moral white man who could transmit to children the best from both native and white cultures.

It is likely that my skill as a hunter contributed to the ascription of supernatural powers to me. Hunting prowess was erstwhile attributed to such powers. At a time when three shamans were rumored to have been seeking to destroy my increasing status as white shaman, motivated by "jealousy," since I had successfully "cured" clients whom they had been unable to help, I went hunting with various Indians for several days. It soon became clear that I was able to see deer and other game when they could not, and, with my powerful rifle and telescopic sights, I could kill game at distances far greater than they. My feats earned me the name of *enjadeh*, great hunter, and were taken as evidence that my supernatural powers were obviously greater than those of the shamans who were seeking to make me impotent.

Pumpian-Mindlin (1961) has described a facet of self-development which occurs frequently among white youth of our dominant culture. He said, "It consists primarily of the feeling on the part of the teenager that he can do anything in the world if only given the opportunity, and if it is not given, he will create it. He knows of no limits of fantasy, and accepts grudgingly any limits in reality." The great majority of Apache youth undergo no such adolescent or postadolescent phase. They see themselves as products of defeated parents in a deteriorating culture. They have little optimism concerning the future and but vague life goals. Girls, while also pessimistic, are less so. A few can realize their optimistic dreams of having "nice" clothes and a "white" home and succeed in graduating from secretarial or beauty culture schools. They rightly anticipate that if they are to have "nice" things, they will have to supply the wherewithal from their own earnings, in the majority of cases, or marry an outsider.

CLINICAL MATERIAL

During the first twelve of my nineteen months in the field, my professional help was sought exclusively for the treatment of neurotic symptoms and chronic alcoholism and as a marriage counsellor. At last a young man whom I shall here call Hanging Hairlock was hospitalized after he had been treated unsuccessfully for alcoholic hallucinosis by a shaman. My aid was sought by the USPHS doctors and the family. A year later, a second victim of the syndrome spontaneously came for assistance. It had become rumored I had cured the first patient.

Case 1

Hanging Hairlock was a man in his twenties, a sometime cowboy. His natural parents had died during his infancy. His foster family will henceforth be referred to as though he were their blood relative.

Almost every person in his extended family was promiscuous and was or had been a drunkard. The nuclear family lived largely from cattle income. The family rarely engaged in money-earning activities. They had *much* leisure time which was spent almost exclusively in the pursuit of carnal pleasures.

The mother had died a year previously. She and one sister had been prostitutes. Two sisters had been charged repeatedly with child neglect or abandonment by the tribal court. One had "thrown away" illegitimate children and undergone abortions.

The father and older brothers were drunkards. The latter, when intoxicated, were violent men. They and their wives were frequently charged with child abandonment. The father had, throughout the life of Hanging Hairlock, been a singer for the Horn Dancers (Mountain Spirits, Mountain Gods, Devil Dancers), a group of men who perform sacred ceremonies. Traditionally, they have been thought to possess supernatural powers and to use those powers for good purposes. They dance routinely at the annual puberty ceremony for girls. Their role is primarily protective and they are viewed as benevolent but potentially vindictive (Bourke, 1892; Breuninger, 1959a; Goddard, 1916; Harrington, 1912; M. E. Opler, 1938, 1941, 1946).[3] They are thought by some Apaches to be capable of curing illnesses caused by ghosts and witchcraft. They can be viewed as projections of the loving and beloved as well as the punishing superego introjects.

Although he spent his first six years with his nuclear family, he spent the next four with classificatory grandparents. He had little contact with his parents and siblings thereafter, until he returned from off-reservation school during his early teens. Then he usually slept and ate at the homes of various relatives and friends. It would have been diffi-

---

[3] Currently, they are generally believed to possess ritual songs and dances which have the capacity to prevent harm to people and property and to cure sicknesses caused by ghosts and witchcraft. They are rarely shamans, but one man, who has the status of a shaman, is also a leader of the Horn Dancers (L. B. Boyer, 1962, 1964).

cult on any night to learn where he might be staying, and, as is usual among these Indians, his parents had but vague knowledge of his whereabouts.

When with his grandparents, he was lonesome for his parents, particularly the father. He blamed his mother for his having been sent from home and thought his being placed under the care of the grandparents was punishment for incestuous sexual activities.

Before he began to drink at thirteen, he was passive in his sexual activities. Then, however, he began to initiate intercourse. At first, he chose girls five to eight years his junior, but soon began regular relations with cousins his own age and older. From the age of fifteen, he had numerous affairs with married and other women who were his senior by from five to twenty-five years. All sexual relations in which he was the seducer were accompanied by fortifying, preparatory alcohol intake.

His reservation court record was not unusual for a man his age. There were indictments for theft, injury to public property, drunkenness and disorderly conduct, malicious mischief and paternity charges.

He was first interviewed by me after he had been hospitalized for two days. We had never met previously, but he had been told by relatives that I was a shaman, and, although I conducted my cures in English and used no songs or rites, I knew the Apache language and Apache medicine and religion. He was also informed I had cured cases of chronic alcoholism and that three shamans had been or were my patients.

He willingly accompanied me to a consultation room and, after a short period during which he was guarded, poured out the following story:

Five weeks previously he had tired of working as a cowboy. He had been "hard up." He quit and spent the next two weeks in a drunken orgy with a fifteen-year-old girl. One day after he returned to camp, he began to feel "spooky." That night he hallucinated a sister of his mother and her daughter. Although he lay in bed, he saw them outside the cabin. They were gesturing obscenely and saying, "You can make up your mind if you want relief, or die." He saw the devil, pictured as in Christian church books, black, horned and tailed. The devil urged him to drink and consort with his aunt and cousin. At the same time, his mother's voice forbade the incest. He became terrified. He said to me, "I was too scared to get a hard-on." He attempted to strangulate or smother himself with his blanket. At one time, the devil's head stuck out from an unconnected stovepipe, situated on the wall of the room. After he had been prevented from choking himself, he saw three notoriously loose women and his mother in a car. All four were factually dead. They threatened he must service them sexually or die. Another cowboy and the devil had intercourse with the ghosts. He excitedly related, "Then the devil was in me and I cussed God out. I called to lots of married women to come and fool with me. Then I heard the Horn Dancers and saw the big tipi." He was referring to the ceremonial tipi of the girls' puberty ceremony. Hanging Hairlock was bound at his own request. He feared he would suicide or murder the cowboy, who, with the devil, had intercourse with the ghosts in his hallucination.

From cow camp he was transported to the house of a female shaman. Beginning the following night, he underwent a four-night curing ceremony administered by the woman and designed to remove from him the ghost of his mother. It was assumed by him and others his psychosis had resulted from the presence of her spirit within him.

During the sunlight hours of the four days, he hallucinated the Horn Dancers' singing and dancing and all of the women of the reservation who were suspected of possessing ghost-chasing powers. As is common with toxic psychoses, he regressed during the hours of darkness, continuing to see and hear frightening sights and voices, such as those described above, with decreasing intensity. His belief in the reality of the presence of the hallucinated beings gradually abated.

During the third night of the ceremony, while the shaman sang, he noticed a black purse hanging on a wall of the dwelling. He said to me, "One time I saw my mother hold that black purse out to me with one hand and wave for me to come, with the other hand." He equated purse with vulva but refused to have intercourse with his mother's ghost. His recital continued, "Then the devil sat and waved a huge rattlesnake in the air. It sure rattled loud." The snake crawled up inside his trousers leg, almost to the crotch. Then it disappeared. After the snake left, he again saw and heard the lecherous women who demanded sexual servicing.

Aside from requests that he continue his story, I had made no comments until this point in the interview. Now I asked him what he feared the snake might do. He became embarrassed and silent. I queried further whether he had thought the snake might bite him or crawl into him, but received no answer. He became guarded once again and was able to continue only after I asked him to describe the sound of the rattle. He immediately talked of the noise made by deer-hoof rattles employed by shamans and the Mountain Spirits while they performed their rites. He looked relieved and relaxed. Soon he resumed his narrative, again speaking as though under considerable internal pressure.

The morning after his ghost-chasing ceremony was completed, he attended a Christian church and prayed that he would be forgiven for his immoderate drinking and freed of his mother's ghost. He said to me, "Then I was well."

For the next few days he stayed with various sisters and at the home of his father. However, he became restless and "hard up" after a week. Being a man who was shy except when drinking, he gave himself courage to proposition women by resuming his drinking of wine. The next two weeks were spent in continuous drinking and sexual relations. He slept with various girls and married women, always in the houses of his relatives and at times in the same rooms in which were "sleeping" children of varying ages. On one occasion, he and another man of his age drank with married women fifteen to twenty years older. They went to his father's house and displaced him from his bed. The four spent the night in the parental bed. They did not change sexual partners and no homosexual acts transpired. A nine-year-old boy "slept" nearby. The following morning, Hanging Hairlock, his father and the boy shared a hallucination of the dead mother.

When an Apache dies, it is expected his ghost will hang around the house in which he expired. The spirit will seek to take a loved one with him or to avenge himself on someone, usually a family member. It is customary for the relatives to have someone perform a ghost-chasing ceremony to remove the potential danger before they live again within the dwelling. No such rite had been conducted at the house in which the mother of Hanging Hairlock had died, since her family considered themselves above such superstitions. Because of the vision of the mother's ghost, a shaman was hired to "bless the house." Thereafter the father and boy were at ease, but Hanging Hairlock was more frightened. He ceased drinking. He wondered whether his mother's spirit had returned to reproach him for having continued to have incestuous relations with a cousin, a sexual partner for fifteen years. Two days later, hallucinations such as those previously described reappeared. Among the tempting women seen were all of those with whom he had had intercourse since his previous "cure." He hired a male shaman, but discontinued the ceremony after two days. He felt it unlikely the rite could succeed because the shaman was drunk throughout and stumbled over his songs and prayers. He decided to enter the hospital.

At this point in his recital, he became frightened. Voices said to him,

"Don't tell him. He'll put it down." I said he had begun to worry that I might harm rather than help him. He then heard, "Don't drink no more. You'll drink all your money out." I said perhaps his conscience was speaking to him and the voices he heard came from his own mind rather than from somewhere else. He looked surprised and then relieved. Then he recalled that soon after he decided to enter the hospital he began to see static pictures of Jesus, horses, and the Horn Dancers. In the standard Apache interpretation of dream symbols, the horse represents good luck and is at times equated with the good father. Jesus and the Horn Dancers said he should come to them and they'd be glad to see him. Then he told me, "I really came to the hospital because my belly felt so full and tight I thought I'd burst." He was not constipated. In a later interview, when recounting this material anew, he said his father and his father's voice were in his gut.

The first interview was terminated at this point. Hanging Hairlock gravely and warmly shook hands with me and requested further meetings.

The following morning he was distant and suspicious. He reluctantly went to the consultation room and sat as far as possible from me. Yet, when I said it was reasonable he should distrust me, Hanging Hairlock became warmer and moved his chair close to mine. He said he had dreamed of his mother who was dancing in the manner of old women at the puberty ceremony, with no suggestion of obscenity. At one time he had awakened thinking of his curing ceremony with the female shaman. During wakeful periods, "the devil and those bad thoughts" had troubled him.

A Rorschach test administered at this point revealed clear signs of psychotic regression, in contrast to one given after the sixth interview at which time Hanging Hairlock had abstained from alcohol intake for some ten days and had received heavy vitamin therapy.

The third day found him cool again. He denied further hallucinations but, upon request, presented three dream fragments: (1) "Some man [Indian] was trying to hit me. I called him a son of a bitch." He awoke flailing his fist about. (2) "My little sister [a fourteen-year-old adopted illegitimate girl] said she wanted to take off. I was drunk. I got *mad* and told her to go. I didn't give a damn." (3) "I took a shot of wine."

He spoke spontaneously and continuously. The first manifest associative theme was of the profligacy of the female members of his family. The accompanying emotion was anger, initially at the men involved and subsequently at his mother and sisters. Beneath a spiteful "I don't care" appeared jealousy of their chosen partners. Then appeared sadness and anger toward his parents because he had been sent to live with his grandparents as a boy. He spontaneously recalled lifelong dreams of falling and, immediately thereafter, said that following his mother's death he had dreamed of her walking into a room in which he was sitting, looking as she did in her coffin.

Without pause, he returned to his having been sent to live with his mother's parents. I asked whether he had missed one parent more than the other. He suddenly became angry and refused to speak. I inquired what I had done to offend him, whereupon he cried and revealed he had long felt guilty because, when he was drunk, he'd often told his mother he preferred his father, for which she had frequently reproached him while she was intoxicated.

Each of the previous two interviews had lasted an hour, although no mention was made of time and there was no clock in the room. After about fifty-five minutes had elapsed, he drew his chair closer to mine and sadly spoke of having always wanted to be close with his father. He said, "But my father never talked with me, drunk or sober. Since mother died, he's tried to tell me he loved me by giving me things."

The fourth time he was seen, Hanging Hairlock was eager to talk. He said that so long as he was with people, he had no difficulty. However, when he was alone, he heard women's voices challenging him to get up and service them sexually. The women were daring him to prove his masculinity. At times, he heard the devil singing muffled words over a background of the sounds of the drums of the Horn Dancers. He offered two dreams: (1) "I went to my [classificatory] grandfather's for that ghost cure, but I forgot to take a black-handled knife, so I didn't have any cure." (2) "A crow or something was flying over me. I heard it but I didn't see it. I woke up with a jerk, choking."

One of the four necessary "gifts" which a potential client must offer a shaman for a cure is a black-handled knife. The Indian expression for nightmare is "the ghost covers my mouth." A crow is considered to carry evil spirits, ghosts of dead people.

The third dream fragment was: "My cousin [a girl younger than he] told me 'Here I am. Come to me.' "

His associations emerged under much internal pressure. He related the material cited earlier concerning his childhood sexual life. After a time he became silent and sad. He said he had been thinking of his mother and that he wanted a "fresh start." Then appeared a fourth dream fragment: "I was at a bar. A woman offered me a drink. I didn't want to drink it." The loose, ugly woman was his mother's age. He laughed and said: "I wouldn't want to drink [have sexual relations] with her. She's too old." He said, in response to a query concerning what bar he thought of, that his mother used to drink in the bar which appeared in the dream.

I inquired whether sexual games with his cousins had been sanctioned when he was a boy. He said it had been bad, and then revealed that the punishment for incest was "ghosts." He continued, referring to the recurrence of his alcoholic hallucinosis: "The second time it all started, my father sent the ghosts. The devil sounded just like my daddy but sometimes like a white man. But when I was little boy, it was my mother got after me when I was bad. My father never got after me." He cried and talked of having had intercourse with an older sister when he was sixteen; then again of having "slept with" a girl cousin during all of his remembered life. He said, "I was sleeping with her just before the ghosts came the second time. *Can* I get a good start again? Can I stop drinkin'? I wish I was at cow camp."

During the interview, when he was asked whether he could identify the white man whose voice he had heard in the form of the devil, he was unable to do so. Immediately after the interview, he returned to his bed and began to read the Bible.

During the entire fifth interview, he held his Bible. He denied further bad dreams and hallucinations, but he had continued to hear the sound of the drums of the Horn Dancers. While partly awake, he'd heard the devil tell him to get out of the hospital. He had continued to hear, as background accompaniment to the devil's voice, the sound of the Horn Dancers' drums. When awake, he had decided his hallucinations had been illusions. He said, "The radio was on. I changed that music and the voices into the drums and the devil's voice." He spontaneously postulated that his mother had sent him to his grandparents as punishment for sexual relations with his cousins. He said he had been thinking about the devil's voice and thought it had really been his father's voice, coming from Hanging Hairlock's bowels. When I asked him to what he now attributed his illness, he said he thought he had been "witched" by the mother of a girl he'd impregnated. I inquired whether he had been "witched" or punished by his own conscience. In response, he laughed with relief and said he thought the latter.

The sixth interview, which took place seven days after the first, found him cheerful, friendly, warm and apparently well. He said he thought his illness had been the result of too much drinking of wine. He vowed to turn to religion and to lead a "good life."

He requested but did not keep an appointment scheduled for a week later. After some months he was seen by chance. He was warm but shy. He had resumed drinking and "fooling around," but suffered no further "craziness."

Case 2

Two Waters Came Together sought assistance for recurrent alcoholic hallucinosis, during a period of remission. He was interviewed but once. Extensive data concerning him and his family had been collected by the research team and gaps of clinical knowledge were subsequently filled by information provided by the USPHS physicians.

Individuals of his parental family were more stable than those of Hanging Hairlock. The males drank less heavily, spent more of their time in money-earning work, were fairly regular in attendance of church, and were not known as "chasers." Drunkenness was uncommon among the females, most of whom were reputed to be "good women."

Two Waters was the last-born of a large family. He was always a gentle, shy, quiet boy and youth who was dependent in all his relationships. He had been particularly fond of his father and sought to be with him whenever possible. In grammar school, he was an obedient, passive, silent, average student. However, when he was transferred to another area to attend high school, he became a chronic truant. He explained his running away from school as resulting from loneliness for his family. Peers said he never talked to girls during his boyhood and youth. Largely because he was ridiculed for abstinence by boys of his age, he began to drink at sixteen or seventeen. At nineteen, while he was intoxicated, a girl dared him to have intercourse and he lost his virginity. They had two children premaritally and were finally married by court order. He supported his family marginally to well, working fairly steadily and only occasionally losing time or jobs for drunkenness. He never struck his wife except when she, a teetotaller, refused sexual relations when he was intoxicated.

During his early twenties, he formed a deep, affectionate relationship with a church pastor, a man his father's age who was reputed to be overly fond of boys. He also developed an abiding friendship with a forceful man just older than he. Both relationships were characterized by the dependent behavior and attitude of Two Waters.

Three years before I first saw him, Two Waters' father died after a brief illness. No ghost-chasing ceremony was performed, inasmuch as his family considered itself enlightened and above such "superstitions." Two Waters immediately began to suffer severe nocturnal anxiety attacks. He feared being anywhere without his wife. He lived in terror that the devil, black, horned, and tailed, would find him at night, sit on his chest, and choke him to death. (It will be recalled the word for devil is also the word for ghost and that the expression for nightmare can be interpreted as "the ghost takes my breath.") He feared his father's ghost was lonesome and might take Two Waters for company. He sought to relieve his anxieties by drinking more and more heavily and consistently of wine. Eventually he was jailed. In a cell with an older man, he became unbearably claustrophobic and hallucinated "dead people." He sought to suicide by hanging, "so I wouldn't go crazy." When he spoke with me, he denied recollection of the identity of the "dead people" or the actions within the hallucinations. When speaking of his experience in the cell, before he was hospitalized, he said to me: "I thought after I got out of Purgatory, maybe I'd get to heaven and be with my daddy."

Following his release from the hospital, he worked fitfully for a few months. Periodically, restless, fearful nights led him to drink wine in the company of other men. On many occasions, after he drank for a time, he became acutely fearful the devil would come and get him. Simultaneously, he frequently wished his father would come and transport him to heaven. Unless under sedation, he was relieved only when his wife held him like a baby, rubbed his back, and then initiated intercourse. He said: "I drank with the boys. But after a while I'd get nervous and feel like I had to get home to my wife. I felt safe with her." Unfortunately for his peace of mind, she was often infuriated at his drunkenness and refused to coddle him. At such times, he shook with terror and fled to the hospital. He recalled one "dream" which occurred soon after his return to the reservation from the state hospital: "My father was in the hospital with all those white sheets. I lay beside him. Then I was on top of him and he was holding me in his arms. He told me if those ghosts came, I shouldn't believe them. He said I should take care of myself and go good, so when I died, I could be with him in heaven." Father held Two Waters on his chest, as one would a baby.

A few months after Two Waters' return to the reservation, the pastor suddenly died. There was a severe recurrence of drinking bouts and night terrors. Two Waters was frequently hospitalized for a few days on the reservation. Although he consistently denied hallucinations to the doctors, an Apache-speaking nurse said Two Waters talked with ghosts every night he was immured. During the next year, his friend, too, died suddenly. Two Waters told me: "I got so *scared,* then. I thought maybe his ghost or my father's or the pastor's would come and get *me* to go with them. Just after my friend died, I dreamed I was in bed. A *big* anaconda crawled across the floor toward me." He awoke in terror. When asked to describe the snake, he replied that it had diamonds on its back, which reminded him of a rattlesnake and a design commonly painted on the Horn Dancers, symbolizing snake and lightning.

DISCUSSION

No systematic epidemiological survey was conducted to determine the incidence and types of psychoses from which these Apaches suffer. Descriptions were obtained from informants of the symptomatology exhibited by all individuals considered to be "crazy." Information was acquired from physicians who served at the three principal hospitals in New Mexico in which emotional disorders of Apaches from the reservation are treated, and from doctors who worked at two federal penitentiaries in which Mescalero, Chiricahua and Lipan Apaches have been incarcerated. The diagnostic labels attached were schizophrenia, senile psychosis, delirium tremens and alcoholic hallucinosis. No case had been named mania, psychotic depression or manic-depressive psychosis. The instances of psychosis described by informants, whether or not apparently of organic origin, presented only schizophrenoid and/or organic symptomatology (see also Baker, 1959).[4]

The psychosis of "choice" into which the Apache retreats when psychic strains become overwhelming, then, appears to be one of the group of schizophrenias. In this sense, the typical Apache may be said

---

[4] Devereux (1939; 1961, p. 16) holds that schizophrenia does not occur among "true primitives." He has also stressed that there is much difficulty in translating native symptom complexes into Western psychiatric terms (Devereux, 1961, p. 18). Agreeing with many others, I (1962) have previously noted that the differentiation of schizophrenia and neurotic syndromes is frequently difficult even when patients are under the care of and intensive study by trained personnel for long periods of time. Attempts to differentiate between neuroses and psychoses on the basis of descriptions offered by anthropologists who are psychiatrically unschooled is hazardous. Obviously, no living Apache informants can recall individuals who suffered from mental disorders during periods previous to Apache contact with Western cultures. However, their descriptions of people with psychopathic states, who lived while there was yet no great contact influence, sounded very much to me as though overt schizophrenia did exist during early reservation days. It seems unlikely that Devereux's stand can be tested empirically.

to be preschizophrenic.[5] Perhaps the drunkenness serves as a safety device which permits periodic episodes of minor psychotic outbreaks and safeguards against the development of a more insidious, chronic state of withdrawal. There are few Apaches who do not retain deep involvement in the old-time religion, regardless of the degree to which they participate in the Christian sects. It is my opinion that belief in a religion which involves the concept of diffuse supernatural power and the retention of infantile notions of animation of the inanimate, requires relatively indiscriminate projection of infantile omnipotence onto surroundings, conditions which are consistent with confusion of ego boundaries. People who retain such defects of ego growth are subject to the development of character disorders and psychoses. Montagu (1961, pp. 19-20) has stated that in some cultures mental illness is institutionalized, meaning the behavior of the sick man is incorporated into the society as a normal part of it, and conditions institutionalized forms of emotional expression, such as religion, painting, narrative, and the like. Spiro (1959) suggested that the Ifaluk avoid overt psychosis because of the sanctioned outlet of hostility provided by religion in the form of the malevolent ghost.

The description of modern socialization processes has revealed the care afforded the Apache infant during his early life to be grossly inconsistent. He is confronted with a narcissistic, ambivalent mother who clearly places her immediate desires before his needs, and he has no adequate surrogate for her. He is haphazardly treated with vacillating tenderness

[5] A. C. and H. M. Voth found, through use of the autokinetic phenomenon described by A. C. Voth (1947), that individuals who suffer from manic-depressive psychosis, involutional depression, hysteria, psychopathic personality, alcoholism, and true paranoia are ego-close." Ego-closeness (H. M. Voth, 1962, p. 151) "refers to a high dependence on external stimulation, to a compelling need to invest attention cathexis in external objects and a limited control over impulse. The experience of 'self' is more in terms of external objects and a limited control over impulses. The experience of 'self' is more in terms of external values and circumstances."

They found that individuals who are afflicted with schizophrenia, anxiety state, obsessive-compulsive neurosis, and mixed neurosis are "ego-distant." Ego-distance (H. M. Voth, 1962, p. 151) "implies a greater independence of the ego from external reality. There is less dependence upon external stimuli and a greater ability to shift cathexis to internal objects and stimuli. Impulse control is greater."

The empirical data afforded by the Eastern Apaches are dysmensurate with the Voths' findings. They suffer from all the illnesses subsumed under "ego-close," except for the manic-depressive psychosis and involutional depression. Their psychosis of "choice" is some variant or other of schizophrenia. Some experience anxiety states. Obsessive-compulsive neurosis and mixed neurosis, so far as I was able to determine, are absent, although I found obsessive and compulsive symptoms in one individual. My clinical impression was that these Apaches are indeed, as a rule, "ego-close."

and abrupt abandonments, regardless of the urgency of his inner strivings, physiological or psychological, which cannot be synchronous with his mother's. Escalona (1953) has stressed the need for cooperative, reciprocal interactions for the development of what Mahler (1954; Mahler and Gosliner, 1955) has designated the adequate symbiotic phase, which facilitates id-ego differentiation and the *Anlagen* of satisfactory object relations (Hartmann, 1939, 1952; Hartmann, Kris and Loewenstein, 1946) and the development of a sense of basic trust which Erikson (1950, pp. 219-222; 1959, pp. 55-65) deemed an important heritage of the oral phase.

The waking life of the newborn centers around his attempts to reduce tension through his body (Hoffer, 1949) and his mother's care of him. He learns to distinguish between a pleasurable quality and a painful quality of experiences and the qualities of "good" and "bad" become equated with "edible" and "inedible" substances. Eventually he develops a vague, affective discrimination between self and nonself. The qualities of pleasure-giving and pain-inflicting become attached to the mother and also to primitive memory islands formed through pleasurable and unpleasurable sensations from within his body; this appears to be the start of the formation of scattered part images of the object and of the body self, which are endowed with the same qualities of prevailingly good and predominantly bad as are the scattered part images of the mother. The baby reacts to bad stimuli with ejective and ridding mechanisms; to good, at first with quiet bliss and later with reaching out. Overshadowing both reactions is the unneutralized impetuous drive of aggression and indiscriminative incorporation of good and bad which reaches its peak at the period of oral aggression. As Hoffer (1950) has written, deflection of the surplus unneutralized aggression from the body ego is of the utmost importance for its development. In the further course of normal growth there is a unification of the split images and a unified object becomes demarcated from a unified self-representation.

The maturational growth of locomotion during the second year exposes the infant to the important experience of voluntary and active bodily separation from and reunion with the mother, in normal child development. During the second eighteen months of life, in which the pregenital phases progress in rapid and overlaminating procession, he masters increasing segments of his physical surroundings, provided he feels his mother's encouragement and dependable availability. The characteristic fear of this period is separation anxiety, which is more complex but probably less overwhelming than the fear of annihilation through abandonment to be found in the previous phase. A strong and adequate symbiotic phase is a prerequisite for the subsequent successful disengagement which gradually develops in the separation-individuation phase and leads to a stable image of the self. Provided the environment of the child has allowed the growth of an optimal symbiotic phase and permitted successful individuation, at the end of three or three and a half years, the child should be able to respond to the mother as an entirety and realize one and the same person can both gratify and disturb him. With the advent of latency he should begin to be able to modulate feelings within himself, appraise good and bad by trial acting, that is, thinking.

Anna Freud (1951) wrote of the negativistic phase of the toddler which marks the beginning of disengagement from the mother-child symbiosis. The more parasitic or less satisfactory the symbiotic phase has been, the more prominent will be the negativistic reaction. Early psychic injuries disrupt the process of self-differentiation and object creation. Too massive or continually harassing painful noxae (L. B. Boyer, 1956) may overwhelm the infant and lead to exhaustion, apathy, and finally regression to a more archaic level in which the budding self-awareness and apperception of the good part image of the mother are destroyed. Fused and confused faulty couplings of part images of self and object result, and hinder reality orientation. According to Mahler and Gosliner (1955), the toddler whose ego is constitutionally vulnerable or symbiotically fixated, and then during the separation-individuation phase additionally traumatized, is prone to psychotic defense, a secondary autism they designate a reactive restitution because through it the ego regressively restores the blissful, oceanic feeling of oneness with "the object," and secures a delusional substitute for the child who is unable to endure "the second hatching process," i.e., the actual separation from the good object.

The Apache infant irregularly alternately experiences the bliss of great physical intimacy with his mother and abrupt, terrifying abandonment. The nursing couple stare at each other's faces and become oblivious to their environment; at such times they seem to achieve what I have elsewhere (1956) named a state of psychological syncyntium. If we assume that the progression of psychological development outlined above is true, we must assume that by the time of the separation-individuation phase, the ego of the Apache infant has developed unevenly. His reaction to the sudden rejection upon the birth of a new rival, occurring as a rule during that separation-individuation phase, is violently regres-

sive. He screams, throws himself about, flails out, and desperately strives
for succor. After a time, he frets, wails, becomes withdrawn and to some
degree apathetic. He becomes an inveterate thumb-sucker. As a rule, his
actions are greeted with ridicule and physical rejection. In addition, his
parents begin to use false promises and threats of desertion to cultural
bogies in their attempts to discipline him, that is, they support his
paranoid ideation. He is forced into a position of caring for himself
prematurely: he has to procure his own crust of bread or his own blanket.
He soon learns to control his physical manifestations of rage and develops the passive stoicism characteristic of the frightened or angry Apache
adult who feels any other behavior would be fraught with danger of
some kind, whether in the form of physical damage or ridicule.

Searles (1961) has dealt further with the results of a child's being
reared by an ambivalent mother. He has indicated that the infant who is
faced with an ambivalent mother defends himself against her and against
his own ambivalence by maintaining a symbiotic relationship with her
mental representations far beyond its normal period. Through such a
relationship, he maintains his imagined infantile omnipotence, one
facet of which is the unconscious fantasy of being both male and
female. His sexual image is also distorted (1) by the castrating effect of his
mother's hostility toward him, (2) by the fact that in a setting of psychological symbiosis with a poorly integrated mother, he has introjected
various of her self-concepts, and (3) by his own destructive desires toward
his mother. He therefore lacks a sexual identity. Partly because of this,
he tends to conceive of *all* attributes and behavior traits as bearing a
sexual label, which may make him even more unwilling to accept a sexual
identity, since, in his unconscious view, to do so would be to relinquish a
part of himself. As we have observed in the socialization data, Searles'
remarks concerning the youngster's interaction with his mother would
apply to that with the father.

Sarvis and Garcia (1961) have hypothesized the vulnerable developmental period for the onset of childhood autism as the time during
which the mother is the primary object to the child, usually about six
months to three years. They wrote (p. 308):

During the period of differentiation and gradual perception of the
mother as a separate person, the mother is still the primary object.
Therefore, anything that happens to the child, whether from
the inside or the outside, is apt to impress the child as persecu-
tion by the mother and cause him to adopt the paranoid attitude
which we feel to be central in the promotion of an *autistic reac-*

tion. Feeling the mother to be responsible for his difficulties, the child rejects the mother.... she faces a temptation to counter-reject or withdraw from the child. The reactions of other family members are especially important at this stage.

Should antiautistic factors in the mother, other family members or the child himself be inadequate,

> if the mother seriously counterrejects or withdraws from the child, the child tends to be confirmed in his paranoid reaction and may develop the more intransigent, less reversible state which we have called *chronic autistic disease.*

We observed only a few instances of chronic autistic disease among the Apache. However, autistic reactions commonly occurred following frustration of the displaced child's desperate strivings toward re-establishment of contact with the mother. We have not studied in detail the etiogenesis of the autistic reactions. It is possible that there is an unconscious need within the mother (and perhaps the father as well) for the child to become autistic. Our impression, as previously mentioned, has been that the infant is periodically treated as a narcissistic extension of the mother, who bestows upon it care she wishes for herself. Perhaps she communicates to the displaced child her desire that he seek gratifications from within himself and withdraw his demands from the environment. Sarvis and Garcia (p. 311) wrote: "Tone-deaf mothers promote autistic reactions by virtue of their inability to empathize with the child." The incapacity of Apache mothers to empathize with the needs of the older baby is very clear. Sarvis (1960, 1962) has noted a high incidence of temporal lobe disturbance among autistic children and has written of the role of perceptual distortions in the development of paranoid reactions. Clements and Mohr (1961) have found, through actual removal of blood by syringe, gross chronic subdural hematomata in thirteen per cent of Apache infants. They could not determine with certainty the reasons for the presence of such intracranial pathology, but it appears likely that it may be resultant from the effects of traumata which have occurred to the infant pre- and postnatally, combined with gross neglect and resultant dietary deficiencies. It seems reasonable to assume that brain damage results from the presence of such effusions and also that, if gross hematomata can be demonstrated in such a percentage of babies, smaller ones must be quite common. Greenacre (1941, 1958, 1960) has postulated that unfavorable conditions, ". . . if especially severe, often repeated or long sustained during the early months of life (even during the prenatal, natal and neonatal periods) may establish a permanent tendency to tension. The resultant increased reactivity of young infants in turn elevates the susceptibility to and the intensity of later anxiety reactions" (Greenacre, 1960, pp. 704-705). We have here a hint that Apache socialization processes lead to the early development of autistic tendencies through the promotion of psychological and organic factors. In times past, the development of such intracranial hemorrhages might very well have been more common. I have commented on the apparent choice of one or more of the group of schizophrenias as the psychosis of the Apache. Perhaps here we have one of the *Anlagen,* which are apparently supported by the ethnocentric encouragement of the use of projection, introjection and displacement as defenses and adaptation phenomena.

It is suspected that the principal reason there is not a high percentage of chronic autistic disease among the Apache is that older siblings and other children *have* the capacity to empathize with the needs of the newly displaced child and provide it with succor.

As we have seen, the typical early care of the Apache baby does not provide the necessary ingredients for the development of an adequate symbiotic phase, and the treatment afforded him by the abrupt separation which accompanies the birth of a new sibling causes further traumata. If we had no data but these, the tendency of the Apache to develop schizophreniform psychoses under stress would appear to be understandable. Certainly, the tenuousness of Apache interpersonal relationships and their perpetuation from generation to generation are partially explained.

I do not wish to overstress the possibility that organic components, whether resultant from inbreeding, physical traumata, or neglect, constitute the major predisposing phenomena which result in Apache personality maturational deficiencies. It is my opinion that the psychological socialization processes in themselves provide adequate reasons for the constellations we observe, and that whatever organic elements may exist are probably merely additive.

During the anal phase, the Apache toddler is confronted with abrupt displacement by a new arrival. His attempts to re-establish himself with caretakers are nonrewarding. He is pushed into a situation in which he must develop prematurely a form of relative autonomy. He learns that reaction formation must be developed toward those who are younger and smaller, and passivity, stoicism, and noncompetitiveness will avoid ridicule.

We have seen that the Apache toddler is disciplined with ridicule and the instillation of fears. He is constantly shamed. The Apache does not develop a well-organized sense of guilt. Rather, he develops a determination to get away with things, and, in many, there results deliberate shamelessness, or shamelessness which emerges so easily under the influence of a little alcohol that it appears to be deliberate. He cannot develop stable control of emotions and behavior. Real, inner autonomy is lacking.

R. M. Boyer (1962, pp. 336-337) has hypothesized that the present-day Apache usually develops a negative identity, a concept of which Erikson (1959, p. 131) wrote: "an identity perversely based on all those identifications and roles which, at critical stages of development, had been presented to the individual as most undesirable or dangerous, and yet also as most real." He communicated further (p. 132):

> Such vindictive choices of a negative identity represent, of course, a desperate attempt at regaining some mastery in a situation in which the available positive identity elements cancel each other out. The history of such a choice reveals a set of conditions in which it is easier to derive a sense of identity out of a *total* identification with that which one is *least* supposed to be than to struggle for a feeling of reality in acceptable roles which are unattainable with the patient's inner sense. [See also Bychowski, 1958; Greenson, 1954.]

R. M. Boyer wrote:

> . . . a young child who is frequently told he is a "bad" child, may try to prove such badness in later life although he is fully aware that the cultural ideal is one of "goodness." Among the Apache . . . many children are constantly told they are "no good." One small child of two and one-half years had learned to speak only one English phrase although her understanding was largely bilingual. She was encouraged to repeat this expression over and over for the amusement of guests. The rote consisted of the following: "Me, Susie, me no good. Me, Susie, me no good." As further illustration . . . some Apache young people are reputed to "know nuthin' " throughout their " 'teen" years. By the time they have completed a year or so of high school, their scholastic ratings indicate a general lack of knowledge even though their intelligence is purportedly normal. The Indian society is proud of its members who show knowledge and intelligence—intelligence devoted to outwitting the Anglo or knowledge of old Indian ways or just "common sense" in general. Academic knowledge *per se* is not important, but an Apache should not appear stupid, nor should he become the subject of ridicule. Failing is not an Apache ideal, and yet many Indian children fail in high school. . . . They seem intent on demonstrating that they "just don't know nothin'."

Thus, through the oral period, the Apache baby is traumatized by the inconsistent, narcissistic, ambivalent treatment afforded by his care-takers. Then he is assaulted by rejection at the time of arrival of a new infant and the environment does not consistently assist him in his attempt to master the new injury. He is further damaged by the support afforded his utilization of regression as a defense and as a partially ego-syntonic adaptation mode. But this is not all. Throughout his infancy and child-hood, he is bombarded with the exciting stimuli emanating from his parents' drunken expressions of their own lack of self-control. Periodically, he is subjected to their displays of unbridled fury, during which they will strike out with anything which comes to hand. And in the crowded households, there is utter lack of regard for children when sexual activities proceed, if the parents have been drinking, or, if the children are up to three or perhaps even four years of age, if the parents are sober. The child who is subjected to such experiences judges the external events according to the maturational stage in which he happens to be. We have observed that the Apache child has had scant opportunity to develop to the degree of maturity which would permit him to face life with an orientation rela-tively unhampered by the influences of severe oral fixations. The devel-opment of secondary-process thinking has been thwarted. During the anal and phallic phases, he must continue to interpret his experiences in man-ners which are tinged by his remaining primitive oral view. It seems likely that small Apache children, stimulated as they are by adult aggres-sive and sexual behavior about them, incorporate the excitements of both partners. Probably this supports the identity confusion which has per-sisted from the oral phase. The males leave the oedipal period having retained in part a feminine orientation. According to Searles (1961), a child whose parents are ambivalent and narcissistic has further warped experiences during the oedipal phase. He has to compete with their love for themselves. If their object-relatedness is only weakly established at a genital level, he may have to remain at an infantile level in order to relate to them. His libidinal and aggressive strivings dating from the genital phase of psychosexual development will be poorly integrated with those traceable to the oral stage; as a result, frightening oral ele-ments may appear alternately with adult lustful ones.

The empirical data demonstrated clearly that the Apache have severe outbreaks of destructive rage as a facet of unstable development of ego and superego. Quite apparently, they have not developed the capacity to sublimate or neutralize aggressive energies (Hartmann, Kris and Loew-enstein, 1949) and thus to place aggressive drives in the service of self-benefit.

Although the data from which we must draw our conclusions are the result of inference rather than actual observation, they suggest that infant care patterns in aboriginal periods were similar, in crucial pathogenic respects, to those seen today. We know, from careful reading of M. E. Opler (1941, pp. 5-76) and from our own investigations that there was considerable ambivalence toward pregnancy and young children. From observations of the attitudes of old people toward mothering as practiced by women of younger generations, and from watching those same old people when they are the guardians of youngsters, we have learned that despite some moralizing talk, the actual care afforded children of all ages does not vary significantly by parents and step-parents or guardians of different generations. To judge from the shallowness of emotional relationships seen among many of the very old today, we can judge that formerly, as now, adults had a faulty capacity to develop lasting, deeply meaningful object relations.

Apparently, to some extent, mothers felt their babies to be merely objects requiring physical care until they were one and a half to two years of age, and were able with equanimity, even self-righteousness, to leave them to the ministrations of others at any time they chose, whether the stated reasons had to do with gathering of subsistence products or merely pleasure. It may be that the fact that there was ideally no new childbirth for three years provided a mitigating circumstance, since the baby did not experience a sudden, gross, traumatic displacement until his period of separation-individuation had had more opportunity to flower and wane. Perhaps, then, the displaced toddler received more or less considerate care for a longer period than is the rule today. He may have suffered less from the necessary suppression and repression of hostilities toward parents and siblings because emotional separation was delayed until his ego was better prepared to accept the shock. We do not know to what degree aboriginal fathers assumed maternal roles, but there is every reason to believe there was a clearer differentiation of parental functions than exists today. In all probability, infants were generally left to the ministrations of maternal female relatives. We cannot evaluate with conviction whether the aboriginal child received less trauma from the enforced separation. Although Caplan (1953) and Spiro (1958) have made steps in this direction, so far as I am aware, no thorough study has been done of personality development in a group in which children have relatively free access to a number of mother surrogates and no truly close ties with any single individual. Surely the flowery interpretation of Polynesian child rearing by Mead (1928) smacks of romantic superficiality, to judge from the writings of the Beagleholes (1946). But if we

assume that there was then, as now, a lack of consistent cooperative interaction between mothers and their infants, it would follow that there was
also a lack of the ingredients which are requisite for the development of
an adequate symbiotic phase with its resultant growth of basic trust and
id-ego differentiation. Today, the very old people appear to have the
same incapacity to relate deeply as do the middle-aged and younger. It
seems reasonable to trace this emotional shallowness to early mother-
infant relationships.

There seems no doubt that, with the birth of a new child, the old-
time Apache parent abruptly pushed away the clamoring displaced
sibling and proceeded to support his regressive defenses and precocious
spotty facets of ego growth acceleration. I wrote elsewhere (L. B. Boyer,
1956, pp. 238-239):

> Defenses against the without as well as the within develop in close
> interconnection with object relationships (Arlow, 1952; A. Freud,
> 1949; Hartmann, 1953; Kris, 1950). Trouble in the development of
> object relations may well interfere with growth of stable defenses
> which may again stultify development of object relations. Distorted
> object relations predispose to schizophrenia. One decisive factor on
> the side of the ego is the level of neutralization. In dedifferentia-
> tion of the ego, more differentiated forms of object relations can
> no longer be maintained. Self-object and ego-id relations run paral-
> lel. Withdrawal of object cathexis may well lead to loosening of
> ties with reality. The dedifferentiation of reality testing may be
> related to deneutralization; inner reality as well as outer reality
> become distorted.

I have assumed that the typical mother-infant relations of the Apache
result in suboptimal, uneven development of object relations, defenses,
neutralization, reality testing, and development of secondary-process
thinking—that is to say, id-ego differentiation. At the time of the usual
rejection consequent upon the birth of the new king or queen of the
family, we should expect regression to take place from whatever forward
strides have previously transpired. Thus, there would be a tendency for
a further distortion of object relations, weakening of defenses and reality
testing, deneutralization and dedifferentiation of the ego. The institutionalized child-rearing patterns support some aspects of this regression.
Continued utilization of primary-process thinking is enhanced as are
autism and utilization of primitive defenses. This is most obvious in
the cases of displacement and projection, with the systematic teaching
of the reality of supernatural agencies and cultural bogies and the sanc-

tioning of release of sadistic impulses on small animals. At the same time, precocious development of an aspect of autonomy is demanded, involving the rapid development of reaction formations and muscular and expressional controls. Superimposed upon the formal teaching aspects resultant from shaming and ridicule are the inevitable excitements produced because of the parents' sexual and hostile behavior, particularly when intoxicated, the effects of which are unavoidable in the living arrangements which afford scant privacy and the attitude of the parents that children before the age of six are incapable of learning; such stimuli are present throughout the growing child's maturational phases, all of which are necessarily yet under the influence of the oral phase, and preclude rational perception and integration of the stimuli and their meanings. The Apache child remains primarily identified with his narcissistic, impulsive, ambivalent mother who has sexualized, and to some degree aggressivized, most attitudes and behavior patterns. It follows that the boys, at least, leave their oedipal periods with a partially inverted orientation. In the early days, surely tent living in small groups provided no more privacy than today's housing. We must assume that aboriginal Apache children were psychologically immature for their ages when they reached the period of life when their formal role training began. But there was a sharp difference between the training of Apache children in the old days and that currently offered. Then, men and women had clearly differentiated roles and children of both sexes were offered manifestly distinguishable constellations of behavior and functions with which to identify; they were consistently schooled toward their expected adulthood positions. That the old ways were effective from the standpoint of the group is illustrated by the workability of the relatively stable and internally flexible social structure then prevalent. Childrearing patterns created conflicts then, as they do currently. But institutionalized means were afforded for the expression and reduction of anxieties and the support of dependency needs; that is, means were provided for the use of such conflicts for adaptation (Hartmann, 1939). Aboriginally, the culture provided unambivalently sanctioned outlets for psychopathological symptoms and characterologic defects. Boys had a real opportunity to become men, Apache style. Such conditions no longer obtain. Whereas the same personality configurations are instilled within children as formerly, there are no unambivalent outlets for the release of intrapsychic tensions.

In addition, in contrast to the attitude of pride and arrogance which accompanied being an Apache in past days, today the Indians basically feel pessimism, resignation, and confusion. Acceptable standards of expression of love and hate, occupational behavior, personal responsibility, and moral actions and tenets are contradictory. Not only are "double-bind" messages (Bateson et al., 1956) transmitted by the parents, but by the entire environment. It would seem that the modern Apache child is still prepared psychologically with a personality structure which could have become functionally useful a hundred years ago, but now has at best asymptotic application in the inevitably changing societal and life patterns.

It seems most likely the individual suffered less guilt and anxiety when there were consistent societal outlets for the conditions of psychological abnormality which were stimulated and promoted. Nevertheless, we should not forget Devereux's evaluation that "warlike tribes often have deep-seated conflicts related to guilt over aggression." He wrote:

> Hence, the Mohave Indians' notorious blood phobia, which is a symptom of many types of mental disorders known to them, is by no means unique even in the Southwest. Thus, according to Hrd-lička (1908) a "White Mountain Apache . . . had a boy who, from nervousness, could not eat the red-fleshed pitahaya; 'it looks to him too much like blood'" (Devereux, 1961, p. 14).

Apaches of the groups with which this communication deals, uniformly cook meat until it is completely free of any trace of pink.

Among the Hutterites (Eaton and Weill, 1953), culturally normative trends lead to the internalization of problems through community expectations of the principles of personal guilt and pacifism. Psychopathic personalities and violent crimes do not exist and the dominant type of psychosis is the manic-depressive. Among them, the development of stable ego and superego without the presence of gross lacunae is enhanced. By contrast, among the Apaches, the principle of personal responsibility and guilt is meager. Violence and immorality prevail. The adults are in general narcissistic, impulsive, grossly ambivalent, pleasure-seeking people. All adult Apaches have sanctioned fears and the great majority have phobias. It is likely that most hallucinate at some time before they reach adult age. A great many become drunkards for some period of their lives, and probably most of those who do have episodes of alcoholic hallucinosis. Drunkenness, that societal and personal self-defeating constellation, has become an institutionalized pattern providing for the release of tensions. As Peter Blos has commented in a personal communication, the current-day Apaches lack symbolic representations or derivatives which are detached from the original organ modes (Erikson, 1950, 1959). He wrote: "Other societies—like the Balinese [Bateson and Mead, 1942; Gill and Brenman, 1959, pp. 294-320; Mead and Macgregor, 1951]—formalize in the trance and dance a psychotic transient state which permits a regression and simultaneously protects ego intactness" (see also deZoete and Spies, 1938, and Belo, 1960).

In order to permit a more adequate discussion of the strong, latent, passive, dependent homoerotic yearnings I observed to be typically present among Apache men, we shall now examine the case histories. The material from Hanging Hairlock will be scrutinized in some detail and that of Two Waters Came Together more generally.

Although we have no specific data concerning the infancy of these two men, information concerning their relatives allows the assumption that their early training was typical. They remained the babies in their families and as such may have received more considerate care than they would have experienced had siblings replaced them within a short time. Leighton and Kluckhohn (1948, p. 37) found adult Navahos who had been reared as the youngest members of their families to be more stable, more secure, less suspicious and generally "happier" than others. A preliminary evaluation of our Apache data does not indicate such differences.

In contrast to most Apache boys, Hanging Hairlock preferred to play with girls from early childhood. In games with them, he at times overtly assumed a feminine role, even to imitating childbirth. He began to drink and conjointly became sexually aggressive at thirteen, before which time he had been sexually active, but passively. Information obtained from other men indicates they began to imbibe and become sexually aggressive during their middle teens and that their behavior was often motivated by a desire to prove their masculinity.

Five weeks before he was interviewed, Hanging Hairlock quit his job as a cowboy because he was "hard up."

One of our research team, Dr. MacLachlan, spent the greater part of ten days among the cowboys. His observations reveal Apache men to be much more modest in cow camp than are white soldiers on bivouac. They spend leisure time giggling over very mild pornography. They allude to their sexual prowess and joke about castration. There is tame sexual horseplay which involves slapping of buttocks. If a man's sexual capacities are doubted, he becomes angry. One shooting is thought to have resulted from allusions to a cowboy's potential lack of masculinity, a notorious Don Juan whose intensive pursuit of sexual conquests was interpreted by many Indians to mean that he felt unsure of himself as a man, particul larly since he was one of the very few Apaches who carried a revolver and refused to engage in fisticuffs.

After two weeks of a heterosexual orgy, Hanging Hairlock returned to cow camp. His first toxic hallucinations involved temptations by female incest objects. Since he was sated with sexual relations and yet required further "relief," there is a hint his excitement stemmed from proximity to homosexual objects. The content of a chance interview which took place a year subsequent to the period described above under the category of clinical material affirms such an interpretation. Then, after he related recurrences of hallucinosis with manifest material identical to that cited previously, he said: "I have to drink. I have three girls and I can't even talk to them when I'm not drinking. I'm too shy. I can't stand to be alone because I get too nervous. So I go drinking with the guys and I have to drink because they drink and they'd think I was funny if I didn't drink. Then, after I'm with them for a while, I get hard up and have to go with a girl."

Let us return to the data obtained during the first interview. I assume that Hanging Hairlock was undergoing an identity crisis. Under the influence of vitamin shortage and perhaps alcohol toxicity, he had regressed to a deep psychotic state in which he was confronted with dilemmas which faced him during his infancy and early childhood. Hanging Hairlock was in a state in which he strove to retain both his masculine and feminine identities. On one level of thinking, hallucinatory representations constitute projections of incorporates. The first hallucinations were those of mother and sister surrogates which demanded gratification of sexual urges. It can be assumed that his prolonged heterosexual orgy had threatened his feminine identity and that the revealed incestuous desires were defensive in nature. He was encouraged to "relieve" himself by the devil, symbolizing a forbidden libidinous aspect of his composite paternal mental representations. The devil's head stuck out from a stovepipe. Apaches freely equate stovepipe and rectum. At a later time, Hanging Hairlock said his father's voice emanated from his gut. The site of the paternal introject was considered to be inside the bowel. However, at the time the devil coaxed him to engage in incestuous activities, his mother's voice forbade participation. Stated differently, a facet of his maternal incorporate threatened him with loss of self-love, should he indulge. Faced with the dilemma of loss of self-love through sexual relations with either males or females, he sought relief through suicide.

The choice of suicide is interesting. He tried to strangle or smother himself with his blanket, suggesting that in his regressing he was reliving a period during which he had been in bed with his parents while they were engaged in sexual activities, and he had incorporated the excitement of both partners.

Following the enactment in hallucinations of sexual relations between masculine and feminine introjects, he became briefly elated. It is well known that one defensive function served by the elated state is that of denial (Lewin, 1950). He became the devil, or the devil was inside him, and he defied God or morality. But the denial immediately failed, as he then hallucinated the Horn Dancers, representative of his father and his father's morality. Again he contemplated suicide as relief of his dilemma.

While undergoing a shamanistic cure intended to remove his mother's ghost, or his maternal incorporates, during the daylight hours, his degree of regression was lessened and he hallucinated cultural representations of the moral and loving aspects of the superego, the Horn Dancers, and the women who were thought to be endowed with supernatural powers to be used for purposes of good. At night, the period during which identity loss is a greater threat and during which most Apache sexual relations transpire, his regression increased and he returned to seeking to use defensively heterosexual incestuous relations. The dilemma persisted, although with decreasing anxiety. Its nature was clarified beyond question by the events of the third night, when the hallucinated figure of his mother offered him her black purse and, when he refused to participate in sexual relations with her, his father, the devil, attacked him sexually. However, the depth of his regression had decreased by then, as attested by the fact that mother's genital and father's penis were now represented by commonplace symbols, the purse and the snake. In addition, the snake now had a more clearly defined meaning. Its noise was associated to the rattling of deer hooves. Perhaps, using the primitive mode of introjection, and displacing the function of the mouth to the anus, he sought to obtain added moral support from the snake, which represented the phallus of his father.

His seeking for recathexis of moral and loving paternal introjects continued after completion of the curing ceremony, when he went to the Christian church, attempting to obtain more secure decathexis of the composite maternal introject, mother's ghost. He then resided with various sisters, where he was undoubtedly excited by the noises of sexual activities and drunken arguments which would have revived dangerous childhood memories, and with his father. Among the complex interweaving of meanings of this behavior should be considered its thinly disguised vicarious homosexual significance. The latent homosexual content of group heterosexual activities is well known. The fact that the next morning found him again hallucinating his mother's spirit may support the hypothesis that the actions which took place in his father's bed constituted to him a loss of masculine identification. The projection of the maternal introject as the hallucination had a defensive function intended to enable him to restore his bisexual identity, the least anxiety-producing state of psychic equilibrium he had been able to achieve in his psychosexual development.

An institutionalized attempt at removal of the dangerous maternal introject was performed in the employment of the customary ghost-chasing rite which relieved two of the three sufferers of *folie à trois*. The anxiety of Hanging Hairlock, however, did not abate. He attributed the reappearance of mother's ghost to punishment for his continued incestuous relations with a sister surrogate, his cousin. He again hallucinated libidinous objects with whom he had engaged recently in sexual activities. It would appear the promiscuity had been employed to alleviate heterosexual and homosexual incestuous urges in one of the tried and sometimes successful methods he had learned, denial through action. The sexual activities can again be understood as strivings to regain identity equilibrium. Apparently, however, the primary process was still dominant. He equated the women with whom he indulged in sexual relations with feminine incestuous surrogates, since he then voluntarily sought a cure from a male shaman, rather than the female shaman who had been previously chosen for him by his relatives. But he could not complete the ghost-chasing ceremony with the male shaman. On one level, no doubt, his stated reason, that the shaman was drunk and could not properly conduct the rite, is accurate. On another level, however, we must recall that all Apaches fear and many have phobias concerning drunken men. There seems no reason to doubt that such phobias are based in part upon revival of childhood memories of the activities of drunken fathers. We should suspect, then, that he could not complete the cure with the male shaman because of anxieties aroused by his passive urges toward the drunken father surrogate. Having failed to obtain surcease with both male and female shamans, he sought hospitalization, where he might obtain relief from other logical and magical treatments. That the white constituted a threat to him is indicated by the fact that, during the first interview, at the point where he related his decision to enter the hospital, he became frightened of me. My interpretation that he had projected his conscience onto me was greeted by relief. He corroborated the interpretation by revealing that soon after he entered the hospital, he projected temporarily recathected moral and protective aspects of his tenuous superego in the form of culturally defined symbols, Jesus, horses, and Horn Dancers. He then localized his conceptualization of the site of paternal components of his superego to be within his gut.

During the third interview, a new element appeared in the manifest content of his productions: his lifelong yearning for a father upon whose love he could depend. This theme arose during the interviews of most of the men and some of the women whose conflicts were investigated. As has been noted, when the babies are pushed away from their mothers, either because of the appearance of a younger rival, or because of the intrinsic ambivalence and narcissism of the mothers, they strive to obtain relief from their anxieties from their fathers, who prove to be highly undependable sources of emotional sustenance. In the cases of the boys, they have already learned or soon learn that sexual submission to the father is a means of obtaining at least physical closeness. Such an observation no doubt helps to keep alive feminine components of their identities and re-enforces proclivities to maintain an inverted position from which they cannot grow during the oedipal period. Reasoning from the viewpoint that stable superego structures develop from or are at least concurrent with positive resolution of the oedipus complex, we can hypothesize that we have here a partial explanation for the incidence of weak superego development among the Apache. In a personal communication, Dr. Sidney Axelrad has added:

> It may also be that the fixation at the negative phase of the Oedipus may be one determinant of their delinquency. I've found that many juvenile delinquents have this. Basically, there is an overwhelming identification with an overwhelming aggressor.

During the fourth interview, after having said the punishment for incest was affliction by ghosts, he stated that his father had sent the ghosts which produced the second episode of alcoholic hallucinosis. However, he then added that his mother had been, in reality, the parent who disciplined him. His statements can be understood as meaning he partially recognized that his superego was composed of paternal and maternal introjects. When he delineated more specifically the paternal components of the superego, he added that the devil's voice sounded like his father's and, in addition, like that of some white man. When he was asked to identify the white man whose voice he heard, he responded by turning to the Bible.

The fifth interview found him clinging to the Bible, that is, striving to make secure the recathexis of his masculine identity through further introjection of male superego components. It seems likely that part of his improvement can be attributed to his having dealt with a white "shaman" whose calmness and quietly hopeful expectancy were combined with an attitude of less superego harshness. Without attributing his "cure" to psychological means alone, I believe that he was able to support aspects of his masculine introjects by taking into his psyche aspects of his picture of me. I have written elsewhere of the importance of such introjections during the first phases of psychological treatment of psychoses (L. B. Boyer, 1961a). I believe it likely, too, that an emotional environment had been established which made it possible for him to accept and utilize certain interpretations, dealing primarily with the influences of his superego.

Let us now briefly consider the second clinical case. Two Waters had been, throughout childhood and teens, a dependent, ultimately anaclitic, passive, shy, obedient, fearful boy. According to his word, he began to drink and first engage in heterosexual activities in defense of his masculine status. During adulthood, he continued to seek dependent relationships with men. On the death of his father, his desire to continue to be with his father in a dependent position made itself manifest in the longing to rejoin his father in heaven. His wish was expressed in a culturally determined fear: either father's lonely and loving ghost would enter his body and drive him to craziness, which would result in his suicide, or the devil, the bad father in the other world, would choke him to death. In either case, his own ghost would be rejoined with father's spirit.

We must wonder why the wish to be with his father in the other world was so frightening. On one level, let us consider the evidence that latent passive homosexual strivings were involved. When he drank with young men, ostensibly in order to forget his anxious longings to be with his father, he became nervous and had to return to his wife. If she coddled him and then asked him to have intercourse, he lost his "nervousness" for a period. In the constellation of his wife's first literally babying him and then instigating sexual relations, we have a singularly clear instance of sexual intercourse psychologically constituting nursing with the penis. If his wife refused to mother him so extensively, he became intolerably panicky that his father's ghost or the devil would enter his body and mind. The fear could be mollified by the administration of oral sedatives and physical nursing, either in hospital or in his own bedroom at home. In either place, he was free of the drinking companions in whose presence he had become so "nervous."

There seems no reason to doubt that the pastor and his friend served as father surrogates. The specific nature of his fear of achieving a reunion with the ghost of one of them in the other world was made manifest by the content of the dream or hallucination which followed the death of his friend: the large snake which crawled toward him as he lay in bed.

On another level of reasoning, we can explain his fright on the basis of fear of loss of masculine and feminine incorporates, as demonstrated earlier in the more detailed analysis of the case of Hanging Hairlock. There is one manifest difference in the defensive maneuvers employed by Hanging Hairlock and Two Waters. Two Waters did not indulge in promiscuity. Whether he would have, had he been single, is moot. That he sought to use a mother surrogate to defend himself from loss of masculine identity components is clearly demonstrated by his actions with his wife.

Let us now list the defenses against latent homosexual yearnings which have been illustrated by the case histories. It should be remembered that some of the defensive maneuvers were accompanied by symbolic gratification of the same urges, that is, they constituted portions of true symptoms. Although at times there was contemporaneous coalescence of two or more defensive actions, they can be broken down into (1) regression, (2) denial, (3) projection, (4) introjection, (5) heterosexual relations and promiscuity, (6) desires for sexual relations with actual or substitute heterosexual incest objects, (7) suicidal attempts, (8) homicidal impulses, (9) group heterosexual relations, (10) employment of shamans and doctors, and (11) striving to incorporate loving and authoritative masculine introjects, or, stated differently, attempts to strengthen ego and superego organization and structure.

We have observed that regression, denial, projection, and introjection are defense mechanisms which are used generally by Apaches whenever they are confronted with psychic strains. We can postulate that heterosexual relations and promiscuity serve culturally among these Indians as defenses against passive yearnings unconsciously directed at men. Such an interpretation is consistent with our clinical experience with Western patients as well as with the two cases reported here. Among the Apaches, there appears to be less threat from heterosexual incest than from homosexuality. Stories and legends in which homosexuality is a manifest element are very rare; those in which incest occurs are not uncommon. Also, as indicated in the anthropological data cited earlier, incest has been apparently more common than is homosexuality. Suicidal attempts and homicidally directed assaults are common when people are drunk. It is possible that they frequently partly serve the function illustrated by the cases of Hanging Hairlock and Two Waters. Group heterosexual relations are frequent, whether they involve two or more couples or one woman and several or numerous men. The approved method for the removal of ghosts is the employment of shamans and, as a last resort, attendance by a white physician. It would appear that one aim of such actions is to preserve unconscious infantile omnipotence through the preservation of bisexual identification. Seeking of a strong father figure to guide and protect is almost universal among Apache males, although the father surrogates sought are also expected to have maternal qualities.

Saul and Beck (1961) have written of the psychodynamics of male homosexuality. Although their summary of the analytic literature and personal observations pertain to instances of overt homosexuality, their statements are valid for latent homosexuality as well. The differences between the two forms have to do with psychic phenomena which pertain to the incapacity to make culturally unacceptable infantile desires ego-dystonic rather than ego-syntonic. S. Freud (1905, p. 575) wrote: "The neurosis is, so to say, the negative of the perversion," and

> The well-known fancies of perverts which under favorable conditions may be changed into actions, the delusional fears of paranoiacs which are in a hostile manner projected on others, and the unconscious fancies of hysterics which are discovered in their symptoms by psychoanalysis, agree as to the minutest details.

Saul and Beck grouped the wide variety of determinants and mechanisms which have been described in the genesis of homosexuality into four groups: (1) faulty or inadequate early, fixed identifications. Positive identification with an important female figure may result from the absence of a father figure during childhood or from the boy's having been swamped emotionally by females of his family. Failure to identify with men may result from overwhelming fear or hatred or both of a sadistic or overpowering father. (2) Unusual infantile fixations. In the absence of a mother figure, there may develop a too-exclusively libidinal attachment to a father. (3) Homosexuality as a defense or adaptive mechanism. It may serve as a defense against castration anxiety or may be chosen as a way of appeasing a mother who does not want her son to become masculine or aggressive. Homosexuality may be chosen as over-compensation for or erotization of a son's rage toward his father and used to ward off hostile impulses. A boy may attempt to appease a sadistic father by assuming a noncompetitive, feminine role. (4) Homosexuality as a mode of expression of pregenital drives. An individual who fantasies he has no penis may unconsciously regard fellatio or sodomy as a way of acquiring a penis, ultimately the father's, which would at times simultaneously serve as a means of castrating his rival for his mother's love. The principal element of the homosexual's activity may consist of self-love. He may gratify his narcissistic wishes through receiving love from the partner, through identification with the partner and giving him love, or a combination of the two processes, thus enhancing self-love. Constructive strivings may be embedded in the homosexual wish. The boy is dependent upon the father for learning the secrets of masculinity, acquiring the know-how for dealing with women, and attaining a sense of adequacy and self-confidence. The dependent wishes may become eroticized and he may seek their fulfillment via homosexual relationships. In some cases of homosexuality, there is an infantile wish to please the parents through deviant sexual behavior which affords the parent unconscious, vicarious gratification.

We have only macroscopic information regarding the development of latent homosexuality among Apache males. In consequence, I am able to apply only very tentatively available data to these four groups. (1) Apache boys retain uncertain identifications, as part of strong fixation to the oral phase of their development. It is true that the females of Apache families remain the dominant figures and that female solidarity persists, but the nature of the tie between mother and child would not allow us to assert that boys were swamped emotionally by female figures. Apache fathers do not serve as individuals who are able to encourage and support the development of stable object relations, but neither are the fathers altogether absent, physically or emotionally. (2) What was just stated regarding the father is true, although perhaps to a lesser degree, for the mother. We have no evidence of excessive fondling or actual seduction of sons by fathers. (3) Old-time stories, psychotherapeutic interviews with adolescents and adults, and play-therapy interviews with boys regularly reveal preoccupation with castration fears. Apache mothers have mixed attitudes toward their sons' potentially becoming masculine or aggressive. Apache fathers, no doubt, stimulate rage in their sons, with their periodic expression of brutality and with their neglect of children's needs. We did not gain the impression that consistent sadism was a characteristic of the fathers. It is possible that a confluence of factors stemming from all these areas contributes to the development of passive desires in boys, but our information is too scanty to warrant more than generalizations. Such nonspecific statements, as Erikson (1959, p. 21) indicated, are of little more than suggestive use. (4) It may be that Hanging Hairlock's and Two Waters' snake visions indicate anal incorporative fantasies aimed at acquiring the father's phallus, but data are too meager to permit a certain statement. Two Waters' relations with the various father figures hint that he sought fulfillment of narcissistic fantasies through receiving love from the partner. His reactions to the losses through death of the three men may indicate that he eroticized his dependent wishes.

In brief summary, then, it would appear that the infant care afforded the Apache results in their being unable to become clearly individuated. In the case of the female, because of the position of the woman in the group and because there is a reasonably clear adult feminine model with whom to identify, individuation proceeds to a higher degree than it does among the males, whose psychological growth remains more stunted. They retain more unconscious fantasies of bisexuality and infantile omnipotence. Such fantasies, however, are continually threatened by all too obvious external realities. It would appear that the male Apache retains unconscious desires to fuse with each of his parents. The sexualization of all relationships, which is characteristic of all his attitudes, makes it necessary for him to perceive the means of such union with others to be sexual in nature. Ultimately, it seems that the latent homosexual strivings of the Apache male stem from his need to preserve a bisexual identity, that is, to retain satisfying unconscious fantasies of infantile omnipotence.

Various discussants and critics of this communication have asked whether it would be possible to do mental health work with the Apache so that future generations would be less stigmatized by the products of inadequate id and ego differentiation. Some have suggested that changed and consistently administered governmental policies might play a beneficial role. It is my opinion that such an alteration would be beneficial but that, since the psychopathology seems firmly established during early infancy, more drastic steps would have to be taken. The only two which occur to me as remotely feasible would be the transfer of infants to suitable foster homes or an attempt at the establishment of carefully supervised organizations modelled after the Kibbutzim. However, each of these notions has definite drawbacks which would lead, in all probability, to a more rapid disappearance of Apache societies. It may be that, with the current growing spate of intermarriage with outside groups, socialization processes will be changed for the betterment of the individual. The intermarriage tendency will also doubtlessly lead to gradual change in Apache social structure, but perhaps with sufficiently small steps so that the results will not constitute total ethnosuicide.

Summary

This study has been devoted to the delineation of certain identity problems of the present-day, reservation-bound Apaches on the Mescalero Indian Reservation. In it have been summarized what is known of aboriginal and current social structure and socialization processes and clinical case studies of two men who suffered from alcoholic hallucinosis.

The data suggested that in the old days internally flexible, yet stable, social processes encouraged the development of a "typical" personality structure which, defined in Western terms, closely resembled the hysterical combined with impulse character disorder and a proclivity to develop schizophreniform psychoses. Sanctioned modes for discharge of anxieties inherent in such a personality structure were formerly provided by the social organization which had caused its growth.

With the advent of subjugation by the United States Government, the influences of cross-cultural infusions and the administration directed by the Bureau of Indian Affairs, the aboriginal social structure was destroyed, although derivative influences are clearly traceable in the current social organization. However, socialization processes, with effectually minor exceptions, have not changed fundamentally. In consequence, the Apaches are still reared in such a manner that the same "typical" personality configurations persist, but culturally sanctioned outlets are only haphazardly provided for the resultant conflicts and anxieties.

The modern child grows up in a "protected" environment in which tribal, state, and federal governments tacitly and overtly encourage dependency and lack of personal responsibility. In his transitional culture he is confronted with contradictory expectations and examples. The governing bodies encourage permanency of residence, but the ancient roaming patterns persist. The legal system is based on Western white patterns, but Apaches respect only those laws which appeal to them as concordant with their aboriginal and individual philosophies, and there is scant group onus for infractions. Formal education is officially enhanced, but many parents have little interest in effectively supervising school attendance and ambivalently belittle their children's acquisition of the white man's book learning; students who achieve the educators' recognition for school performance are ridiculed and beaten by their peers. The steady worker is praised but in fact almost half the income-earning males work less than three months a year, and there is little prestige to be derived from regular employment. Men are supposed to be tribal leaders and ultimate family authorities, but women subtly and increasingly openly influence tribal administration and obviously constitute the final household administrators. Western religions and health practices are espoused but the influences of aboriginal customs and beliefs pervade every aspect of life. Restrained personal behavior is idealized. The group sanctions ancient rules of courtesy, formal obligations, generosity, gentleness, strict morality related to sexual activities, and restriction of or abstention from alcohol intake. However, almost no formal training persists which enables children to learn the desirable rules of behavior. Sexual experimentation and promiscuity are covertly encouraged, and drunkenness is rife, and any behavior is excused provided the participant has been or can convince observers he has been drinking. Knowledge of ancient lore constitutes perhaps the greatest single attribute which earns group esteem, but the young are denied education in the old stories and ways. Boys and girls are supposed to be prepared for adulthood roles but, although the girls receive lackadaisical informal training for their expected functions of mother and homemaker, no systematic preparation is afforded boys and they have no clearly defined adulthood functions to learn.

Because of unrelatedness on the parts of their caretakers, a fundamental trauma is inflicted upon most infants resulting in a basic stunting of id-ego differentiation which persists throughout the life of the average Apache. Apache parents are grossly ambivalent toward their babies and small children and handle them with startling inconsistency; doting tender care alternates with utterly inconsiderate handling, gross neglect, and frequent abandonment.

The Apache infant is king or queen of the household, within the limits provided by the ambivalence and unrelatedness of the parents, until the birth of the next baby, an event which currently usually transpires at an interval of less than two years. Then the toddler is abruptly displaced. His reactive regressions avail him little in the way of reward and he quite soon learns he must depend largely upon his own resources for satisfactions, resources obviously highly influenced by the oral mode. The primary-process thinking which until then comprised much of his manner of mentation is now reinforced as are concomitant primitive defensive maneuvers. Projection, displacement, and introjection are consistently encouraged and reaction formation is now taught systematically. Although the development of muscular control directly related to sphincter functions affords scant reward, he quickly achieves muscular and expressional controls related to the overt exhibition of anger toward the new rival and other smaller and younger children. He learns that sadism directed toward animals is acceptable behavior as are displacement and projection of hostility onto witches, ghosts and other cultural bogies, and outsiders. He is taught that competition with peers is disapproved and that the attitude of adults toward him is colored by fairly consistent ridicule, shaming and denigration of his capacities and knowledge.

A third principal trauma which hampers the Apache child's development of a personal identity consists of his exposure to repetitive exhibitions of sexual and brutal aggressive actions perpetrated by drunken adults. He incorporates the excitements of individuals of both sexes, and is unable to successfully repress and modify his archaic instinctual urges. These have remained strongly fused with his oral fixation which has been reinforced by the abrupt sibling displacement. Not only do his ego boundaries remain diffuse, but the development of a clear sexual identity is seriously hampered. There is little opportunity for the healthy growth of an Oedipus complex and almost none for its satisfactory resolution. As would be expected under such circumstances, superego development is spotty and shame is much more prevalent among the Apaches than is guilt.

A fourth psychic injury which affects the boys is the absence of a clearly defined adult model to emulate. The identity confusions which have been with boys before the latency period are reinforced by that absence. One obvious aspect of the identity confusion which exists among males is general, powerful, latent homosexual drives which are defended against both by various individual and group defensive maneuvers.

It is not surprising to observe widespread drunkenness in a group among whose members id-ego differentiation has remained indistinct, who have remained strongly fixated to the oral phase of psychosexual development, and who have a readily available supply of intoxicating liquors. This constellation exists among these Apaches. The drunkenness is used as a culturally ambivalently approved outlet for poorly integrated sexual and aggressive energies. Its use contributes to individual and societal destruction.

The administration afforded by the Bureau of Indian Affairs has strongly resembled the relationships between adult Apaches and their children, and has reinforced the Apaches' dependency and lack of personal responsibility.

BIBLIOGRAPHY

Albert, M. H. (1957), *Apache Rising*. Greenwich, Conn.: Fawcett.

Arlow, J. A. (1952), Discussion of Dr. Fromm-Reichman's Paper. In: *Psychotherapy with Schizophrenics*, ed. E. B. Brody and F. C. Redlich. New York: International Universities Press.

Baker, J. L. (1959), Indians, Alcohol and Homicide. *J. Soc. Therapy*, 5:270-275.

Basehart, H. W. (1959), *Chiricahua Apache Subsistence and Socio-Political Organization*. University of New Mexico Mescalero-Chiricahua Land Claims Project, Contract Research 290-154, mimeographed.

———(1960), *Mescalero Apache Subsistence Patterns and Socio-Political Organization. Ibid.*

Bateson, G., Jackson, D. D., Haley, J., & Weakland, J. (1956), Toward a Theory of Schizophrenia. *Behav. Sci.*, 1:251-264.

———& Mead, M. (1942), *Balinese Character: A Photographic Analysis*. New York: New York Academy of Sciences, Special Publication, Vol. 2.

Beaglehole, E. & Beaglehole, P. (1946), *Some Modern Maoris*. New Zealand Council for Educational Research, Series 25. New Zealand: Whitcomb and Tombs.

Belo, J. (1960), *Trance in Bali*. New York: Columbia University Press.

Benedict, R. (1949), Child Rearing in Certain European Countries. *Amer. J. Orthopsychiat.*, 19:342-350.

Betzinez, J. (with Nye, W. S.) (1959), *I Fought with Geronimo*. Harrisburgh, Pa.: Stackpole.

Boas, F. (1911), *Handbook of American Indian Languages*, Part I. Washington, D.C.: U.S. Govt. Printing Office.

Bourke, J. G. (1892), *The Medicine-Men of the Apache*. Ninth Ann. Rept., Bureau of American Ethnology. Washington, D.C.: U.S. Govt. Printing Office.

Boyer, L. B. (1956), On Maternal Overstimulation and Ego Defects. In: *The Psychoanalytic Study of the Child*, 11:236-256, eds. R. S. Eissler et al. New York: International Universities Press.

———(1961), Notes on the Personality Structure of a North American Indian Shaman. *J. Hillside Hosp.*, 10:14-33.

———(1961a), Provisional Evaluation of Psycho-Analysis with Few Parameters Employed in the Treatment of Schizophrenia. *Int. J. Psychoanal.*, 42:389-403.

———(1962), Remarks on the Personality of Shamans with Special Reference to the Apaches of the Mescalero Reservation. In: *The Psychoanalytic Study of Society*, 2:233-254, eds. W. Muensterberger & S. Axelrad. New York: International Universities Press.

———(1964), Folk Psychiatry of the Apache of the Mescalero Indian Reservation. In: *Magic, Faith and Healing: Studies in Primitive Psychiatry*, ed. Ari Kiev. Glencoe, Ill.: The Free Press, in press.

———(1964a), An Example of Legend Distortion from the Apaches of the Mescalero Indian Reservation. *J. Amer. Folklore*, 77:118-142.

Boyer, R. M. (1961), The Apache Success Story. Paper presented before the Kroeber Anthropological Society. Berkeley, California, May.

———(1962), *Social Structure and Socialization Among the Apache of the Mescalero Indian Reservation*. Ph.D. Dissertation, University of California, unpublished.

———(1962a), The Apache "Toddler." Paper presented before the Southwestern Anthropological Association, Berkeley, California, April.

Breuninger, E. (1959), Debut of Mescalero Maidens. *The Apache Scout*. Mescalero, N.M.: Mescalero Indian Agency, 2:1, 3-4. Newspaper.

———(1959a), Dance of the Mountain Gods. *Ibid*, pp. 5-6.

Burnett, W. R. (1956), *Adobe Walls*. New York: Bantam.
Bychowski, G. (1958), Struggle Against the Introjects. *Inter. J. Psychoanal., 39*:182-187.
Calhoun, J. S. (1849), Communication to the Commissioner of Indian Affairs, Oct. 1. Cited by Kelleher, W. A., *Turmoil in New Mexico*. Santa Fe, N.M.: Rydal Press, 1952, p. 52.
Caplan, G. (1953), Clinical Observations on the Emotional Life of Children in the Communal Settlements in Israel. In: *Problems of Infancy and Childhood*. Transactions of the Seventh Conference, pp. 91-120.
Castetter, E. F. & Opler, M. E. (1937), *The Ethnobiology of the Chiricahua and Mescalero Apache*. The University of New Mexico Bulletin, #507.
Chittenden, H. M. (1902), *A History of the American Fur Trade of the Far West*. Stanford, Calif.: Academic Reprints, 1954, Vol. 2.
Clements, W. W. & Mohr, D. V. (1961), Chronic Subdural Hematomas in Infants. Paper presented at the Ann. USPHS Nat. Clin. Soc. Meeting. Lexington, Kentucky, April.
Cohen, Y. A. (1961), *Social Structure and Personality, a Casebook*. New York: Holt, Rinehart & Winston.
Cremony, J. C. (1868), The Apache Race. *Overland Monthly, 1*:201-209.
Davis, A. (1929), Apache Debs. *New Mexico, 15*:10-11.
Davis, B. (1929), *The Truth about Geronimo*. Detroit: Burton Historical Coll.
Dennis, W. & Dennis, M. G. (1940), Pueblo Cradles and Cradling Customs. *Amer. Anthropol., 42*:107-115.
Devereux, G. (1939), A Sociological Theory of Schizophrenia. *Psychoanal. Rev., 26*:315-342.
———(1956), Normal and Abnormal: The Key Problem of Psychiatric Anthropology. In: *Some Uses of Anthropology, Theoretical and Applied*. Washington, D.C.: Anthropological Society of Washington, pp. 23-48.
———(1961), *Mohave Ethnopsychiatry and Suicide: The Psychiatric Knowledge and the Psychic Disturbances of an Indian Tribe*. Bur. Amer. Ethnol. Bull. 175. Washington, D.C.: U.S. Govt. Printing Office.
Eaton, J. W. & Weill, R. J. (1953), Some Epidemiological Findings in the Hutterite Mental Health Study. In: *Interrelations Between the Social Environment and Psychiatric Disorders*. New York: Milbank Memorial Fund, pp. 222-234.
Erikson, E. H. (1945), Childhood and Tradition in Two American Indian Tribes. In: *The Psychoanalytic Study of the Child, 1*:319-350, eds. R. S. Eissler et al. New York: International Universities Press. Also, revised, in: *Personality in Nature, Society and Culture*, eds. C. Kluckhohn & H. A. Murray. New York: Knopf, 1948, pp. 176-203.
———(1950), *Childhood and Society*. New York: Norton.
———(1959), *Identity and the Life Cycle. Psychological Issues*, Monogr. 1. New York: International Universities Press.
Escalona, S. (1953), Emotional Development in the First Year of Life. In: *Problems of Infancy and Childhood*. Transactions of the Sixth Conference, ed. M. J. E. Senn. New York: The Josiah Macy, Jr. Foundation, pp. 11-91.
Forster, L. A. (1958), *Proud Land*. New York: Bantam.
Freud, A. (1936), *The Ego and the Mechanisms of Defense*. New York: International Universities Press, 1946.
———(1949), Aggression in Relation to Emotional Development. In: *The Psychoanalytic Study of the Child, 3/4*:37-42, eds. R. S. Eissler et al. New York: International Universities Press.
———(1951), Negativism and Emotional Surrender. Paper read before the International Psychoanalytic Congress, Amsterdam.
Freud, S. (1905), *Three Contributions to the Theory of Sex*. In: *The Basic Writings of Sigmund Freud*. New York: Modern Library, 1938, pp. 553-629.

————(1920), *Beyond the Pleasure Principle*. London: Hogarth Press, 1948.

————(1938), *An Outline of Psychoanalysis*. New York: Norton.

Gill, M. M. & Brenman, M. (1959), *Hypnosis and Related States*. New York: International Universities Press.

Gladwin, T. & Sarason, S. B. (1953), *Truk: Man in Paradise*. New York: Wenner-Gren Found. Anthropol. Res.

Goddard, P. E. (1916), The Masked Dancers of the Apache. In: *The Holmes Anniversary Volume*. Washington, D.C., pp. 132-136.

Greenacre, P. (1941), The Predisposition to Anxiety. *Psychoanal. Quart.*, *10*:66-95, 610-638.

————(1958), Toward an Understanding of the Physical Nucleus of Some Defence Reactions. *Inter. J. Psychoanal.*, *39*:69-76.

————(1960), Regression and Fixation, Considerations Concerning the Development of the Ego. *J. Amer. Psychoanal. Assn.*, *8*:703-723.

Greenson, R. (1954), The Struggle Against Identification. *J. Amer. Psychoanal. Assn.*, 2: 200-217.

Hall, E. T., Jr. (1944), Recent Clues to Athabaskan Prehistory in the Southwest. *Amer. Anthropol.*, *46*:98-106.

Harrington, M. R. (1912), The Devil Dance of the Apaches. *Museum J.* (Philadelphia), *8*:6-9.

Hartmann, H. (1939), *Ego Psychology and the Problem of Adaptation*. New York: International Universities Press, 1958.

————(1952), The Mutual Influences in the Development of Ego and Id. In: *The Psychoanalytic Study of the Child*, 7:9-30, eds. R. S. Eissler et al. New York: International Universities Press.

————(1953), Contribution to the Metapsychology of Schizophrenia. In: *The Psychoanalytic Study of the Child*, 8:177-198, eds. R. S. Eissler et al. New York: International Universities Press.

————Kris, E. & Loewenstein, R. M. (1946), Comments on the Formation of Psychic Structure. In: *The Psychoanalytic Study of the Child*, 2:11-38, eds. R. S. Eissler et al. New York: International Universities Press.

———— ———— & ————(1949), Notes on the Theory of Aggression. In: *The Psychoanalytic Study of the Child*, 3/4: 9-36, eds. R. S. Eissler et al. New York: International Universities Press.

Henry, J. (1936), The Personality of the Kaingang Indians. *J. Personal.*, *5*:113-123.

Hoffer, W. (1949), Mouth, Hand, and Ego-Integration. In: *The Psychoanalytic Study of the Child*, 3/4:49-56, eds. R. S. Eissler et al. New York: International Universities Press.

————(1950), Development of the Body Ego. In: *The Psychoanalytic Study of the Child*, 5:18-23, eds. R. S. Eissler et al. New York: International Universities Press.

Hoijer, H. (1938), The Southern Athabaskan Languages. *Amer. Anthropol.*, *40*:75-87.

———— (1938a), *Chiricahua and Mescalero Texts*. Chicago: University of Chicago Press.

Hrdlička, A. (1908), *Physiological and Medical Observations among the Indians of the Southwestern United States and Northern Mexico*. Smithsonian Institution.

Huscher, H. A. & Huscher, B. H. (1942), Athabaskan Migration via the Intermontane Region. *Amer. Antiquity*, *8*:80-88.

Kardiner, A. (1939), *The Individual and His Society*. New York: Columbia University Press.

————(1945), *The Psychological Frontiers of Society*. New York: Columbia University Press.

Khan, M. M. R. (1962), The Role of Polymorph-Perverse Body-Experiences and Object-Relations in Ego-Integration. *Brit. J. Med. Psychol.*, *35*:245-261.

Klopfer, B. & Boyer, L. B. (1961), Notes on the Personality Structure of a North American Indian Shaman: Rorschach Interpretation. *J. Proj. Tech.*, 25:169-178.

Kluckhohn, C. & Leighton, D. (1946), *The Navaho*. Cambridge: Harvard University Press.

Kris, E. (1950), Notes on the Development and on Some Current Problems of Psychoanalytic Child Psychology. In: *The Psychoanalytic Study of the Child*, 5:24-46, eds. R. S. Eissler et al. New York: International Universities Press.

Kunstadter, P. (1960), *Culture Change, Social Structure and Health Behavior: A Quantitative Study of Clinic Use among the Apaches of the Mescalero Indian Reservation.* Ph.D. Dissertation, University of Michigan, unpublished.

Leighton, D. & Kluckhohn, C. (1948), *Children of the People*. Cambridge: Harvard University Press.

Lewin, B. D. (1950), *The Psychoanalysis of Elation*. New York: Norton.

Lummis, C. F. (1952), *The Land of Poco Tiempo*. Albuquerque: University of New Mexico Press.

MacLachlan, B. B. (1962), *The Mescalero Apache Tribal Court: A Study of the Manifestation of the Adjudicative Function of a Concrete Judicial Institution.* Ph.D. Dissertation, University of Chicago, unpublished.

Mahler, M. S. (1954), On Normal and Pathological Symbiosis. Paper read before the Baltimore Psychoanalytic Society.

———& Gosliner, B. J. (1955), On Symbiotic Child Psychosis. In: *The Psychoanalytic Study of the Child*, 10:195-212, eds. R. S. Eissler et al. New York: International Universities Press.

Marinsek, E. A. (1960), *The Effect of Cultural Difference in the Education of Apache Indians*. The University of New Mexico Research Study, College of Education, University of New Mexico, mimeographed.

Mason, O. T. (1889), Cradles of the American Aborigines. *Rep. Nat. Mus.*, Smithsonian Institution, U. S. Nat. Mus. Washington: U.S. Govt. Printing Office.

Mead, M. (1928), *From the South Seas*. New York: Morrow, 1939.

———(1932), *Changing Culture of an Indian Tribe*. New York: Columbia University Press.

———(1954), The Swaddling Hypothesis: Its Reception. *Amer. Anthropol.*, 56:395-409.

———& Macgregor, F. C. (1951), *Growth and Culture: A Photographic Study of Balinese Childhood*. New York: Putnam.

Montagu, A. (1961), Culture and Mental Illness. *Amer. J. Psychiat.*, 118:15-23.

Nicholas, D. (1939), Mescalero Apache Girls' Puberty Ceremony. *El Palacio*, 15:110-115.

———(1961), Personal communication.

———(1961a), Apache Bands and Chiefs. *The Southwesterner*. Columbus, N. M.: 1:4-12. Newspaper.

Opler, M. E. (1933), *An Analysis of Mescalero and Chiricahua Apache Social Organization in the Light of Their Systems of Relationship*. Ph.D. Dissertation, University of Chicago. Private edition distributed by University of Chicago Libraries, 1936.

———(1935), The Concept of Supernatural Power among Chiricahua and Mescalero Apaches. *Amer. Anthropol.*, 37:65-70.

———(1938), The Sacred Clowns of the Chiricahua and Mescalero Indians. *El Palacio*, 14:75-79.

———(1938a), *Myths and Tales of the Jicarilla Apache Indians*. American Folk-Lore Society, Mem. #31. New York: Stechert.

———(1940), *Myths and Legends of the Lipan Apache Indians*. Ibid, Mem. #36.

———(1941), *An Apache Life-way*. Chicago: University of Chicago Press.

———(1941a), Three Types of Variation and Their Relation to Culture Change. In: *Language, Culture and Personality*, eds. L. A. Spier, A. I. Hallowell & S. S. Newman.

Menasha, Wisconsin: Sapir Mem. Publ. Fund, pp. 146-157.

———(1942), *Myths and Tales of the Chiricahua Apache Indians*. American Folk-Lore Society, Mem. #37. New York: Stechert.

———(1945), The Lipan Apache Death Complex and Its Extensions. *Southwest. J. Anthropol.*, 1:133-141.

———(1946), The Mountain Spirits of the Chiricahua Apache. *The Masterkey, 20*:125-131.

———(1946a), The Creative Role of Shamanism in Mescalero Apache Mythology. *J. Amer. Folk-Lore, 59*:268-281.

———(1946b), Reaction to Death Among the Mescalero Apache. *Southwest. J. Anthropol.*, 2:454-467.

———(1947), Notes on Chiricahua Apache Culture, I. Supernatural Power and the Shaman. *Primitive Man, 20*:1-14.

———(1955), An Outline of Chiricahua Apache Social Organization. In: *Social Anthropology of North American Indian Tribes*, enlarged edition, ed. F. Eggan. Chicago: University of Chicago Press.

———& Hoijer, H. (1940), The Raid and Warpath Language of the Chiricahua Apache. *Amer. Anthropol., 42*:617-634.

———& Opler, C. H. (1950), Mescalero Apache History in the Southwest. *New Mexico Hist. Rev., 25*:1-36.

Opler, M. K. (1959), Dream Analysis in Ute Indian Therapy. In: *Culture and Mental Health*, ed. M. K. Opler. New York: Macmillan, pp. 97-117.

Pellman, E. (1950), The Mescalero Apache Tribe Presents the Debut of Its Most Honored Maidens. Program for Annual Fourth of July Indian Celebration, Mescalero, N.M. El Paso, Texas: McMath.

Pumpian-Mindlin, E. (1961), Omnipotentiality, Youth and Commitment. Paper presented before the West Coast Psychoanalytic Society, Los Angeles, October.

Santee, R. (1956), *Apache Land*. New York: Bantam.

Sarvis, M. A. (1960), Psychiatric Implications of Temporal Lobe Damage. In: *The Psychoanalytic Study of the Child, 15*:454-481, eds. R. S. Eissler et al. New York: International Universities Press.

———(1962), Paranoid Reactions. *Arch. Gen. Psychiat., 6*:157-162.

———& Garcia, B. (1961), Etiological Variables in Autism. *Psychiatry, 24*:307-317.

Saul, L. J. & Beck, A. T. (1961), Psychodynamics of Male Homosexuality. *Int. J. Psychoanal., 42*:43-48.

Schwatka, F. (1887), Among the Apaches. *The Century Magazine, 12*:41-52.

Searles, H. F. (1960), *The Nonhuman Environment*. New York: International Universities Press.

———(1961), Sexual Processes in Schizophrenia. *Psychiatry* (Suppl. to #2), pp. 87-95.

Shepardson, M. T. (1961), *Developing Political Process Among the Navaho Indians*. Ph.D. Dissertation, University of California, unpublished.

Sjoberg, A. G. (1953), Lipan Apache Culture in Historical Perspective. *Southwest. J. Anthropol., 9*:76-98.

Sonnichsen, C. L. (1958), *The Mescalero Apaches*. Norman, Okla.: University of Oklahoma Press.

Spiro, M. E. (1958), *Children of the Kibbutz*. Cambridge: Harvard University Press.

———(1959), Cultural Heritage, Personal Tensions, and Mental Illness in a South Sea Culture. In: *Culture and Mental Health*, ed. M. K. Opler. New York: Macmillan, pp. 141-171.

Steck, M. (1863), Apache Agency, New Mexico, Sept. 15, *Steck Papers*, University of New Mexico Library.

Thomas, A. B. (1959), *The Mescalero Apache, 1653-1874*. University of New Mexico Mescalero-Chiricahua Land Claims Project, mimeographed.

——(1959a), *The Lipan Apache, 1718-1856*. University of New Mexico Mescalero-Chiricahua Land Claims Project, mimeographed.

——(1959b), *The Chiricahua Apache, 1695-1876*. University of New Mexico Mescalero-Chiricahua Land Claims Project, mimeographed.

Voth, A. C. (1947), An Experimental Study of Mental Patients Through the Use of the Autokinetic Method. *Amer. J. Psychiat., 103*:793-805.

Voth, H. M. (1962), Choice of Illness. *Arch. Gen. Psychiat., 6*:149-805.

Winnicott, D. W. (1961), The Effect of Psychotic Parents on the Emotional Development of the Child. *Brit. J. Psychiat. Social Work, 6*:13-20.

Worcester, D. E. (1947), *Early History of the Navajo Indians*. Ph.D. Dissertation, University of California, unpublished.

Zintz, M. V. (1957-1960), *The Indian Research Study*. College of Education, University of New Mexico, mimeographed.

deZoete, B. & Spies, W. (1938), *Dance and Drama in Bali*. London: Faber & Faber.

IS THE OEDIPUS COMPLEX UNIVERSAL?

The Jones-Malinowski Debate Revisited and a South Italian "Nuclear Complex"

ANNE PARSONS

INTRODUCTORY REMARKS

In the 1920's a famous debate took place between Ernest Jones and Bronislaw Malinowski which set forth some outlines of theoretical differences between psychoanalysis and anthropology which are still unresolved today.[1] On the basis of field work in the matrilineal Trobriand Islands, Malinowski drew the conclusion that the Oedipus complex as formulated by Freud is only one among a series of possible "nuclear complexes," each of which patterns primary family affects in a way characteristic of the culture in which it occurs. In this perspective, Freud's formulation of the Oedipus complex as based on a triangular relationship between father, mother, and son appears as that particular nuclear complex which characterizes a patriarchal society in which the most significant family unit consists of mother, father, and child. The alternative nuclear complex which he postulated for the Trobriand Islands consisted of a triangular relationship between brother, sister, and sister's son, this in function of the nature of matrilineal social structure in which a boy becomes a member of his mother's kin group and is subject to the authority of his

---

From McLean Hospital, Belmont, Mass.

This paper is based on research carried out in Naples, Italy, in 1958-1960 on two grants from the National Institute of Mental Health, Bethesda, Md. (M-2105 and M-4301) and was written during the term of an interdisciplinary grant from the Foundation Fund for Research in Psychiatry. I am very much indebted to Merton J. Kahne, Donald S. Pitkin, David M. Schneider, Alfred H. Stanton, and to my father, Talcott Parsons, for many comments and discussions which have gone into the formulation of the ideas in ways which would be difficult to acknowledge specifically.

[1] Jones (1924) in a paper read before the British Psycho-Analytical Society first discussed three prior publications by Malinowski: "Baloma: The Spirits of the Dead in the Trobriand Islands" (1916) and two articles which were later published together as the first two sections of *Sex and Repression in Savage Society* (1927). The last two sections of this latter work were written in response to Jones's paper. For the most complete summary of the Trobriand field data, see Malinowski (1929).

maternal uncle rather than the biological father. One of his most important observations was that in the Trobriand Islands ambivalent feelings very similar to those described by Freud with respect to father and son can be observed between mother's brother and sister's son. Relations between father and son, on the other hand, are much more close and affectionate; however, Malinowski felt that the father should not be considered as a figure in the kinship structure since the Trobrianders do not recognize the existence of biological paternity. The child is seen as conceived by a spirit which enters the mother's womb and later the father appears to him as the unrelated mother's husband.

In addition, Malinowski noted that the Trobrianders give a very special importance to the brother-sister relationship. While the brother has formal authority over the sister and is responsible for her support, their actual relationship is one of extreme avoidance, to the point that an object may be handed from one to the other by means of an intermediary. He characterized the brother-sister incest taboo as "the supreme taboo" from the Trobriand standpoint; while incest with other primary biological relatives and within the matrilineal kin group at greater biological distance is also forbidden, in no instance are the taboos as strict or surrounded by intense affects as in the brother-sister case. He also discerned, with his acute clinical eye, many evidences of the real temptations underlying the avoidance pattern, for example, in that while no Trobriander would admit to having such an incest dream, the questioning itself aroused a great deal of anxiety and often the assertion that "well, other people have such dreams, but certainly not me." He noted brother-sister incest to be a primary theme in Trobriand mythology, for example, in that love magic is seen as originating in a situation in which brother and sister actually committed incest and died as a result of it. He considered these variations from the European pattern of sufficient significance to uphold the view that the Oedipus complex is not universal.

Jones, in his 1924 paper, upheld with considerable vehemence the classical psychoanalytic point of view that it is. Thus while he felt that Malinowski's field data were in themselves interesting, he came to the conclusion that they did not point to the need for any important theoretical revisions in the psychoanalytic framework. For the data on the Trobriand failure to recognize the biological relationship between father and son, he provided an alternative explanation, namely, that the nonrecognition was a form of denial covering affects originating in the Oedipus situation.[2] Much to Malinowski's dismay, this argument was carried to the point of the assertion that matrilineal social organization can itself be seen as a defense against the father-son ambivalence universally characteristic of the Oedipus situation. He also pointed out that Malinowski's observations of ambivalence between mother's brother and sister's son concerned adolescent and adult life, so that, theoretically, it is possible to see it as a secondary displacement in that there is an initial oedipal rivalry between father and son, but that in adult life the hostile feelings are displaced to the mother's brother. He also commented that similar patterns can be observed in Europe, for example, in that the hostile father figure may later be an occupational superior or rival, while the actual father remains a positive figure.

A re-examination of the debate in a contemporary perspective indicates that actually there are a number of intertwined issues. In the first place, it is characterized by a highly polemic character related to the newness and consequent defensiveness of both fields: for Jones "the" Oedipus complex appears as a kind of point of honor upon whose invariance psychoanalysis would stand or fall, and exactly the same is true of some elements of Malinowski's argument, in particular those which touch on the resemblance between Jones's views and those of the older evolutionary anthropology which he himself did so much to overthrow. Thus, concerning the question of whether matrilineal social organization can be seen as a defense against oedipal affects, it seems difficult now to see how a complex social pattern could be based on the "denial" of an affect which occurs in the individual. But on the other hand, one can regret that Malinowski, in his rebuttal, went into a tirade against the evolutionary implications of this view rather than attempting to answer Jones's much more cogent point, namely, that Freud's concepts concern infantile life, and in this perspective it is quite possible that the hostility toward the mother's brother observed in adolescent and adult Trobrianders might be displaced from hostility initially experienced toward the father. What is perhaps most regrettable of all, given his status with regard to the psychoanalytic theory of symbolism, is that Jones never discussed in detail Malinowski's observations concerning the special im-

---

[2] Not all anthropologists have accepted Malinowski's observations on this at face value; however, the data he presents indicate that the Trobrianders had formulated a reasonably coherent and intelligent picture of the facts of biology for a people lacking in any scientific framework.

portance of the Trobriand brother-sister relationship and the integrally related material concerning dreams and mythology.

When we look at the present state of theoretical knowledge, we might come to the conclusion that the question of whether or not the Oedipus complex is universal is one which should not be asked in such a way as to create the impression that there is a yes or no answer. In the first place, the theoretical assumption that there are infantile sexual wishes is one which has proved so useful, and has brought together such a variety of clinical facts, that it seems simply foolish to abandon the general Freudian scheme until such a point when we have an alternative that appears scientifically more valuable. In retrospect, one might say that the major point that Jones wished to maintain was simply the idea that there is an infantile sexual life. Secondly, the main point which Malinowski was supporting is now also so well established that we need not any longer be defensive about it—that human societies do structure family patterns in different ways according to laws of kinship, or particular phrasings of the incest taboo, that by no means can be derived directly from the biological facts of mating and reproduction. These latter simply cannot explain facts such as the extreme significance given to the brother-sister incest taboo by the Trobrianders in comparison to ourselves.

Taking these two points for granted, we might then proceed to ask again the same questions which were asked by Jones and Malinowski and to re-evaluate some of the major points made by each in the light of contemporary psychoanalytic and anthropological knowledge. It is this task which we have set ourselves in this paper. After some general theoretical considerations, we will discuss a particular case with respect to the possibility of formulating a third distinctive "nuclear family complex" differing both from Freud's patriarchal one and from the Trobriand matrilineal case.

THEORETICAL POINTS

Much of the Jones-Malinowski argument centered on the evidence presented by Malinowski to the effect that Trobriand Islanders are unaware of the facts of physiological paternity. The main importance of this material to Malinowski lay in its value for demonstrating the independence of social from biological kinship; certainly one of the major points which troubled him and has troubled many other anthropologists since about psychoanalytic theory is the implication that these two must overlap. However, while Jones's formulation leaves itself open to just this objection, one might now wonder whether in fact psychoanalytic theory does presuppose such an equivalence. One of the fundamental tenets of instinct theory is that an instinct is displaceable according to source, aim, and object; but if we use the term "object" in a social sense, referring to either an external person who is the focus of a drive or to an internalized representation of a person, we might then say that the possibility of variant family structures is built into even Freud's earliest formulations. Moreover, Freud's theory, while it anchors affects and fantasies in biological concepts of instinct, might also better be seen as a psychological than a biological one; so that to the extent that it postulates universals, we should also see these psychologically rather than biologically.

Contemporary concepts of object relations and object representations[3] may make it possible to bring this point out more clearly than was done by Jones. Any clinician can cite from immediate experience a great many instances in which the object focus of oedipal affects has been a person other than the biological mother or father—an adopted parent, a more distant relative, or as in many cases today, a child therapist. Actually, Freud himself was very much concerned with the role played by domestics in the early sexual life of the Victorian upper status child. We might then say that the question of the Oedipus complex has two sides to it, the first related to instinct and fantasy, and the second to identification and object choice. But it is hard to believe that the latter processes are not in some way directly dependent on social structure and social norms, or the available possibilities for object choice and object representation.

In this perspective, the idea of the distinctive nuclear complex for each society becomes much more compatible with the psychoanalytic idea that there is an invariant series of developmental phases which is rooted in instinct; the social factor need only influence the object side. Using this assumption, we might interpret Jones's displacement hypothesis as saying that the passing of the Oedipus complex in the Trobriand Islands is equivalent to assimilating the polar distinction between two socially represented figures, the mother's brother and the mother's husband. Each of these then comes to have a differing or contrasting affective valence and one can even say that the boy identifies with both, but that each identification represents a different social function or aspect of personality. According to this view,[4] it is the social distinction which lies at the basis of the conscious representation, which could not even arise

[3] See Jacobson (1954), T. Parsons (1958), and Stanton (1959).

[4] Which utilizes Durkheim's concept of collective representations (Durkheim, 1915).

without the mediating effect of social exchange; if there were none, the biological drives would presumably arise nevertheless, but they would not give rise to a personality. Such a formulation seems much simpler and less awkward than to say that first the Trobriand child goes through an Oedipus phase centered on the father, somehow acquiring a knowledge of biological paternity which adults in his society do not possess, then represses this knowledge and displaces the affects to the mother's brother. What we are saying is rather that conscious representation of objects by definition depends on collective representation, though their affective charge or valence may be rooted in unconscious or instinct-based constellations which are prior to culture.

This formulation would permit us to say that it does not make much difference whether the relevant figure is father or mother's brother; psychoanalytic theory requires only that the small boy have some available figure for masculine identification. However, a second aspect of the Oedipus theory raises a more difficult problem. This is that, according to Freud, the boy's hostility to the father arises from the fact that the latter has sexual relations with his mother; in other words, the Oedipus complex is rooted in sexual jealousy. However, in the Trobriand Islands, it is the biological father and not the mother's brother who has sexual relations with the mother. In fact, though it is not impossible that the mother have other sexual involvements as well, the one person who could not be a sexual object for her is precisely the maternal uncle, since he is, of course, her brother.

Here it seems that we have reached an insoluble impasse; either we must abandon the Malinowskian attempt to isolate distinctive nuclear complexes, saying that the initial oedipal object must always be the father since he is the actual sexual rival, or we must take the more empiricist "culturalist" viewpoint which abandons the idea of infantile sexuality altogether and says simply that various role patterns are learned in direct relation to social interaction. But since neither solution seems satisfactory (the second because it does not utilize instinct theory), we might do better to look further. Perhaps in reconsidering some of the various possible phrasings of psychoanalytic theory, we may find that some are more compatible with Malinowski's attempt than others.

It is well known that Freud's thinking contains many, not always compatible, interwoven strands. One of his earliest conceptionalizations was the trauma theory; this is the one which most directly influenced Malinowski and, moreover, most of the early workers in the field of culture and personality. According to the trauma theory, specific sexual events

or observations take place in childhood which then have crucial consequences for adult personality and attitudes. In much of Freud's writing
about infantile sexuality (before he reached his more general structural
and dynamic formulations), he acts as if he were taking the trauma
theory for granted, for example, when he portrays the Oedipus crisis
as the point when the child observes or becomes aware of the "primal
scene," asks questions about sexuality and comes to some conclusion about
this matter and his own future sex role. This formulation presupposes a highly rationalistic child and a very direct relationship between
environmental factors and psychosexual development. However, over the
course of psychoanalytic history, the trauma theory has gradually slipped
into the background; much of it today might well be given the status
of myth. The main reason for this may well be that it simply has not
worked; we certainly cannot try to predict today, nor does anyone, complex adult personality patterns from specific and limited kinds of infantile
events. Applied in the anthropological field, however, the trauma theory
very readily lent itself to the view that almost any kind of cultural difference could give rise to variations in the nature of the oedipal situation, and
many of Malinowski's own convictions, like those of the later culture and
personality theorists, were certainly derived from this kind of rough empirical evidence.

However, here we are concerned with the question of global structures
rather than with specific items of socialization or other kinds of cultural
behavior. With respect to family structure, trauma theory would lead us
to believe that if it is in fact the father who has sexual relationships
with the mother, then he should be the object of oedipal jealousy. However, in a somewhat different framework we could also reach the conclusion that this need not be so. It is often said that psychoanalysis began
precisely at the moment when Freud abandoned the trauma theory, i.e.,
when he began to consider the verbal productions of his hysterical
patients as fantasies. At this critical point he became much less concerned with the environmental question of whether or not his patients
actually had been seduced in childhood and much more concerned with
the questions which were formulated and reformulated throughout his
later life: what are the instinctual roots of fantasy, and what are the
inhibiting factors which can prevent instinct discharge on the biological
plane and how do they operate? The work on hysteria, of course,
led Freud right into the problem of the incest taboo, since his explanation of the genital inhibition associated with it was precisely that
later objects may represent tabooed incestuous ones; moreover, he, at this

point, began to interpret the relevant genetic sequences and drive constellations retroactively from fantasy and symbolic productions, rather than to postulate environmental events *ad hoc*. This shift went along with very close attention paid to the actual mental content of patients in all its details. In this perspective, we might come to the conclusion that if the brother-sister-sister's son triangle is most emphasized by the Trobrianders themselves in mythology and dreams, that this one indeed has a primary unconscious significance in Trobriand culture. Jones's main methodological mistake would then be that he did not pay sufficient attention to Malinowski's clinical detail and rather postulated a paternal trauma on the basis of theory alone. On this level, his formulation is logical, but it is as if he had tried to apply the genetic theory of hysteria to a schizophrenic patient without having tried to modify it to fit what the patient actually had to say.

But if we abandon trauma theory, it might be possible to postulate a distinctive genetic sequence that does not depend on the actual sexual relationships of which the child may be aware. Lacking the necessary material, we can only make a hypothesis, but to do this we might begin by summing up the three major facets of the brother-sister-sister's son triangle as it operates in adult life. First, it is very evident from the dream and myth material that even though there is a strict taboo, or just because there is one, brother and sister are to each other very highly cathected libidinal objects. Second, not only is the expression of any wishes for sexuality or intimacy forbidden, but also the relationship is one of respect, so that the expression of aggression is inhibited as well; the sister must show deference to her brother as an authority figure, and he, in turn, owes certain responsibilities to her. Third, the sister's son comes into this relationship in that he also owes respect to the mother's brother, and for social continuity to be preserved, he must identify with him; for in time, of course, he will become a mother's brother with respect to his own sister's son.

Translating this into the genetic perspective, two difficulties arise. First, although this is not true in some other societies, the mother and father do share a habitation which is independent from that of the mother's brother. Second, as Jones points out, it may be difficult to conceive of the sister as a primary object (for example she may be younger and not present or an infant at the oedipal crisis), and later feelings about her may be displaced from the mother. In any event, one would expect the mother to form a part of the Oedipus triangle in almost any society since oedipal affects arise from the body closeness which is experienced in early infancy.

However, we can include the mother as a primary object and also make the mother's brother into the primary focus of masculine identification if we presuppose that much of the boy's early feelings about him derive from the special place which the uncle, as her brother, occupies in his mother's eye. Presumably, at a very early age the small boy becomes aware of the special importance which he has to her, both as an authority figure and as a primary object in her fantasy life. In this perspective the idea of sexual jealousy can be built into the triangular situation involving mother, brother, and son in that we might say that, by some process which is not yet fully understood, the boy becomes aware of the strong affective importance which the brother has for his mother; and when his jealousy and anger are awakened, he deals with them by identification. The mother's brother then becomes the primary rival. Moreover, assuming that the passing of the Oedipus complex is equivalent to an assimilation of social representations of objects into the child's mind, we could also assume that much of his perception of his own mother is based on her role as sister, linked to the maternal uncle in the kin group to which he belongs. Having made this supposition, we could then suppose that the representations of the brother-sister relationship which are assimilated, in which the boy identifies with the brother role, then become transferred to the actual brother-sister relationship, within which the taboos are taught in the home very early in childhood. Such a formulation presupposes that identity and jealousy can both be transmitted through symbolic processes alone, without depending on particular observations or knowledge of parental sexual relations, but it would bring in the mother as a primary object, the distinctive aspect of the complex lying in the inclusion of her brother and the emphasis on her role as sister rather than father's wife.

Much of this is, of course, speculative since our knowledge of the possible range of perceptions of the oedipal child still has many gaps. However, such a formulation could reconcile the two assumptions with which we began, and moreover, could place the Oedipus complex in a more dynamic and wider social perspective, in that it would link up psychological knowledge with anthropological knowledge of kinship structure, given that we already know that this triangular relationship has a crucial status in the functioning of the matrilineal kinship system.

In a more general perspective, it should also be possible to say that each culture imposes restrictions on primary drives according to a particular pattern, and from the pattern of restrictions it should be possible to predict much of the cultural content from the assumption that symbols arise when a primary impulse is denied gratification. Such a possibility is found in the concept of repression, but perhaps comes out more clearly if we use the recent formulation of David Rapaport (1960), according to whom it is the fact of delay in drive expression which gives rise to the symbol, than in at least one facet of Jones's (1912) summary of the psychoanalytic theory of symbolism according to which there are biologically given types of primary symbolic content.

Returning to the Trobriand example, we could then say that the model for delay, or for the elaboration and maintenance of complex cultural productions, is provided by the brother-sister relationship. This latter would then be seen as the key relationship in a distinctive nuclear complex which can be used or interpreted on a number of levels: it is manifested directly in the myths of which brother-sister incest is the theme; it appears integral to matrilineal social structure; it presumably has genetic roots; and if we look to the actual experience of childhood and adolescence, we can see that quite concretely the brother-sister relationship is presented as the symbol of delay, for example, in that while infantile sexual games are generally rather freely permitted, this is not the case between brother and sister, just as later in adolescence rather casual affairs are the rule, but between brother and sister the taboo is very strict. In other words, for the Trobriand Islands the brother-sister relationship has a special place on the borderline between instinct and culture; but it should also be possible to isolate such specially important relationships for other cultures as well.

SOME SOUTH ITALIAN CULTURAL COMPLEXES

At this point, I should like to attempt the description of a third nuclear complex, resembling neither the matrilineal one of the Trobriand Islands nor the patriarchal one described by Freud. The material concerns Southern Italy, but descriptions by other researchers indicate the existence of similar patterns throughout the Latin world and possibly even in pre-Reformation Europe. My own concrete observations were made primarily in the city of Naples where I carried out a study of working-class families; however, the basic pattern does not seem fundamentally different in other areas of Southern Italy or in other social class groups, though, of course, there are many variations in details. What I shall try to do is to bring together a number of facts from quite diverse areas—general cultural patterns, intrafamily behavior, and projective test material—in a way which depends on the framework sketched above.

The South Italian family system, similar in this respect not only to other Latin countries but also to much of the Mediterranean world, is in a certain sense intermediate between the kind of lineage system found in the Trobriand Islands and the discontinuous nuclear family characteristic of the industrial world. As we have seen in the Trobriand Islands, it is quite possible that units other than the biologically based mother-father-child one serve as the key axis of social structure; this is very often true of primitive societies where the latter unit usually is enclosed in some wider kinship unit which in turn defines patterns of social organization for the society as a whole. In industrial societies, on the other hand, it is often said that since there is such an elaboration of alternative nonkin-ship social structures (religious bodies, bureaucratic organizations, governments, etc.) the functions of the family have contracted to an irreducible minimum, i.e., the satisfaction of intimacy needs and the caring for small children. The family is discontinuous in the sense that it lasts only as long as particular individuals are alive; as children grow up they gradually move into a wider society and eventually form new families on their own rather than acquiring adult roles in a continuing social group. The world outside the family is seen in this perspective as a locus of positive achievement.

The South Italian family is an intermediate form in two senses. First, although there is no corporate lineage, since religious, economic, and political functions are handled by nonkinship organizations just as in any complex society, there is a rather loosely organized body of extended kin, the "parenti" which has some significance; one's "parenti," or relatives in a generic sense (usually meaning siblings of parents and their offspring), form the most immediate field of social relations and in theory at least are the persons on whom one can best count for aid in time of trouble. Second, while the family unit is the immediate biological one (with monogamous marriage, no legal divorce, and co-residence of husband, wife and minor children), this latter tends to be centripetal rather than centrifugal. In other words, parents, or in particular the mother, bring up children in such a way as to strengthen loyalties toward themselves rather than to move increasingly into a wider social context. This latter tendency is in turn associated with a definition of the world outside the family as hostile and threatening and very often as a source of temptations toward sexual or other forms of delinquency and dishonesty.

We can begin on the level of global culture patterns by examining a key complex of attitudes, namely, those surrounding the Madonna. The importance of the Madonna complex throughout the Latin world is evident to even the most casual observation; in the South Italian villages she stands in every church and along with the saints may be carried through the streets in procession, and in even the poorest quarters of the city of Naples she is likely to occupy some niche or other, decorated with the flowers or even gold chains brought by her children grateful for her favors. Moreover, every home has a private shrine, in which pictures or statues of the Madonna appear along with photographs of deceased relatives illuminated by a candle or lamp.

As a figure in Roman Catholic theology, the Madonna, of course, is only one element in a much wider religious complex. However, popular religion in Southern Italy does not always conform to theological doctrine, for example, in that it has a considerable admixture of magical beliefs and in that the Madonna and the saints are conceived of more as persons of whom one can ask a favor (Italian *grazia,* or a grace) than as ideal figures in a moralistic sense. The Madonna may also be seen in characteristic folk manner as a quite familiar figure who is very much part of daily life. One older woman has said, "The Madonna must have had a hard time when she was carrying the Savior, because people couldn't have known about the Holy Ghost and they always gossip about such things." Religion in general is seen in this concrete and living way, and religious vocabulary as exclamations, for example, *Madonna mia* and *Santa Maria,* are very much part of daily conversation.

The most important characteristic of the Madonna is that her love and tenderness are always available; no matter how unhappy or sinful the supplicant, she will respond if she is addressed in time of need. Acts of penitence may be carried out for her, for example, pilgrimages or even licking the steps of the church one by one and proceeding to the altar (today only in the most traditional rural areas). Even such acts of penitence, however, are apt to be conceived of as means of showing one's devotion in order to secure a favor, such as the recovery of a sick child. In this sense, the Madonna complex is based on an ethic of suffering rather than sin; the devotee seeks comfort for the wrongs imposed by fate rather than a guide for changing it.

The Madonna is quite obviously the ideal mother figure, and the relationship of the supplicant to her is conceived of as that of a child. The other family figures in the Christian pantheon are, of course, not lacking, that is, the father and the son. However, God the Father is usually conceived of as being so distant that he is unapproachable except through the intermediary of the Madonna or a saint; in Naples, the first cause theory of creation is very common, according to which God set the world in motion and then let it run according to its own devices. Christ, on the other hand, is perceived not as in many Protestant denominations as a representative of moral individuality, or even as an alternative comforting figure, but rather either as the good son who is truly and continually penitent or else in the context of suffering; as dramatized in Lenten rituals, the Madonna weeps when he dies martyrized by a hostile world. Of the three figures, it is the Madonna who has by far the greatest concreteness in the popular eye. Moreover, of all her characteristics one of the clearest is her asexuality: she conceived without sin and so became mother without being a wife.

Not only is the most apparent deity a feminine one, but also religion is defined as a primarily feminine sphere. Thus, while small boys may attend mass regularly in the company of women, as they approach puberty most of them are teased out of this by their male peers or relatives. The level of participation in religious functions (except for those touching on the secular such as fiestas) is in general very low for adult males; but at every Sunday mass one can observe crowds of young men waiting outside the door. The reason they themselves give for being there is that the girls are inside; thus, at the courtship phase religious participation becomes an opportunity for escaping surveillance, but with the difference that the girl's overt devotion increases and the reverse is true for the boy. Moreover, Southern Italy is noted for its anticlericalism, but, along with some socioeconomic aspects, a major feature of this anticlericalism is a joking pattern whose main consequence is to raise doubts concerning the ideals of purity which religion represents. This joking pattern is an important part of interaction in the male peer group which crystallizes around adolescence. It thus seems as if religion and adult male sexuality are conceived of as incompatible with each other.

The oppositional or skeptical trend which is represented by anticlerical joking is seen in a number of other cultural patterns as well; first, in swearing and obscenity which are extremely widespread. The particular expressions used can be divided into four groups: those wishing evil on someone else (e.g., "may you spit up blood," from the extreme anxiety evoked by the idea of tuberculosis); those reflecting on the dead ("curse the dead in your family"); those reversing religious values (the most common oath being "curse the Madonna"); and those reversing the values of feminine purity. The latter group includes graphic expressions for a variety of possible incestuous relationships with mother or sister, anal as well as genital, and can also be linked with the horn gesture (index and little finger extended) implying infidelity of the wife. Cursing may be engaged in by women as well as men, but it is far more characteristic of the latter, particularly the last two types.[5]

The context and seriousness of insult and obscenity is extremely variable; one may curse the Madonna on the occasion of stubbing one's toe, but raising the possibility of the "horns" or using the incestuous expressions with enough seriousness may also lead to murder. It is this subtle distinction of style and context which differentiates Neapolitan patterns from those found in association with lineage systems where there are more formalized distinctions between those kin relationships which permit joking or obscenity, and those which do not because they are based on respect.[6] But the essential point is that the frequency of obscenity as used by men is such that one might talk of any positive value as reversible into a potential negative one; the reversibility relation is in turn confirmed by the particular content choices.

A second index of the same oppositional or skeptical trend is found in the style of masculine behavior and in social interaction within the male peer group. From adolescence on, an important segment of male life takes place on the street corner, at the bar, or in the club setting which at least psychologically is quite separate from either the home or the church. But in this setting in contrast to the other two, it is masculine values which predominate over feminine ones. Not only are swearing and anticlerical joking characteristic, but most social interaction has a particular style which is partly humorous and partly cynical in quality; many features of both language and gesture point in the direction of skepticism. Moreover, attitudes toward all forms of higher authority, secular as well as religious, are far more negative than positive in emphasis. Much of this style has a ritualized quality to it, but again we have a further index of the reversibility in the masculine setting of values defined as positive in the feminine context. In addition, many male peer group patterns, in particular the emphasis on gambling and risk, are such that they provide a kind of counterpoint to the extreme emphasis on protection and security found in the Madonna complex.[7]

---

[5] Women may in quarrelling with each other call each other prostitutes, but without reference to incest. They may also substitute euphemisms for actual curse words, such as *mannaggia alla marina*, literally "curse the seashore" for "curse the Madonna."

[6] See Radcliffe-Brown (1952, pp. 90-116). For the Trobriand Islands, obscene jokes are freely exchanged with the father's sisters but not with the mother's brother, and there are obscene expressions referring to mother, sister, and wife. Of these the most serious insult refers to sexual relations with the wife, a fact which is not quite congruent with the emphasis we have placed on the brother-sister taboo (see Malinowski, 1927, pp. 104-108).

[7] See Vaillant (1958), Whyte (1943), and Zola (1963) for descriptions of relevant patterns.

The second cultural complex which we will describe centers on courtship. Courtship is highly dramatized, and in the very important tradition of Neapolitan drama one can find over and over again the same
plot: girl meets boy, this is kept secret from the family, or in particular
from the father, father finds out (by catching them or by gossip from
others), there is a big fight in which the girl or the fiancé stands up for
the couple's rights against the father, father gives in at last, and here the
play ends. Sometimes there are attempts on the part of the parents to
marry a daughter to an old and ugly man for reasons of *interesse* or
financial gain, but they are apt to be frustrated and never go without
protest from the daughter. Says Rita in the early nineteenth-century
play *Anella* when her father tries to marry her off to a rich but effemi-
nate rag dealer:[8]

> You can cut me up piece by piece, but that Master Cianno, I'll
> never take him. Poor me! Even if I had found him while Vesuvius
> was erupting, I wouldn't have gone near him. If I weren't your
> daughter but your worst enemy, even then I wouldn't think of
> marrying that sort of man. What sort of life would it be?

The same play also serves to point up the very high degree with which
courtship is romanticized and the particularly humble and supplicative
position attributed to the young man. The following dialogue is addressed
to Anella, standing in the balcony, by her suitor, Meniello:[9]

> What sleep, what rest! What sleep, what rest can I have if I am
> in love, and the man in love is worse off than the man who is hang-
> ing on a rope and as soon as he gets a bit jealous, then the cord
> tightens. What sleep, the minute I close my eyes from exhaustion,
> jealousy makes me see my Anella up on her balcony surrounded
> by a crowd of lovers all looking up at her from below . . . what
> sort of sleep can you look for. And the worst of all is that I haven't
> even any hope of getting out of torment because I can't even ask
> her mother to give her to me as a wife because my dog's destiny
> made it happen that just to make a baker's dozen her mother is in
> love with me, too. You see what terrible things can happen in
> this world to torment a poor man in love!
>
> (Anella appears) Oh, Menie, is that you?
>
> (Meniello) Oh, beautiful one of my heart!
>
> (Anella) What on earth is wrong? I haven't even dressed yet, and
> you are up already. Why on earth are you so early?

[8] Davino, Gennaro: *Anella: Tavernara A Portacapuana.* In: Trevisani (1957), p. 125.
[9] *Op. cit.,* Trevisani (1957, pp. 118-119).

The dialogue continues between Meniello's supplications and Anella's much more self-assured and often more mundane reassurances against his jealousy.

Courtship is not only a theme of popular drama; it is also one of the major topics of conversation and joking in everyday life. In one sense, the social norms surrounding it are very strict, in that there are patterns of chaperonage, parents have many active rights of control, and the whole area is surrounded with an aura of taboo. Above all, it is considered highly important that the young girl keep her virginity until she is able to stand in church in the white veil which symbolizes it. Thus, there is a very sharp polar distinction between the good woman and the bad woman, the virgin and the prostitute. The assumptions underlying courtship are linked up in turn with a metaphorical image from which one can derive many specific customs and sayings: in a similar bipolar fashion, the home is defined as safe, feminine, and asexual, while the street is defined as inherently dangerous, tempting, and freely accessible only to men. Thus, a woman of the streets is one who has violated the taboos and in a sense has taken over masculine prerogatives. Coming into the girl's home is a very crucial step in legitimate courtship (popular terminology distinguishes between the often quite casual "so-so engaged" or "engaged in secret," and the more formalized "engaged in the house," i.e., with parental knowledge and approval), and the doorway occupies a particularly strategic intermediary position. Young girls usually become very excitable and giggly when they have the occasion for a promenade, and street phobias are a very common neurotic symptom in Italian women.

But a second aspect of the courtship complex is that in spite of the apparent strictness violations continually occur nevertheless, and the whole topic is treated with a particular kind of humorous ambiguity. Thus, while sexual matters are never referred to in serious or "objective" ways in everyday conversation, in a teasing or joking way they are an almost continuous focus of social exchange. The actual atmosphere or attitudes created by the strictness are far from puritan; it is rather as if the mothers and aunts and cousins who watch over the young girl with terrible threats about what will happen if she is "bad" are at the same time very much enjoying the possibility with her. One might by analogy to the many primitive societies in which there is a polar distinction between social relationships based on teasing or joking and those which are based on seriousness or formal respect, distinguish along the same lines between the Madonna complex and the courtship complex. For this reason, the distinction between the good woman and the bad woman is not as absolute as it might seem; often these may be alternative asexual and sexual images for the same woman, as when a father in anger calls his daughter a prostitute because she has come in late.

However, there is one point at which the sacred and the profane come together, and this is at the point of marriage, which almost without exception is symbolized by a church ceremony. Thus, while courtship is a secular process and while the idea of violation of chaperonage norms is often treated with humor, its more serious aim is nevertheless that it should end up in church with the young girl being able to stand "in front of the Madonna" in the white veil.[10] At the same time, marriage for the man symbolizes a kind of capitulation to the feminine religious complex, whose importance is denied in the male peer group setting by the pattern of sarcasm and secularization. In contrast to the girl, whatever prior sexual entanglements he has had lack significance. Thus, while at least in peasant areas even today the girl's "honor" may be verified by relatives after the wedding night, the whole question is seen as simply irrelevant on the sexual plane as far as men are concerned: said one informant, "How would anyone ever know if a man had it or not?"

There is, nevertheless, a sense in which the idea of honor is relevant to masculine identity as well as feminine. This is that the task of chaperonage is seen by the father (or brother) as a matter of maintaining his personal honor as well as the collective honor of the family. Thus, if a girl falls into disgrace, it will be said that the family honor has been lost, or that her father is also a *disgraziato* or lacking in grace. Moreover, whenever insults are cast at female kin, as in the oaths which reflect on the purity of mother, sister, daughter, or wife, the man is expected to consider this as a violation of his own personal integrity and to immediately come to their defense—in some instances with a knife. There are areas where the violation of the honor of a daughter or sister can lead to socially approved homicide, necessary to the defense of the family honor. This pattern is particularly characteristic of Sicily, where the brother's role is more important than in Naples. In eighteenth- and nineteenth-century Naples the task of protecting the honor of slum women was taken over by the Camorra, the most highly organized form reached by the Neapolitan underworld, which was not averse to using knives in order to force a reluctant man who had violated virginity into marriage.

We can now try to sum up some of the respective implications of the

[10] Voluntary abstention from public church ceremony sometimes occurs when wearing the veil would be a shame in front of the Madonna.

courtship complex and the Madonna complex as two contrasting sides of a global cultural pattern. One of these we have seen as a joking pattern and the other as a pattern of serious respect and desexualization, although the two meet and cross each other both in the male peer group rebellion against the Madonna and in the culmination of legitimate courtship in the church wedding. The symbol that unites them is that of virginity, or an initial asexual image of femininity that can only be violated in the appropriate social circumstances. These contrasting but interdependent patterns in themselves give us some of the elements of a distinctive nuclear complex; the two most important elements are that of the sublimated respect of children for the ideal mother and that of the game in which erotic temptations continually come into clash with this image of feminine purity. In the latter context, the most important actors, as Neapolitan drama would suggest, are the girl, her father, and the prospective son-in-law. The key value is that of virginity or honor, and the father seeks to preserve it against all comers; it is here that we can look for a distinctive triangular situation.

FAMILY STRUCTURE

At this point, we can turn to the more direct consideration of the family. We noted earlier that the primary unit is the nuclear family but that it is embedded in a larger kin group, and there is a high degree of continuity to the mother-child tie. The family is close in a certain sense, at least in that family ties and obligations outweigh all others, but family life is also characterized by a great deal of aggression and conflict. One way in which conflict is handled is by various patterns for the separation of roles, a result of which is the extrafamilial male peer group. After marriage, as well as before, many of the man's needs for comradeship and mutuality continue to be filled by the male peer group and much of the time he is out of the home. The woman, on the other hand, continues in close daily exchange with her natal family (perhaps less in the city than in the villages, and neighbors may also be important) so that many needs for mutual sympathy are fulfilled by mother and sisters or by other women. The division of the sexes is such that the marriage relationship is not often a focus of continuous intimate or reciprocal affective exchange. After the courtship phase and the honeymoon, it more often than not becomes very conflictual, principally because of the emotional ties which both partners retain to the natal family.

In actual fact, of course, there are a great many varied families as

well as the noted regional variations; however, many of the observable
norms and patterns can be interpreted from the above structural givens.
For example, there is a variety of possible balances to the husband-wife
versus primary family conflict. For Naples, the most common type of residence is in the vicinity of the wife's family, but the husband as an individual is likely to maintain important contacts with his own. Sometimes
the couple together becomes assimilated into one family or another;
women, for example, who have had particularly unfavorable relations
with their own families, or who have lost a mother by death, are more
likely to accept the mother-in-law as a mother surrogate, thus achieving a
better relationship with her than is generally expected. The same may
happen in the case of the man who marries into a fatherless family or
one consisting of girls alone who may take over male roles in that
family with relative success. This is unlikely if there are competing figures.
Quarrels concerning where the couple should reside are very common,
and they are accompanied by a great deal of mutual projection; thus, a
man may complain that his wife is much too dependent on her mother
and pays little attention to him, and then suggest as a solution to the
problem that they move to the house next door to his mother. In extreme
cases the two families may end up with quite violent feelings about each
other; in studying schizophrenic patients, we found this to be common,
and many marriages, while maintained in form, actually dissolved with
each partner returning to his own home. The uncertainties of the conflict
are intensified by the fact that in contrast to many simpler societies, there
are no fixed rules of choice or subordination. A result of this uncertainty
is that in situations of choice and conflict, it is more often the feminine
point of view than the masculine one which prevails, since it is the
woman who in daily life is most concerned with and most emotionally
involved in matters pertaining to the family.

It is also the mother who is the primary personage in maintaining
family unity, and many results of this can be observed; for example, ties
with father or siblings are very likely to break up or become more distant
on the death of the mother. Another consequence is seen in differential
attitudes toward the remarriage of widows and in differing consequences
of the death of parents. If a man is left without a wife, it is taken for
granted that he will need a woman, and whether or not he has children,
he is likely to find one, though often outside of legal sanction. Thus,
many persons who have widower fathers simply state that they have
drifted off somewhere, and the ties are no longer very real. On the other
hand, a widow or a woman deserted by her husband may be condemned

if she seeks alternative sexual attachments before her children marry; it is assumed that her primary loyalty is to them. Marriage, which in Naples is likely to take place either in the late teens or not until the late twenties or thirties, often in this latter instance follows very closely on the death of the parents. Remarriages when both partners have children are often conflictual on the grounds that each prefers his own offspring, and the stepmother is seen as in the Cinderella legend. She may do her best by the children, but even then the tie is never the same; the best possible solution to the loss of a mother is seen to be adoption by the mother's sister, who, because related by blood, will come much closer to fulfilling the maternal role. Marriage to the deceased wife's sister is not uncommon in the case of widowers, though practiced more in rural than in urban areas.

The importance of the mother-child tie as the axis of family structure is seen in some additional patterns characteristic of lower-class Naples. Where illegitimacy occurs, the child is legally recognized and brought up by the mother in about 50 per cent of the cases; such status is not formally approved but it does occur.[11] Fathers very rarely recognize illegitimate children, but there are, on the other hand, certain forms of semi-institutionalized polygamy, according to which a father may have two distinctive families, one of which is legal while the other is not. In contrast to the pattern of the affair where it is assumed that if the relationship is not socially sanctioned, precautions will be taken to avoid reproduction, it seems that aside from prostitution it is usually assumed that children are the necessary and wanted consequence of any sexual relationship; thus, the rapid multiplication which often characterizes monogamous families also characterizes polygamous ones.

The major requirement for a husband is that he be able to feed and support his family. However, in the urban working class, it very often happens that he is not able to fulfill this task; thus, one common source of arguments is that the husband has not brought in any money. It is also the case in urban areas where the married woman often works in her own right; for example, women may be street vendors, artisans, domestics, etc. At the lower socioeconomic levels it is often the woman who has a better opportunity of earning money than the man. She is more motivated to work since she more willingly accepts a low-prestige or low-reward position because of concern for children, while for the man, peer

---

[11] Of the illegitimate children born in Naples in 1956, 51 per cent were legally recognized by the mother alone, as compared with 9 per cent by the father alone, 10 per cent by both parents, and 29 per cent remaining unrecognized. See Office of Statistics of the Commune of Naples (1959, p. 22).

group relationships or a kind of pseudo identification with the higher status groups offers a more immediately rewarding proof of masculinity. One of the primary symbols of peer group belongingness in Naples is the ability to offer food or drink to others, so that the man is faced with an inherent conflict in that what he spends to gain status in relation to other men is bread lost out of his children's mouths. Thus, a vicious circle may be set in motion in which the wife accuses the husband of irresponsibility, and the husband in turn goes off in anger and tries to recapture his self-esteem by taking risks at cards or by treating his friends to coffee. It is, moreover, the way of dealing with this situation which differentiates male relationships with wives and mothers; the mother, if she has anything at all, will give it to her son, but the wife expects the husband to hand everything over to her in the interests of the children. Thus, financial conflicts are one factor which can push a married man back to ask for support at home.

A second factor is the degree to which intrafamily behavior is characterized by rivalry between husband and children for the attention of the mother in her food-giving role. One symbolization of the difference between South Italian society and the more truly patriarchal Victorian one can be found in the nature of eating patterns and their relation to family social structure; in contrast to the regular ritualized mealtimes of the Victorian epoch, with father taking a commanding position at the head of the table, there is a highly irregular eating pattern (space often makes a regular dinner table impossible) in which each member of the family may eat according to his own preference at his own time, but in which the mother is almost continually involved in the process of feeding. In this structure the superior position of the father, and of sons as they grow up, is symbolized by the right to demand what they want and the right to complain if not pleased. When a man complains, the woman will try to do what she can, and as long as she has anything at all, she will give it; but the pattern also puts the husband on an equal subordinate basis with his children.

Thus, the ties to the primary family, the high significance of the maternal role, and the very great difficulties in making a living which characterize most of the working-class groups are such that in spite of appearances the husband and father does not actually enjoy much prestige or authority in the home. From this standpoint the male peer group can be seen as an escape; the man who gets totally "fed up" always has the possibility of leaving. Likewise, many of the male rage reactions, which give the impression that the Italian family is patriarchal, though much more stylized, have the quality of the child who throws his plate on the floor when he has had enough. Moreover, many of the status-gaining activities of the peer group can be seen as identifications with the feminine feeding role, for example, the high importance attributed to offering food or coffee. However, a second aspect of the masculine role in the home and its relations to sex segregation should not be neglected. This is that male rage may be seen as truly terrifying to women, so that kicking men out becomes necessary, and this goes with an image of masculinity as a kind of threatening force which is a disruptive factor in the feminine circle; images used in daily conversation clearly suggest the idea of phallic intrusion.

A few details on socialization can serve to round out the picture of family life. Children become a center of attention as soon as they are born and receive a great deal of physical handling which does not undergo systematic interruption; moreover, as they are weaned, substitute gratifications are provided so there is no significant discontinuity ending the oral phase of development. However, it would be a mistake to conclude from this that they simply receive that much more of the "security" and maternal warmth which are currently so highly valued in the United States. In the first place, the mother may give little attention to any individual child, being busy and often having many; moreover, maternal behavior (in the sense of giving food and physical caresses) is so widespread that in actual social reality the maternal attachment is far from being exclusive. Rather, one might say that the circle of maternal objects progressively widens to include the family as a whole and in many respects strangers; along with this goes the learning of certain kinds of politeness and formality having to do with eating and giving.

In the second, handling of children is often very rough and unsubtle and includes a very high aggressive component.[12] As physical motility appears, it can be systematically frustrated by anxious adults who immediately bring back the wandering or assertive child to thrust a cookie into his mouth; one can see here the beginning of the forced feeding pattern which characterizes moments of tension in the family throughout life. An illustrative example concerns a three-year-old son of a gardener who picked up his father's tools and was immediately called back by mother with the tacit support of father. Children at this age may show considerable diffuse aggressivity and put on an unnatural amount of weight.

[12] It is roughest among the poorest and here also may be quite erotically stimulating as well. I am indebted to Vincenzo Petrullo for the suggestion that this latter may be the case because when children have to go hungry, erotic stimulation may be a means of maintaining their interest in life.

Later, most of them learn to "talk back" with verbal rhetoric and gesture; these important components of South Italian culture might be seen as developed in counterreaction to muscular inhibition in that they become a major means for expressing individuality. A second relevant example concerns an eighteen-month-old girl who seemed hardly interested in learning to walk and was not yet able to talk; yet, held by her father she was able to perform fairly complex symbolic operations with her hands, such as snapping her fingers ten times when asked to count to ten.

For these early phases there seems to be little difference between the handling of the small girl and of the small boy, with the single exception that the small boy is more likely to go unclothed from the waist down and to have his penis singled out for teasing admiration.[13] This open phallic admiration is characteristic of the behavior of mothers to sons, and in teasing intrafamily behavior the genital organs may be poked or referred to with provocative gestural indications. Children may also share beds with their parents or with each other even at advanced ages (crowding often makes this necessary)[14] though precautions are taken to prevent their observing parental intercourse. One young man was asked what he would do if he saw this; the answer was "I would kill them." Except for small children, modesty taboos are very strict, and while physical proximity within the family is very close with respect to anything except genital activity, this latter is surrounded with some secrecy.

There are, however, two crucial points at which sex difference is more prominent. The first is in the ritual of First Communion which ideally takes place at the age of six or seven. Around this age the growing attractiveness of the little girl is the focus of considerable teasing admiration from father or older brothers, uncles, etc., though these have not taken much interest in the very small child. One Neapolitan informant, for example, told me how his seven-year-old daughter had taken to getting into bed with him in such a seductive way that he finally had to slap her and kick her out. It did not surprise him in the least when I said that a famous Viennese doctor had made quite a bit out of this sort of thing. However, once the small girl's oedipal affects have been excited to this degree, it is also necessary that the culture find a resolution for them which it does in the ritual of First Communion; the small girl is dressed

[13] This pattern is even more characteristic of Puerto Rico (see Wolf, 1952), where sex differences in modesty rules are also sharper.

[14] I know of examples of mothers sharing beds with adult sons, and also of a case of a mother who lost a child in infancy whereupon she asked a thirteen-year-old son to take the milk from her breast; he, however, refused on the grounds that "she was my mother and I was ashamed."

as a miniature bride, and at this point it must be impressed on her fantasy that she must delay fulfillment of her wishes until such a time as she can again appear in church in a white veil. Thus, a particularly elaborate cultural symbolization is provided for feminine oedipal wishes.

For the boy, on the other hand, there is much less in the way of such cultural elaboration of the Oedipus crisis, nor for that matter is there any ritual symbolization of masculine status at adolescence, as there is in many other cultures where socialization at earlier stages is so exclusively in the hands of women. First Communion does take place, but masculine emphasis and degree of symbolization is simply less. Moreover, in many ways the boy's position at home is much more passive than that of the girl; the beautiful warm-eyed docility which one can observe in many boys in the Neapolitan slums might make for the envy of the American mother in the Hopalong Cassidy phase. The same degree of aggressive tension does not appear to be present, nor for that matter is there as much elaboration of the phallic "I want to be when I grow up" type of fantasy. What does differentiate the small boy from the girl is, first, the open admiration which may be shown for his purely sexual masculine attributes, and second, the fact that he has much less in the way of home responsibility and is in many ways favored by the mother; but since the father is so often out of the home, his socialization is placed in feminine hands almost as much as that of the girl.

In other words, while cultural ritual can be seen as providing a complex symbolic framework for feminine oedipal wishes, this is not true in the case of the boy, who may receive special privileges and an open acknowledgment of his physical masculinity, but no such elaborate social symbolization of it. Presumably, this should result in much stronger motivation for the delay of sexual wishes in girls than in boys. This kind of differential in turn becomes extremely important in adolescence, at which point the pattern of sex differentiation becomes a much sharper one, for it is then that chaperonage rules begin to apply to the girl, and the boy in turn acquires a special freedom to move out into the inherently dangerous and sexualized world of the street.[15] It is at this latter point that the prerogative of adult masculinity crystallizes, especially with respect to the quasi taboo on feminine inquisitions concerning masculine activities which take place outside the home.

[15] Boys are of course outside earlier too, the actual age and amount of time depending on the specific social milieu. The street gang in the slums may include girls and in some groups much of the family income may come from small boys. The important fact is the lack of any very formalized masculine authority over the boy.

One of our initial assumptions was that culture appears in the individual in the form of object representations which crystallize in the conscious mind at the time of the passing of the Oedipus complex. In this perspective, the norms of the intrafamily behavior should be reflected on the psychological plane in the form of more or less uniform representations of the significant family figures in relation to the self. This dimension is one which can be measured through the use of projective tests. Such material will be presented as a supplement to the cultural and social observations which we have already made.

In two separate studies, a number of cards from the Murray TAT were presented to working-class informants in Naples. Four cards (6GF, 6BM, 7BM, 7GF) will be discussed here. They were presented to the informants with the specific directive that they represent family scenes (mother-daughter, father-son, father-daughter, and mother-son), and they were to describe the scene as it appeared to them. Though few very elaborate stories were given, the subjects saw the cards in an amazingly vivid way with a high degree of sensitivity to the immediate perceptual and gestural details of the figures.[16] The high degree of uniformity of response is in itself a proof of the psychological reality of culture. This uniformity was greatest for the mother-son and father-daughter scenes.

A. *Mother-Daughter Card*

The mother-daughter card was presented to twenty-six female informants with a specific directive: "The mother is advising the daughter, what do you think she is telling her?" Additional questions such as "How does the daughter feel about it?" were also asked. Thus, we purposely biased the situation in the direction of emphasis on maternal authority. However, only to a certain extent was this the major theme; rather, the responses fell into three distinct groups, of which the first is most directly relevant to the question of authority as such.

For eleven subjects, the mother appeared as giving some very definite form of censure or advice. In only one such instance is the reaction of the daughter to this seen as wholly positive; in one other instance the reaction of the daughter is openly rebellious, and in the remaining nine, the daughter accepts the advice as "for her own good" but with expressed resentment; however, the mother is finally vindicated since "things don't turn out well in the long run":

[16] "Stories" more often took the form of "well, from the way his eyes are you can tell that...," followed by a conclusion about motivation or feeling.

> The mother is giving good advice to the daughter; the mother tells the daughter to behave well, not to go out much, to pay more attention to things at home. She has to help her mother to do the housework. The picture is beautiful because there is nothing bad in it.

> The mother is yelling at the daughter because with the excuse of the child who is her little brother she goes out walking and comes in late. The daughter talks back to her mother saying "What do you want with me? You made this baby and now you go around finding out bad things about me."

> The mother is moralizing. The daughter is a bit fed up with the mother's words. . . .

> The mother tells the little girl that she has to do housework and the daughter is not looking at the mother as if she had not heard and did not want to do this work. . . . Things won't go very well because the daughter won't listen to the mother.

The first reaction is particularly interesting in that by implication it so clearly brings out the asexual nature of the home in contrast to the outside world where there may always be "something bad." The second is equally interesting in that where there is open rebellion on the part of the daughter, the mother is also portrayed as a sexual being. The remaining responses show a very classic pattern of internalized but ambivalently accepted authority; the mother is clearly a superego figure, but considerable rebellion and resentment are experienced toward her.

For the next group of subjects, the card itself provided a particular difficulty. The Murray card shows a girl in the latency period being read to by her mother and holding what could be either a doll or a live baby. The situation of a mother reading to the daughter is, of course, somewhat out of the ordinary in this group, but in addition a number of informants were led to comment from the girl's age that this could not actually be an authority situation since "the girl is too young to be given the most important advice."

Thus, these responses were limited to fairly factual and emotionally neutral kinds of advice ("the mother is telling the daughter how to bring up her little brother"), and more crucial attitudes of mother and daughter were not made clear. The responses are important principally for their value in pointing up just how crucial the courtship situation is as compared to any other area of performance with respect to the question of authority in general.

For the third group of three respondents this was true as well, but they simply ignored the age of the girl on the card and perceived the situation as involving a mother, her daughter, and the latter's illegitimate child:

> The mother talks with the daughter that is married and has a child, no, I mean the daughter is not married. The mother tries to help her and get her married, the mother is good and does not throw her out of the house.

> The girl is not married and it seems to me that her mother gives her advice on how to bring up the child. It seems that the mother has forgiven her and tells her to treat the child well. The mother gives advice to the daughter about how to behave and how not to fall a second time. Because the mother is understanding she says to the daughter to be careful because the mother should try not to say to the daughter that she is guilty because the girl could do something to hurt herself, she could commit suicide or fall into the same error again thinking that she doesn't have anyone who cares.

This is, of course, a crucial and dramatic situation where norms have actually been violated. The responses make clear that fear of loss of maternal love is a major threat preventing more frequent violations; but also in the actual crisis situation the mother may not really kick the girl out of the house. Another evidence of the internalized nature of maternal authority is seen in the respondent who conceived of suicide as a possibility in the event that such forgiveness did not take place.[17]

B. Father-Son Card

The father-son card was presented to ten men and ten women in a second study. No specific directives were given beyond the statement that the scene involved a father and a son. Authority, however, turned out to be the most important theme, found in the responses of seven men and three women, but in contrast to the mother-daughter responses the specific content of the advice or censure given by the father to the son was left indeterminate. However, there is no doubt but that fathers were seen by the majority of men as censuring figures:

[17] Low suicide rates are often taken as evidence of the lack of internalized superegos. However, material from Southern Italy, including the fact that depressive symptoms are not at all rare, might suggest that instead there are secondary social mechanisms (i.e., the possibility of forgiveness) which alleviate guilt whose subjective intensity may nevertheless be very great. The high suicide rates found in modern industrial countries may result then from the lack of these, or what Durkheim (1897) calls anomie.

. . . the father reproaches the son . . . the son is a delinquent, you can see from his face that he is not a nice person and I think he will not listen to the father's advice. . . .

The son is bitter and the father displeased because the son would like to talk about something and doesn't. During the family life, the father asks the son what trade he would like to have while the son takes the matter unhappily. He would like to be a chauffeur and the father makes him learn carpentry and the result is that he practices his trade against his own will and cannot succeed in it. After a few years he begins to hate the father and so he remains without any trade at all. The son on his side would like to be a chauffeur. As a result father and son fight, the son curses the father, the father says "you ought to listen to me."

The second response was stated to be an autobiographical one; the respondent was the son of an artisan and, as the result of having gambled away his youth and refusing to learn a trade, was at the time I saw him a very despondent man, father of eight children whom he tried to support as a street vendor. Moreover, while all the male respondents were themselves fathers with children, they seemed not to take the perspective of the father. The exceptions to the rule that both were seen negatively were only partial ones; one respondent did unconvincingly portray the father as affable while another (particularly intelligent and outward seeking) was the only respondent to think of the possibility of positive rather than negative assertion against the father:

The son is affable and absolutely convinced of the father's counsels.

The father is decided and authoritarian, ugly. The son *might* be bad, he has an independent spirit and does not want to listen to the father. The son follows something else, as if the father's wisdom were something annoying, not very important for him.

Two of the remaining three men saw the situation as one of shared sorrow for the death of a woman and the third presented an alternative comradely view of their relationship:

There is a close friendship between the father and son, they confide in each other.

But for women it was themes of common sorrow and depression which took precedence over those concerning authority. Thus, three saw authority themes and three a common sorrow over death; but the remaining four show the two as sharing a common sense of helplessness with respect to the (primarily economic) external reality:

> They are desperate (for money)—they worry. Nothing more.
>
> They are worrying about something, the office, work, because they are melancholy.
>
> What a shame, the father is completely blind! Don't you see he has his eyes completely closed and an absent expression? The son is as if he were listening to something, it must be a radio, but the father has the look really of a blind man. (Don't they say anything to each other?) No, the father minds his own business, really with the look of a blind man, and the son on the other hand is listening, he must be listening to the radio.

In this the women seem to be able to portray a socially very real aspect of their relationship, that it is hard for a man to be an effective authority when he cannot provide anything for his son, which the men themselves have to deny.

The most striking features of the responses to the father-son card are, thus, the lack of a clear social agreement concerning the nature of this relationship, and for the men the lack of effective internalization of paternal authority. By the latter, we mean that sons are simply seen as "bad" or "delinquent" in relation to the father, without, as was the case in the mother-daughter situation, there being a view of how the son ought to accept the authority for his own good, etc. One might say that this provides further evidence that the society is not patriarchal, and masculinity is defined more in terms of rebellion than positive identification. In simplest terms, the conflict is that portrayed by one informant who says, "They seem against each other."

C. Father-Daughter Card

For a contrast with responses to the father-son scene, we might again quote the street vendor, who turned to this card with considerable relief and pleasure:

> This case here defines a father, he is sociable. Here it is no longer a job problem, the girl must know a man and he knew from the information that he has been a delinquent. He says "look for another path, there are millions of men." The father wants happiness for his daughter, he wants her to marry someone who will give her something to eat. (Q) The daughter answers "it's my business," no daughter ever listens to her father. (Q) They get bitter but then they make peace after a child is born.

Unfortunately, we do not have enough male answers to this card to analyze quantitatively; however, this one indicates that while the father does have authority over the daughter, its overthrow is to be expected even by the father himself and while they may "get bitter," the bitterness is nothing like the real hostility of the father-son antagonism. The same card was administered to thirty-two female respondents, and it was among these that the highest degree of uniformity was found. Twenty saw the situation as conflict between father and daughter related to courtship:

> The father does not want the daughter to get engaged to a man he knows and does not want this man to marry his daughter. The father is making her ashamed. The father seems bad to me. He is jealous of the daughter and does not want her to get engaged. The daughter is a beautiful girl. She cares a lot about this man that her father doesn't want to give her to and she wants to get married at any price.

> The father is mortifying the daughter. The father is having it out with the daughter because other people have told him something. He makes her ashamed and she remains surprised and amazed. The father wants to know the story of his daughter's engagement. She does not want to tell about her affairs and probably the father heard about this engagement from other people. The father wants to know if it is a good marriage for his daughter.

> The daughter seems like an actress. The father is reasoning with the daughter. They are probably talking about the daughter's fiancé; the father wants to know how things are going in her engagement. The father is happy and the daughter is a bit fed up because her father wants to know many facts about her relationship with the fiancé. For this reason she is not answering spontaneously.

Nine of the remaining twelve respondents gave generally very inhibited answers or denied that the scene could actually be father and daughter in such a way as to suggest some neurotic inhibition.

> I don't know how to say anything about this picture. The father is mad and the daughter is calm. They are talking about not very important problems that have to do with family life.

> (Informant says that the test seems a bit complicated here.) The father is upset because the daughter didn't do something in the house; she should have done some errand and didn't do it. The father says to the girl, "You got dressed up to go out and didn't do the errands." The father doesn't let her go out but the relations between father and daughter aren't bad.

And finally three informants saw the scene as one in which the father was
making seductive advances toward the daughter.

> The father is looking at the daughter in a strange way, that is
> more like a man than like a father. She looks at him perplexed and
> almost struck dumb. The father will not succeed because the daugh-
> ter has understood his intentions, she will control herself unless
> he attacks her. The father is not behaving very well; he has gone
> astray . . . maybe because the girl is attractive.

All three saw the girl as able to control the situation. An additional two
among the above nine, while denying that the scene could be father and
daughter, saw, respectively, a husband and wife, and an older Don Juan
boss seducing a secretary.

As far as we know the incest responses were not given by seriously
disturbed women and they show fewer signs of inhibition than the
respondents who did not perceive any shame or conflict between father
and daughter at all.

For the first group there was not a single informant who failed to
perceive the situation as a conflictual one in which the conflict lay between the father's censure or possessiveness and the daughter's wish to
have a boyfriend. Moreover, the card typically evoked a complex of affects
which included pleasure (blushing and giggling), shame, and embarrassment. When we look for the outcome of the conflict, we find one
element in common with the father-son card, namely, the tendency is in
the direction of expected rebellion rather than internalized acceptance of
paternal authority. In ten out of twenty instances the daughter is specifically stated to win the battle with father, while in only three does she
concede; in the remaining cases the fact of conflict is simply stated. In
other words, the TAT responses repeat the same dramatic pattern which
we have already seen in the play *Anella* in which the courtship situation
is a triangular relation between father, daughter, and prospective son-
in-law, and the expected outcome is the ritual termination of the father's
possessive relation to the daughter.

D. *Mother-Son Card*

The most important characteristic of these responses is the extent to
which they show a close correspondence to the Madonna complex, just as
the father-daughter card corresponds to the courtship one. One theme
occurs over and over again, more frequent among male than female re-

spondents, namely, that of the penitent son who is returning to the mother:

> . . . the son is asking forgiveness of the mother, repenting of the evil he has done. . . .

> The mother pushes the young man away and he asks for something insistently. Or maybe he did something very serious, probably he went away, and so now he has come back to ask her forgiveness and the mother no longer wants to receive him.

> The mother has a son she has not seen for many years . . . he returns after having done many bad things, stealing and other things. He returns to the family to ask forgiveness. Who knows whether or not the mother will give it to him but I think she will.

> The son is asking forgiveness for something . . . a mother would always forgive her son, even if he were an assassin, even if he were Chessman.

> The penitent son who returns to the mother and the mother cannot or does not know how to forgive him.

In comparison to the responses concerning the father, what is most striking is the extent to which the son places the burden of guilt upon himself, in that asking for forgiveness implies an internalized sense of wrongdoing.

There was some variation among the respondents as to whether the mother was seen as certain to provide forgiveness or not; the fact that some expressed doubt or uncertainty is evidence that maternal love is not conceived of as wholly unconditional. In two instances informants were known to have marked difficulties in their actual relationships with the mother. One of these is the informant who states that "the mother cannot or does not know how to forgive"—but he portrays the son as the saint who forgives the mother unable to forgive. The second, recently kicked out of home, is the only one who saw the mother as acting aggressively ("The mother pushes the young man away," etc.), but after in a sense blaming the mother, he changes pattern and like the others puts the burden of guilt on the son.

For ten male and ten female respondents, what we call the penitence response was given by seven men and four women. Among the other responses, three portrayed simple sadness ("The mother is sad because the son will leave"), and three anger. All of the anger responses were given by women, who, on the whole, presented a less romanticized view of the relationship. One response given by a beggar is particularly interesting in that it shows a relation between psychic abnormality and open anger and sexual deviance on the part of the mother:

> As if he (she?) were all upset. You can see the son is arguing with the mother, he has turned his back, maybe they had a family fight. (About what?) Mama and son because the mama you can see made a lot of scandals and the son wants to find out something, who knows what, and so mama and son are arguing . . . because you can see that the mother is a bit off in the head because she turns her back on the son. (Yes, you can see that she is a bit angry. But how does the son feel about it?) The son has an enraged face, he has his nerves out of place too. (In response to further questions, she shifts subject.)

In many instances the fact that the American card portrays a mother looking away from her son was sensed as disturbing but that it could imply psychic distance was denied. Thus, while it may be perceived by women, there seems to be a taboo on perceiving anger in the mother-son relationship by men. In this respect there is a very clear contrast with respect to the father-son relationship.

Conclusions

We began, with reference to the Jones-Malinowski debate, by considering the possibility that each culture is characterized by a distinctive nuclear complex whose roots lie in its family structure. Our subsequent task has been to pull together various orders of data concerning Southern Italy in such a way as to portray such a nuclear complex which differs both from the brother-sister-sister's son triangle characteristic of the Trobriand Island and from the patriarchal complex isolated by Freud. In the South Italian data we have found that two cultural complexes, the sacred one centered on respect for the feminine Madonna figure and the secular joking pattern surrounding courtship and embodied in popular drama, also have their reflections in the actual patterning of family life and childhood experience and in the intrapsychic life of the individual as seen in projective tests. It is this continuity which has led us to the conclusion that it is possible to define a single global complex which can be perceived simultaneously either as intrapsychic or as collective, the representations which are passed on from generation to generation on the social level coming to be internalized in the individual in the form of representations of the self in relation to objects. The task which remains is the more precise summary of the outlines of the South Italian nuclear complex, comparing it with Freud's patriarchal one, and the drawing out of some more general implications with respect to research methodology and application.

Our principal supposition is that the two most significant among the biologically given family relationships are those between mother and son and between father and daughter. In the former instance the son occupies a subordinate position in the sense that authority stemming from the mother is fully internalized, and violations of it are subjectively sensed as inducing guilt, in comparison to the father-son relation where the son may openly express hostility or rebellion in such a way as to put the father in a negative light. In other words, respect for the mother is much stronger than respect for the father. We do not mean by this to say that women dominate in any simple sense, since it is evident that many other taboos, such as the barring of feminine interference in areas of activity defined as masculine ones, act against this result, not to mention the open admiration and permissiveness which women usually show toward the masculinity of their sons. However, in many ways the mother-son relationship is qualitatively different from that of our own society or that of Freud, most notably in the continuation throughout life of what might be referred to as an oral dependent tie, i.e., a continual expectation of maternal solace and giving rather than a gradual or sudden emancipation from it.

It is this fact that might lead an American observer to speak of an "oral" culture, or one based on feeding as the dominant mode of libidinal interaction, in contrast to a hypothetical "anal" or "phallic" based one. However, this type of formulation we would consider quite inadequate both with respect to theory and the empirical facts. It is evident that types of interaction based on the exchange of gifts and food do have an extremely important role, though these result in very complex types of adult interaction which can by no means be derived directly from infantile roots. More important, however, is the theoretical postulate which would lead us to believe that the phallic phase of development nevertheless occurs. In other words, although he may not give up oral types of gratification, the boy nevertheless passes through a phase at which the wishes he experiences toward the mother are sexual and masculine in nature, and that, moreover, this phase will be associated with aggressive reactions against the subordinate feeding position. We can then trace some of the implications of these postulates rather than simply stopping with the "oral culture" formulation.

In this perspective we can better see some of the more general consequences of the fact that the masculine role is so little emphasized within the home and that cultural values center on the feminine image. From the genetic standpoint, we might say that while oral gratifications do not have to be renounced (although they do come to take more complex social forms), this is not true with respect to phallic and aggressive wishes toward the mother; these in fact must systematically undergo repression as they arise. In fact, to characterize the relation to the mother as one based on respect, in social language, is exactly the same thing as to say in psychodynamic language that sexual and aggressive wishes cannot be expressed directly. We then can ask what happens to these wishes, assuming that in some form they persist, and arrive at three kinds of formulation, each of which is relevant to the understanding of culture patterns. Through all of them the important contrast with Freud's formulation lies in the greater continuity of the relationship with the mother and the lesser continuity of that with the father.

First, referring back to the concept of the symbol as arising in precisely those areas where a culture both exploits (by actual affective closeness) and inhibits (by imposing of taboos) primary drives, we can say that the erotic wishes of the son toward the mother come to be sublimated, and it is precisely this fact which gives rise to the representation of the Madonna figure. Moreover, in her characteristics we can see both derivatives of the actual cultural reality, e.g., in that the dependent relationship of the penitent to the maternal figure is preserved, and some unrealizable aspects of fantasy, e.g., in that the Madonna became a mother without being a wife. This latter is, moreover, the characteristic which in itself represents oedipal repression, in that the Madonna is perceived as an asexual maternal figure. But in addition, and in contrast to the "oral culture" view which might say simply that mothers are more permissive, the Madonna is a "superego" figure; she could not be forgiving if she did not have a concept of sins which have to be forgiven. In this perspective we can say that oedipal wishes are repressed in such a way as to give rise to an internalized representation of the tabooed object, who then comes to play the role of conscience. However, the complication in this case is that the internalized object is in the case of men a feminine one; it is this which we mean by speaking of a matriarchal rather than a patriarchal "superego." What it leads to then is a masculine identification with a set of cultural values identifiable as feminine, or even as very concretely perceived according to a feminine body image. The most important of these is the respect for virginity, shared by men and women alike and manifested in the courtship taboos on entering the home of the girl who is sought before the relation is formalized. The identification of the girl who is legitimately courted with the idealized mother is seen in the similar submissive relation adopted by the male; the infantile wishes underlying the image of the pure woman are also seen in a sometimes extreme degree of defensiveness concerning the issue of whether or not the purity is real and to be believed.

Second, however, impulses which are repressed can also be dealt with by displacement. It is in this respect that the significance of the masculine peer group and the definition of the sphere of life outside of the home, i.e., the sum total of masculinity as defined by the rebellion pattern which we have discussed, become apparent. Many of the patterns of the outside peer group are distinctively phallic in nature. Moreover, in many more concrete senses one can conceive of the outside world as the focus for aggressive and phallic wishes which must be displaced outside the home, e.g., the common situation of the male in anger who simply picks up and leaves, or the great importance of cursing. Thus, aggression which arises within the home may be dealt with by displacement outside it. One characteristic of the Madonna is that she is an ideal figure; ordinary mothers of course rarely approach her, in that they may not forgive, they may very often get angry or impatient, or they may in fact dominate in a very aggressively matriarchal way and in this event the recourse of the male is the privilege of exit. Women in turn support this form of expression of masculinity by respecting the taboo on interference and often by direct admiration and encouragement of even delinquent extrafamilial activities. In addition, anger which arises in a mother-son relationship conceived of as exclusive in fantasy may also be dealt with in a complex series of intrafamilial rivalries and jealousies within which the affective consequence of reality frustration vis-à-vis the mother may be expressed with respect to other family objects. Thus, displacement both within and outside the family is used to deal with aggressive impulses whose direct expression toward the mother is tabooed.

Third, erotic wishes may be displaced as well as aggressive ones, and it is here that we can find the source of the bipolar distinction between the good woman and the bad woman. The contrary image to the Madonna is, of course, that of the prostitute, and the close intertwining of the two images is seen at a great many points, e.g., in the obscenity patterns that reverse the values of feminine purity and in the family quarrels where even closely associated women may be accused of promiscuous impulses. The persistence of the early sublimations in later life is manifested in two crucial assumptions: first, that the sexualized woman may be appreciated in a naturalistic way but she is always perceived as on a lower spiritual plane than the pure one; and second, the idea of sexuality is almost inevitably associated with the possibility of betrayal and pluralization of the relationship, i.e., in that wives, sweethearts, and mistresses are continually suspected by men of wanting other partners than themselves as soon as the idea of sexuality comes into play.

It is facts such as these which lead us to postulate an underlying and persistent fantasy of an exclusive maternal object as a theoretical assumption. Because of repression, we cannot, of course, acquire direct information concerning the sexual aspect in most cases. One particularly important area of research, however, is found in schizophrenic cases where one may see gross breakdowns of cultural sublimations. One of two South Italian schizophrenic men whom I have seen intensively showed the sexual aspect of the mother-son relationship and the associated Madonna complex in a very transparent form: having many religious delusions; while praying to the Madonna he had open and bizarre erotic experiences and he was unable to distinguish consistently between maternal and erotic objects. The early history was probably one in which prolonged nursing merged into the awakening of genital feelings. However, the second case points up the need for care in separating local and individual variations from global patterns. Coming from a mountainous area where patriarchal patterns and a lack of sentimentality are more typical, the patient showed a much more autistic form of pathology of which the most conspicuous elements were warded-off homosexuality and an extremely submissive identification with the father. He rejected the breast of a wet nurse at an early age, and a crucial traumatic experience was a childhood seduction by an older brother.

One consequence of such a relationship, which fits many of the data we have concerning the South Italian family, is that it acts against social mobility in the broadest sense of the term by making for a very strong centripetal tendency. In other words, if a key axis of family structure is the relationship between mother and son, and if this relationship tends to maintain itself by the preservation of an infantile fantasy which is then dealt with by a complex series of social sublimations and displacements, rather than by attenuating its significance by dispersal or replacement by other objects, then we should have no theoretical basis for explaining the formation of new families. Rather we should expect each mother-son combination to simply continue until the death of the mother; the incest taboo alone does not seem sufficient for explaining the process of change, since nothing in South Italian norms prevents the adult son from obtaining immediate sexual gratification outside while continuing to occupy the emotionally more important position of son. It is at this point that we might turn to the examination of the father-daughter relationship, which can be seen as complementary to the mother-son one in defining a total structure.

The most important difference between these two lies in the dimension of continuity. The father is not continually and lovingly interested in his daughter as the mother is in her son, but rather his interest becomes particularly important at two points in the daughter's life history: the oedipal phase and the courtship phase. At both of these points the father is highly sensitive to the daughter's femininity, and the daughter is given considerable scope for exploiting this sensitivity in what is often a very active way. Moreover, while the taboo on incest between mother and son is as in all societies a very deep-lying one, it is very easy to come to the conclusion that the desexualization of the father-daughter relationship is not nearly as complete. Thus, in particular in instances where the mother has died, father-daughter incest is not an unheard of phenomenon and the possibility may be referred to even rather casually, as in the many stories about "that case in our village" that go around. We noted this on the TAT responses. In an American setting an openly incestuous perception might be taken as an indication of serious pathology, but we have no reason to believe this was the case for our informants. Their counterpart in the normal case where the taboo is preserved is found in the teasing behavior or embarrassed avoidance which characterizes the relation between the father and the sexually mature daughter or in the giggling embarrassment which women associate with the idea of being found out in their love relationships.

In other words, the incestuous impulses in the father-daughter relationship are quite close to the surface, in such a way that we might speak of a lesser degree of repression than is implied in Freud's concept of the Oedipus complex. There is of course a taboo but one might well speak of a persistence of the incestuous impulses on a preconscious level in such a way that they are openly expressed in cultural idiom, as in the frequent use of the word jealousy to describe the father's feelings about the daughter's suitors, and transformed into the joking pattern which is characteristic of the courtship complex.

The major significance of the triangle involving father, daughter, and prospective son-in-law, moreover, lies in the fact that it is to a much greater extent with respect to the daughter than to the wife or mother that the man plays an active role. When he himself is courting, he has to beg at the balcony for a well-protected woman whose virginity he has to respect, but in the case of his own daughter it is he who does the protecting and whose consent has to be sought by the prospective suitor. Thus, the most fully institutionalized masculine role in Southern Italy, one which is defined positively and not by rebellion, is that of the protection of the honor of the women who are tabooed. In turn, if the sexual affects felt toward these are quite close to the surface, considerable fantasy satisfaction must take place in a way which is active and masculine in contrast to the mother-son relationship, which in so many ways spreads into the marital one, where the male role is passive.

But in addition it is in the father-daughter relationship that we can find a mechanism of change which acts against the centrifugal family tendency. The courtship situation not only gives the father an active role but also has a particular affective style, namely, that of a sudden explosion in which erotic impulses break out with a dramatic intensity which suggests some underlying dynamic force. Moreover, in spite of the chaperonage norms, the behavior of young women at this point is not such as to suggest much innocence or ignorance of sexuality; they just as well as the young men seem propelled to rebel against the taboos, and they are very often teasers. We have also commented at length on the ambivalent nature of the taboos themselves, in that while violations may be severely condemned explicitly, it often seems as if they were just as much encouraged. It almost seems as if the entire pattern of restriction and parental control were a kind of cultural fiction whose actual purpose is to cover something else; this is what we mean in characterizing it as a joking pattern.

In this perspective it is not at all difficult to postulate that much of the actual source of tension lies in the socially exploited incestuous tie between father and daughter. Thus, the South Italian girl does not appear as inhibited or naïve for precisely the reason that even though carefully kept away from outside men, she has in a great many indirect ways been treated as a sexual object by father (and brothers or other male relatives) both at puberty and during the oedipal crisis. Within the family the incestuous tension may be handled by joking (or avoidance[18]), but to the extent that the wishes generated seek a biological out-

---

[18] Casual joking and teasing between men and women within the family is characteristic of urban areas; in some country ones (where courtship taboos may be taken more seriously), there is more likely to be embarrassed avoidance, or *vergogna* (shame), between father and daughter.

let, the daughter has to seek an object outside of the family—and the father has to rid himself of a woman whom he perceives as very desirable but cannot possess. We would then say that it is the strength of the incestuous wishes which accounts for the dramatic and explosive quality of the courtship situation; and the father-daughter relation, by accentuating incestuous tension and at the same time by imposing a taboo, acts as a kind of spring mechanism which running counter to the strong centripetal forces inherent in the mother-son tie has sufficient force as to cause the family unit to fly apart, resulting in the creation of a new one. In this context the insufficiency of the oral culture view again becomes apparent.

One can then see the father's role in defending the honor of the daughter as the masculine counterpart of the Madonna identification; the father's incestuous impulses are sublimated in the active role which he plays toward the daughter in competition with her suitor. Since the sexual wishes cannot be fulfilled, the symbolic assertion of authority is much more important than the actual outcome, a consideration which can explain the ritualized nature of the father's control over courtship and the gracefulness with which he eventually backs down. As the street vendor stated, his real wish is for his daughter's happiness, but in order to show that he is a man he has to be able to demonstrate the power he has over her, and over the still subordinate prospective son-in-law. The principal means he has at his disposal for doing this is by being obstinate in such a way as to increase the excitement of the drama—of which one could say the most important member of the audience for him is the daughter. Likewise, the complementary wishes of the daughter are sublimated in the pleasure which she experiences over the fact of being controlled, a pleasure which is evident in the courtship descriptions of women, however much they may verbally express resentment or rebellion. Moreover, just as the Madonna fantasy provides a feminine identity for men, so the courtship complex provides masculine modes of expression for women, in that in participating in an active teasing pattern the daughter may also identify with the father, as seen in the great importance which women attribute to their own capacity to make a stand in front of him which demonstrates that they really want a suitor.

In other words, while the mother-son tie acts primarily as a centrifugal one, in that it maintains itself in such a way as to make for an unbroken continuity of the primary family, the father-daughter tie acts in the inverse sense in that the incestuous tension, being much closer to the surface, has to seek an external outlet so that a kind of spring mechanism is generated. The two together make up a viable structure which can be differentiated from our own on two counts: first, it emphasizes the romantic cross-sex ties within the family far more than same-sex identifications, and second, it preserves incestuous fantasies in such a way that they may never be fully replaced by the actually sexual husband-wife relationship. Thus, though courtship is based on the idea of individual romantic love, this latter does not appear as a prelude to an intimate emotional interdependence between husband and wife, but rather as a temporary suspension of an equilibrium in which intergenerational ties are in the long run more significant. One might say that after the wedding the supplicant suitor returns in fantasy to his own mother, and at the same time comes increasingly to resent the maternal aspects of his wife in such a way that he is again driven outside, much as in adolescence. The wife on the other hand may experience a parallel disillusion when she discovers that the husband is not the father of fantasy, and she comes increasingly to transfer her own affective needs to her son, and so the pattern repeats itself. The husband will of course have a reawakened interest in the family later, namely, when he has a daughter.[19] Thus, on both sides, it is having children, and in particular children of the opposite sex, which provides the principal affective source of commitment to the family.

We have up to this point given little systematic attention to the mother-daughter and father-son relationships, which we have conceived of as having a lesser cultural significance than the cross-sex pairs. This is, of course, not to say that they are inexistent or unimportant; but what we mean by a lesser cultural significance might come out more clearly if we draw a few brief contrasts with our own society and with the Oedipus complex as formulated by Freud.

The TAT responses for the mother-daughter card indicate a pattern that is quite classic in that the daughter appears to internalize maternal

[19] The importance of the father-daughter relationship becomes particularly apparent when we contrast South Italian patterns with those seen in other cultural groups where the rule is the matrifocal family, in which there is no stable husband-wife attachment and the only constant relation is between mother and child. The matrifocal family (found throughout the Caribbean and among working-class American Negroes) seems regularly to appear where masculine identity cannot be easily maintained on the basis of some real occupational achievement. The same conditions hold in Southern Italy and should be seen as underlying the matriarchal trends which we have described; however, with a few exceptions the monogamous family is nevertheless maintained. But the active role which the father has vis-à-vis the daughter must be one of the primary reasons for this, a view which should be considered by social agencies that often too readily seek to save daughters from fathers whom they see as acting solely from cruelty.

authority but she does so in an ambivalent way—contrasting with the romantic internalization found in the case of the son. Moreover, the actual mother-daughter relationship corresponds to that found in most societies; it is the mother who teaches the daughter the routine techniques of daily life. However, an additional feature of the TAT responses was that the informants themselves often stated that "these counsels are not very important," implicitly by comparison with those given during the courtship phase. But this comment gives us the possibility of tying together one global feature of South Italian values with the family nuclear complex: utilitarian accomplishments, notably in contrast to Protestant value systems, simply do not receive much emphasis. As our society sees the Oedipus complex, its outcome is that the child gives up the sexual fantasies centered on the parent of the opposite sex and then identifies with the parent of the same sex, whom he or she takes over as an ego ideal. Thus, the small girl wants to grow up to be a woman like her mother, and fantasies that when she is, then she too will have a husband, this depending on how well she learns to carry out womanly tasks. But in small girls or young women in Southern Italy there is remarkably little in the way of the ego ideal, or the superior person one hopes to emulate. The necessary tasks are taken for granted, but the affectively more important matter is not becoming something one is not yet but rather guarding something one has already, namely, virginity. This in turn can be related back to the fact that the infantile wish is dealt with to a greater extent by symbolic replacement (the First Communion enactment of the role of the bride) of the cross-sex fantasy than by identification with the same-sex parent. In other ways the mother-daughter relationship acts as a centrifugal force in much the same way as that between mother and son, and the two go together in defining a somewhat static social tendency rather than an active accomplishing one.

The father-son relationship on the other hand seems to constitute an unresolved cultural problem, a fact which may have roots in economic conditions which make continuity of identity from father to son through occupational or social achievement very difficult to attain, though the nature of the family may in turn help to create such conditions. It is in examining the father-son relationship that the contrast between South Italian patterns and those described by Freud becomes clearest. The TAT responses do indicate that the father may be perceived by the son as a judging or condemning figure. However, when we have said that this does not give rise to an internalized paternal superego figure, what we meant was that on the whole our male informants did not present any social values going beyond their immediate relationship which the father represents, e.g., according to a pattern of "well he was tough but he did it to teach me to act like a man." Moreover, although they were adult men, they identified with the son figure far more than the father, and they saw the outcome as a simple mutual antagonism in which the father accuses the son of delinquency but the son justifies himself and his own rebellion, rather than channeling the rebellious forces into any kind of sublimated form.

In other words, father-son hostility simply leads to fights and antagonism rather than being restrained in the interest of higher social goals or symbols. The clearest case in this respect was that of the street vendor, who very explicitly relates the kind of decreasing social energy with respect to occupation—for which he is one of a great many representatives —to a failure to solve the problem of antagonism with the father in any creative way. But for Freud, of course, the exact opposite is true: in perceiving the great importance which hostile wishes against the father on the part of sons may have in psychodynamics, he also provides a cultural resolution in his view of repressed father-son rivalry, and its many derivatives in adult life, as a dynamic which can underlie superior creative achievements—including his own creation of psychoanalysis which resulted from his reactions to the death of his father and the contemporaneous intellectual competition with Wilhelm Fleiss.

In this perspective it is possible to look at Freud's formulation of the Oedipus complex in its wider cultural context in such a way as to bring out some of the contrasts with the South Italian complex. First we might sum up some of the essential characteristics of the latter in such a way as to make a comparison possible. We have seen the mother-son relationship as the primary axis of family continuity and emphasized the degree to which the son maintains a dependent position vis-à-vis the mother, dealing with sexual and aggressive feelings in a variety of ways among the most important of which is an identification with the feminine values of purity; we have also brought out the extent to which the father-daughter relationship provides a counterpoint pattern by a failure to repress deeply the incestuous element. We have also noted that cross-sex relationships are emphasized more than same-sex ones and have suggested that this may build both romantic and conservative elements into the social structure, in that the strength of intergenerational ties wins out over individually formed ones and in that the cross-sex emphasis acts against the creation of ego ideals which the individual seeks to achieve. Both the conservative and feminine emphasis are summed up in the importance given to virginity as a social symbol: virginity is something which is given and not acquired and it is given to women and not to men.[20]

But in discussing the Oedipus complex Freud is quite explicit about the fact that oedipal wishes are given up in such a way as to be replaced by identifications with the same-sex parent; where this does not take place the resulting phenomena are seen as pathological. Moreover, his formulations start from the assumption that the primary factor is rivalry between father and son; these two struggle with each other for the possession of a woman whose background position is taken for granted, just as is that of Sarah who waited until the age of ninety-nine for a son with only one outbreak of skeptical laughter and then did not complain when Abraham took Isaac off as a sacrifice to a patriarchal God. And finally he assumes a very high degree of capacity for delay or sublimation which takes the form of an ability, based on identifications, to turn instinctual impulses into future-oriented creative achievement. This in turn in his own thinking primarily takes the form of masculine imagery, e.g., penetrating reality in the interests of scientific conquest and overcoming resistance, whether in patients or in any other facet of reality.

What differentiates his view of the father-son relationship is then the very high degree of sublimation which he assumes to characterize the conflict: identification with the father, in his view and in his own life, even if ambivalent, does not result in the kind of open hostility and decreasing social energy which we saw in the case of the street vendor, but rather in a complex identification with a continuing tradition. As opposed to the South Italian view, it is the feminine sphere which is the lower and more naturalistic one, while father-son conflict gives rise to the most complex social sublimations, e.g., the many intellectual ties based on a patriarchal model which characterize Freud's life. This is not to say that he was insensitive to other human possibilities—the work on hysteria, and in particular the paper on transference-love, bear witness to a kind of paternalistic but subtly seductive appreciation of women, in many ways a more sophisticated variant of the South Italian father-daughter pattern; and of course his fantasy view of Rome as a romantic opposite to the active competition of his Viennese life is well known. But it is hard to doubt that Freud was a patriarch with a patriarchal view of man.

[20] At least from the South Italian perspective, where the body referent is very clear: as a humorous response to the assertion that Freud defines femininity in terms of a lack of masculinity, we could again refer to the Neapolitan informant who, when questioned about the double standard, replied, "But how could you ever tell if a man had lost it or not?"

The sources of his patriarchal bias can be seen as twofold: the first in the Hebraic tradition which, as discussed in *Moses and Monotheism* (Freud, 1939), was of considerable symbolic importance to him, and the second in elements common to Western society since the Reformation. From both perspectives one can see ways in which the Oedipus complex formulation ties in with broader cultural features. The historical importance of Moses lies in his having organized what was initially a series of patrilineal kin groups into a larger collectivity. The Old Testament makes many of the specific taboos and perceptions of the patrilineal kin group very clear: in the image of the thundering patriarchal God (which we can think of as arising when demands for respect taboo the expression of aggression against the father), in the emphasis on rivalry between brothers, in the tracing of lines of descent solely through men, and in the strong taboo against homosexuality (as seen in the story of Ham who was cursed for looking on his father's nakedness, and perhaps in the extreme anxiety which surrounds the idea of seeing God). From the second point of view, Freud does nothing more than reinforce and deepen our genetic understanding of values of active accomplishment and mastery of external reality, which in the degree of emphasis contrast post-Reformation Western society with many others and which can be thought of as masculine in style. In this perspective, moreover, the continuity between Freud's society and that of contemporary United States becomes apparent—the common elements being the emphasis on active mastery, the delay of gratification for future rewards by means of identification and ego ideals, and the emphasis on separation from early feminine attachments.

However, questioning of some of Freud's more narrowly patriarchal bias has been characteristic in this country and has had many reflections in psychoanalytic thinking, for example, in the much greater emphasis given to the mother-child relationship. This must certainly be related to the more egalitarian concept of the family, and one might say that psychoanalysis itself has been crucially involved in the elaboration of some new cultural values and images which are feminine in quality: the terms "warmth," "security," and "support," with all of their psychological and social ramifications, are evidence of this, and they in turn serve in the definition of norms for intimate relationships, for example, that the mother should send the child into the outside world, but not in such a sudden or traumatic way that he loses the sense of support of security.[21] In the same way, the ideal wife furthers her husband's extra-

---

[21] Cf. the harsh separation characterizing early school life both in the Puritan and Orthodox Jewish traditions.

familial activities by giving her support, in a way which may imply far more submissiveness than the Italian image of an intruding male presence which may on occasion be kicked out, and this goes with the positive rather than negative definition of the extrafamilial world. In addition, family patterns may in many ways make for a lack of differentiation between maternal and erotic aspects of love, in that the latter are not defined as "bad" or forbidden in themselves, but rather, in current American morality, tend to be legitimized precisely to the extent that they are assimilated to qualities such as "warmth" or "security." Thus, in contrast to many societies, we perceive no inherent conflict between family continuity and the sexual instinct. The details of this pattern and its cultural ramifications have yet to be described, but while it certainly involves major changes from nineteenth-century ideals of discipline and control or emphasis on masculine authority in the direction of a higher cultural valuation of the feminine role, it also seems likely that values such as warmth and security will nevertheless remain subordinate to the primary social goal of mastery; we would not see these changes as working in the long run in the direction of matriarchy.[22]

In conclusion, we should like to say a few words on the subject of research methodology. Psychoanalysts who have continued to base their work on Freud's theory of instinct have often commented that work based on the concept of culture is likely to deal with motivation in a way which is behavioristic or even superficial. That many of the potentialities of Freud's theory were overlooked in much of the early work on culture and personality is, we believe, quite true. Among the reasons for this is a too-hasty attempt to take over the trauma theory in such a way as to postulate uncertain and often mechanical relationships between specific features of child training and adult personality or culture patterns, e.g., culture X is oral because it has a long nursing period, and culture Y is anal because toilet training is surrounded with anxiety. At the same time, in particular where it has not hesitated to deal with cultural patterns of meaning as expressed in symbolic form—for example, Mead and Bateson's (1942) attempt in *Balinese Character* to relate an entire ritual sequence to infantile experience—the field of culture and person-

---

[22] Grete Bibring (1953) has commented on some differences between European and American family patterns as reflected in comparative analytic case material. While noting important matriarchal trends in the latter setting, she comments that these are nevertheless not congruent with the total social context and may become pathogenic for this reason. One could add that matriarchalism in the sense of uncompensated female dominance in the family may be quite common as the result of various processes of social change, but that in the long run compensating social mechanisms should appear.

ality has also produced some quite new modes of thought. Similarly, beginning with Malinowski's work, the use of the psychoanalytic concept of affect and the emphasis on the more intimate dynamics of the family have added an entirely new dimension to the comparative study of kinship, the field which makes up the most solidly founded and scientifically based area of social anthropology. In contrast to the field of culture and personality, this latter is almost completely unknown in psychoanalytic circles, a fact which can lead one to believe that the assertion that the "culturalist" approach is a superficial one is as much based on attitudes concerning differences on theory and technique which have arisen within the psychoanalytic movement as it is on serious study of the actual work of anthropology.

Moreover, at the present time psychoanalysis is facing a crisis as the result of increasing pressures both from without and from within for more careful scientific demonstration and elaboration of its conceptual apparatus. One of the potential dangers of this situation is that psychoanalytic research will itself take an increasingly behavioristic direction, i.e., attempt to reduce concepts whose initial originality derived from their immediate perception of meaningful or symbolic phenomena to a form which is quantifiable or experimentally testable in a way which is independent of the interpretive sensitivity of the observer. But this latter, for the anthropologist just as much as for the clinically oriented psychoanalyst, is a factor which cannot or should not be left out of any attempt to create a truly human science of human behavior, however sophisticated we may become concerning the inevitable emotional or normative bias of individual observations. In this perspective the moment when Malinowski, alone in the Trobriand Islands, had to turn to the Trobrianders themselves for companionship—because in his isolation he had lost interest in the questions concerning evolution and the nature of primitive man which he had so heatedly debated with his colleagues in London—is to modern anthropology what Freud's discovery of transference is to psychoanalysis: both make the observer's sensitivity to what is happening around him a primary instrument of research, and both focus research on living human situations rather than artificially created ones.

But today one might say that the initial supposition of Malinowski and numerous other anthropologists that comparative work provides a particularly important means of testing and elaborating psychoanalytic concepts is no less relevant than it was a generation ago, both in that the variety of living cultures provides a natural laboratory setting and in that participant observation, or the attempt to at least hypothetically adapt the framework of a culture different from one's own, may provide an antidote for that part of observer bias that stems from the taking for granted of particular cultural suppositions, i.e., normative bias. In the latter respect, in fact, one might say that comparative work is perhaps all the more necessary now that psychoanalysis, rather than being an isolated and badly misunderstood field of endeavor, has in itself become a source of social norms. One of the dangers of the latter situation is that personality attributes favoring psychoanalytic investigation may be postulated as components of an ideal "human nature" and in turn may be built into a theoretical apparatus. Many qualities common in Southern Italy, for example, may well appear as "ego weakness" from the standpoint of a therapist, but if we look at them in their own setting we may find ways in which they are adaptive and in turn use such observations to enlarge our concepts of the ego and adaptation.[23] A great variety of concepts and postulates also takes on new meaning or leads to new questions if they are applied in the comparative framework.

This paper in itself, moreover, raises many theoretical questions which we have not even tried to answer; for example, can one really say that some kinds of incest wishes are closer to consciousness in one society than in another, and if so, what does this imply for the concept of repression? Or, what are the theoretical consequences for concepts concerning psychopathology and delinquency of what we have called the lesser internalization of paternal authority in Southern Italy and its related social consequences such as the importance of negativism in the peer group setting? It is clear that failure to show a positive masculine identification in the occupational sphere cannot in itself be taken as an indication of psychopathic personality, if by the latter we mean the lack of any superego restraint, because it is by no means incompatible with a fully internalized respect for women and family norms: witness the affirmative role played by the Neapolitan underworld in the protection of virgins. But such facts should in turn lead us to seek a more careful definition of the superego, which, if it is indeed a universally found psychic apparatus laid down in early infancy, should be definable independently of variations in norms relevant to adults.

In other words, in a great many areas more careful and self-conscious comparative thinking might help us to tighten up some of our theoretical concepts and in particular to separate that which refers to early infan-

---

[23] See A. Parsons (1961).

tile life from that which defines normative expectations for the adult. Such attempts can in turn have immediate clinical implications for matters such as diagnosis and prognosis. Many social scientists have pointed out the ways in which normative bias may appear in diagnostic judgment when there are social differences between psychiatrist and patient; moreover, such biases follow some fairly consistent and predictable patterns. Thus, diagnoses such as "character disorder" and "psychopathic personality" are certainly overused for Italian male patients; when the neurotic acts out his difficulties outside the family, or even within it (as in the common example of the depressed and dependent man who beats his wife), he quite often gets into trouble with the law. Similarly for women, "oral" elements are commonly overemphasized (in the sense that significant areas of competence or of genital focus in intrapsychic conflict are overlooked) in the light of the greater restriction of life to the family setting. It would be our view that in this group one can individualize the major genetically rooted personality structures predictable from psychoanalytic theory (schizoid, depressive or cyclic, obsessional, and hysteric), but that the overt differences in phenomenology can be such that even the experienced diagnostician may have difficulty if he does not know the cultural expectations. Such difficulties in turn may have important implications for the evaluation of the depth of pathology or for treatment decisions.

In summary, we believe that comparative research has a potentially very important contribution to make in the light of the current need for further testing and elaboration of psychoanalytic concepts with respect to a variety of materials. Moreover, this is the case both for general social or cultural formulations and for more specific studies of psychopathology in ways which are relevant to the understanding of personality dynamics and which can have immediate applications for diagnosis and treatment. For the original question of whether the Oedipus complex is universal or not, we would sum up by saying that it is no longer very meaningful in that particular form. The more important contemporary questions would rather be: what is the possible range within which culture can utilize and elaborate the instinctually given human potentialities, and what are the psychologically given limits of this range? Or in slightly different terms: what more can we learn about what Claude Lévi-Strauss (1949) has characterized as the "transition from nature to culture"? To answer fully questions such as these will require the equal and collaborative efforts of psychoanalysis and anthropology.

BIBLIOGRAPHY

Bibring, G. L. (1953), On the "Passing of the Oedipus Complex" in a Matriarchal Family Setting. In: *Drives, Affects, Behavior,* ed. R. M. Loewenstein. New York: International Universities Press, pp. 278-284.

Bushnell, J. (1958), La Virgin of Guadalupe as Surrogate Mother in San Juan Atzingo. *Amer. Anthropol., 60:*261-265.

Cancian, F. (1961), The Southern Italian Peasant: World View and Political Behavior. *Anthropolog. Quart., 34,* 1:1-17.

De Jorio, A. (1832), *La Mimica degli Antichi investigata nel Gestire Napolitana.* Naples: dalla stamperia e carteria del fibreno.

Durkheim, E. (1897), *Suicide.* Glencoe, Ill.: Free Press, 1951.

———(1915), *The Elementary Forms of the Religious Life.* Glencoe, Ill.: Free Press, 1958.

Freud, S. (1900), *The Interpretation of Dreams.* New York: Basic Books, 1955.

———(1939), *Moses and Monotheism.* New York: Vintage Books, 1958.

Hartmann, H., Kris, E., & Loewenstein, R. M. (1951), Some Psychoanalytic Comments on "Culture and Personality." In: *Psychoanalysis and Culture,* eds. G. B. Wilbur & W. Muensterberger. New York: International Universities Press, pp. 3-31.

Jacobson, E. (1954), The Self and the Object World: Vicissitudes of Their Infantile Cathexes and Their Influence on Ideational and Affective Development. In: *The Psychoanalytic Study of the Child, 9:*75-127, eds. R. S. Eissler et al. New York: International Universities Press.

Jones, E. (1912), The Theory of Symbolism. *Papers on Psychoanalysis.* Boston: Beacon Press, 1961, pp. 87-145.

———(1924), Mother-Right and Sexual Ignorance of Savages. In: *Essays in Applied Psychoanalysis, 2:*145-173. New York: International Universities Press, 1964.

Lévi-Strauss, C. (1949), L'Analyse structurale en linguistique et en anthropologie. *Word, 1:*35-53.

———(1949), *Les Structures Elementaires de la Parenté.* Paris: Presses Universitaires de France.

Malinowski, B. (1916), Baloma: The Spirits of the Dead in the Trobriand Islands. *J. Royal Anthropolog. Inst., 46:*353-430.

———(1927), *Sex and Repression in Savage Society.* London: Routledge and Kegan Paul, 1953.

———(1929), *The Sexual Life of Savages.* London: Routledge and Kegan Paul, 1953.

Mastriani, F. (1871), *I Vermi: Studi Storici Sulle Classe pericolose in Napoli,* 4 Vols. Naples.

Mead, M. & Bateson, G. (1942), *Balinese Character: A Photographic Analysis.* New York: Special Publication of the New York Academy of Sciences.

Moller, H. (1951), The Meaning of Courtly Love. *J. Amer. Folklore, 73,* 287:39-52.

———(1959), The Social Causation of the Courtly Love Complex. *Compar. Stud. Soc. & Hist., 1,* 2:137-163.

Moss, L. W. & Thomson, W. H. (1958), The South Italian Family: Literature and Observation. *Human Organiz., 18,* 1:35-41.

Office of Statistics of the Commune of Naples (1959), *Annuario Statistico del Commune di Napoli: Anno 1956, 21.* Naples: Stabilimento Tipografico Francesco Giannini & Figli.

Parsons, A. (1960), Family Dynamics in South Italian Schizophrenics. *Arch. Gen. Psychiat., 3:*507-518.

———(1961), A Schizophrenic Episode in a Neapolitan Slum. *Psychiatry, 24,* 2:109-121.

Parsons, T. (1958), Social Structure and the Development of Personality: Freud's Contribution to the Integration of Psychology and Sociology. *Psychiatry, 21,* 4:321-340.

Petrullo, V. (1937), A Note on Sicilian Cross-Cousin Marriage. *Primitive Man, 10,* 2:8-9.
Pitkin, D. (1959), Land Tenure and Family Organization in an Italian Village. *Human Organiz., 18,* 4:169-173.
Pratt, D. (1960), The Don Juan Myth. *Amer. Imago, 17*:321-335.
Radcliffe-Brown, A. R. (1952), *Structure and Function in Primitive Society.* Glencoe, Ill.: Free Press.
Ramirez, S. & Parres, R. (1957), Some Dynamic Patterns in the Organization of the Mexican Family. *Int. J. Soc. Psychiat., 3*:18-21.
Rapaport, D. (1960), The Structure of Psychoanalytic Theory. *Psychological Issues,* Monogr. 6. New York: International Universities Press.
Schneider, D. & Gough, K., eds. (1961), *Matrilineal Kinship.* Berkeley and Los Angeles: University of California Press.
Stanton, A. H. (1959), Propositions Concerning Object Choices. In: *Conceptual and Methodological Problems in Psychoanalysis,* 76:1010-1037, ed. L. Bellak. New York: Annals of the New York Academy of Sciences.
Trevisani, G., ed. (1957), *Teatro Napoletano dalle origini,* 2 Vols. Bologna: Tip. Mareggiani.
Vaillant, R. (1958), *The Law.* New York: Knopf.
Verga, G. (1953), *Little Novels of Sicily.* New York: Grove Press.
Whyte, W. F. (1943), *Street Corner Society: Social Structure of an Italian Slum.* Chicago: University of Chicago Press.
Wolf, K. R. (1952), Growing Up and Its Price in Three Puerto Rican Sub-Cultures. *Psychiatry, 15,* 4:401-433.
Zola, I. K. (1963), Observations of Gambling in a Lower Class Setting. *Soc. Prob., 10,* 4:353-361.

CRUSADERS

K. R. EISSLER, M.D.

Society, particularly modern Western society, is involved in a process of continuous change. Much thinking and research has been devoted to obtaining an understanding of the causes underlying that continuous process; yet, the great number and variety of the theories put forward undoubtedly reflect the ignorance still prevalent on this question, probably one of the most important questions that man has ever asked himself. Of the many facets of the problem, I shall select one.

Whatever sociology or related disciplines may ascertain in the future regarding the forces responsible for society's changes, we know for certain that man himself almost always wishes, plans and undertakes to change society. The conscious desire to change society varies, to be sure, from one time and/or place to another. At certain historical periods, it is intensive; at certain other periods, or in other societies, it would never dawn upon man's mind to even consider an essential change in the current structure of the society. Sometimes it happens that man changes his society without intending to and even without being aware of so doing. Many an inventor has set out to solve a mere mechanical task only to wind up actually exerting through his invention a fundamental influence on the structure of society. On the other hand, many a man has devoted his whole lifetime to the task of propagating a new system of government; yet few of his contemporaries have taken notice of his existence, and his system has rapidly fallen into oblivion.

Whether man—individually or collectively—causes society to change, or whether man is only the medium of impersonal, suprapersonal and supracollective forces, cannot be decided by sociology. From a study of historical events, it often seems as if great individuals have impressed their intuitions, schemes, fantasies or rational systems on groups. Such solitary phenomena are not the subjects of this essay, however. They are often preceded, surrounded or followed by satellites—persons of minor

This is a chapter of an unpublished manuscript on the psychopathology of army life, based on experiences during wartime activity between 1943 and 1945.

prestige, whose names may appear only in the footnotes of history but whose great importance must not be underestimated. I want to call a certain type among these satellites "crusaders."

It is not easy to differentiate "crusaders," in sociological terms, from agitators, politicians or reformers. Furthermore, the importance of the crusader does not always spring from his historical connection with a great leader, as in the case of, let us say, John the Baptist; more frequently he seems to travel his road unconnected with his contemporaneous historical structure. I would reserve the term "crusader" for that type of (mainly social) innovator whose crusading is primarily a matter of conviction. This conviction, furthermore, is an emotional matter, which, to my way of thinking, makes him different from the sort of reformer whose activity stresses planned rationality, even if only pretendedly so.[1] The term "agitator" is generally understood to denote a person who follows his feelings predominantly and whose social activities serve in the first place to facilitate the discharge of his rather intense emotionality. The agitator is not susceptible to reasoning; he may use reasoning as the springboard for his work as an agitator, but he is not concerned about having to face an argument which may disprove the correctness of his claims. He is compelled to engage in activity as an agitator just as a gambler is addicted to gambling. This attitude toward reasoning comes sharply to the fore in one of Lasswell's (1930) case histories of agitators. The popular imagery regarding "politicians" in our times generally refers to persons who are involved in their pursuits for purposes of enrichment, or for the aggrandizement of their prestige. The "crusader," by contrast, is mainly interested in the victory of a cause, or in the spread of an idea or an interest or a conviction, quite independently of his personally faring well or badly with the rise or fall of that cause or idea.[2] He is genuinely interested in the soundness of his cause, and never lightly bypasses a valid argument against it, although,

[1] The list of sociological as well as psychological types who deliberately and purposely try to change their society is long. A psychological analysis of these various types must start with an investigation of the identifications which the socially active person has made. Then a comparison between identification and object relation must follow. I think that the great variety of types can be understood within the framework of identification and object relation, their consciousness or unconsciousness, the conflict between both, and many other factors involved. It would be a challenging task to show how these factors combined to produce a man like Lincoln Steffens (1931), a unique personality supremely endowed to participate successfully in the great struggle for social change without causing destruction.

[2] See Deutsch (1934) for a discussion of the relationship of the idealist to the realist and of the effect that the unrealistic idealist has on others.

of course, his emotionality may lead him to misjudge the significance of an argument which threatens his feeling of harmony with regard to his particular cause. The sociological types briefly outlined here often overlap, sometimes changing from one to another, depending on external vicissitudes or on personal development. These remarks are definitely not meant to be taken as delineating rigid categories or well-defined types.

As I have mentioned previously, two groups of crusaders must be distinguished: those whose aims and goals fit into broad developmental movements which later on acquire historical import; and those who propagate, so to speak, a "private affair"—a system appealing to small groups only, without contemporary or later interest to any other section of the broad stream of political or spiritual development. The latter are among those who may easily develop into "cranks" or harebrained people, the propagators of unusual schemes, who believe that they have found salvation in the abstruse and the bizarre. It would be of interest to know how far these two groups of crusaders actually represent two different psychological types, or whether they are made up of similar personalities, drawn by *imponderabilia* either into the broad stream of a historical movement or into the blind alley of sectarian isolation. Crusaders do not usually earn the thanks of their contemporaries; those who herald the coming of a new time especially are likely to arouse the ire of their community. The crank is far more often forgiven, precisely because of the innocuousness of his effect on society; in the crusading reformer, however, whose credo harbors the seeds of impending and consequential social action, society scents a person who may bring to an end its cherished inertia and tradition. Rather than adapting itself to necessities by way of social change, society tries to smother the spark of change which may grow into a fire.

In the following, only what might be called the "constructive crusader" will be discussed, the one who may have the chance to be an actor in a drama of historical importance. He is really the salt of society: at the least, he will prevent social stagnation; at best, he prepares the way for some leader or mass movement which will move toward a new goal. The crusader, if his goals are to be evaluated in group terms, seems to be trying to transform morality into mores. He is evidently a man who does not feel satisfied with merely having developed a code of conduct satisfactory to himself. His own moral conduct, even if it is estimated by him as important, does not stand at the center of what he considers to be his main responsibility. He aims chiefly at seeing his morality accepted by the community as binding upon the whole society. He wants to force a matter of personal conscience directly or indirectly on his contemporaries as a universal maxim.

In general, his interest in actual conduct is more significant of him than his interest in laws. The hero is the man of action, the crusader of selfless action. His field of action is not limited merely to mediation between morality and customs; he creates a morality by his own personal example, or he will change the structure of society, or try to change it, by violence, by force, even by crime. A crusader may become a martyr-hero as soon as society makes him pay a price for his "interference." The transition from one type to another is gradual; sometimes, it is difficult to decide whether a crusader has reached the lofty heights of heroic action, or a hero has degenerated into a mere crusader. The notion that the crusader's activity takes place between the realms of morality and customs may make it possible to distinguish more clearly between the two types.

The crusader who is regarded as a crank spends his energy in a way that appears to be wasteful. He wants to introduce mores which, if they were integrated, would not enrich personal morality but rather imply mere inhibition or the enforcement of a behavior pattern with no recognizable relevance to moral values. The "crank" even may provide the rest of the community with a feeling of moral superiority in that he betrays adherence to a moral code which seems to be inferior to the current one. He tries to elevate trivialities of routine to the dignity of ethical principles—a sure sign of immaturity. The other type of crusader—who usually arouses opposition, sometimes resulting even in violence, against him—extends his endeavors to innovations which are consciously or unconsciously felt by the community to be of a higher moral value than those embedded in the mores of the society. The forceful opposition which that type of crusader encounters is the product of the group's guilt feeling. The majority of group members fight the dawning enlargement or sharpening of their own consciences by trying to defame the "invader" or to silence his voice.

In view of the great importance the crusader has with regard to the momentum of social change, it has been of interest to observe the role he might play in the army. The army, as an organization, was offensive in many respects to the truly democratically-minded. A representative cross section of our able-bodied and sound male population was involved in it, and nearly all of them were exposed to military institutions most of which are intrinsically offensive to the civilian mind. The very young, who do not yet possess a frame of reference sufficiently fixed to encourage deliberate action deviating from the social norm, and the overmature, who by experience and insight are resigned to a merely philosophical registration of human wickedness in place of combative action against it, were for the most part excluded from participation in the army. The age groups which were inducted took in those very years in which the willingness and readiness for "social action"—the impetus of an active thrust toward society with the purpose of impressing one's own will on it rather than adapting to it—might be assumed to be at their peak.

It was thus all the more astonishing to find so little constructive endeavor to enforce the army's adaptation to minimal democratic standards. The tendency was present, but it exhausted itself in two main channels. There were the so-called "psychopaths," some of whom are in continuous rebellion against society, and whose rebellion is therefore likely to flare up in a society as rigid as the army. Their rebellion, however, was of such a personal nature, so clumsily carried out, and so offensive to group standards, that no general constructive action could grow out of their propensity to take the law into their own hands.

Then there were the millions of soldiers who expressed their dissatisfaction by griping. Griping was an institution: it might have had value as a means of discharge; it was an accepted channel of "letting off steam." How far it really led to the relief of tension is questionable precisely because of its institutional status. More often than not, it was performed mechanically because it was the accepted and expected behavior of a soldier. The contents of griping took in all sectors and subjects of army life; there was nothing which it would not have included. From the extremely childish to the pertinent and sagacious, it included every range of observation but it rarely led to constructive discussion or action. How little effort of reason there was to griping may be seen from the fact that nonparticipation gave any soldier a stigma: anyone who said a word in favor of the army at once became *persona non grata* to all the rest. Griping did not grow out of wrestling with a problem; it did not serve the purpose of clarifying a situation; it was merely the empty repetition of a standardized pattern with possibly some wholesome side effects, as a way of giving vent to unpleasant emotions.[3]

It has its counterpart in civilian life: a citizen assumes a higher status

[3] For an excellent analysis of griping, see Janis (1945). Janis rightly describes griping not as intended to change objective conditions, but as providing the feeling that the present life situation is not being taken without protest. "The illusion that he (sc. the soldier) is doing something about the deprivational state of affairs is based on the expectation built up during many years of his past life that verbal complaints are an effective weapon for improving his situation." A different opinion is expressed by Fox (1945).

by being critical of the administration. Opposition to the party in power is a respected mode of behavior; yet, the citizen is expected to act in conformity with group standards. "Opposition in opinion, conformity in action," may well describe the behavior of the "ideal citizen." The concept of opposition, however, needs to be qualified. If opposition goes so far as to become a rallying point for social action, if it may lead to active steps of interference with those in power, then it stands at the threshold of being looked at askance. Opposition should be witty, more in the nature of an epigram; it must not smell of resistance. To be sure, a multiplicity of examples can be adduced to show the limitations of that statement, but I think it covers fairly adequately a current type of behavior in democratic society. It was certainly very strongly expressed in the army, where the discrepancy between critical words and conforming action was marked. Just as the group expected the soldier to be a good griper, it also expected him to be a good conformist. The institution of griping may even have been one of the obstacles in the path of desirable or necessary social action.

I myself encountered two officers to whom the foregoing description was not applicable. As will be seen, only the *seeds* of the crusader can be observed in them; but in the light of the infrequency with which the crusader is to be met in the army, the little that I could learn from them may be worth presenting.[4]

A young officer was referred for neuropsychiatric examination. The reason which made his commanding officer request the examination was that he had sent a letter to a newspaper, in which he complained about certain features of the physical aspect of the post administration. His complaint centered on the housing conditions at the camp and the quantity of food soldiers received. Since the letter was published, it caused a great flurry at headquarters. There was no report of any behavioral abnormality in the officer, unless the fact of his writing to a newspaper was to be considered as such. At least, no other reason was mentioned by the referring command, and further investigation did not reveal any conspicuous or deviated behavior or neglect of duty prior to his using the newspaper letter column.

---

[4] The sketchiness in important details of the two following histories must be excused. The author is aware of their shortcomings. The proper place for the study of crusaders would have been in the camps for conscientious objectors. However, I never had the opportunity to work at such places. From this point of view the title of my paper may appear to the reader to be a misnomer since essentially it refers to the surprising *absence* of the crusader type among American males exposed to a situation which is at once more provocative and more rigid than their customary civilian mode of life.

The officer was a quiet young man who made a favorable impression. He appeared during the interview to be a stable, sincere, and congenial, although somewhat reticent person. His answers gave the impression of truthfulness; one would assume from the personality facets that he presented that he took life and his duties more seriously than the average officer did. There may have been an indication of a mild depression; yet this could easily have been a permanent feature of his character structure rather than a symptom of an acute condition. The officer reported that his interest in the army had been aroused during childhood; although he could not remember the particular events leading to the development of that interest, he never had any doubts about making the army his career. He had volunteered for the army and was later commissioned; he had been overseas, where he was injured but recovered without ill-effect. He was in excellent physical condition and had no complaints on that score whatsoever.

It turned out later that throughout his life, from the age of three, as far back as he could remember, there had run a series of temper tantrums precipitated by a variety of circumstances. The frequency of these tantrums decreased during puberty, and at the time of the interview he estimated that they occurred at intervals of two to three years. Before the onset of acute temper tantrums, he had been given to running away from home, which he did habitually up to the age of three. Leaving home abruptly also occurred later but was no longer a frequent or regular event. The runaway had become an irascible child (a sequence, by the way, that is more frequently observed in reverse). He remembered some of the situations in which he had lost control over his anger. Once, he had beaten up a boy who had taken advantage of a playmate's being smaller in size and of inferior physical strength. At sixteen, he seriously intended to kill a young man who, in his estimation, had offended his younger sister by not accompanying her home from a date but letting her walk home alone. The offender, being warned in time, had left the community. Once he had slapped a noncommissioned officer's face because of a refusal to obey and disrespectful language. After his release from the hospital following his injury, he had been challenged in a tavern by a civilian, who called him a "sucker" for having gone overseas. He hit him over the head with a beer bottle and would have gone further had not others prevented him from causing more damage.

He thought that he remembered that, between the ages of eleven and fourteen, he had worked himself out of the habit of frequent tantrums and learned to reduce them to a tolerable number. He had never got entangled with the courts or with the police because of these outbreaks of anger, and his military record was similarly spotless.

There had been frequent fights between him and his father about his sister. The father treated her in a gruff way whenever she had difficulties with her home tasks. Once he attacked his father physically, taking a swing at him. The occasion was a disagreement about a chore he had been asked to perform. Physical punishment was used profusely at home, and he was frequently beaten by his father with a razor strop; he himself thought that this was well deserved. After the age of three, he ran away only twice. At fourteen, he took off with a friend to the latter's farm without telling his parents, even though there was no indication that his parents would object to the trip. On his return he received the usual corporal punishment. Two years later he joined a labor gang and stayed with them for three weeks. This time he was not punished upon his return; his father merely remarked: "Did you get your belly full?" The fact that he took up his former habit of running away shortly after he got at least a half-hold on the temper tantrums may indicate an essential connection between them. As a child, he ran to his grandmother, who apparently approved of his coming; once when his mother was looking for him, his grandmother hid him. On his way home, he met a policeman, and became frightened: he dashed home and hid himself under the bed. His parents tried to make him stay by tying him down, but he howled so that the neighbors complained to the police. His parents were told to let him go free; they consented, but told the police that they would have to be responsible for getting him back home.

There was a lot of arguing between the parents. The mother was the outgoing, sociable, talkative type, who would have preferred to visit with neighbors. The father was quiet and, feeling tired after work, preferred to stay home. The father never went to church; the officer read the Bible at least once a week, but he was not particularly interested in religion and was not affiliated with any church. The parents had become divorced after he had left home; his mother had remarried, and both parents seemed to be happy as things were. The officer himself was married to a divorcee, who had a daughter by her first husband. He thought that she had probably become divorced because her husband had had to move to another place, while she preferred staying in her home community. When he was overseas, she wrote him once that she was no longer willing to go on with him. He never found out what had made her think of divorce and the topic was never broached again. She was angry with him for returning home from overseas unannounced; he thereupon left for his father's home and spent his furlough with him. The father lived now happily, undisturbed by his wife's longing for social activities.

At the time of the interview, the officer's wife was pregnant. She did not want to join him at his post. She was suffering from some physical disorder in conjunction with her pregnancy, and she had already expressed the desire to be sterilized after the delivery.

The officer had been unfaithful to his wife with two women. One affair was long drawn out, and the girl wrote to his wife. The officer maintained that there was no conflict between them at that time, and that he was undisturbed by his wife's pregnancy, although he had not wanted to go overseas the second time before the birth of the baby.

The officer liked the army: he felt deeply attached to his profession, in spite of some of the criticism that he had made publicly. He had repeatedly requested the repair of huts, yet his requests had been without avail. He had made a valiant effort to provide his soldiers with an adequate diet. It was customary to acknowledge the receipt of all the rations he was entitled to de jure; but he had never received the prescribed amount, there always having been a significant margin between the de facto and the de jure rations. Hence, he had had to contact other mess halls, and to try supplementing his soldiers' diet by ingenious bartering. When he read in newspapers that the army announced an increase in the diet of prisoners of war, he had one of his temper tantrums and wrote the letter which brought him to the psychiatrist.

From this history it can easily be recognized that, behind the officer's composure and the excellent surface that his personality presented externally to society, there were plenty of indications of severe psychopathology. It can be assumed that he permitted only glimpses into the serious conflicts which were simmering inside him. Since his surface structure was firmly established, and so far his pathology had not caused any serious threat to his army status, no therapy was instituted other than superficial discussion of the evident. Any deeper probing into his history might have precipitated acute reactions, and the time when therapy could have resulted in substantial benefit to him would have been put far off. Acute temper tantrums in the adult—probably even in the adolescent—are always a sign of serious psychopathology. The officer's general background, the little known about his parents, and his marital relationship only confirmed the foregoing opinion. I was certain that the officer had revealed only a small sector of pertinent material, although he gave the impression of having made a serious effort at cooperation. There are automatic, wholesome, self-defensive mechanisms in some very sick individuals, which prevent them from rushing into deep self-revelation and thus precipitating a phase of acute disturbance.

In this context, it would be of importance to get an inkling of the specific factors which may have led to the writing of the letter. That action occurred after repeated attempts at correcting an apparently harmful and unlawful situation. Up to the moment when he sought a public medium for remedial action, he had stayed in keeping with army customs. The only circumstances that had made him overtly different from the average had had to do with the seriousness with which he tried to fulfill his obligations, which were being taken lightly by the majority of his fellow officers. In spite of his seriousness, however, he was flexible enough to participate in the customary (and unlawful) practice of signing for the receipt of goods never delivered to him. I emphasize this point because, whatever this officer's full psychiatric diagnosis might have been, he did not act in that regard like a frequently encountered type of the so-called "psychopath," who readily picks up the differences between custom and tradition and the behavior requested by law, and thus not only becomes extremely keen in discovering breaches of that kind,[5] but also makes capital out of such deviations, even when society readily condones them. This officer, however, was not a stickler; he tried to improve conditions by partly lawful, partly mildly unlawful means.

He put in requests for the repair of huts—which was the "regular" way; and he also tried to draw rations from other mess halls— which was customary but not in conformity with regulations. In acting so he revealed flexibility. Although he was probably a compulsive personality, he did not apply rigid principles in his efforts to fulfill his official or self-imposed duties, but was ready to play the game of his particular group, even when it came to playing an unprincipled game. Viewed realistically, it must be understood that the officer did not have a fighting chance of reaching his goal by the customary means at his disposal. Further, it is of interest to note that his act of writing to the newspaper—a highly unusual undertaking, from the viewpoint of army customs—was far more efficacious than the sum total of his previous endeavors. Actually, a crew of carpenters was very quickly ordered to make at least the minimum repairs. As far as the diet of his soldiers is concerned, it is questionable whether he was equally successful.

Furthermore, it must be emphasized that the run-of-the-mill psychopath most often selects tangential items as the subjects for his accusations. When the psychopath rebelled against the caste system or against saluting,

---

[5] Cf. Schmideberg (1946).

he was probably right *sub specie eternitatis;* but he was wasting his energy under prevailing conditions. There was not even the semblance of a possibility that the army would change such institutions at the request of a soldier. It is important to stress, however, that the officer under consideration was sound in his program. The element of bizarreness or of the fantastic was lacking here—an element which is so significant of the reforming tendency of the psychopath.

All the military personnel that I questioned agreed that the housing conditions about which the officer had complained were miserable. The insufficiency of the diet had also been noted by others. One officer was known to have made a record of the soldiers' diet, over a significant period of time, and even to have consulted a medical officer for an evaluation of his records. A reliable and thorough-going calculation was made by an expert leading to the conclusion that the diet did not meet minimum medical requirements, and was lacking in calories. The officer filed a report (including the expert opinion), whereupon a board of officers was assigned the duty of investigating the complaint. That board called in a "dietician," who testified that the diet was sufficient. And, without requesting the testimony of the medical officer who had made the original calculation, the board of officers decided that the food was adequate, and that there was no need for further measures. This incident, it may be mentioned in passing, was highly characteristic of army techniques— a beautiful example of the illusory world in which the army moved. The report of that board of officers was final: the soldiers *must* have been receiving an adequate diet, because a board of officers had decided so. There was *ex definitione* no possible evidence that could have disproved the board's decision.

Hence, this officer had been right in taking such steps as might force the army into a realistic handling of a defective situation. The request for an adequate diet and for humane housing of soldiers was not exaggerated, theoretical or beyond the limits of the possible. It was in keeping with a realistic outlook on society. Racial discrimination was also forbidden, and whoever tried to combat it in the army might have succeeded perhaps in stopping one leak, but would surely have only succeeded also in opening hundreds of others. He would have been doomed to failure in his efforts to reform a deep-seated psychological attitude, inaccessible to physical measures. Yet our officer's efforts were aimed at something which could be measured, which was accessible to the senses, and the repair of which was within the confines of the possible and wholly realistic.

Nevertheless, the action that the officer took must be recognized as being not only deeply connected with his central psychopathology but also motivated by it. There is some likelihood that, had the officer not read the particular news item by which a temper tantrum was precipitated, he might not have secured sufficient impetus to carry through an action which, even though it caused him some serious personal inconvenience, did nevertheless result in the partial repair of deficiencies which he had striven in vain to correct previously, by means legalized by custom or by regulation. The details of the connection between his psychopathology and his appeal to the public, even though such connection may appear evident merely from the concurrence of a temper tantrum, can only be reconstructed.

It appeared that the problem, or the assumed duty of defending the helpless or the weaker—in some instances the "female" against superior forces—was a permanent part of his inventory. This conflict had taken concrete form around the protection of his sister against the strong father. That his mother had also played her part in the conflict may be concluded from his peaceful association with his father, after she moved away. The mother—or rather the "female"—played a dual role. The grandmother had been a protective refuge in his early years when, for some unknown reason, he would feel an urge to abandon temporarily his parental home. In view of the women in his life having thus been both protectors and simultaneously in need of protection, it may be assumed that he had an ambivalent attitude toward the object of his protective care and against the assumed aggressor.

The repetition of this basic situation in the army may be conceded. Military authority, as so often in other cases, represented the father; but the helpless, exploited, abused soldier, particularly the trainee, stood for the weaker—which, in his childhood constellation, had signified the sister. Military life was attractive to him. He apparently needed an authoritative frame of reference, although he lacked the willingness to accept its overbearing highhandedness. It is questionable what meaning the assumed favoritism toward prisoners of war, which had precipitated his temper tantrum, really held for him. Particularly because of his combat experience, he felt acutely ill-disposed toward members of the enemy forces. Yet prisoners of war are people of lowered standing. If possibly overstrained speculation may be condoned, the repetition of an archaic triangular situation can be hypothetically assumed. The series sister-mother-father may have been revived in the series trainee-prisoner-military authority. It is tempting to establish more detailed correlations, but they would not contribute much more than to demonstrate anew the fact that the acute reappearance of an unresolved conflict resulted in pathological action, which precipitated an impulse beyond his control. That impulse in turn led to a social action with significant reverberations. Nothing is known as to why the earlier behavior pattern—namely, that of the runaway—did not become the governing principle here. It seems to have been without any relevance in his relationship with army authority.[6]

The reaction of the group to the officer's procedure was significant. The fact of his having been sent for psychiatric examination demonstrated that, somewhere along the line of the military hierarchy, the connotation was: "An officer who uses a public medium to wrest remedial action from the army must be crazy." The immediate reaction of a superior officer, who was not personally acquainted with this officer but based his decision on the mere fact of the letter, betrayed a significant philosophy endowed with serious consequences. A cartoon in the *New Yorker* expressed a "sounder" philosophy; it depicted a sergeant addressing some rookies with: "If you have complaints, tell me; don't write to Mrs. Roosevelt."

The correctness of the officer's complaint, as to the facts concerned, was not questioned by anyone I spoke with. Some had praise for his courage, but no one dared to join him publicly or to give him official support. But one officer—who was, incidentally, in process of separation from the army at that time, and who had become well acquainted with prevailing conditions at camp in the course of official duties, and agreed with the facts—was asked to throw his authority in favor of the young man who had attempted to help others. The appeal was without avail. Although the officer was of mature age and in a secure position, and the requested step did not involve the slightest risk for him, he nevertheless refused to do anything. His opinion approximated the attitude that to remonstrate against drawbacks in the army was just not done, that such behavior was "psychopathic," that some action could be taken privately

[6] This officer's problems are, in my mind, connected with the psychopathology investigated by Freud (1919) in "A Child is Being Beaten." The question to be answered is the extent to which the officer corresponded to a conjuncture which Freud made regarding one aspect of paranoia. Freud wrote of certain unconscious masochistic fantasies: "People who harbor fantasies of this kind develop a special sensitiveness and irritability towards anyone whom they can include in the class of fathers. They are easily offended by a person of this kind, and in that way (to their own sorrow and cost) bring about the realization of the imagined situation of being beaten by their father. I should not be surprised if it were one day possible to prove that the same fantasy is the basis of the delusional litigiousness of paranoia" (p. 193).

by personal contact from man to man, but not by social means. Hence, the crusader's venture was left without one single voice of succor or of support.[7]

As soon as the officer's acute anger had evaporated and he became aware of the unforeseen effect that his action had, he regretted what he had done. He felt embarrassed and discouraged, and fearful of a possible court-martial procedure (which might have been planned initially by higher authority but was never instituted). He signed a statement in which he revoked all his previous accusations. He really turned out to be a week-end crusader only. He showed no intention of pursuing his former course of action once he had recovered from his initial shock; and when he was permitted to take an investigating newspaperman to any place in the camp that he wished, he decided that he would just take him around, but not give him any information. The "why-should-I-stick-my-neck-out" attitude had by now taken full possession of him. He had evidently become victimized by a feeling of guilt. Subjectively, his action belonged in the realm of psychopathology, and seemed to justify one officer's opinion—which, by the way, was encountered frequently—defining psychopathic behavior as "individual deviation from the average."

The other example I wish to present in this context concerned a twenty-seven-year-old soldier, my association with whom lasted only a short while, being discontinued because of external circumstances. He had been sent for a neuropsychiatric examination in conformity with the ruling that all soldiers, before being tried by a general court-martial, must first be examined by a psychiatrist. The soldier had been AWOL for about five years. He had gone AWOL eight months after he had joined the National Guard, and six months after he had volunteered for the army. At the time of his leaving the army, he had been through with his basic training for some time. He was not under any particular tension. He had had no difficulty in getting along and nothing unusual had happened during his time of service. Shortly after his departure, he joined

---

[7] I tried, for various reasons, to keep the officer as long as possible in the ward. The officer himself had no objections to it. Yet one of the medical officers became quite angry with me for this extensive hospitalization. It was not quite clear by what he was irritated. I knew little of his past. In spite of many years of army service, he was still serving in the lowest rank of medical officers. He maintained that his failure regarding promotion was due to an argument he had had with his superior officer at his previous post. He had allegedly disproved the correctness of a diagnosis made by his superior, and thus incurred his resentment, which resulted in a bad report. Be that as it may, he was not liked by many, brimming with dissatisfaction and showing himself to be incapable of getting accustomed to army life. It was noteworthy that he strongly identified himself with the officer patient on the ward, as if the latter's hospitalization stigmatized him (the medical officer) as a mental patient.

the air force of a nation which later became one of our allies. He remained with that organization throughout the war, fulfilled his duties in it in an exemplary way, and the rank he reached in the course of his service there spoke by itself for the excellence of his contribution. He was arrested shortly after his return to this country.

The soldier explained his desertion by the conviction that he then held that this country would never enter the war, and that it was his highest duty to make the largest possible contribution to the war effort. He felt quite desperate about Hitler's seeming success, and what he thought to be this country's inertia. At the training camp, he felt ashamed of the callous ways of the soldiers and of their anti-British attitude. In general, he seemed to be quite critical of Americans, although of American stock; he had never left his native country prior to his desertion. He regarded Americans generally as braggarts and ill-informed. He criticized the way they behaved overseas and was resentful of their supposedly provocative conduct. His critical attitude extended to current food habits and other national attributes, which he considered childish. Yet, his attitude could not be called essentially hostile; it was rather one of good-humored joviality. Nevertheless, he showed a certain alertness to patterns which were susceptible to reproof. The source of his attitude was unclear. There was no doubt that he held the average Englishman superior to his American counterpart; yet it could not be said that he was uncritical of the English. He censured the Conservative party, but there was an unquestionable disposition in favor of British culture, civilization and politics.

The soldier's past had been uneventful in its gross outlines. He had been rather aloof to his mother, as compared with his relationship with his father. He had held long discussions with his father about religion, politics and general philosophy. The mother was quite religious: she was a Methodist, the father a Baptist. By preference he read books on religious subjects. He did not believe in a personal God but in a supreme power, and he was interested in the harmony of the universe. The soldier had been religious up to the age of ten or twelve. He described himself as never having been unduly preoccupied by religion; yet, later he reported that he had had nightmares about being in Hell. Most of the discussions between him and his father had been controversial. For example, his father thought that Negroes were of inferior intelligence, and should therefore not go to school. The soldier, though agreeing with his father as to the general intelligence level of Negroes, considered this insufficient reason to exclude the individual Negro from educational institutions. He had had the opportunity to observe Negroes in a plant, and he maintained that the Negro did not absorb knowledge but needed instruction in any new situation which might come up. He thought that only ten per cent of Negro students would be able to graduate from a university, whereas he was certain that two thirds of the white population would be able to do so. His father had opposed his enlistment. He had not discussed with his father his plan to go AWOL and join an allied army, as he recalled, merely because the latter was not at home; he was positive that he would have consulted his father's opinion had he been at home.

At home sex had been one of the taboos, and he had accepted his parents' attitude toward it. During his army service in this country, he had read books whose titles he could not remember but which had changed his outlook on sex. Abroad, he joined an adventurous crowd which apparently indulged freely in alcohol and sexual freedom. Whereas up to then he had shunned sexual contacts, he had intercourse twice there, both times in a state of drunkenness. The first intercourse took place a year after he had left this country; the second, shortly after the first. During his leave, following these two episodes, he became engaged to a girl whom he had known since childhood days, and with whom he maintained sporadic contact. He was married two months after his engagement. He referred his change of mind in his outlook on sex partly to the books that he had read, partly to the influence of the crowd he associated with abroad and partly to the change of climate arising out of living in a foreign country. After he had earned his wings, he had the feeling "that something was missing"; it was that feeling, he thought, that had induced him to marry.

He had graduated from high school at the age of eighteen. Then he had gone hitchhiking alone for six months, during which time his father had supported him. After his return home, he had worked in a plant for two years. His father had wanted him to be a white-collar worker, but he had preferred mechanical work in order not to be disturbed in his thoughts, which he liked to indulge in. He was preoccupied with geography, which became his hobby. One of his favorite thoughts had to do with the possible shift of the zero meridian. He wanted to see it shifted from Greenwich to a location where it could cross the ocean throughout its full course, thus avoiding offense to any nation by favoring any one of them. He liked to spend time alone and was considered "harebrained" by others. He seemed to be quite preoccupied with a lot of bizarre ideas, the shifting of the meridian being only one of them; but there was no opportunity to get any more out of him about them.

The only other element of bizarreness may be seen in his writing to higher authority under an assumed name, informing it of his presence in this country. Yet he insisted that he had been advised by another source, whose reliability he had had no reason to doubt, to proceed in just that way. There was no insight into the lawlessness of his conduct in deserting the army. He did not regard an oath as binding, and arrogated to himself the prerogative of acting on an important matter in a way contrary to what he had accepted as his duty by oath. He was eager to be court-martialed, resenting the possibility of being separated from the army by a medical discharge; he maintained that he wanted a court-martial in order to satisfy his conscience. He became restless, and complained about the time it took to investigate his case and to reach a decision on it.

When he was told that the army had decided to separate him without further procedure, he accepted this without raising any objection. Yet the impression remained that he would not have minded becoming a victim of red tape, or being given the status of a hero by the injudicious sentence of a military court. His action unquestionably made him liable to a severe sentence. The army psychiatrist felt greatly relieved by the army's decision to separate him. The question of what stand to take in this instance would have been very hard to resolve. In view of his prolonged and brilliant performance during the war, and the soundness of his external behavior, a psychiatric diagnosis was out of the question; it would not have been fair to him under those conditions. In my interpretation, he was not a free agent at the time of the desertion, since he was acting under an irresistible impulse to participate in the destruction of Germany. The assumption of such an impulse might have seemed to imply that he was not able to adhere to what is right. But was it not exactly the right thing to do what he did? Here was a man getting into a conflict with society because his concept of right was of a higher order than that held by society. As political conditions stood at the time of his desertion, he was exchanging a life of comparative leisure and safety for one of danger, strain and discomfort.

In view of the unpredictability of a military court's decision, the psychiatrist felt the desire to preserve his organization from the ridicule which would have occurred in the case of a sentence. Fortunately, in this instance the army carried the matter to a happy ending, satisfactory to all parties concerned, with the possible exception of the central person in the juridical dilemma.

Again, as in the previous illustration, it is impossible to write a complete history of the events which led to the soldier's taking the law into his own hands—deciding what was right, against the expressed will and intention of the nation, and yet achieving a goal which later found approval in the very nation against whose will and intention he had acted previously. There was his intellectual propensity for disagreeing with his father in debates, as a constant element in the pattern of his life history. That deviation from his father's tenets, views, and doctrine, the habitual dissent and demur which pervaded his mental development, probably starting at an early age, became a significant aspect of his relationship with the community at large. His mental nay-saying apparently became the principal tool with which he maintained his identity, or could establish the differentiation of self. The reasons why it was so important to him to establish a sharp line between him and his father in the mental sphere are not known.

Yet the structure of his "heresy" was never so provocative as to lead to an open breach with his father. He was not a revolutionary son; his convictions did not lead to offensive actions. This was also due to certain facets of the father's personality. Another father might have resented the son's hitchhiking and have refused to go on supporting him. Yet, as a matter of fact, the son seemed to have sensed how far he could go in his struggle to attain his self-identity without rupture of a superficially amiable relationship. He stayed within those limits and therefore the history of their association remained devoid of turbulence. Apparently, what the son needed was simultaneous contact with and deviation from his father. The outstanding feature was that he was able to keep both requirements in harmonious balance.

A second feature was the dynamic value that thinking held per se in his personality configuration. He was forced to think, with full awareness of its purpose all the time; thus, his predilection for mechanical work. It did not permeate the realm of thought, which he kept isolated and in which he proceeded in conformity with his own needs, and to a far lesser degree in correlation with the requirements of external situations. The valence that thinking held in his personality setup may be indicative of the presence of a schizophrenic element. The bizarreness of some of his preoccupations would tend to point in the same direction. His idea about shifting the meridian is expressive of most of the elements described. He did not invent a new system of geographical coordinates, as would probably have happened had there been the evolvement of a paranoid system; but an existing system of order had to be adapted in such a way as to eliminate rivalry between countries. The new system would guarantee the integrity of those partners who participated in it, without infringement of their prerogatives.

It would be of interest to compare this soldier's life history with those of some who have developed a communistic political system, with a preponderance of attitudes favorably inclined toward present Russian ideals. In those instances, a political system was developed which deviated from the common American conception to such a degree as to make integration or compromise impossible. In the instance of our soldier, his British preferences—which may be called by many "British fads," and which may be as offensive as Russian fads to these same people—did not lead to such a profound aberration from the national norm as to result in an irremediable break with his native community. Here we encounter a replica of his relationship to his father: a deviation which does not lead to discontinuance of smooth contact, and which is able to provide the subjective feeling of prestige without creating a manifest conflict. The soldier's ability to proceed in conformity with that pattern was marked.

The issue involved must be considered in order to grasp fully the broad margin which the soldier was permitted to fill out with his acting out, without getting into conflict with society. This soldier broke an oath, and committed a crime which was liable to capital punishment during wartime—a crime on which there rested a strong social taboo. Nevertheless he succeeded in performing it in such a way as to provide himself in the end with an increment of internal and external prestige. There is no doubt that he was a deserter. Article of War 28 reads in part: "Any soldier who, without having first received a regular discharge, again enlists ... in any foreign army, shall be deemed to have deserted the service of the United States. . . ." There must have been a special constellation of conditions active in him that enabled him to win for himself the privilege of committing such a crime in full public view, without having to pay the heavy price that humans must usually pay under such circumstances.

There were indications that psychologically his desertion was an act of aggression. He had not been drafted: society had not imposed on him nor had it forced him to take any step which might conflict with his convictions. It was he who had volunteered and had asked to be accepted as a member of the Armed Forces. He did not learn, during his service, anything new about the national character of his native country, such as might have made him acquire new convictions. At the time of his desertion America's entry into the war appeared, if anything, far more probable than at the time of his enlistment. Hence, his claim that he felt desperate about his country's aloofness from the war does not bear realistic scrutiny; such desperate feelings might have been far more in place at the time when he sought enlistment.

It is known, however, that during his service a change took place in him concerning an essential sector of life: the familial taboo on sex lost its compelling force. He tried to explain the transformation by way of the inculcation of new ideas from books whose titles he did not remember. Be that as it may, he must have been exposed to the usual upsurge of sexual tension, to which the sexually ascetic man is exposed in the army, through his new contact with looseness. He complained about the "bragging" of Americans, which "got on his nerves" during that time. Perhaps this was a reflection of that sexual bragging which is rampant in army group life. How little he had really changed his puritanical outlook may be seen from the fact that the two instances of infringement of his traditional outlook on sex were performed when he was drunk. When he left his post in this country, he might have felt that his puritanical habits were on the verge of giving way. A breach of his sexual tradition might be more tolerable if it occurred in a foreign society. Absence from home sometimes makes a superego somewhat more pliable, for then the superego may permit indulgence in behavior patterns which would be considered intolerable during one's continued presence in the initial group. Both instances of intercourse, he reported, were with females of non-Anglo-Saxon stock. Furthermore, his shift to the foreign country gave him the opportunity of becoming an officer.

There was no opportunity for us to investigate possible conflicts in his relationship to officers during his service in this country. Military authority was certainly not a social structure which would have permitted him to apply his customary ways of handling authority. That set of well-established techniques, which he had so successfully used in his dealings with paternal authority, must have become pretty useless for him as a private. Here authority was removed from the plane on which partial deviation or partial participation were still regarded as permissible. Officer status, however, left room for the possible play of such mechanisms. All this tended to establish the assumption that his desertion, even though it had been carried out under conditions providing for excellent rationalization in terms of justification to the group, rather furnished him with solutions and gratifications than it reflected the frustrations unavoidably involved in a true sacrifice. Even from the viewpoint of the realistic future waiting for him had he been a private and one of the first to go abroad after Pearl Harbor, it may be said that his desertion was indirectly a lifesaving device. To be sure, there was not the slightest reason to believe that such a motivation played an active part in his decision to leave the United States. No American could have foreseen the turn historical events would take a few months after he left. But it is of interest to observe how an eagerness to make sacrifices may, through the inscrutable course of fate, often save an individual from the far greater burdens that he would have had to carry had he followed the beaten path. Psychologically—if a general conclusion may be permitted in view of the scarcity of the material at hand—his desertion was a flight from and an aggression against his father in order to carry out a sexual action which could not contain any element of compromise, but constituted an open breach with the official morality, handed to him along the lines of a traditional familial pattern.

His appearance was that of a friendly, cooperative, interested young man. He kept himself neat and clean; the compulsiveness of his personality showed up but mildly in the way in which he presented himself to society. He admitted that it was important for him to do everything in a way calculated in detail beforehand. His ethicopolitical convictions were marked also by some compulsive rigidity (which is not designed as passing judgment on the content of his system). He censured American soldiers severely for eating ice cream in England, and for paying high prices, thus effecting a detrimental economic situation in a country laboring under dearth and a lack of essentials. He might have been basically quite right in such an estimation of the impact of the American character on the economic situation of an ally; yet the way in which he made an absolute, rigid measure of that observation betrayed the compulsive personality. In his political views, I would judge that he took a position somewhere between Thomas Paine and Thomas Jefferson. He defined the American system in terms of the defiance of intolerance and the eternal privilege of every citizen to disobey the government when this was done for the common good. His bent for the English was a personal excrescence which had no necessary or logical place in his political philosophy.

This soldier could not be called a crusader to the same extent as the first example. The former's philosophy reached the level of public repercussion for a short while because of a coincidental combination of circumstances. Yet his stamina as a crusader flagged as soon as he reached the point at which he aroused society's interest. The second soldier was not at all a crusader in the true sense of the word: he did not try to induce others to follow his course of action. He had an indirect influence on public opinion because his past became known to the community when he was arrested, and the public became interested in the impending decision of the army. Yet certain features of his life were of such a kind as to include him in the context of this essay.

He lived with the feeling that his opinions and his actions ought to have pragmatic value for other members of the community. This attitude must be differentiated from the attitude of most people who have the feeling that their opinions are the only right ones, and would be shared by all if only those others were capable of logical thinking. The claim to universal validity does not extend to the realm of action as frequently as it holds for the realm of thought. The capitalist does not believe that all people should be capitalists: the producer of chewing gum, even though he were convinced that his product contributes to salivation, would oppose the idea of all group members contributing to salivation the same way he does. Yet, our soldier thought that all of his actions which he regarded as significant should be imitated by the rest of the community.

It is one of the highest achievements of personal life for the mode of one's own existence to become a symbol of conduct for the entire community. This symbolic content of a life history found its strongest expression, perhaps, in Christ's life. Not only did the contents of his preaching acquire binding power over every member of the Christian Church, so did the symbolic aspect of every episode in his life. His life was without accidentals; its minutest details are of equal symbolic value. The living of such a life is not merely a personal, subjective matter; it is a continuous process of the taking shape of a principle or of an ethical system. The soldier's way of living certainly did not reach such heights, but potentially it rested in him to do so. The most important decisions he made were arrived at as containing a symbolic value, which would be taken up by a thousand others if only they were desirous of living up to the requirements of the hour. Hence, he may be called, in a sense, a potential crusader. In a sense, he may have been even more of a crusader than many so-called crusaders who reach the level of social recognition. The conduct of their crusades is often meant to serve as a gospel binding on others, yet the crusader does not feel himself to be under any obligation to realize those same goals, because the mere fact of spreading the gospel is regarded by him as merit enough to warrant his being exempted from the duties of the rabble. The soldier, by contrast, demonstrated in his own life history the obligations which his opinions imposed on his actions.

The two instances reported here are the only ones I can remember of men who tried to clutch at the social wheel, and to impose their will on the army, in a constructive action which was outside the customary or permitted confines of army traditions. I do not say that there was a lack of criticism with regard to special performances, traditions, or even the army at large. The viewpoint of that criticism depended in every case on the political convictions, general philosophical outlook, specific occupation of the particular censor. Yet the profusion of the criticism was out of proportion to the events which gave cause to criticism. Instead of their being directly correlated with the degree of criticism, just the opposite was to be noted. An emotionally or mentally adverse attitude toward the army was customary and was found in the average soldier. Neglect of duty, slipshodness, unreliability—all these may have been the direct outgrowth of such attitudes, but no systematized or organized pattern of action grew out of them. Once, a group of physicians organized to give vent to their complaints, concerning the overstrain of work under which they were laboring. This took the form of a personal talk of the chief with his staff, carried on against that background of familiarity that automatically establishes itself within the "team" framework of professional people.

Those two exceptions to that general rule, however, were marked by psychopathology; the actions these two soldiers took were the direct outgrowth of their subjective pathology. Now, it may be said that nearly all of a person's behavior patterns fall into line with the subjective history of his life and are not correlated solely with external reality. That may be quite true; yet not all behavior patterns fall into line with unresolved conflicts. If a person volunteers for the army because he considers it his duty to contribute his share that way to a national emergency and if during the course of his service ancient ambitions and childhood dreams find revival, his volunteering need not have been genetically connected with the impact of those unresolved childhood dreams. Military service may have created a conflict by bringing those early fantasies to an acute level. In the two instances quoted, however, the two particular actions were directly caused by psychopathology. The first officer would never have written the letter without his first being victimized by a pathological affect; the second officer would not have joined a foreign army had there not been a tension due to the lack of gratification of biological needs.

If one studies the history of any great movement in this country—such as that, for example, which led to the Civil War—one obtains the impression that the crusader made his great contribution to it. It is questionable whether the Emancipation Proclamation would ever have been written without the preceding movement of the Abolitionists, without John Brown's self-sacrifice, and without Senator Sumner's incessant raising of his demanding voice. There was a group of men then, courageous, carried by intense conviction, and ready to bear the awful stigma that society attaches to any person who dares to touch cherished traditional views, especially those pertaining to important forms of economic or political association. It must be emphasized that society is often tolerant to a certain extent—so long as "touching" traditional views means no more than establishing a doctrinal viewpoint. As soon as the viewpoint is presented in such a way as to lead to action, or as soon as the doctrinal viewpoint makes action the inescapable consequence, that same tolerance disappears. It is impressive to see with what equanimity society can bear doctrinal deviations from tradition. For example, the writings of George Bernard Shaw are now the accepted readings of the educated. One may even incur censure as a person pretending to be a member of the educated class if one is discovered to be ignorant of his social philosophy. Yet in what disastrous complications would a person instantaneously become involved if he tried to make Shaw's philosophy the guiding principle of his *actions!* The problem becomes more serious once it has to do with the basic doctrines of a society—for example, the Christian doctrine, about which much the same can be said as about Shaw's philosophy.

The crusader fills the gap between a society's theory and its practice. He oils the ever-rusty wheels of social change and is usually crushed between those very wheels. Yet the fact that the crusading type was scarcely ever encountered overtly in the army may give reason for some deliberations. Since a society which tries to exist on what is called "the democratic principle" must abstain from force as much as possible, yet needs the cooperation of group members as much as does any other society, it tries to institute conformity by means other than the direct application of force. How a democracy enforces conformity without the direct use of force cannot be made the subject of investigation in this context. It is a matter of fact that, among the vast majority of members of the American community, the desire for conformity is found to an amazing degree. The demand for conformity is never officially raised. On the contrary, individuality, freedom, and the pursuit of personal happiness are made official and important parts of the national philosophy, and have more than once found touching expression.

Yet, the individual member shrinks from filling out those very patterns. There cannot be any doubt that the remotest necessity of deviating from conformable behavior precipitates acute anxiety in a surprisingly large number of group members. It is likewise surprising to observe how many people are preoccupied with the ideal of acting like social automata, of behaving in minutest conformity with the group ideal. This desire frequently finds expression in a wish to possess poise, which, to my mind, means in reality a desire to renounce individual behavior patterns in favor of one structured according to group demand. Since democracy, because of its having dispensed with outward force, would easily be thrown off balance by "determined and resolute deviation," it needs voluntary conformity, to a great extent merely for its survival.

One reason for the antagonism against the crusader in democratic society may be precisely the great danger into which it could easily be brought by a misguided crusader. Unfortunately, it is only in retrospect that one can determine who was the "Messiah," and who the misguided crusader. On the other hand, because of the great need for conformity in democracy, conformity may become so widespread that it loses its great advantage for society's stability, and instead prevents or unduly retards necessary social development. A society which is completely wrapped in conformity would lose its flexibility; it would be condemned to die a slow but certain death. The prevention of the petrification of society is one of the heroic historical functions of the crusader. The question must be seriously raised to what extent our democracy has already lost its flexibility and its readiness to undergo changes, partly because of the extinction of a type which, in spite of its great contribution, has been ostracized by society. To that extent, society has been victorious in the spread of a conformity so profound that what was benefit has grown into a plague.

If people are forced by coercive means, these may precipitate resistance, as we can already observe in the child. If they can be induced to accept certain behavior patterns without apparent coercion, rebellion does not find a point around which it can crystallize. This, again, can be observed among children who are raised in families which consistently satisfy their needs.[8] Since conformity is, in democratic society, a latent group demand—not even verbalized, but ever present in the national climate of the group—the opportunity and the urge for rebellion decrease. Furthermore, the type of person who may feel inclined toward opposition against society, and whose personality encourages the development of a longing for action which expresses that opposition, meets organized groups, at present devoted to the goal of introducing reforms. The crusader who joins an organization, and becomes integrated into an established group structure, more often than not is bound to become gradually deprived of that very element which has the greatest appeal to masses—namely, his passionate participation in the crusade. The modern crusader, caught up in the workings of an organization corresponding to his own principles, becomes interested in the organization of mass action and of political action, and he may in turn use the prevalent tendency toward conformity for his own ends. At that moment, however, he may stop engaging the fantasy of the broad masses: he may lose the role of a symbol and sink to the position of a salesman.

It is possible that present democratic society has reached such a degree of rigidity and conservatism that it has, in effect, eliminated the constructive crusader, with the result that the crusader now grows only on the soil of severe psychopathology. Yet, his psychopathology will more often than not prevent the crusader from applying himself to the execution of a broad program, anticipating necessary social change correlated to the true needs of the community. The probability is great that, under such circumstances, the crusader will be alienated from the masses. He will probably waste his efforts in fantastic and unrealistic schemes, which may prove highly gratifying to his personal needs but antagonistic to the historical course that the community should take. The problem of the crusader is closely related to the more comprehensive problem of conformity and nonconformity (see Merton, 1938), and of society's reaction to social change (cf. Trotter, 1919).

I do not know how far my personal experiences in the army with regard to crusaders were significant and how far merely accidental. They taught me one new lesson: not to rely on theoretical conclusions regarding social reality. The official philosophy, as taught and professed in this country, would hardly have made me expect to find griping without subsequent social action—a general reaction pattern among young men

[8] One aspect of the problem concerns the vicissitude of aggression in human development. See S. Freud (1923 and 1930).

in a situation of the greatest degradation of the democratic way of life. The appearance of the great man in a time of distress depends on accidentals and therefore cannot be anticipated. The crusader, however, is not only a sociological type: he is a psychological one as well. There ought to be in every one of us, so to speak, a crusader. It has to do with that function of the superego which insists that moral precept and action coincide. The isolation of these two, one from the other, in the overwhelming majority of our young men, is a remarkable fact. It deserves our attention.

BIBLIOGRAPHY

Deutsch, H. (1934), Don Quijote und Donquijotismus. *Imago, 20*:444-449.

Fox, H. M. (1945), Neurotic Resentment and Dependence Overseas. *Psychiatry, 8*:131-138.

Freud, S. (1919), A Child is Being Beaten. *Standard Edition, 17*:179-204. London: Hogarth Press, 1955.

———(1923), The Ego and the Id. *Standard Edition, 19*:12-66. London: Hogarth Press, 1961.

———(1930), Civilization and Its Discontents. *Standard Edition, 21*:57-145. London: Hogarth Press, 1961.

Janis, I. L. (1945), Psychodynamic Aspects of Adjustment to Army Life. *Psychiatry, 8*:159-176.

Lasswell, H. D. (1930), *Psychopathology and Politics*. Chicago: University of Chicago Press.

Merton, R. K. (1938), Social Structure and Anomie. *Amer. Sociolog. Rev., 3*:672-682.

Schmideberg, M. (1946), On Querulance. *Psychoanal. Quart., 15*:472-502.

Steffens, L. (1931), *The Autobiography of Lincoln Steffens*. New York: Harcourt, Brace.

Trotter, W. (1919), *Instincts of the Herd in Peace and War*. New York: Macmillan.

SOME DYNAMICS OF UNCONSCIOUS AND SYMBOLIC COMMUNICATION IN PRESENT-DAY TELEVISION

MARTIN GROTJAHN, M.D.

SOME OBSERVATIONAL FACTS ON VIEWING HABITS

In a three-year study, Schramm, Lyle, and Parker (1961) questioned 6,000 children, 2,000 parents, and 300 teachers about their attitude toward television. They collected questionnaires and had personal interviews; they went to San Francisco, Denver, and an unnamed suburban area; they compared what they call "Television Town" with a "Radio Town," where atmospheric conditions made television reception impossible. Here are some of this report's main points:

For most children, under most conditions, television is probably not particularly harmful nor particularly beneficial. Children do not just sit passively in front of their television sets. They learn how to *use* them.

The television industry has developed only in the last ten years. It is now the greatest source of national entertainment, and one sixth of the children's waking time is given to television viewing. Until the sixteenth year of life, a child spends at least as much time on television as in school. It is the greatest source of common experience in the life of children. The age of radio has changed into the age of television. Children begin viewing television programs when they are two years of age, and they are at the peak of their viewing while they are in the sixth grade. A child will spend three or three and a half hours on weekdays, and four or five hours on Saturdays and Sundays in front of the set. After the age of twelve, there is a sudden shift from television viewing to reading: the more intelligent children lead away from the group of heavy viewers.

The brighter the child, the earlier will he be interested in public affairs, such as congressional elections and news. Where the family listens to educational programs, the children will do so too. However, the influence of the peer groups is greater than that of the family.

Television is cherished with affection and respect by children and parents. There is very little critique; there are very few suggestions for improvement. Children want the same, only more so. When the television set is sick, the whole family is sick. It is more missed than any other media. Children trust television; mothers are undecided; fathers trust the newspapers more. Television is no longer considered a miracle; it is fun and entertainment.

No one seems to complain much about commercials; still, no one seems to be satisfied either. Most parents are worried about too much violence and too much crime. The more educated parents are more worried about crime and law breaking, while working-class parents are more worried about sexual delinquency.

Children view television for passive pleasures: they like fantasy, thrill, getting away from real life problems and real life boredom. Television viewers may be classified as fantasy seekers and reality seekers. The fantasy shows facilitate dependency and emotion. They offer escape from threats and anxiety, and offer wish fulfillment and pleasure. Reality shows lead to the problems of the real world, invite alertness, activity, effort, cognition and working through. They lead to understanding of realistic situations and make the children aware of threats and anxieties in return for better understanding of the problems in life and living. Fantasy shows are Westerns, crime drama, popular music, variety shows; realistic shows are documentary interviews, public affairs, and educational programs.

Television is used only secondarily and incidentally for learning. Children learn to play baseball, and perhaps how to fix a fence, as they may have seen in a Western. A child cannot space his learning, since television has no contact with the viewer. He cannot get needed information by asking for it; he must wait passively until it is offered to him. There is no search and there is no research. Parents complain that children do not learn enough in school, but that they learn too much about the wrong things from television.

Children take television as "really real" because they do not have "adult discount" (meaning the secret reservation of the adult: "it is only a movie"). Children are by no means always aware that that which they see is not real.

Television City compared with Radio Town shows that there is hardly any difference in newspaper reading; however, children from Television Town read less books.

Television absorbs some of the discontent resulting from the child's socialization. It helps him withdraw from the real world; many shows encourage confusion of reality situations with fantasy. This may cause special difficulties for the troubled child. It may build up aggression more than it drains it, and therefore may increase the difficulties of a child already burdened with troubles.

The children of Television Town begin school with a quicker start and with a larger vocabulary. Certain advantage is given to the children of Television Town when they are above or below average intelligence. Television becomes less attractive and rewarding in higher grades, and students turn to reality-oriented media. Girls change a little sooner than boys. The higher economic groups change earlier, faster, and to a higher percentage. The present-day-oriented working-class family turns more to TV than does the future-oriented family of the upper middle class.

The heavy viewers among the fantasy seekers are frequently antisocial. Reality-oriented groups show little antisocial aggression, and seem to feel the most anxiety about it. They are the ones who would be considered the best adjusted to reality, and they have the least conflicts in their homes.

The more driving and ambitious the parents are, the more time is spent in escaping them. It seems as though television does not spoil children, but that spoiled children turn to television. Children in conflict remember more from television violence than other children. The less trouble in the family, the less viewing. Television does not reduce tension; it changes tension to attention and directs it to another world. It uses aggression and violence to hold attention.

The children's hours on television, lasting from four o'clock in the afternoon to nine o'clock in the evening, are overloaded with crime, Westerns, and drama, showing an incredible amount of violence. There are some hair-raising statistics: In one hundred program hours of children-time, the authors tabulated: 12 murders, 16 major gunfights, 21 persons shot, 21 other violent incidents with guns, 15 fistfights, 15 incidents in which one person slugged another, an attempted murder with a pitchfork, two stranglings, one stabbing in the back with a butcher knife, three successful suicides (and one unsuccessful attempt at suicide), four people pushed or falling from cliffs, two cars plummeting from a cliff, two attempts made to run over persons with automobiles, a raving psychotic loose in an airliner, two mob scenes (in one, the wrong man is hanged), a horse grinding a man under its hooves, two robberies, a woman killed in a fall from a moving train, a tidal wave, an earthquake, a hired killer stalking his victim, and, finally, one guillotining. Since this sampling was taken, the amount and refinement of crime and violence has been further intensified.

This violence does not frighten children. They are more frightened by the dark and the mysterious. It is not proven nor disproven that television crime influences children to act out delinquency. Even children who claim that it was television which seduced them to delinquent behavior, show that they come from broken homes and that television may contribute but not *cause* delinquent behavior. Any child would rather be like a strong villain than a weak hero. The great statistical increase of juvenile delinquency is due in part to the fact that more and more courts have been opened in the last ten years for juveniles. The worst television can do is to feed malignant impulses that already exist.

American television has not ushered in a new age of enlightenment. It does not raise a better-informed generation. It has not created a new medium of esthetic expression. Television has not fulfilled its potentials. Perhaps it is not even a medium of communication, only of commerce. More and more, it has become a hindrance for the intelligent child, rather than a help. Television has not stimulated intellectual, creative activity, nor has it raised intellectual standards of living just because it was invented.

Parents are often more relieved than concerned over their children's immobilization. Television is a reliable baby sitter and is always available, never too busy. The automobile removed adolescents from the surveillance of their homes, and parents were concerned for their morals. Now TV immobilizes them in the living room, and parents deplore their passivity.

UNCONSCIOUS COMMUNICATION IN TELEVISION

The analytic observer will not regard crime and violence, detective and mystery stories in the way they are presented on television. Instead, he will turn from the manifest content of dreams to their latent, unconscious meaning, so the analyst will try to understand and to interpret the symbolic meaning of the mystery stories and other television programs. Only then can we hope to understand their hold on the fantasy of the child.

Horror is experienced when an old and long-repressed childhood fear seems to come true. The child fears ghosts, dead people returning, magic mystic beliefs being enacted, murder and crime taking place no longer in fantasies, but in front of his eyes. An old, long-forgotten childhood fear returns from repression. The projection of repressed images into the reality of stage or screen may have a chance to lead to working through and to final solution. We try to do this in the theatre in one way; we attempt the same, unsuccessfully, in the nightmare.

In the horror drama of television, a working through of unsettled childhood fears is hardly attempted or intended. Television is aimed at the switching of tension from the conflicts of living, conscious or unconscious, to a play with thrills and threats. Television is not a problem-solving activity; it is a change from tension to attention.

A television performer uses tension in order to distract, to reassure, to postpone integration of conflicts. In other words, television entertains where the art of the theatre does not avoid our conscious or unconscious conflicts. Art offers a chance to project conflicts on the screen, on the stage, or on the pages of a book, in order to see them there with the eyes of a creative artist outside of ourselves and yet experience them inside of ourselves. The truly artistic performance gives us a chance for working through. Exposure to art leaves us a little better, a little more mature, a little more human.

Television does not allow the child to keep former stages of development safely suppressed and hidden in the unconscious until it emerges for further integration. Television teases the child to toy with all kinds of trends from the unconscious without helping him to deal with them and to integrate them. When, in such situations, the outside reality does not offer help and does not invite socialization, then acting out in the form of juvenile delinquency may be the consequence. It seems as if many juveniles turn to crimes as if they need self-administered initiation rites, marking dramatically the end of adolescence, the beginning of maturity, death of one, life of a new phase. Much delinquency is a desperate call for help in order to get the authorities to re-enforce the necessary controls of threats from the unconscious. If this cry for help is not heard, if authorities do not react to the crime, then the unconscious activated by environment and inner needs may break down all defenses. The results are either suicidal depressions or short psychotic episodes, which nowadays seem to replace the neurotic reactions we used to see fifty years ago.

The Teasing Effect of Television and the Unconscious Meaning of the Cowboy Story and of the Mystery Drama

The true hero of the cowboy story is not the pioneer who conquers the land. The true hero is a boy—a cowboy. He rides into focus from nowhere. He is independent, asexual, self-reliant, trusting, resourceful, and perhaps sort of foolish (Grotjahn, 1957). The cowboy seems to be

homeless, like Moses when he was found in the rushes along the Nile. He
seems to have neither father nor mother. His only friend is his horse.
He is involved in disaster, treason and gunfire, murder, unlawful action and shooting. He rescues an old man in a helpless village, restores
peace, law and order; he disregards the village virgin when he finally
rides off into the lonely landscape of the Plains. He is a man of all men,
but boy does not get girl—he gets horse.

Cowboy stories symbolize the whole wealth of oedipal childhood fantasies, including the rape of the mother (or of the ranch) and her
rescue. Different aspects of the mother are symbolized in various women:
as for instance, the virgin or the tough prostitute in the gambling joint.
The Westerns are a contemporary variation of the ageless oedipal theme.
The hero is not the tragic Oedipus, but the victorious son and brother.
The hero does not commit a crime as Oedipus did; he remains guiltless.
The cowboy repeats a dream of glory, which was dreamed through
childhood and puberty. Conflicts are avoided, disguised, sidetracked.
Guilt is replaced by suspense and thrills. The whole show takes place on
the level of daydreaming. The cowboy is a good son whose actions serve
the good of the father after all.

Oedipus is put into the cowboy boots; the Sphinx is disguised as the
all-knowing, silent, faithful horse; the tragic guilt is transformed into
wish fulfillment and dreams of glory. The punishment is turned regressively into a return to the mother, endorsed by all participants. After all,
the rebellious and heroic deed of Oedipus is changed to a rescue fantasy.
The murder of the father has been turned from a God-given fate to a
gunplay. The emotional experience of living through an oedipal situation
on the stage of the legitimate theatre or on the screen of a truly great movie
is changed into sentimentality and wishful thinking. A maturating experience is changed to entertainment and can therefore be enjoyed instead of
suffered. Tension replaces solution.

The censorship in a television presentation distorts, falsifies, degener-
ates, renders harmless and cute the essential features of the Oedipus
drama: it stimulates and teases the unconscious in need of working
through. It denies true and necessary integration. Where it should help, it
hinders.

A peculiarly distorted childhood curiosity explains our interest in the
mystery story. There was a time when we all would almost risk our lives
to see and hear and learn what transpired on the hidden stage of the parental bedroom. The primal scene appears to the child as a bloody, cruel, wild
and lustful performance, with the father as a rapist or murderer, the

mother as the victim, and the child as a clever little detective who collects the clues and explains it to the stupid Dr. Watson. The police protect the vested interests of the parental authorities and do not help in discovering the mystery of crime and sex. Actually, the facts of life are obvious: in the mystery story, the facts of the crime can be deduced from obvious clues by anyone who wants to see them. Clues are all around us, and so is murder and crime and lust, if we only are allowed or allow ourselves to see them.

The mystery fan is a perennial Peeping Tom, who looks desperately and persistently through the wrong keyhole. No longer does he look at the facts of life, but at the facts of crime. He wants to follow his natural curiosity, but does not dare to rebel against this taboo. He displaces his curiosity from sex to crime. Since he will never find the answers this way, he will avoid trouble, but may become addicted to the wrong search. The mystery story does not represent just another variation of the Oedipus theme. It is more regressive and leads us back to the time when we all wanted to find out mysteries of sex and lust, when we thought that sex was a bloody fight for life and death between father and mother.

All participants in this childhood drama are present: a crime is committed and it is a bloody crime of violence, committed with a "blunt instrument"; everyone is suspected: father, mother, and son, as everybody seems to indulge in this kind of crime. The clues are obvious; we must only be able, willing and courageous to see them. The police are of no help; like teachers and doctors, they tell stories about the stork. The clever detective represents the Peeping Tom, the child: courageously and with good conscience, he tries to put two and two together. Everybody is suspected since everybody is guilty.

The mystery story writer plays with primal scene material. He implies by his technique of avoidance and disguise that sex is bad, and suggests regression to pregenital levels. He further implies that we all are murderers anyhow and may as well enjoy it. He suggests a slight punishment later—but what child would not prefer to identify with the strong villain rather than with the weak, moralistic hero?

Television does not rebel as all art does. It is neither revolutionary nor rebellious, nor is it liberating. Therefore, the viewing experience cannot lead to progress, working through, understanding and maturation. Since it is commercially motivated, television must keep its audience on infantile levels because there people are more inclined to listen to the hucksters and their slogans. The advertisers behave like parents of idiots, who tell their children what to do, what to buy and what to consume. This is why television in America today trains idiots but not criminals. It sidetracks our children's natural trend to work on their conflicts and teases them without offering a way to the solution.

It is as if the television writer says: "All of you are murderers, so let's enjoy it. Of course, we do not really mean it, but let's pretend as though at the end we take a mild punishment and continue the teasing game." Just because the television writer is partially right, he will activate a response from the unconscious of his listeners. The religious person in a similar situation would say: "Murder is in all of us. Let us fight it; let us all become children in the Family of God." The attitude of the therapist is still different: "We are not as bad as we fear we are, and we are not as good as we hope we could be. Let us know ourselves and let us be ourselves." The artistic approach is: "Let us turn death into immortality." In his artistic creation, the artist shows his attempt at restitution and tests it in our esthetic experience.

SOME DREAMS ILLUSTRATING THE TEASING EFFECT OF TELEVISION ON THE UNCONSCIOUS

A man, sixty-two years of age, analyzed eighteen years ago, told the following dream to his analyst during one of his occasional, informal visits with him:

> I was with my wife. She was very small, half-sized, and in the nude. She opened the door—a double door—and saw a murderer. She jumped back. I rushed out and there was a pirate; he had only one eye, the right one, while the left one was bandaged. He had a red dotted handkerchief over his head. He threatened me with a hook which he had on his right arm instead of a hand. The hook was actually a needle or poisonous tooth of a rattlesnake. A scratch of it would kill instantly. The door was closed with paper folders and newspapers, making it unmovable. I called my wife: "Lock yourself up!" Without fear and in murderous rage, I attacked the bandit. I could not understand how other people were kept in check by a threat of this kind, no matter how real. When I jumped on him, I woke up.

The patient had observed his wife watching television the previous night. The wife is a kind, beloved lady, helpful and unobtrusive—almost the type of the Parson's wife in the movies; she loves to watch mystery stories. She goes through real suffering while watching these shows; her hands and feet get ice cold; occasionally she has to hide her face from the screen—only to return again to the frightful experience. The most dreadful moment for her is to see a crime committed after it has been planned and expected and not to be able to prevent its execution. She behaves like a child but knows her bedside stories by heart but still insists on hearing them and "to die in anxiety." She behaves like a child who knows the secrets of the primal scene but must watch it, nevertheless, in horror and fear.

The husband, who reported the dream, is not interested in television, but is amused by and curious about his wife's behavior. He watches her and feels obliged to remain with her in her hour of need. In the dream, he sees his wife as a child, in the nude, symbolizing sexual excitement. He opens the door to the parental bedroom wherein the parents commit the bloody and beastial crimes.

The one-eyed bandit is the pirate of the movies, the psychoanalyst, who is allowed to see and to show. Like Oedipus, who lost both eyes, the analyst has sacrificed at least one. Symbolically, one eye is directed to the outer world, while the other eye, the blind one, is directed inward.

The symbol of the poison in the syringe or in the rattlesnake's tooth is taken from television, but simultaneously symbolizes the dreamer; he is a parent himself, powerful and dangerous, ready to penetrate and solve the problems of the primal scene.

The dreamer pictures his wife, who symbolizes his own "better half," ultimately himself, caught between a lustful television father and a one-eyed, but all-seeing bandit-analyst, who also represents death.

The true analytic problem, which is also the essential issue in the analysis of television crime drama, is the dreamer's murderous rage, his disregard for danger, his being beside himself. It symbolizes his wish and determination to break through the infantile taboo; it represents his murderous rage at the mother who leaves the child alone while she enacts the primal scene. This rage is very real for the child, is felt very deeply, and is older than the Oedipus conflict, during which this original rage is reactivated by the frustrated child. It is this activation of incompletely repressed bloodlust and violence, with rage and with murder, which makes television dangerous. It may activate trends to bloody action, or it may activate anxiety and deeply repressed material concerned with death and dying.

In the unconscious, the fear of death and dying is symbolically connected with the wish to murder. The fear of dying often hides the wish to kill. The play with the horror of the primal scene activates this fear of murder and of dying. This teasing of unconscious trends does not necessarily lead to acting, but it deepens a conflict and asks for a new repressive effort or increased defenses. It does not lead to insight and integration.

Another patient, a writer, a man of fifty, was in analysis because of angina-like symptoms with considerable anxiety. After a quiet evening at home watching television, he had the following dream:

> I was in a forest and climbed a hill. I looked down on a river. A cowboy came and led his horse to the water. It was very thirsty and drank enormous quantities. The horse looked pregnant. The cowboy was cruel to the horse and beat it. I ran down the hill and saw the man coming, wearing tattered clothes and with an emaciated, starved horse which could hardly move. There was a big dog, and I called out to the man to watch his dog, lest he bite me. The man turned and came right up to me. I saw that the dog could hardly move; his right legs had been crushed, tied together, and had grown together. Suddenly, a little boy, like a war orphan, appeared and showed me their completely ruined shack. He said that a lady comes there occasionally and had left her gun. There were two guns. He also showed me that they were making a moonshine whisky there, and the old man said that anyone who could drink his whisky was a strong man. He showed me a bottle of it, and it looked like poison or urine. I woke up.

As the analysis of this dream shows, the dreamer took from television the symbols of the cowboy story in order to disguise his concern with life, death, and sex. The cowboy, in this case, is an old man, who mistreats and cruelly tortures his pregnant horse: the mother. As the dreamer witnesses the horrible scene and rushes to protect the horse, he is petrified by the sight of it and, in his fear, is immobilized. The motive of the pregnant horse, emaciated and dying, is repeated in the symbol of the crippled dog: the bitch, who represents sexuality. The horrible team is headed directly at the patient, who is almost at the point of awakening. The little boy represents the dreamer. He holds out hope by talking about the lady with the shining, well-functioning gun: a denial of castration, which in turn is a symbol of death in a man with angina pectoris.

A third representative example is of special interest, since it is taken from the analysis of a young man of nineteen, who came to analysis because of a deep, prolonged identity crisis, so frequent among our younger generation today:

> I walked through the campus and suffered from leprosy or from severe radiation burns, like after an atomic bomb. It was dark, but here and there were a few lighted windows. A car came by with a

couple sitting inside, and they asked for directions. I did not want them to be embarrassed at the sight of my distorted face, so I kept my back turned to them as I spoke, and I kept on walking. I knew I was going to die. I was dangerous to touch, so I crawled under a bush to die there without endangering people. Mr. Starr, who is a very strict disciplinarian, came and wanted to help me; but I could no longer talk and wanted him to leave in order not to suffer from my radiation. I had the most horrible burns on my face and on the right side of my neck.

This young man used television material like a day residue as an illustration for his unconscious needs and conflicts. However, this is only part of the story. It is as true as if somebody were to say that he saw a bloody car accident in all its gory details and then concludes in his analysis that his horror and shock were "only" an activation of a long-repressed childhood dread and not in need of being analyzed. Without such activation, this unresolved, unconscious material may have remained undisturbed for years. Eventually, it might have been solved and integrated to a degree which would have kept it at a safe distance from traumatization.

Here again the dreamer takes a threat from present-day reality: the threat of the atomic bomb and its terror. Young people with any intelligence and any independent thinking will be concerned with this threat, which endangers them more than anybody ever before in human history and prehistory. This external threat is combined with an internal threat of this man's struggle for independence. The son of his parents had to die, so that the man might be born. He was aware that the people in the car, by whom he did not want to be seen, were his parents. He did not want them to be embarrassed by seeing in him what he feared to see in them.

What fifteen years earlier had been a wish to kill his mother (or both parents), now returns as a fear to die himself. The situation is so totally horrible and so without escape because the realistic threat reflects great inner turmoil. It is almost as if the primal scene is no longer an intimate secret of the parental bedroom, but is now an event of universal dimension, re-enacted in reality. This makes our present-day world so schizophreniogenic *(Weltuntergangserlebnis)*. The experience of seeing the doom of outer and inner world can also lead to outstanding artistic-esthetic expression.

Television penetrates the defenses and teases the unconscious. It is essential for the understanding of the visual arts to note that they facilitate this bypassing of defenses. Television stimulates and activates without providing fulfillment or showing a solution. By doing so, it turns from an esthetic experience or a maturating influence into a damaging trauma. It operates like the trainer of a tightrope dancer who constantly and consistently points out the dreadful consequences of a fall from the rope without providing skill, confidence, safety and relief.

The young man of the dream has conceived the meaning of television horror on the level of his unconscious and applied it to his own anxiety. The dreamer of the cowboy story unconsciously understood the latent meaning of the cowboy stories. The result in both cases is increase of unconscious turmoil, which may lead to an aggravation of psychopathology.

In my clinical work (Grotjahn, 1960), broadened by supervision and consultation, I have found undeniable increase of conscious and unconscious preoccupation with death and dying, violence and morbid lust (instead of healthy pleasure in sex), which leads either to delinquent acting out or to the need for especially strong repressive efforts. If these newly required repressions do not work successfully, we frequently see short-lived, often self-curative, psychotic episodes with suicidal attempts, which are so significant for present-day pathology. Many of these suicide attempts appear like television horror stories turned inside.

In other cases, increased and powerful repression may be victorious, even if we would not call the results successful adjustment. Since repression consumes energy, this kind of repression or suppression is wasteful and the result is mediocrity and conformity of the seemingly adjusted personality. These people then become television addicts who constantly need the assurance that their repressions hold firm in the face of persistent stimulation by the television programs.

SYMBOLIC THINKING AND TELEVISION

The dreams reported here pose the questions: How does the projection of unconscious trends onto the visual reality of the television screen influence repression, defenses, action, integration and creativity? Are there differences between the dynamics of working through and the teasing of unconscious stimulation into tension, thrill and fun? When does an experience become maturing? When does it become traumatic, or simply thrilling, or boring?

The combination of unconscious needs, a threatening reality, and a show of violence invite the trespassing of the borderline between fantasy and reality. The results are not necessarily acts of violence, but many different kinds of psychopathology, which would defy all statistics and could be verified only by interviews in depth. Conformity and mediocrity are also pathology, since they are symptoms of energy-consuming repression.

Television cannot equal the esthetic experience of true art. It should not even try to do so. Its place in the living room or bedroom, rather than in the theatre, church, or concert hall, makes such emotional depth unlikely—even inappropriate. In ancient times, the pilgrimage to the place of worship was an essential part of the mystery plays. Time and place do not nowadays invite such experience and ask for modification of maturing or esthetic experience. Our culture has developed away from this form of maturation and has not yet formed new ways of education. This does not mean that such new ways and new forms of artistic expression cannot be found for television. They must be found.

Beside the pleasure and reality principles, a third principle of mental functioning emerges: the principle of magic-mystic thinking, with which all higher, truly human mental activity starts. Infants try to govern the world by magic-mystic thinking (Róheim, 1956; Sterba, 1960). Later, men learn to correct magic action by realistic experience. This feedback of reality is missing in television. There is no action, and there is no correction. There is mostly—like in schizophrenia—fantasy, tension, occasionally wish fulfillment. A schizophrenic patient can no longer correct his symbolic thinking and ritualistic acting through the feedback of realistic experience. He has lost this ability to learn; he has broken his ties with reality and withdrawn to happier fields of narcissism.

Television is almost a training for schizophrenia. It trains not only by violence and fantasy, but also by an invitation to withdraw from adequate reaction. In the retreat from reality, we alienate ourselves from even our own feelings by the brisk interruption through the commercials. They are not the introductions of reality into the world of television fantasy. They are not like awakening from a dream. They are invitations to emotional denial or withdrawal.

Here is an example: On Easter morning, television took its audience to Rome, showing the Holy City as only a skillful and gifted artist could show it. The viewer really felt the almost ecstatic peace of the Eternal City on Easter morning. From Saint Peter's, we were led to the Coliseum and were shown the great wooden cross—beneath which stood a huckster selling pressure cookers. If such crass denial of emotions is repeated often, the viewer will defend himself against such brutal abuse of his submission to the beautiful; he will not allow himself to be moved again.

The abuse of emotions for commercial profit is the second offense of television. The result is a schizoid withdrawal from adequate emotional experience and participation, leaving in its wake a peculiar "beatnik" detachment. The withdrawal from reality is followed by a withdrawal from emotion. The denial of honest and mature emotions is deepened by television. The esthetic experience of the theater shows that free communication with our unconscious can be of great maturating importance. The constant teasing of our unconscious by the violence and crime on television, combined with emotional denial and the schizoid withdrawal, is further complicated by the depreciation or neglect of values. This leads to existential despair and the "beatnik" philosophy. It deepens the reluctance of young people to form a dependable ego identity. It has failed to fulfill its educational promise, as it has failed in its esthetic potential. Television offers a fun culture. It does not invite creativity and does not inspire learning. It does not offer an esthetic, maturating experience.

BIBLIOGRAPHY

Grotjahn, M. (1948), The Primal Crime and the Unconscious. In: *Searchlights on Delinquency*, ed. K. R. Eissler. New York: International Universities Press, pp. 306-314.
———(1957), *Beyond Laughter*. New York: McGraw-Hill.
———(1959), On Bullfighting and the Future of Tragedy. *Int. J. Psychoanal.*, *40*:238-239.
———(1960), *Psychoanalysis and the Family Neurosis*. New York: Norton.
Róheim, G. (1956), *Magic and Schizophrenia*. New York: International Universities Press.
Schramm, W., Lyle, J., & Parker, E. B. (1961), Television in the Lives of Our Children, with a Psychiatric Commentary on the Effects of Television by Lawrence Z. Freedman. Stanford, Calif.: Stanford University Press.
Sterba, R. (1960), Therapeutic Goal and Present-Day Reality. *J. Hillside Hosp.*, *9*:195-417.

ART

THE UNDIFFERENTIATED MATRIX OF ARTISTIC IMAGINATION

ANTON EHRENZWEIG

The psychoanalytic concept of the unconscious is often criticized as unscientific because it is impossible to prove unconscious processes empirically. This is a narrow view. The unconscious mind is not a physical fact that can be demonstrated, but an explanatory concept which allows us to understand phenomena that could not be accounted for otherwise. Neither, for that matter, can an electron be observed directly. A few flickerings on a screen can be seen; all the rest is deductive reasoning that leads to explanatory concepts which themselves are not open to direct demonstration. In the case of the unconscious, it follows from its definition that it cannot be observed directly.

I myself had to expand the use of the term "unconscious" to a new field. I needed the concept of an unconscious undifferentiated imagery underlying the conscious imagery of art in order to break the deadlock which has held up the progress of psychoanalytic aesthetics for half a century. It has been known all along that unconscious fantasy does not differentiate objects and concepts in the way in which our conscious mind sees them. Opposites like "high" and "low," "inside" and "outside," are treated as the same thing. What has not yet been realized sufficiently is the possibility that the unconscious mind could shape these undifferentiated *con*cepts into *per*cepts (images), equally undifferentiated. Of course, an image that did not make a distinction between top and bottom, inside and outside, cannot be visualized; but this is precisely the point. The quality of being "unconscious" need not be brought about by the repression of censored content; it can be due solely to structural processes of dedifferentiation. But I am hastening too far ahead. Let me begin by discussing the first truly spectacular successes of psychoanalytic aesthetics that did not yet require the concept of an undifferentiated unconscious imagery. It seemed at the time that the typical primary-process structures of the dream would imprint themselves on any creative work where the unconscious mind participated in shaping the structure. One of the first applications in the aesthetic field was surprisingly the joke, a not unimportant border subject of aesthetics. Classical aesthetics, as it was practiced by men like Hogarth, sought to connect specific emotions with definite structural elements; for instance, feelings of the sublime would be linked with large-scale structures, the graceful with slender forms. The laughter-raising quality of the joke was related with its brevity of expression. But gradually aestheticians lost heart in their search for objective foundations; there was too much uncertainty about the most important aesthetic experience, the feeling of beauty. What seemed ugly at first sight gained beauty as it grew more familiar. The frequent failure in establishing objective laws of beauty led to a gradual change of aim in nineteenth-century aesthetics. Instead of searching the objective structure of aesthetic objects, aesthetics turned to analyzing the subjective experience. Fechner and Lipps (Freud, 1905) helped in this reorientation of aesthetics toward psychology.

It seems paradoxical, though gratifying, that Freud, himself a psychologist and aesthetician influenced by Fechner and Lipps, should have solved the aesthetic problem of the joke's laughter-raising quality on truly classical lines. He compiled an exhaustive catalogue of all possible forms of a joke and then identified them with the typical primary-process structures of the dream. Freud's achievement of compiling an exhaustive catalogue of possible jokes could have been emulated by anyone who cared to have a closer look at the joke's structure. But Freud's achievement went further. If the joke assumed the structure of the primary process, it proved that the joke, like the dream, was formed spontaneously on the same deeply unconscious levels. The stage was set for Freud's triumphant entry into the heart problem of aesthetics, the origin and character of artistic structure. Art, more than the relatively shallow joke, could claim spontaneous roots in the deep unconscious. Though a large part of artistic structure is no doubt composed consciously and deliberately, any truly original creation in art will involve utter spontaneity as indeed any creative work. Freud was pleased when he could transfer the entire inventory of the dream's symbolism to a new understanding of art's unconscious content. It was more than legitimate to expect that the spontaneously created components of artistic structure should carry the impression of the primary process more securely than the relatively shallow joke. After all, the joke's point expresses only lightly suppressed aggressive or obscene fantasy, while art's symbolism is fed from deeply repressed fantasies. Otto Rank (1907), the first psychoanalyst to explore art form systematically, duly searched art for the same primary-process structures, e.g., condensations, representations by the opposite, displacements, which characterize the formulation of jokes and dreams. Rank pointed out that the German word for poet, *Dichter,* meant the condenser. Myth, folklore, and also art abound in dreamlike apparitions, composite monsters condensed from several animals and the human form, such as sphinxes, chimaeras, winged angels. But these intrusions of primary-process structures, however frequent, do not add up to an exhaustive catalogue of all art forms, even if the more deliberately shaped portions of artistic compositions are excluded and the search be confined to spontaneously created elements. Apart from the impossibility of repeating Freud's success in cataloguing all possible structures of a joke—nobody has yet succeeded in a catalogue that would have to include also all future art—it is equally impossible to describe the spontaneous form elements of art in terms of primary-process structures. Art form generally excels by its almost logical coherence and rigor that seems a far cry from the incongruous and paradoxical twists which the primary process gives to the dream and to the joke. It is true, however, and this leads one to the problem of structural undifferentiation, that spontaneously created elements of art, such as the inarticulate scribbles of artistic "handwriting" and other types of texture in art form, lack the logical rigor and simplicity that characterize more deliberately created compositions. In fact, these textures seem to lack any recognizable structure and could therefore not be identified as condensations, displacements, and the like. It appears that Freud's analysis of primary-process structures in the dream and in the joke has not opened the way to a similar analysis of unconsciously created art form. Half a century has gone by since Freud wrote on the joke, yet psychoanalysis has not made substantial progress toward solving the central problem of aesthetics, the unconscious origin and character of art form. In reason, one has to accept the failure as final.

It has often proved possible in the history of science to break a deadlock of this kind by ceasing the frontal attack against the closed door and examining instead the possible methodological reasons for the failure. Non-Euclidean geometry arose from the interpretation of a centuries-old failure to prove all the Euclidean axioms. The acceptance of this failure as final led to a new conception of space that proved fruitful in spite of an impossibility to visualize this kind of space. A similar difficulty of visualization may be the cause of our failure to find the unconscious origin and character of art form. The apparent lack of structure in spontaneously created form elements such as textures or artistic "handwriting" was already mentioned. Could it not be that our normal powers of visualization fail to appreciate their structure?

One can interpret the long-standing failure to discover the unconscious structure of art in two ways: one can either deny that an unconscious substructure of art exists (this is what the current theory of psychoanalytic aesthetics as expounded by E. Kris [1952] ultimately did), or one can assume that we have failed to find the substructure because it defies our normal powers of visualization. The latter approach is chosen here. It has already been indicated that the structural undifferentiation of low-level form processes may be sufficient reason in itself to keep such imagery unconscious, or to put it more precisely, to keep the principle of their organization unconscious. The chaotic, unorganized appearance of textures in art is certainly deceptive. Only a bad commercial artist will treat them as accidental and lacking in structural significance. In an etching by Rembrandt, the intricate scribbles of his handwriting are inextricably interwoven with the large-scale composition and, no doubt, were created in a single act. Only the commercial artist will compose the main structure of his work and then add decorative texture and a suitably nervous handwriting as an afterthought.

In music, the performer may distort the clean line of a melody by the textures of vibrato, portamento, rubato, etc., all of which (like graphic textures) add decorative richness. Again, the commercial musician will strive for richness in his tone quality by an indiscriminate use of vibrato, portamento, rubato and the like, but the inspired performer will apply them intuitively only in certain places, without being able to account for the reasons of his choice. The rigor of the intuitive discipline is nonetheless stringent for him for not being capable of rational formulation. The inspired artist will agree with the psychoanalyst in his basic attitude that nothing can be deemed accidental and insignificant in the artistic structure. Our growing intimacy with the working of the unconscious mind has put us on guard against taking the appearance of accidentality and insignificance at face value. More likely than not, the superficial guise of accidentality and disconnectedness indicates a superior unconscious significance. We are indebted to Arnold Schoenberg (1911) who saw in the hidden and fleeting phenomena of musical form the secret workshop where the musician's unconscious form sense experiments with the form innovations of the future. The chaotic-looking textures of music and visual art may well contain the form principle of unconscious creation. When I wrote first on the undifferentiated form elements of painting, I stated, on scanty evidence, that the scribbles of handwriting in traditional painting foreshadowed the less differentiated structure of modern art. The subsequent development of American painting vindicated this prediction in the most spectacular manner. Jackson Pollock and his followers blew up the seemingly unstructured loops and dabbings of artistic handwriting into the main structure of their work. The initial reaction of the art critics denied their work any organization whatsoever. It was even contended that Pollock's canvasses could easily be cut up into arbitrary fragments without losing in their aesthetic substance. But what I said about the secret discipline of musical textures applies of course also to Pollock's work and to the seemingly accidental textures of traditional painting.

There is formal discipline, but it can only be applied and sensed intuitively. If the musical performer tries to control his application of textures deliberately, he is bound to interfere with the apparent irregularity of this discipline; he will automatically stereotype his application of vibratos, rubatos and the like and thereby destroy their structural significance. This conflict between conscious and unconscious intuitive form control is of great theoretical significance. Critics of my aesthetic analysis of unconscious form elements in art suggested that I was merely dealing with preconscious, not truly unconscious phenomena. But preconscious form processes are syntonic with conscious thought; they prepare and assist it. Their formal discipline is identical or at least consistent with conscious form principles. If, as the evidence suggests, the application of textural elements in art and music is disturbed by conscious attention, then their discipline is dystonic and indeed antagonistic to conscious form control. To call them preconscious does more violence to existing terminology than my proposed extension of the term unconscious. I am averse to terminological controversies which are largely unfruitful. But in our case, any lingering doubt about a possibly preconscious character of the phenomena discussed here prevents their proper evaluation. The terminological question of preconscious versus unconscious will be taken up again whenever new facts come into view that could cast doubt on the unconscious quality of art's deepest substructure.

The conflict between the conscious and unconscious form principles is best conceptualized as a conflict between differentiation and undifferentiation. We can identify the principle of differentiation as the *gestalt* principle of academic psychology. According to the gestalt theory of perception we are compelled by an inborn tendency to organize the assembly of color patches in our visual field, for instance we have to bisect it into a relevant figure (the chosen gestalt) and an irrelevant background. Koehler, one of the founders of this school of psychology, went even so far as to deny the structural elements of the background any psychological existence whatsoever. The differentiation of the visual field into significant and insignificant areas runs counter to the aesthetic discipline of art discussed here. Bisecting the field of vision into relevant figure and irrelevant ground is precisely what the artist cannot afford to do. He needs to treat the scribbles of textures and artistic hand-writing as structurally significant, if not more significant than the prominent (gestalt) patterns of the large-scale composition. Every detail, however paltry-looking, has to be firmly related with the over-all structure in a complex maze of overlapping crossties determining the balance of line, tone, color, etc. Even the most austere geometric construction possesses this complexity. It defeats the normal powers of visualization which can attend only to a single gestalt configuration at a time and cannot scan the entire visual field with impartial attention. Yet the artist must be able to judge the impact of every dab of his brush as it affects the countless formal interrelationships set up between the smallest details of his work. Obviously, he must possess a kind of attention that can transcend the narrow focus of normal attention and can control all these superimposed patterns in a single act of attention. This scattering of attention has to do with the dedifferentiation of perception obtaining in my view on a lower level of ego functioning.[1]

It is now assumed that perception evolves from generalized, less differentiated techniques to more individualized differentiated techniques. The child does not differentiate the shapes around him in the way in which the adult distinguishes them. He calls all males "dada" while his mother has already become an individual in his eyes. I say "in his eyes" quite deliberately because it appears that the child's generalized concept of all males as "dada" corresponds to an actual perception. It is feasible that the child really sees all males as having the same undifferentiated shape. Only under the spur of his developing object relationships, branching out beyond the charmed circle of mother and child, does he learn to make finer distinctions in his concepts and percepts. This link between individualization of perception and individualization of object relationships can be observed with greater accuracy in adult perception. Even in adults, individual percepts fail to develop if the incentive of object relationships is not forthcoming. We fail to pick out the individual shapes of

[1] I will speak of *un*differentiation when describing a primitive still undeveloped state of perception, of *de*differentiation when speaking of the active process that destroys a more highly developed state of differentiation.

the flies buzzing around the lamp shade even if we make a determined effort to do so, while the more discerning entomologist has no such difficulty. Members of foreign races really look the same to us though, objectively, their features may differ in abstract form more decisively than Europeans among each other. The minutest ethnological study of face measurements and the like will not help us to make finer individual differentiations, while friendship or hate toward a single person will suddenly transform all members of his race into separate individuals.

Differentiation of the ego's perception, then, follows or is geared into the parallel differentiation of object relationships sustained by the id. This parallelism fits into the general model of ego functions devised by Hartmann and his associates. They assumed that the ego as well as the id develop from a common undifferentiated matrix. It would not have been necessary for me to fit the differentiation of perception into this model had not these writers exempted perception from it, possibly in deference to the then current gestalt theory of perception. If, as the gestalt theory maintains, we possess an inborn compulsion to differentiate the visual field into definite patterns, then it is impossible to maintain that perception—like other ego functions—has developed from an undifferentiated matrix, slowly progressing from primitive, hardly differentiated blurs to the more precise imagery of adulthood.

But the old concept of an inborn differentiation of the visual field has been severely shaken during recent years, largely owing to the belated translation of von Senden's (1960) collection of case histories concerning patients who were born blind and acquired vision late in life. The old gestalt theory predicted that these people, opening their formerly blind eyes to the world, would immediately differentiate the visual field into prominent figures and ground, choosing preferentially "good" gestalt patterns, such as nearly perfect geometrical shapes like circle, square, etc. Later, they would learn to associate these incisive patterns with the objects of the real world. Fortunately, so the gestalt psychologists thought, important objects happen to possess good abstract shapes. None of these predictions was confirmed by the reaction of these patients; rather, the reverse happened. Though they were perfectly familiar with the distinction between circle and square from their sense of touch, they were unable, nor did they care, to make the proper distinction between them. In fact, the most important effort of the attending physician went into keeping alive their interest in the still meaningless forms—a striking demonstration of the fact that the differentiation of perception is linked with that of object relationships. A child who was an animal lover soon learned to make clear distinctions between animals while she failed to pick out humans. We have since learned from R. Spitz's experiments with young babies that children, like animals, recognize objects from schematic cues rather than from an appreciation of abstract gestalt.

I have maintained in my writings that thing perception was different from and indeed in conflict with abstract gestalt perception. We recognize a face instantly without having memorized the infinite variety of aspects which a face offers as it turns from a profile to a full-face view. The various "constancies" in our perception help us to identify an object in spite of the constantly varying distortions of its shape through perspective, chiaroscuro, and other vagaries of illumination. We are aware of an object without being aware of its shape. Awareness of an abstract shape as such is a highly sophisticated achievement which no doubt we owe to the artists. This independence of our awareness of reality from an appreciation of shape is the reason why, as Gombrich (1960) has shown, realism in art is not based on a precise copy of our perceptions of shape, color, etc., but on a seemingly arbitrary invention of a "schema." The child can use the same circular scribble as a faithful equivalent of his father, mother, his dog or of the house he lives in, because to his still weakly differentiated perception almost any geometric shape can be made into a suggestive cue, and so appear realistic to him. Because realism in painting is not based on the copy of abstract shapes, the convention of old Egyptian painting to choose one particular aspect (the face in profile, the chest frontally, a pond from above, trees from the side, etc.) was just as realistic in its own way as the realism of the Renaissance. The awareness of reality is based on the suppression rather than the appreciation of abstract shape. A round plate looks the same to us, though perspectivic distortion will make it assume the shape of various elliptical patterns while only a view from above will reveal its circular shape. If the Egyptians represented a round plate by a circle, they did not copy this particular perception from above, but invented a schema that served as an adequate cue to its corporeal reality and so must have appeared perfectly naturalistic. How little the illusion of plastic reality depends on awareness of shape is more evident in mental imagery. A vivid dream image is often composed of several interpenetrating things possessing quite incompatible outlines so much that when we try to remember its shape after waking the image may melt into a white fog. Yet, while we were dreaming, it appeared quite real and solid. The child's undifferentiated vision which fails to distinguish between things of very different appearance (of different appearance, that is, to the adult's eye) would be capable of the same feat. In this sense, the child has not only undifferentiated concepts, but actual percepts that allow him to see the world in an undifferentiated manner.

Of course, once the adult has achieved a certain advanced state of differentiation in his vision, it becomes impossible for him to imagine, on a conscious level, a less differentiated form of perception. That is why interpenetrating dream things dissolve into a white fog in waking memory. We have to make a careful distinction between a dream condensation where several things can interpenetrate freely without cancelling each other out and a condensation where the things become unyielding; they obliterate each other owing to their incompatible shapes, so that only some dismembered particles are telescoped into an overconcrete mixture thing. This mutual obliteration allows the condensation to be remembered in the waking state, but only at the expense of losing much of its original substance. However, when we speak of primary-process structures we should only include the first kind of fluid interpenetrating condensation which is still undifferentiated and can, therefore, true to the spirit of the primary process, reconcile incompatible things. The joke, admittedly, produces mostly condensations of the more superficial kind where partial obliteration has occurred. The condensation "famillionaire" in Heine's joke which Freud quotes has torn the word "familiar" apart; true undifferentiation would have preserved the incompatible words intact, though we could not mould its sound into an articulate shape. We begin to understand why Freud's analysis of the more superficial primary-process structures of the joke did not lead directly to an equivalent analysis of art's unconscious substructure which belongs to a much lower level of the mind.

Fortunately for us, more recent research into dream images has tapped lower levels of image making that resist conscious visualization. B. Lewin (1953) began his work on the dream screen and the blank dream by drawing attention to the still very tangible dream screen which at first appeared as an indistinct ground behind the more concrete dream things (the figures of gestalt psychology). When viewed on its own, the dream screen reveals its undifferentiated structure and uncertain localization in space. Lewin reports a dream where the dreamer stood opposite an immense wall expanding into the infinite. While he faced the wall he also felt he was inside it. Adrian Stokes (1963) has drawn attention to a similar "enveloping" quality of modern painting which he himself compares to the dream screen. The onlooker faced with the immense canvasses of some abstract art feels drawn into it and made to wander in all directions.

Stokes, like Lewin, traces this feeling of envelopment to the child's oceanic fusion with the breast, which is also the basis of all mystic experiences. Stokes seems to deprecate this irrational enveloping quality of much modern painting which to his mind seems to undermine the "otherness" and individual existence of a work of art. But it is not easy to decry a quality of artistic structure which points to spontaneous creation from a deep level of the mind, from a level of dedifferentiation moreover which allows the artist to control the extreme complexity of all artistic structure. It is difficult to do justice to a mode of mental functioning which defies proper introspection.

In the mystic orison proper we see the same disintegration of precisely differentiated vision. The visionary, like St. Anthony in his temptations, may be visited by monsters that are composites from fragments of human and animal forms equivalent to the more superficial kind of condensation in which incompatible shapes overwhelm each other. Progressing toward lower levels of differentiation, the apparition may lose its localization in space in the manner of the dream screen. Ibsen makes Peer Gynt meet such a monster on the way up from the dream world of the Trolls. The monster has definite form—it is bent—but refuses to be pinned down in a definite point in space. On the lowest level, the true mystic orison becomes empty yet filled with intense experience that is highly esteemed by the mystics themselves. Bertram Lewin, who like all genuine depth psychologists progressed to ever deeper levels of the mind, at last came up against the totally blank dream filled with intense emotions that point to the fullness of fantasy on an unconscious level. This full emptiness, smacking as it does of the mystic, is a paradox attaching to all extreme phenomena of dedifferentiation. It is the direct result of our conscious failure to grasp imagery formed on more primitive levels of differentiation. The emotional fullness of great abstract art, as distinct from empty decoration, is a similar paradox. The simplest abstract patterns have retained, on an unconscious level, their role as primitive schemata that can stand for a diversity of incompatible things. These things, owing to their incompatible shapes, cancelled each other out on the way up to consciousness and so produce in our surface experience a blank "abstract" image still replete with unconscious fantasy.

Róheim (1953) has made the undifferentiated experience of the dream screen, where inside and outside become dedifferentiated, into the central theme of his last book *The Gates of the Dream.* For Róheim the tension as well as fusion between the inner (dream womb) and outer space of the dream belongs to the core of a basic dream conflict and, significantly, also to diverse cultural material. The dreamer enters and leaves the gates of the dream in a single act. While he enters the dream womb—where all differentiation is suspended—he rebuilds an outer dream space with the help of residual sensations streaming in from his body. It is interesting to ponder on Róheim's assertion that a similar dedifferentiation of the space experience should pertain to waking cultural activities. The "enveloping" quality of modern painting certainly exists in a less extreme manner in all art where the "aesthetic distance" between the work of art and the onlooker remains ambiguous.

The dedifferentiation of any flat painted surface also involves a fusion between an inside and outside. I mentioned the gestalt principle of surface vision which forces us to bisect the visual field into an "inside" area containing the chosen figure, and an "outside" area relegated to an indistinct ground. I contended that the artist could not afford to differentiate his visual field in this manner, at least if he wishes to control the immense complexity of form events which every stroke of the brush sets into motion. Every line he draws circumscribes a figure within and the negative shape outside cut from the ground. Paul Klee speaks of an endotopic (inside) and exotopic (outside) area of the picture plane. Klee states that the painter can either emphasize the "boundary contrast" (bisection of the painted surface) by keeping his conscious attention on the inside of the line he draws, or he can disperse his attention and watch both inside and outside at the same time. Klee was not a psychologist and so did not realize that such dispersed attention would be deemed impossible according to academic psychology. He instinctively used a language that indicated the ineffability of such attention. According to Klee, the attention dispersed to both inside and outside makes a picture "multidimensional." This recalls the language of non-Euclidean geometry which, too, refers to a kind of space that cannot be visualized. He also, with great insight, compares the interpenetration of inside and outside space with the interaction of polyphonic voices in music. Here we have reached firm ground where we can show that the blankness of a conscious experience does not preclude precision and fullness of information. Hearing polyphonic voices in music has received a technical name—horizontal listening—as opposed to the normal vertical hearing of a single melody underscored by a harmonic background of merely accompanying voices. The narrow focus of normal perception can attend only to a single "figure," the melody, and must necessarily suppress the rest into an indistinct "ground." Listening to one melody will automatically prevent us from attending to the other accompanying voices which recede into the harmonic background. But the control of the polyphonic structure requires from the composer and performer that they keep an equally firm grip on the entire fabric of music, not merely on a single melody.

The multidimensional type of attention, of which Klee speaks, allows precisely this. But—and this is the important point—horizontal hearing is totally blank as far as conscious memory is concerned. The several voices, each contending for exclusive attention, cancel each other out in conscious hearing. Again it is a full blankness. The trained musician can extract from it at an instant all the information he needs about the submerged voices of the polyphonic structure. So prompt is this information that it tends to cover up the blankness of the preceding experience. Attention will seem utterly mobile and speedy, capable of turning at once to any disturbing detail; yet this recurring lighting up of a hidden detail, a shred of melody here and there, does not detract from the essential blankness of dispersed attention spread out as it is to comprehend the entire structure of a work of art.

There is no doubt that the unconscious scanning that goes on under the cover of conscious blankness is indispensable for rational thought generally. This may once again induce doubt in the reader's mind whether unconscious scanning should not be better described as preconscious inasmuch as it assists conscious rational thought. But preconscious processes, unlike unconscious scanning, are readily accessible to conscious introspection; they are outside the focus of conscious attention solely because another thought happens to occupy attention. The process of unconscious scanning, by contrast, is disturbed by any attempt at introspection; it depends on conscious "blankness" and to that extent disrupts conscious thought. The results of unconscious scanning may, but not always, be available for rational evaluation and criticism. Sometimes not only the process of scanning, but also its outcome remains withdrawn. The control of musical textures—portamento, vibrato—and of artistic handwriting in the graphic arts must be totally automatic and unconscious. Not only would any attempt at conscious control regularize and stereotype the execution of these textures, but their resulting structure remains incomprehensible to conscious inspection and retains the accidental chaotic impression of all truly unconscious form creation. Some may prefer to restrict the term unconscious only to such cases where both the scanning and the results of scanning remain inaccessible to conscious analysis. Then horizontal hearing in music would be deemed merely preconscious, though it too disrupts conscious thought into blankness. I personally prefer to call all cases of blank scanning unconscious.

A very similar technique of dispersed "horizontal" attention is found in the graphic arts. It is a common experience to see a painter stop in his work: a mien of doubt creeps into his face; he steps back from his canvas and views it with a vacant stare that focuses on nothing in particular. Through this stare he can divert his attention from the prominent, obtrusive "figure" pattern and is able to take in the entire field of vision. All details, figure and background alike, are scanned with equal acuity, just as in horizontal listening all polyphonic voices are given the same significance. Now and again some inconspicuous detail will momentarily come forward and sink back into the surrounding blankness. At last some obscure detail is found that had upset the balance of the painting; the search is over.

Musician and painter alike will be loth to admit the conscious blankness of their fruitful scrutiny. Detached self-observation in moments of creative tension presupposes powers of introspection not necessarily associated with artistic gifts. Nor are such powers of introspection a necessary equipment of the depth psychologist. It is for this reason that I suggest with diffidence that the psychoanalyst's free-floating attention is none else than Paul Klee's multidimensional attention or the horizontal attention of the musician.

The psychoanalyst's normal attention is structured according to the gestalt principle which lifts prominent features from a receding ground. Freud found that inconspicuous, seemingly disconnected details, lacking properties of good gestalt, are more likely to contain the key to the meaning of unconscious fantasies. Hence it is necessary to counteract the conscious attraction of conspicuous features and treat the entire material with equal diligence. After all that has been said such a free interpenetration of figure and ground material must lead to a total blotting out of all conscious imagery. However, most analysts, interested as they are solely in the results of their scanning, will not care to hold on to the twilight states of mental imagery that precede the emergence of these results. When I once discussed the blankness of free-floating attention before a psychoanalytic audience, a member of the audience suggested, not unreasonably, that free-floating attention was merely highly mobile and ready to be shifted at the slightest provocation rather than empty and blank. The same objection is apt to arise in a discussion of the artist's unfocused stare. I once listened to a debate among young musicians as to how many polyphonic voices they could attend to at the same time. Some claimed that they could follow two voices simultaneously, others even three; none claimed that he could keep track of all four voices that are the normal complement of a full harmonic sound. They would have been very astonished had I told them that in fact they had the choice of following only one single voice or else none at all. It has been my experience that musicians are ready to accept the blankness of the painter's unfocused stare and painters the emptiness of horizontal hearing. It may well be that a creative use of unconscious scanning may produce unfavorable conditions for detached self-observation. It is too much to hope that by drawing on the psychoanalyst's personal experiences I have strengthened rather than weakened my argument. But to omit the example of free-floating attention would have been intellectually dishonest. My difficulty has wider methodological implications. Empirical proof of a hypothesis requires that its confirmation should be open to all and sundry. But if the confirmation rests on the results of introspection —as happens with most hypotheses in the aesthetic field—then proof is only available to observers with introspective gifts. It is difficult to accept that hypotheses of this kind should be excluded from scientific validation because of their aristocratic character which limits their confirmation only to the few.

It may be helpful here to bring out the common features in the many varied examples of undifferentiated perception adduced so far. Their most important property is a freedom from the need to make a definite choice. The narrowly focused beam of normal attention can select only one of many possible constellations. The unfocused dispersed type of attention is free from the compulsion to make such a choice. It can grasp in a single act of comprehension several mutually incompatible constellations. I have called these mutually exclusive possibilities of organization the "or-or" structure of undifferentiated perception. For instance, the choice between figure and ground is unnecessary for a subliminal vision that can comprehend figure and ground together. For this reason undifferentiated perception of this kind is uniquely capable of scanning a complexity of choices which would have to be examined one by one by conscious attention. A computer differs from human thought by the incredible speed with which it goes through countless possible constellations. The undifferentiated mode of perception postulated here could go one better by comprehending a great number of possibilities at once, cutting down the time required to nil.

In serialized composition, for instance, the composer has to hold all possible permutations of the serialized musical elements in a single undifferentiated view. It has been said that serialization destroys all vestiges of recurrent pattern and has therefore only an intellectual, not an aesthetic significance; its regularity cannot be appreciated by hearing, but can only be read in the written score. This is certainly true as far as conscious experience is concerned. The acoustic gestalt of a theme depends entirely on the preservation of its temporal order. A variation which tampers with the temporal sequence of the tones constituting a theme also destroys its identity. Yet serialization is nothing else but a series of variations that scramble up just this order in time. No doubt, it can become, and often does become, an intellectual device for constructing a certain type of empty wind-blown music. But in the hands of an inspired composer it must be handled by an inner view that can transcend the conscious differentiation of time and can scan the typical or-or structure of serialization in a single perception. Here neither the scanning process nor its aesthetic results can be grasped on a conscious rational level. All that we can fall back on for judging a true work of art and distinguishing it from an intellectual artifice is a feeling of inner necessity, of an inner life that is the only conscious signal of a well-made unconscious structure. Once the conscious order of space or of time, the two main principles of conscious differentiation, are suspended, we are dealing with modes of perception that cannot be called preconscious even by the widest stretch of the term; they are truly unconscious.

The scanning of or-or structures can, of course, have fully accessible results and I would be less confident in claiming unconscious qualities for such cases. For instance, the experienced bridge player evaluates the possible distributions of the still unplayed cards in a split second and decides accordingly on his strategy. I myself, being neither gifted nor experienced in such games, am only too painfully aware of the irrational or-or structure of such an evaluation. I would go through all possible permutations in the distribution of the unplayed cards and, not surprisingly, would arrive in the end at a wrong evaluation. The relaxation, in my view, which difficult combination games like bridge or chess afford comes from the dedifferentiation of our normal narrow attention and its replacement by the wide-open inner stare that is nearer to the structure of the dream than to waking consciousness. "Relaxation" is not the right word for this shift in ego functioning; it is rather a substitution of a more intense concentration for our normal one. These shifts between dedifferentiation and redifferentiation constitute an ego rhythm which must go on undetected for most of the time; in creative ego functioning the rhythm is deepened until it touches on levels of dedifferentiation that are beyond all rational understanding.

The progress of scientific thought, for instance in a mathematically formulated argument, can be described as a series of or-or structures. Each step of mathematical transformation opens up a new network of possible further transformations. We cannot see many steps ahead and anticipate the choices which will meet us at a later juncture. While the permutations in a combination game like chess are strictly finite, limited as they are by the rules of the game, no such rules exist in truly original work in science or art. There future choices that lie well ahead have to be scanned and evaluated according to rules that can be formulated only at a much later stage. Creative work makes its own laws. In spite of this obscurity, the creative thinker has to consider somehow the future course of his search in order to make the right decisions at an early stage. Conscious analysis cannot help him. The mathematician, Hadamard (1945), who studied mathematical creativity insists that the right decision depends on scanning all possible (or-or) structures of a mathematical argument and that a too precise conscious visualization leads the mathematician astray. To put it into my words, only the blotting out of conscious attention into blankness can stimulate unconscious scanning.

The dedifferentiation of mental imagery into or-or structures thus helps the ego in performing complex technical tasks. Through overdetermination, the same process of dedifferentiation also serves the id in its symbol formation. It has already been suggested that primary-process forms, such as condensations, displacements, representations through the opposite, rest on an undifferentiated matrix of image making. The or-or structure of this matrix allows incompatible object forms to interpenetrate without mutilating each other. Condensed objects can coexist without being compressed into nonsensical mixtures. Opposites and displaced meanings are held in a single view. According to Freud, the symbol was, at a primitive stage of human development, identical with the object it now merely symbolizes. The or-or structure of unconscious imagery can still perceive this identity. In my view every new symbol formation would be preceded by the temporary dedifferentiation of mental imagery into or-or structures where symbolic and symbolized objects are equated. This complete interpenetration, of course, is impossible on a conscious level. Either symbol or symbolized object must give way. Condensation into a mixture thing may occur or, more frequently, the symbolic substitution of one concrete object for the other. In order to symbolize the other object efficiently, it must remain identified with it on a lower unconscious plane. Once a symbol becomes dissociated from its unconscious matrix where the symbolic identification occurs, its symbolizing power withers and ultimately vanishes. This loss of symbolic power is a common occurrence. Writers like Ernest Jones would exclude the age-old artefacts of civilization—plough, house, knife, etc.—from their study of symbolization; the daily use of such things has become too independent from their unconscious meaning. I suggested earlier that truly potent abstract art owed its impact to its unconscious matrix of conflicting images that cancelled each other out on the way up to consciousness. Abstract art tends to turn into empty ornament when it is severed from its unconscious matrix. The all too facile use and abuse of ornamentation is explained by its dissociation from unconscious imagery. Elsewhere I have tried to show that creative abstraction in science served to resolve inconsistencies in our view of the world. A new abstract concept "sees together" incompatible objects and images. An abstract concept will be debased into an empty and facile generalization as soon as it cuts itself free from its unconscious matrix of equated images.

There is a constant tug of war between differentiation and dedifferentiation. As long as the way down to renewed dedifferentiation is not cut off, new symbols will be freely formed to take the place of images that have lost their symbolizing power. Ego rigidity and a schizoid dissociation between surface and depth functions will block the rhythm of dedifferentiation and redifferentiation and so induce creative sterility. Ego rigidity is not infrequent in the immature artist. An important aspect of good art teaching consists in softening this rigidity and inducing the student to let go and allow unconscious form control to take over. Unconscious form control is indispensable in creative work because conscious attention is incapable of dealing with the complex or-or structure of art and science. The smallest addition to the work of art affects the total web of formal relationships. It will affect the flow of the linear composition, the balance of tone and color, the distribution of light and shade, smooth surface and texture, and many other such conflicts and harmonies. Attention must be dispersed, and therefore blank, in order to scan all these effects in advance.

A fussy art teacher can be too eager in pointing out to the student his manifold responsibilities. A gifted student may well be overwhelmed by his task. His attention will be pulled into opposing directions and may fail to function altogether. He may then be afflicted by "Centipede's Paralysis," recalling the centipede of the fable who was asked how he managed to control the independent movements of his countless legs. The poor animal reflected on his achievement for the first time and could not move a single leg.

It is clear that conscious control of several simultaneous events is impossible. Only unconscious scanning sustained by conscious blankness can succeed in this. Even a gifted student may feel unable to relinquish conscious control because, to him, the lapse of conscious control means letting in unconscious chaos. He may well be right in his fear.

Letting go of conscious control alone will not ensure that an unconscious form control will necessarily take over. The very rigidity of the immature ego will prevent proper integration between conscious and unconscious levels of ego functioning. Without this integration the intrusion of undifferentiated unconscious form processes will only cause the destruction and chaos which we usually associate with the primary process.

Schizoid ego rigidity exaggerates the vicious circle. The common denominator of all schizophrenic art is its rigidity. It serves a defensive function and prevents the normal dedifferentiation of imagery. In spite of its rigidity, schizophrenic art is fragile. As the illness deteriorates, rigidity will not gradually soften, but will suddenly disintegrate into inarticulate chaos.

The schizophrenic cannot afford dedifferentiation because, to him, it means self-annihilation. It has been pointed up how, in dedifferentiated imagery, several normally incompatible objects can interpenetrate freely without causing mutual damage. Only on a higher, near-conscious level will such object forms press against each other. They may then be telescoped into the familiar condensations which are no longer dedifferentiated, but are squeezed into crudely concrete mixture forms. The overconcreteness of schizophrenic imagery points to the same intolerance of unconscious dedifferentiation. Abstraction in art and science is based on the unconscious interpenetration of incompatible images which, on their way up to consciousness, cancel each other out into abstract blankness. In the schizophrenic's concretized thought, the incompatible images partially or totally overwhelm each other. Hanna Segal (1957) reports the case of a psychotic patient who refused to play the violin because he "did not want to masturbate in public." Segal rightly states that the symbolic object, the violin, is overwhelming by the symbolized sexual object. Segal's term, "symbolic equation," does not describe adequately this violent conflict between symbol and symbolized thing; it fits better the free interpenetration between symbol and symbolized thing on the unconscious dedifferentiated level of image making, which underlies all successful symbol formation. The schizophrenic's obliteration of the symbol, of course, prevents successful symbolization.

It seems that the schizophrenic cannot tolerate the dedifferentiation of incompatible objects even on an unconscious level because it threatens his tenuous hold on reality. His tendency toward confusion, his doubts about his identity, the proper separation of sexes, and the like give psychic reality to his fear of dedifferentiation so that indeed it can signify to him annihilation and even death.

I have met with many borderline schizophrenic cases in the art school. At least one of them has become a major artist. His work is now in public collections. When he came under my care, his work displayed full-blown schizophrenic traits, not only rigidity, but also the intolerable admixture of sweet decoration and anxiety which is another characteristic of psychotic art. He was fortunate to be taught by an artist whose intuitive facility and apparent casualness were at first deeply disconcerting for the young man. What he had to learn was to bear chaos and destruction and the severe anxiety attendant on lack of conscious control. He attacked his work with a ferocity which was a measure of his anxiety. Collage of torn fragments suited him best and he assembled the torn bits with utmost sensitivity. The initial fragmentation of his collage material certainly bordered on fragmentation found in schizophrenic art. But in tearing his collage material to bits, he already anticipated the ties established between them by subsequent collage. For the schizophrenic the fragmented bits remain concrete and separate and so resist mutual attraction. His splintering represents the vain attempt to overcome the concrete separateness of his imagery. Instead of melting the concrete entities down into dedifferentiated unity—a feat of which he is incapable—he only breaks them up into ever smaller bits. Like the magic broom of the "sorcerer's apprentice," every little fragment turns into another concrete and complete entity. The artist, by comparison, in breaking down his collage material, already scans in advance the or-or structure into which the bits can be reassembled.

This sensing in advance of the possible recombinations of disconnected elements is a characteristic accomplishment of the artist. It is another example of his capacity for scanning or-or structures. Modern composers like Stockhausen provide the performer with a number of disconnected passages which the performer himself can fit into any temporal sequence he wishes. But of course, the composer has somehow anticipated all possible combinations, however incredible such an achievement may seem to the pedestrian music critic.

The fragmentation of objects need not be physical. Picasso, in his portraits, tears, as it were, the features of a face into disconnected bits and reassembles them in what seems a most arbitrary fashion. Yet, surprisingly, just the more extreme dislocations lead to the most convincing likeness. This points to an undifferentiated unconscious vision which transcends the rational concept of space and perceives the features of a face jumbled up into an unlimited number of possible reassemblies. This or-or structure, unconsciously seen, allows us to recognize a familiar face in spite of Picasso's fragmentation and seemingly arbitrary reassembly of its features. The painter Harry Thubron, teaching at Leeds College of Art, used dislocation and fragmentation in life drawing. He kept the model moving and twisting. The student had to catch a fleeting pose in a single groping line. As the pose changed, he had to superimpose the incompatible outlines into a composite. If he was sensitive enough, the conflicting shapes added up to a stronger physical presence than ordinarily found in a more orthodox life drawing. Thubron went further and asked his students to tear their finished drawings into bits and reassemble them into collages. Even this fragmentation, if successful, did not destroy the likeness of a human body but could still be read as a potent presence. Perhaps the feeling of a presence was all the stronger because the work could only be read and understood on an unconscious (dedifferentiated) level of vision.

These practical examples drawn from highly controversial works of modern art are not out of place in a theoretical treatise on unconscious perception. E. Kris (1952) once criticized my theory of perception because it was built on facts that are not available in clinical work. But is this necessarily a disadvantage? It follows from my findings that certain modes of ego functioning can be more easily discerned in creative activity than in the disconnected material which the patient produces in his free associations. Creative work differs from psychopathological disturbance in the decisive point that, in illness, dedifferentiated fantasies act disruptively and display the unstructured chaos of the primary process as described in clinical theory. In creative work the same dedifferentiation of unconscious fantasy leads to heightened ego control. It assists in that scanning of or-or structures which plays so important a part in original work. But the danger of ego disruption is always there to the extent that every sane person retains a measure of ego rigidity (schizophrenic "pocket"). This is why it is necessary to emphasize the truly unconscious character of dedifferentiated imagery. In spite of the highly constructive role it may play in creative work, any lapse of ego control will bring into the open the imminent danger of disruption inherent in the ambiguity and possible confusion of dedifferentiated imagery. Even the most gifted mind is exposed to danger, as it is always possible that the id's propensity for confusing wildly different images may sweep aside the creative ego's more controlled construction of or-or structures. Then and only then the chaos usually associated with the primary process will manifest itself.

But in successful creative work a proper balance is achieved. The same process of dedifferentiation will allow the id to fuse different objects into symbolic union and the ego to construct its precise or-or structures. The id and the ego once worked harmoniously in harness when they emerged from their common undifferentiated matrix which Hartmann (1952) postulates. As the id learned to differentiate its aims with greater refinement and accuracy, the ego developed more finely differentiated perceptions and images exactly fitted for the id's progress. New id content was adequately expressed by new ego structure. Creative dedifferentiation simply reverses this process. It produces fusion between objects befitting a more primitive and coarsely aimed id content, expressed in images possessing the coarser differentiation of a more primitive ego. Owing to the dynamic tension inherent in all sublimation, creative work utilizes the primitive undifferentiation of imagery for performing highly advanced technical tasks like unconscious scanning and the formation of elaborate or-or structures.

It would be wrong to interpret the dedifferentiation of imagery purely as a regression to a more primitive stage of development. Dedifferentiation seems to be built into the fundamental techniques of perception from the outset. For instance, our compulsion to divide the visual field into figure and ground confines the ground to unconscious perception. Similarly, the subliminal threshold of perception pushes a large number of potentially conscious experiences to the unconscious. The narrow pinpoint of precise vision in the focus of the visual field reduces peripheral impressions to the vagueness and ambiguity of dream vision. All these phenomena involve processes of structural dedifferentiation. For example, at first sight, the unconscious quality of subliminal vision seems to depend solely on the weakening of the physiological stimulus. But the causal nexus is perhaps more complex. The weakening of the physiological stimulus, such as the split-second duration of tachistoscopic exposure, first brings about structural changes in the image that faithfully reflect the now familiar symptoms of progressive dedifferentiation. It is this dedifferentiation which is directly responsible for the blankness of subliminal vision and its conscious inaccessibility. We remember how the progressive disembodiment of concrete dream images into an insubstantial dream screen gradually approaches the totally blank dream, or how in creative vision the vagueness of intuitive imagery is ultimately dissolved into the totally blank stare. In all these cases the progressive dedifferentiation reaches a threshold where the gestalt techniques of conscious perception begin to fail. If we apply the term unconscious to all these blank images, there is no reason why we should deny the same unconscious quality to subliminal vision. Cutting down the tachistoscopic exposure toward the critical subliminal threshold first induces typically dreamlike ambiguity and distortion with parts of the images already sinking below the threshold, until at last the entire image is swallowed up by total blankness. As in other cases of dedifferentiation, the increasing unconscious quality of the image will open the door to the participation of id fantasy. It is well known how easily subliminal experiences enter subsequent dreams.

Tachistoscopic and subliminal perceptions have the great advantage of being open to laboratory experimentation; they supply welcome empirical confirmation for my thesis that the apparent vagueness and ambiguity of dedifferentiated vision are misleading. In creative work, dedifferentiated imagery can serve precise technical tasks. Experiments with subliminal perception bear out that unconscious perception, in spite of its apparent vagueness, excels conscious perception by its superior scanning power. I mentioned Paul Klee's insistence that the artist can disperse his attention to figure and ground in a single act of comprehending both at the same time. Normal conscious attention is certainly incapable of this feat, but not subliminal perception. Charles Fisher (1959) who experimented with subliminal imagery, exposed typical ambiguous patterns to his observers where figure and ground are easily interchangeable. In normal vision, we are compelled to choose one of the possible readings. Fisher found that subliminal vision can comprehend both figure and ground at once. A significant number of his observers produced freely associated drawings that showed two objects corresponding to the shapes of figure and ground. Subliminal vision is thus able to scan the or-or structure of such ambiguous patterns in a split second and gathers more information than a conscious scrutiny lasting a hundred times longer. Because of this hidden organization, we must accord subliminal vision the full status of an unconscious perception. It is more than a passive "registration" of unorganized stimuli as is sometimes suggested.

Subliminal perception can serve as the prime example for the way in which the ego provides for dedifferentiated unconscious imagery owing to an autonomous built-in technique. The pull of id fantasy toward dedifferentiation is not needed. A similar consideration may account for the equally puzzling fact that by far the larger part of the visual field is biologically useless. An extremely narrow central pinpoint of precise vision is surrounded by a broad fringe of dreamlike peripheral imagery. An image is formed by the pinpoint of central vision oscillating around the viewed object. The final image is composed of a series of such pinpoint glances. The object is never viewed in its entirety. The vagueness of peripheral vision is not due to physiological factors, at least only to a small degree. In cases of hemianopic vision—where exactly one half of the visual field has become blind—the dividing line between blindness and vision cleanly cuts through the pinpoint focus of precise vision. Some patients restore the normal situation by creating a new focus of precise vision in the remaining half of the visual field. In such a case, the mutilated former focus becomes engulfed by the usual vagueness of peripheral vision. As almost any part of the periphery can be chosen as the new focus, it stands to reason to assume that potentially we could have precise vision over most of the visual field. That we have no such vision can only be due to psychological causes. The problem seems the same as that of subliminal vision. There too we have the physiological equipment for a far larger range of conscious vision. But a purely psychological limitation ensures that a large part of perception remains subliminal-unconscious. It is the ego which thus provides the id with ample opportunity for symbolization in ambiguous unconscious imagery.

The same explanation may hold true for the vagueness of peripheral vision. The structure of the visual field, divided into a precise and narrow focus and a large fringe of vague and almost blank vision, is identical with the structure of attention generally. Attention can only fasten to a single and very restricted object; the rest of mental imagery recedes into an indistinct "halo" (William James, 1901) of indistinct and unstable shapes. It needs great gifts of introspection to become aware of the imagery swimming in the peripheral fringe. They are easily distorted by fantasy and often bear little resemblance to reality. Normally, they evade attention because the central pinpoint of attention swiftly scans an object and supplies an all-over view which is really composed of several successive glances. Any strange object entering the visual field from the side instantly attracts attention and is duly scanned. Thus the fantasy structure of the initial glance is not retained in conscious memory. One can, of course, by a determined effort, keep the pinpoint of the central focus steady and prevent it from scanning some new object appearing on the fringe of the periphery. If we are in entirely unfamiliar surroundings, it will be quite impossible to identify the peripheral object. Moreover, any initial impression can be modified almost at will by the play of fantasy and be turned into any fantasied apparition. However, once an object has been scanned consciously, it will retain its identity even after slipping back into the vague periphery. That is the reason why we so seldom become aware of the fantasied objects swimming in the fringe of our vision. We are invaded by this hidden world when, during twilight, the central focus of vision begins to fail while the rod cells of the peripheral retina are still functioning. Then terrifying phantoms may lurk in the periphery of our vision. They will promptly disappear as we train the now blinded central focus on them only to re-emerge in a more frightening shape in another corner. In cases of nyctophobia, unbridled id fantasies may wholly overwhelm all external perception.

It is not impossible that the censorship of the superego adds to our difficulties in becoming aware of peripheral vagueness and distortion. I became aware of this possibility at a lecture on recent advances in the physiology of vision, given by a leading specialist in this field. I expected that a scientist who gave his whole professional life to the study of vision would have come across the phenomena of peripheral distortion. During the following discussion, I asked a somewhat leading question about the nature of peripheral distortion. The lecturer seemed mystified. After a pause, he quickly passed a pencil across his visual field and exclaimed: "I cannot see any distortion!" I did not try to insist that a familiar object, once it is identified by central vision, would not display vagueness and distortion. I realized that the lecturer's failure to notice the irrational structure of peripheral vision had something to do with its truly unconscious quality. Precise observation alone had never led to the discovery and understanding of unconscious phenomena. A specific depth-psychological attitude is necessary to realize the existence of a problem and then to open one's eyes to observable facts. Often, the observation of facts follows the realization of the theoretical problem.

No definite solution of these obscure problems is offered here. They are mentioned only to substantiate the possibility that the ego autonomously provides for a large range of unconscious perceptions, all of which show characteristics of dedifferentiation. Owing to this dedifferentiation, the shape of any outer object can readily merge with objects of id fantasy. Outer perception and inner mental imagery can no longer be held apart. For this reason, the term "image making" is suggested for unconscious vision which is outer perception and mental fantasy at the same time.

It has been said that the wide range of unconscious perceptions underlying conscious experience is built into the mechanism of perception from its earliest inception. Conscious differentiation is poised against the pull of unconscious dedifferentiation. This dynamic tension is greatly reinforced in creative work. This is also true for the earliest forms of the child's creativity. The child's powers fully awaken during the anal phase, in the second year of life. Then he becomes socially adaptable, learns to talk, acquires cleanliness and imaginatively works out his own games. His powers of differentiation also increase at a great pace, and with them his orientation in outer reality. Considering the dynamic tension between conscious and unconscious imagery, we should expect that his unconscious fantasy life would develop in the opposite direction, i.e., toward extreme dedifferentiation. This is indeed the case. The concept of dedifferentiation helps to throw new light on the familiar, yet obscure traits of anal fantasy. In the second year of life, oral fantasy begins to give way to anal fantasy. The latter differs from oral fantasy by its lack of differentiation. The already acquired distinction of the oral zone as part of the body image is undone and is merged with other, anal and genital, zones. Mouth, vagina, and anus are equated not merely symbolically, but as an actual experience of the body image. Abraham pointed out that such an undifferentiated body image fitted only an utterly primitive organism possessing a single body cavity and opening to do service for oral, anal, and sexual functions. But he did not suggest that the child, in forming such a primitive body image, "regressed" to the subhuman experience of an animal so far down on the ladder of evolution. The creative adult dedifferentiates his imagery in an even more extreme manner; he cannot be said to have "regressed" to the child's primitive vision. Both child and adult, in unconscious fantasy, perform active feats of dedifferentiation that have no equivalent in reality, even on the most primitive level. At an extreme limit, a near oceanic fusion of all distinctions is reached which in its unreality borders on the mystic. Psychoanalytic theory and practice have not been very successful in interpreting these ubiquitous oceanic fantasies as regression to a prenatal state when the child felt physically at one with the mother (it is questionable that the child could ever have felt such a concrete unity, even in a parasitic existence in the womb). The womb fantasy may be due to an active suspension of already established frontiers which goes even beyond the very extreme dedifferentiation of anal imagery.

Oral fantasy may be very early in the ontogenetic development, but this alone does not make it the deepest and least accessible material. That anal fantasy tends to be neglected over oral material may be due not so much to the greater significance of the earlier oral material, but to the greater inaccessibility of undifferentiated anal fantasies. Winnicott (1957) warned against the prevalent assumption that what is earlier in life must also be more deeply unconscious. Ernest Jones, speaking after Winnicott, paraphrased this formulation by saying that the earliest material need not necessarily be the least accessible. This paper may serve as a further comment on this warning.

In summary, one could say that the purely structural dedifferentiation of later fantasies, particularly in creative work, could make them less accessible and, to that extent, more deeply unconscious than fantasies that belonged to a much earlier stage. Also, clinical work, preoccupied as it is with very early material, may cut less deeply than applied psycho-analysis which has at its disposal the still highly obscure fantasies of the creative mind. Writers dealing mainly with cultural material, like Rank or even Róheim, are likely to be pushed out into the wilderness of incom-prehensibility because some of their statements fail to make sense for clinical analysts. In this paper I was content with stating new problems rather than proposing solutions. Only in a single point do I feel strongly. Psychoanalytic ego psychology, after the lead given by Hartmann and Lewin, could be bolder in the development of its theory and the expan-sion of classical concepts, particularly of the concept of the unconscious, in order to cast its net a little wider and, in the end, bring about the much needed integration between cultural and clinical psychology.

BIBLIOGRAPHY

Fisher, C. & Paul, I. H. (1959), The Effects of Subliminal Visual Stimulation on Images and Dreams: A Validation Study. *J. Amer. Psychoanal. Assn.*, 7:35-83.

Freud, S. (1905), Jokes and Their Relation to the Unconscious. *Standard Edition*, 8:9-238. London: Hogarth Press, 1960.

Gombrich, E. H. (1960), *Art and Illusion*. London: Phaidon Press.

Hadamard, J. (1945), *The Psychology of Invention in the Mathematical Field*. Princeton, N. J.: Princeton University Press.

Hartmann, H. (1952), The Mutual Influences in the Development of Ego and Id. In: *The Psychoanalytic Study of the Child*, 7:9-30, eds. R. S. Eissler et al. New York: International Universities Press.

James, W. (1901), *The Principles of Psychology*. London: Macmillan.

Kris, E. (1952), *Psychoanalytic Explorations in Art*. New York: International Universities Press.

Lewin, B. D. (1953), Reconsideration of the Dream Screen. *Psychoanal. Quart.*, 22:174-198.

Rank, O. (1907), *Der Kuenstler*. Vienna: Hugo Heller.

Róheim, G. (1953), *The Gates of the Dream*. New York: International Universities Press.

Schoenberg, A. (1911), *Harmonielehre*. Vienna: Universal-Edition.

Segal, H. (1957), Notes on Symbol Formation. *Int. J. Psychoanal.*, 38:158-165.

Senden, M. von (1960), *Space and Sight*. London: Methuen.

Stokes, A. (1963), *Painting and the Inner World*. London: Tavistock Publications.

Winnicott, D. (1957), Address to International Psycho-Analytical Congress, Paris.

INDEX

INDEX

401